For the [illegible] ?ug,
which [illegible] o
look [illegible] h"

+ For Medieval Studies Students,
who taught me so much!
March 2004

Public Piers Plowman

Public Piers Plowman

MODERN SCHOLARSHIP
AND LATE MEDIEVAL ENGLISH CULTURE

C. David Benson

THE PENNSYLVANIA STATE UNIVERSITY PRESS
UNIVERSITY PARK, PENNSYLVANIA

Library of Congress Cataloging-in-Publication Data

Benson, C. David.

Public Piers Plowman : modern scholarship and late medieval English culture /

C. David Benson.

p.   cm.

·   ISBN 0-271-02315-5 (alk. paper)

1. Langland, William, 1330?–1400? Piers the Plowman.

2. Literature and history—England—History—To 1500.

3. Literature and society—England—History—To 1500.

4. English literature—Middle English, 1100–1500—History and criticism.

5. Art and literature—England—History—To 1500.

1. Title.

PR2015 .B4 2003

821'.1—dc21

2003009908

Published by The Pennsylvania State University Press,

University Park, PA 16802-1003

It is the policy of The Pennsylvania State University Press to use acid-free paper. Publications on uncoated stock satisfy the minimum requirements of American National Standard for Information Sciences—Permanence of Paper for Printed Library Material, ANSI Z39.48–1992.

Contents

For My Grandmother, Carolyn June Farnum (1892–1982)
"Wel may the barn blesse that hym to book sette"
(B 12.186)

Girton College, Cambridge
"For if hevene be on this erthe, and ese to any soule,
It is in cloistre or in scole, by manye skiles I fynde"
(B 10.299–300)

Acknowledgments

I owe special thanks to Girton College for a Helen Cam Fellowship in the Arts (in addition to intellectual and social fellowship), which allowed me to begin this project, and to the National Endowment for the Humanities for a fellowship that enabled me to finish it. In between, I have been aided by the University of Connecticut by means of a Chancellor's Fellowship and support from the Research Foundation and Dean MacKinnon and the College of Arts and Sciences.

I was fortunate to have outstanding guides to medieval fields that were new to me. For London, I am particularly grateful to the incomparable Caroline Barron, and to Martha Carlin, Vanessa Harding, and Derek Keene. For parish wall painting, David Park could not have been more gracious and helpful to a beginner, as later was Miriam Gill.

Many distinguished Langlandians read drafts of this work to my great benefit, though they are not responsible for its conclusions: Robert Adams, John Bowers, Charlotte Brewer, Vincent DiMarco, Hoyt Duggan, Derek Pearsall, and Beth Robertson. Other colleagues and friends kindly helped with conversation and comments on parts of this work: Christine Cooper, Mary Clemente Davlin, O.P., A. S. G. Edwards, Katherine French, Brian Goldberg, Katharyn Horsely, Tamarah Kohanski, Rebecca Krug, Francine McGregor, Linne Mooney, Rebecca Schoff, A. C. Spearing, Paul Strohm, Nicholas Watson. Charles Muscatine offered encouragement when it was needed.

I was kept from many errors by the research assistance of Erin Heidkamp, Vladimir Kleyman, Heather Masciandaro, and Chandra Wells. I have learned much from the wonderful students with whom I read *Piers Plowman* at Virginia, Harvard, and especially Connecticut, as I have from the audiences before whom I have been privileged to speak, in particular the annual meeting of SEMLA a decade ago.

Two groups have contributed more than they know to this project: the Amherst Chaucer reading group and the extraordinary participants of the 1995 Chaucer/Langland NEH Summer Institute organized at Boulder by Elizabeth Robertson. I am grateful to the *Yearbook of Langland Studies* for permission to use material that first appeared (in a different form) in its pages.

I am honored to be published by The Pennsylvania State University Press and indebted for the skill and poise of Peter Potter, Cherene Holland, and Lisa Tremaine. The critiques of the conscientious readers for the press, who turned out to be Frank Grady and Derek Pearsall, were immensely helpful.

From the beginning to the end of this project, I have benefited from the unrivaled learning, energy, generosity, and good humor of James Simpson.

Once again my most constant and best reader has been my wife, Pam.

List of Illustrations

Introduction

I have long been convinced that *Piers Plowman* is the least-read great poem in our language. Many students of literature know little more than its title, and even some Middle English specialists ignore the work. It was not always so. *Piers Plowman* was widely popular with its original audience in the late fourteenth and fifteenth centuries: it may well have been the first poem in Middle English to achieve a national readership, and the number of its surviving manuscripts ranks just below those of Chaucer's *Canterbury Tales.* The modern neglect of this rich and demanding work is a serious loss, for there is nothing quite like *Piers Plowman.* Although it emerged from the fourteenth-century revival of alliterative poetry in England, it was never confined to that tradition, nor do later imitations begin to match its achievement. One need only compare *Piers* to *Winner and Waster*, perhaps its closest alliterative analogue and possibly a direct influence, to be struck by the differences in length, variety, and ambition. Likewise, the poems that follow *Piers* in the fifteenth century as part of the so-called *Piers Plowman* tradition—such as *Mum and the Sothsegger* or "London Lyckpeny"—are narrower in the issues they address, less accomplished in style, and more explicit in their didacticism.

Useful comparisons can (and have) been made between *Piers Plowman* and other Ricardian poetic masterpieces, but the contrasts are just as striking. *Piers* lacks the fundamental commitment to narrative and clear, sophisticated literary structures that distinguish the works of Chaucer, Gower, and the *Gawain*-author. *Piers* is always interrupting itself and offering readers something completely different: the bursting of the emperor Trajan into the story, for instance, with his cry, "Ye, baw for bokes!" (B 11.140; C 12.76) or the layering of dreams within dreams.[1] With a plowman as its hero and ordinary life as its frequent subject, the poem offers social perspectives rarely found in the works of its

---

1. Citations to *Piers Plowman* in this study are from A. V. C. Schmidt's 1995 parallel-text edition of the poem. Quotations are from the B-version unless otherwise noted and are slightly modernized in spelling.

more courtly contemporaries. The uniqueness of *Piers* also extends to its reception: in addition to reaching a broad early readership, it seems to have supplied slogans for the Rising of 1381 (how many other English poems have been put to such dramatic political use?); then, after being ignored by the early printers, it was first published in 1550 by Robert Crowley to support the Protestant cause.

For many modern readers, *Piers Plowman* has become a difficult, ungainly work, hard to understand and harder to enjoy. Extracting selections that are capable of standing alone for classroom use (so simple for the *Canterbury Tales*) is almost impossible with *Piers*. At the same time, the poem is so intricate and dense that reading it straight through as if it were a novel tends to produce confusion and dizziness. Two popular modern critical strategies (often combined) for making sense out of this formidable poem are to read it as a personal or as a privileged work. The personal approach sees *Piers* as a vehicle through which the poet speaks about his own experiences and spiritual struggles. The poem is taken to be fundamentally autobiographical and to promote, more or less directly, its author's individual religious and political views. A related, more recent, and more learned approach treats the poem as the erudite work of an unconventional intellectual, who was perhaps writing for a limited coterie: the poem is taken to be an expression of elite thought that draws on material found in canon and civil law, biblical commentary, anticlerical satire, monastic psychology, apocalypticism, and the scholastic *moderni*. Both approaches—the personal or individual and the privileged or learned—have produced valuable studies of *Piers*, but they tend to overlook those elements of the poem that do not accord with the author's supposed life or abstruse learning. This study is intended as a corrective: it goes beyond both the personal and the privileged to explore the poem's engagement with the common culture of late medieval England. It emphasizes the public in *Piers Plowman*.

THE LANGLAND MYTH

Public Piers Plowman is divided into two parts, each containing three chapters. The first part prepares and explains the need for the second by demonstrating the limitations of treating *Piers* as a record of an individual poet's life and views. The second part then offers an alternate way of interpreting *Piers* that is not restricted to the personal and elite by approaching the poem through three different aspects of the public culture of late medieval England: writing, art, and urban life.

I begin this study by charting the lasting influence of one of the major achievements of nineteenth-century Middle English scholarship: the coherence that the great Victorian editor W. W. Skeat brought to the centuries-old confusion about the authorship and text of *Piers Plowman* by constructing what I call the "Langland myth." Skeat's formulation has two related components, each of which supports the other: the myth of the poet (a biography Skeat assembled from various scraps in the poem) explains and is explained by the myth of the poem (three versions written in a specific chronological order). Today, well over a century after its creation, Skeat's Langland myth still dominates *Piers* scholarship.

My use of the word *myth* to describe what Skeat formulated, and so many Langlandians have believed, is intended to be provocative and not merely dismissive. I might have spoken of the "Langland hypothesis" or "Langland theory," but such quasi-scientific language would have implied that its claims could be convincingly proved or were able to be falsified, which they cannot be (or, at least, have not been). I believe that *myth* is the better term for what I mean, though it is a difficult concept that has been used in various ways by modern thinkers (see R. Williams, *Keywords*, 210–12). I do not use the word in either its familiar negative meaning of something that is false or deliberately deceptive (a mere fable), nor in its grand psychological and structural meaning of universally valid principles of thought. Rather, *myth* in this study refers to a narrative that explains what is unknown and perhaps unknowable. Myths are "useful explanations of inexplicable mystery," as Patrice Higonnet, in discussing myths about the city of Paris, paraphrases Hans Blumenberg (*Paris*, 2). Like literature, myth constructs "persons, scenes, even worlds which arouse responses uncircumscribable by rational knowledge or empirical description" (Brogan, *New Princeton Handbook*, 200). Myths often deal with origins (of a city, a people, or the gods) that are lost in time: thus the story of Romulus and Remus is one myth of the founding of Rome, and Aeneas's escape from Troy another. Myth may have some basis in historical fact (as the myth of Arthur is often thought to have) even though solid proof is lacking. Myths must ultimately be taken on trust. Indeed, they are often associated with religion (a common anthropological description of them is "sacred tales"), and although the Langland myth is a purely secular narrative, we shall see that its adherents often accept and refer to it as a matter of faith. The core assertions of the Langland myth (such as the order of composition of *Piers* or its status as autobiography) conform to Roland Barthes's influential view that the authority of modern myths comes from making highly charged claims as if they were simple facts that needed no explanation. They are regarded, he notes, as that which is obvious and goes without saying (*Mythologies*, 109-59, esp. 143): "[M]ythical beliefs transform complex cultural processes into apparently natural, unchangeable and self-evident ones" (Edgar and Sedgwick, *Key Concepts*, 250). I revere Skeat and his work, as I hope the following chapters make clear, and admire the originality of his Langland myth, whose explanatory power is proved by the value it has had in *Piers* scholarship for more than a century. But it is precisely because Skeat's influential myth, as we shall see, was presented by him as natural and obvious (and accepted as such by so many) that its history deserves to be examined and its limitations explored.

In my first chapter I trace the evolution of the Langland myth by looking at four crucial stages in its development: *(a)* the initial creation of the myth by Skeat in the late nineteenth century and its immediate acceptance; *(b)* the attack on the myth of the poet at the beginning of the twentieth century by John Manly, who argued for multiple authorship of the poem, and the defense of the myth, especially by J. J. Jusserand and R. W. Chambers; *(c)* the adoption of the myth in the innovative Athlone edition of *Piers Plowman*, even though its own editors, especially E. T. Donaldson, had recognized some of the myth's weaknesses; *(d)* the persistence of the traditional myth today, even in writing by some of the best and most original scholars of *Piers*, including Anne Middleton and Ralph Hanna III.

In my second and third chapters I examine the limitations of the myth of the poem and the myth of the poet, respectively, and suggest ways of going beyond each to new understandings of both the texts of *Piers* and its authorship. In Chapter 2, "Beyond the Myth of the Poem," I argue that *Piers* ought to be understood as a social text. The different forms of *Piers* need not be only the product of the author's compulsive personal spiritual or aesthetic struggles but may also have been shaped (either by the poet himself or by others) to address specific audiences. I demonstrate the diverse reception of individual manuscripts of *Piers* and its life in the late Middle Ages as a public, interactive text. In Chapter 3, "Beyond the Myth of the Poet," I explore the difficulties of locating the poet and his opinions in the poem. If we do not automatically assume that the poem is autobiographical, we can respond to its many discourses without trying to interpret them as the direct, personal expression of the author. Deeply engaged as it undoubtedly is with social and religious questions, *Piers Plowman* nevertheless offers no coherent message, or, more accurately, it offers too many messages. The figure of the poet is fragmented into different characters and voices throughout the work, the meaning and value of which challenge its readers.

PIERS PLOWMAN AND THE PUBLIC CULTURE OF LATE MEDIEVAL ENGLAND

Like other myths, the Langland myth depends on the faith of its supporters. I do not insist that we have to be atheists about the myth of the poet or the myth of the poem, but I do suggest that critics consider a tolerant agnosticism or perhaps polytheism. The most serious objection to the Langland myth is not that it is necessarily untrue, but that it is reductive. It offers a narrative of poet and poem that obstructs other interpretive approaches to this most provocative of Middle English works. In Part 2 of *Public Piers Plowman,* I offer an alternative to personal and elite interpretations by reading the poem in the context of the general culture of late medieval England.[2]

Before I settled on *public* as my title, I considered other related adjectives.[3] The most obvious alternative was *popular,* but I rejected it, not only because the word can mean so many different things (as can *public*), but, primarily, because it suggests too strict a separation between high and low culture. The same binary restrictiveness caused me to reject *lay* and *vernacular.* Although I certainly deal with popular, lay, and vernacular elements in *Piers,* I do not thereby exclude the recondite, clerical, and Latinate. Public culture comprehends both. Thus *public* is used here as a broad and nontechnical term, similar in significance to *common* and *general.*[4] *Piers Plowman* is a public work, for all its individual artistry, especially in its interests and its audience. It directly addresses diverse contemporary readers (lords one minute, clerics the next, then ordinary married folk), while drawing on

2. Culture, as Raymond Williams observes, "is one of the two or three most complicated words in the English language" (*Keywords,* 87). Some of the most important work on culture in the last generation has been done in anthropology, especially by Clifford Geertz (e.g., his *Interpretation of Cultures*). Perhaps the most useful way to understand culture is to see it as a system of symbols and meanings, following Geertz, and also as practice (see the evaluative essay by William Sewell ["Concept(s)"]).

3. It is not a requirement that academic work on *Piers* have an alliterative title, preferably on the letter *p,* but it does often seem to happen. I want to thank Paul Strohm for first suggesting to me the relevance of the concept of *public.* As a title, which he did not suggest, it has the added advantage of echoing and acknowledging his own groundbreaking achievement in *Social Chaucer.*

4. I decided not to use *common,* because of its pejorative modern connotations, though it seems to be the word most frequently used in Middle English for what I mean by *public* (see the quotations in Middleton, "Public Poetry"; cf. Kempshall, *Common Good*). The term *general* is perhaps too inclusive, without the political or social connotations of *public.*

a range of widely accessible discourses: commercial, political, literary, and religious. The second part of this study thus explores ways that the poem drew on, transformed, but always remained connected to the public culture of its time.

The writings of two scholars, Anne Middleton and Jürgen Habermas, have been especially helpful to me in thinking about the public in relation to *Piers Plowman*, though in each case I have modified their ideas for my own purposes. Any discussion of public poetry in late medieval England must start with Middleton's influential 1978 *Speculum* article, "The Idea of Public Poetry in the Reign of Richard II." Middleton argues that writers such as Langland and Gower produced a new kind of writing that speaks with "'a common voice' to serve the 'common good'" (95). Neither satiric nor directly addressing contemporary abuses, and certainly not courtly, this general voice is pious, but "assigns a new importance to secular life, the civic virtues, and communal service" (95). I adapt Middleton's pioneering work to support a concept of the public that is even more inclusive and dialogic: *Piers* constructs public discourses and spaces that permit a variety of competing voices rather than a single authorial voice speaking on behalf of others. Middleton defines her idea of public poetry by a series of oppositions: "'lay' (as opposed to clerical), 'popular' (as opposed to learned), 'vernacular' (as opposed to Latin)" (100). But I insist on the blurring and overlapping of such categories: the public spaces discussed in this part of my study are lay *as well as* clerical, popular *as well as* learned, vernacular *as well as* Latin—and, also, poor as well as rich, female as well as male.

Jürgen Habermas, whose book *The Structural Transformation of the Public Sphere* also lies behind my title, has been useful to my thinking about the public in *Piers Plowman*, but, as with Middleton, I have used his ideas for my own purposes. Habermas's major interest is the emergence of a "bourgeois public sphere" in the early modern period and its transformation in the contemporary world. Supported by forces such as markets and reading, forums emerged in the modern Western world, according to Habermas, "in which the private people, come together to form a public, readied themselves to compel public authority to legitimize itself before public opinion" (25–26). In its most idealistic form, according to one commentator on Habermas, the public sphere fosters "a rational-critical debate about public issues conducted by private persons willing to let arguments and not statuses determine decisions" (Calhoun, *Habermas and the Public Sphere*, 1). Habermas believes that there were no genuine public spheres in his sense during the Middle Ages; instead, he says, medieval publicness (or publicity as it is also translated) was confined solely to rulers who presented themselves before the people as the embodiment of a higher power. They made that which was invisible visible through the display of their persons by means of personal attributes such as badges, dress, demeanor, and rhetoric (*Structural Transformation*, 8), as Theseus does so effectively in Chaucer's *Knight's Tale.*

Habermas's focus differs from mine. His concern is with political life rather than literature or general culture, and his notion of a *bourgeois* public sphere, in which adversarial ideas could be debated on their merits without regard to status, does not fit the inescapably hierarchical Middle Ages. Nevertheless, Habermas's concepts, while not directly applicable to my study, have helped me to recognize that late medieval England did have spaces, both real and metaphorical, that deserve to be called public, even if they do not completely fulfill the requirements of Habermas's "public sphere." Status, gender, and power were never wholly forgotten in the Middle Ages (nor, despite Habermas, at any other time in human history), but there were places in late medieval England where groups of differing individuals could gather and interact. The public spaces I discuss are not only physical locations, such as the local church or city streets, but also discourses, including writing and art, that were available to the many and not just to the few.

The idea of public culture in late medieval England counteracts the tendency of some scholars to explain the period in terms of rigid dichotomies. The most prominent example of this in Middle English literary criticism during the preceding generation was undoubtedly the work of D. W. Robertson Jr., and his followers, whose totalizing Christian irony insisted that there was little historical change or ideological struggle from Augustine to Chaucer and who read even the richest medieval literature as dramatizing the clear opposition of good and evil, charity and cupidity (see especially Robertson's *Preface to Chaucer*). A different binary model for late medieval England, from the left rather than from the right, has recently been offered by David Aers in the opening chapters of the book he co-wrote with Lynn Staley, *The Powers of the Holy.* In Aers's account the "dominant" model of Christ's humanity in late medieval England, which stressed "the tortured, bleeding body on the Cross" (37), has had the effect of occluding, in medieval orthodoxy and modern scholarship alike, both dissenters then, like the Lollards (and Langland), and those now, like Liberation Theologists (and Aers), who imagine a more humane, social, and reforming Jesus. Instead of Robertson's view of the Middle Ages as always valuing charity over cupidity, Aers's more

political analysis imagines a small band of reformers standing against the hege-
mony of medieval ecclesiastical power. Both scholars present stark contrasts—
love versus sin or resistance versus power (and thus right versus wrong).

I Yet late medieval England also had public spaces, in art and in life, where different groups and ideas met and interacted. These places may lack the reassuring
clarity of binary opposition: rather than a middle ground they may seem something of a muddle. But the messy middle is where much cultural work gets done,
then as now. Understanding medieval public spaces as imprecise and shifting, as
ambiguous rather than definite, may prevent any nostalgic idealization of them
from whatever ideological position. The public areas I shall discuss are certainly
not lost worlds of peace and harmony, not a preindustrial dream of organic
community, but neither are they primarily sources of militant opposition and
resistance. The real and metaphorical spaces I shall explore (vernacular writing,
parish art, and civic practices) are sites of contestation, negotiation, and cooperation—in short, ordinary public life.

I begin the second part of my study by reading *Piers Plowman* along with two
vernacular prose works, *Mandeville's Travels* and the *Book of Margery Kempe.* Although
not previously discussed much with *Piers,* both works, like the poem, use the
materials of high medieval culture (often originally in Latin) to address a wider
readership. The *Travels* and Kempe's *Book* provide a variety of insights about *Piers*
that range from its textual multiplicity to its unstable narrative "I." The attempt
of these two different kinds of works (a travel book and spiritual testament) to
refigure Christianity as a more open faith (respecting even non-Catholics and
finding the sacred in ordinary life) further demonstrates that the daring
reformist religious ideas of *Piers* were not extreme, eccentric, or merely academic,
but were shared by familiar examples of contemporary public writing.

Chapter 5, "Public Art: Parish Wall Painting," moves from writing to an even
more public discourse, the art that once covered the walls of parish churches.
Murals, though often overlooked by literary and cultural historians, were the
most common and accessible visual images in the period when our poem was
first written and read, available to all regardless of class, sex, or education. Parish
wall painting offers many analogues, in both matter and style, to *Piers Plowman.*
The murals of the church nave, for example, express a "lay theology" similar to
that found in the poem, just as both emphasize the centrality of doing well in
the world. Readers accustomed to the jumble of mural subjects on parish walls

would not have been disoriented by the narrative and structural discordances in *Piers* that so often bewilder modern interpreters.

In the final chapter, I turn from written and visual art to public life: the civic practices of late medieval London. I concentrate on a single area of the city, the ward of Cornhill (mentioned once by the narrative "I" in one version of the poem as his dwelling place), not for autobiographical information about the poet, but for what Cornhill can show us about a range of urban activities that are central to the poem (especially those associated with guilds, markets, and the pillory). For instance, even though market frauds are strongly denounced in the poem, the everyday life of London (even the explicitly commercial) is also used to point to the divine. A dramatic example can be seen in the judicial spectacle of the pillory, whose exposure and punishment of crime at first suggests the thirst for social justice in the poem. Yet *Piers* is much more than a poem of strict equity and punishment: behind its pillory stands the Cross with its hope of a public and saving fellowship, more inclusive than any London parish guild, that unities all humans with Christ.

Although I question the effects of Skeat's Langland myth, in this study I follow the great editor in believing that *Piers Plowman* is anything but a marginal or eccentric work. In treating *Piers* as public, I not only stress the role of others besides the poet (now as then) in its production and reception, but also show the relationship of the poem to various discourses and practices of its time and place. This is not to say that *Piers* merely reflects its cultural environment; it transforms what it finds in the public world of late medieval England into one of the most demanding poems of the fourteenth or any other century. It is finally as a work of literature that *Piers Plowman* demands our attention and rewards being read with all the care and subtlety we can bring to it. My hope is that *Public Piers Plowman* will contribute to making this great poem more accessible, exciting, and necessary to modern readers.

PART ONE

Piers Plowman *and Modern Scholarship*

1. The History of the Langland Myth

In the "Note on the Author" at the beginning of his 1995 Everyman edition of the B-version of *Piers Plowman*, A. V. C. Schmidt expressed an understanding about the poet's life and the shape of his poem that is generally accepted by most (though not all) scholars today: "William Langland lived from c.1330 to c.1386. He was born near Malvern, in Worcestershire, and educated for a career in the Church, but appears to have married and never proceeded beyond minor orders. Little is known about his life apart from what can be learnt from the work on which he spent the years from 1360 or earlier to the time of his death, earning his living as a psalter-clerk in London, mainly, and possibly returning to the West Country in his last years. His great alliterative poem *Piers Plowman* exists in three versions, A, B and C" (vii).[1]

If there is little surprising about this account of poet and poem, it is because all its essential claims were made nearly a century and a half ago by the first modern editor of *Piers*, the great W. W. Skeat.[2] Derek Pearsall has declared that Skeat's work on *Piers Plowman* marks "the end of the 'myth' of the poem, and the beginning of a more accurate historical appraisal of it" (*Bibliography*, 218). Skeat's monumental labors did indeed sweep away many previous fancies, but in so doing he established a new and more persistent Langland myth. To be more

1. Schmidt goes on to suggest the possibility of an earlier Z-version of *Piers*, which was first proposed by A. G. Rigg and Charlotte Brewer and is still much debated.

2. Skeat edited the three versions of *Piers Plowman* for the Early English Text Society in individual volumes beginning in 1867, to which he added two volumes of commentary and annotation in 1877 and 1884; he then produced a two-volume parallel-text edition for the Oxford University Press in 1886, which became the standard edition of the poem for almost a hundred years. Skeat's most influential statement about the life of the author is in this edition (*Three Parallel Texts*, 2:xxxii–xxxviii), but see also his many other writings on the life cited in the text and notes that follow. The biography of Langland first constructed by Skeat has been widely accepted, though some of its details (such as birth at Cleobury Mortimer and life as a wanderer) have tended to drop away. In this chapter I am much indebted to the pioneering work of John Bowers, to Vincent DiMarco's magisterial *Reference Guide*, and to Charlotte Brewer's splendid *Editing "Piers Plowman."*

accurate, he established two closely related and interdependent myths: the myth of the poet's life (including youth in Malvern, marriage, marginal clerical life in London, and final return to the West Country), which explains and is explained by the myth of the poem (the writing of a single work at least three times over a working life in a specific chronological order). By using the term *myth* for these ideas about poet and poem, I do not casually dismiss what so many have for so long found so useful, as I have already discussed in my Introduction. Myths can be productive and are not necessarily false.[3] The Langland myth is a plausible explanation of the available evidence and may well be true, in whole or in part, but almost none of it can be verified, so that it remains a narrative that is, in the Scottish legal verdict, "not proven."

Skeat's construction of a Langland biography in the 1860s was a major achievement that satisfied a real need. Curiosity about the elusive author had been strong from the beginning, but little was known.[4] In a preface to the first printed edition of *Piers Plowman* in 1550, Robert Crowley declared that "[b]eynge desyerous to knowe the name of the Autoure of this most worthy worke," he consulted "such men as I knew to be more exercised in the studie of antiquities," from whom he learned that "the Autour was named Roberte langelande, a Shropshere man borne in Cleybirie [Cleobury Mortimer], aboute viii myles from Maluerne hilles" (Crowley, *.ii).[5] This information apparently came from the circle associated with the Protestant polemicist John Bale, though exactly what materials Crowley possessed is unknown.[6] A later sixteenth-century tradition begun by John Stow and accepted by Anthony à Wood and others identi-

3. Somewhat later in the fourteenth century, Dick Whittington, three times mayor of London and the subject of many modern pantomimes, did actually journey to London from his home not far from Malvern, with rather more public success than William Langland.

4. For example, ten of the sixteen relevant B-manuscripts in some way call attention to the famous line of narratorial self-identification "'I have lyved in londe,' quod I, 'my name is Longe Wille'" (B 15.152), though none provides any additional information about the poet. For the manuscript annotations to this line, see Benson and Blanchfield, *Manuscripts*.

5. Bowers observes that given that Crowley was born close to the Malvern Hills, "we may glimpse an early indication of the ways in which an editor might identify personally with his author" (J. M. Bowers, "Editing the Text," 68).

6. See the notes in Bale's manuscript (written after 1546) and now published as *Index Britanniae Scriptorum* (383, 509, 510) and his 1557 edition of *Scriptorum Illustrium Maioris Brytanniae*, which identifies Langland as a priest (DiMarco, *Reference Guide*, 3–4, 6). Similar information, apparently in Bale's hand and written about 1540, appears on the front pastedown of a B-version manuscript, Huntington Library, San Marino, MS HM 128 (Dutschke, "Guide," 163). Bale's principal informant may have been Nicholas Brigham, the constructor of Chaucer's tomb in Westminster Abbey, though Bale's notes also mention others and the

fied the author of *Piers* as John Malvern, a fellow of Oriel College; additional candidates for the authorship were also proposed, including John Lydgate and Piers Plowman himself.[7] None of these claims supplied more than a name and local habitation, in most cases clearly derived from the poem, and for a long time there was no consensus. Robert was the most popular first name for Langland during the four hundred years from Crowley to Skeat (and he was sometimes awarded John Malvern's Oriel fellowship), but many of the best authorities, such as Thomas Tyrwhitt and Richard Price, argued for William (DiMarco, *Reference Guide*, 4–50, 30–31, 40).

Knowledge about the shape of the text of *Piers Plowman* was equally uncertain. In the century before Skeat, there was growing acknowledgment that the manuscripts contained distinct forms of the poem, though there was no agreement about the number, order, and authorship of these versions. The first published statement that *Piers* had been revised was made by Joseph Ritson in 1802, and Price publicly announced a third version in 1824 in his edition of Warton's *History of English Poetry*.[8] Hearne, Ritson, and even Crowley wondered if the poem was the work of more than one person (DiMarco, "Eighteenth-Century Suspicions" and *Reference Guide*, 21–22, 35–36; Brewer, *Editing*, 14, 21; Dahl, "*Diuerse Copies*"). The two editions of *Piers Plowman* produced between Crowley and Skeat did nothing to clarify the situation. Thomas Whitaker's 1813 edition of what Skeat would later call the C-version (the first publication of the poem since Owen Rogers's reprint of Crowley in 1561) claimed that this was the earliest form of the poem; whereas in his 1842 edition of what Skeat would call the B-version, Thomas Wright, despite Price, recognized only two versions of the poem and suggested that Whitaker's text might have been a political revision by someone other than the original poet (Whitaker, *Visio Willí*, xxxi; Wright, *Vision and Creed*, xl–xli; cf. DiMarco, *Reference Guide*, 37–38, 44–45; Brewer, *Editing*, 183–84).

---

ultimate origin of this information is not clear. The most obvious mistake in the Bale account, perhaps the result of a scribal error and later pounced upon by Allan Bright, is the claim that Cleobury is only eight miles from the Malvern Hills. See Chambers, "Robert"; Kane, *Evidence*, 37–45.

7. DiMarco, *Reference Guide*, 9, 16–17, 13, 9–10; Edwards, "Seventeenth-Century." Skeat noted that David Buchanan in the mid-seventeenth century "coolly calls our author a native of Aberdeen!" (*Three Parallel Texts*, 2:xxviii; see DiMarco, *Reference Guide*, 15).

8. Thomas Hearne, as early as 1725, may have been the first to suspect revision of the poem, but he confined his thoughts to his journal. Ritson also made a private note of the possibility of a third version. See DiMarco, "Eighteenth-Century Suspicions" and his *Reference Guide* (21–22, 35–36, 40).

Into this confusion about poet and poem, Skeat brought clarity, common sense, and a powerful organizing imagination. Professor the Reverend Doctor Walter William Skeat, the first holder of the chair in Anglo-Saxon at Cambridge (and apparently the first of that university's professors to ride a bicycle), was the very model of Victorian industry and good sense throughout a remarkably productive scholarly career (Brewer, "Walter William Skeat" and *Editing*, esp. chapter 6; Sherbo, "Skeat"). He was an influential member of such innovative projects as the *Oxford English Dictionary* and the Early English Text Society, and his multivolume editions of Chaucer and Langland set new standards for textual scholarship, even as they secured a wider readership for both poets.

Skeat was the first to offer anything like a systematic life of Langland.[9] He constructed this life not from outside historical sources (which were and still are virtually nonexistent), but by stitching together the scattered comments about the first-person narrator (the dreamer/seeker who is sometimes called Will) found within the various versions of *Piers*, especially a passage about his life on Cornhill found only in the C-manuscripts.[10] Not that Skeat ignored documentary evidence when it was available. He was the first editor to recognize the importance of a memorandum that appears among a series of annals about Welsh and Despenser affairs that a later hand (c. 1412) appended to a C-manuscript of *Piers* (Trinity College, Dublin, MS 212 [D.4.1]): "Memorandum quod Stacy de Rokayle pater Willielmi de Langlond qui stacius fuit generosus et morabatur in Schiptoun vnder Whicwode tenens domini le Spenser in comitatu Oxoniensi qui predictus Willielmus fecit librum qui vocatur Perys ploughman."[11] This is the only near-contemporary source that fully names the author of *Piers Plowman* (even if written some quarter century after his presumed

9. Skeat's later work on Chaucer had the opposite effect of demolishing the Romantic life of that poet, as found in William Godwin's influential biography, for instance, based on such poems as "The Court of Love" and "The Flower and the Leaf," which Skeat showed to be apocryphal.

10. Previously, in addition to some contradictory names and birthplaces, the author of *Piers* existed only in a few fleeting images, such as Puttenham's sixteenth-century characterization of him as a "malcontent" (DiMarco, *Reference Guide*, 11) or Whitaker's Romantic wanderer (vi). There was no detailed life of the poet.

11. This memorandum is early, though apparently not as early as once thought—Kane dates it to c. 1400 but Doyle gives c. 1412 (Hanna, *William Langland*, 2n). Even after Madden discovered it (not Skeat as Hanna suggests, 2n [the correct page reference in Skeat's parallel-text edition is 2:xxviii]) and Wright printed it in his edition of *Piers*, it was not much heeded: Wright continued to believe that the poet's name was probably Robert (x–xin). It was left for Skeat to emphasize the importance of the memorandum. For transcriptions, see Kane, *Evidence*, 26; Hanna, *William Langland*, 26. For a report on recent work by Teresa M. Tavormina and Lister M. Matheson on the memorandum, see Hanna, "Emendations," 186; cf. Matheson's review of Hanna's earlier study.

death in the late 1380s). In addition to a name, the memorandum also provides William Langland with a paternity: he is identified as the son of one Stacy de Rokayle, who held lands from the Despensers in Shipton-under-Wychwood, Oxfordshire, though the memorandum says nothing more about the life or status of the poet himself.

Given the paucity of such external information, Skeat's bold innovation was to make a life of the poet by turning to the poem itself, which he described early in his editing as "a true *autobiography*" (*Text A*, xxxviii, his emphasis). With the self-confidence that marked all his work, Skeat insisted that "the internal evidence of his poem really reveals much more [than the external evidence], quite enough, in fact, to give us a clear conception of [Langland]" ("Section VIII," 245). The sources Skeat used for his life were eclectic. He took the name William Langland from the Dublin memorandum and the birthplace Cleobury Mortimer from the Bale tradition. But it was the poem itself that supplied most of the details that were shaped into a coherent biography, which runs as follows: born free and grown tall, William Langland began his first version of *Piers Plowman* while wandering on the hills above Malvern, where he had probably been to school at the priory; he then moved to London and, having taken minor orders, dwelled with his family on Cornhill; unable to rise in the Church because of his marriage, he lived in extreme poverty and supported himself by praying for others and writing legal documents; London was where he wrote the second and third versions of *Piers*; in old age he returned to the West Country and wrote a last unfinished poem, *Richard the Redeless*, while living in Bristol.[12] The ingenuity of this narrative has caused many to ignore the way it begs a central question: did the author of *Piers Plowman* mean to describe himself through the figure of the first-person speaker? The two previous nineteenth-century editors of *Piers*, Whitaker and Wright, thought not, but Skeat, although he was the first to make such a case, believed that the self-portrait was so self-evident that he felt no need to justify it further.[13]

12. Skeat, "Section VIII," 247: "[W]e may now piece together the following account of him, which is probably true, and, at any rate, rests chiefly upon his own statements." The life was first set out in Skeat's contribution to the 1871 edition of Warton's *History* and repeated in subsequent writings. On Langland's authorship of *Richard the Redeless*, now discredited, Skeat stated, "I am not only entirely satisfied on this point in my own mind, but considerably surprised to think that there could ever have been a moment's doubt about it, or any place for a contrary opinion" (*Text C*, cvii).

13. Whitaker, *Visio Willi*, xix, cf. v; Wright, *Vision and Creed*, x–xi. On Skeat's certainty that the dreamer/speaker is an authorial self-portrait, see J. M. Bowers, *Crisis*, 166; Brewer, *Editing*, 173.

In addition to the myth of the poet's life, Skeat invented the related myth of the poem. He argued that *Piers Plowman* was rewritten twice during the poet's lifetime, and he established a sequence for these versions, which he labeled and put into chronological order as A, B, and C.[14] The two conceptions were clearly intertwined in Skeat's mind as they would be for later scholars, for he described the poet and his poem as growing and declining together like the Sphinx's three ages of man. The first shape of *Piers* is the youthful A-version, "written with great rapidity and vigour"; the second is the mature B-version, expanded by Langland's greater learning and experience of London and providing the best example of the poet's "peculiar powers"; and the last is the feebler C-version, in which "there is a tendency to diffuseness and to a love for theological subtleties" ("Section VIII," 245–47).

Skeat assumed that his account of the poem, like his account of the poet, would be obvious to all. His only argument for the ABC order of composition is casual to the point of breeziness: "Now, when we proceed to place the *three* texts side by side, it is at once apparent that the B-text is *intermediate* in form between the other two; so that the order of texts must either be A, B, C or C, B, A; but the A-text so evidently comes *first*, that the C-text can only come *last*; and this settles the question" (*Text C*, xiv, his emphasis). In the best British empirical (not to say imperial) tradition, the true shape of the poet's text is not really difficult to discern, because (to the proper observer at least) it is so evidently apparent.[15] Once again, however, the result is achieved by means of begged questions, including whether the different versions of *Piers* are indeed successive authorial drafts written at different stages of the poet's life. Skeat's myth was a brilliant and imaginative achievement, though it convinced more because of the coherence and sweep of its invention than because of solid verification.

---

14. The ABC order, though without the later alphabetic labels, was announced by Skeat in his earliest publication on *Piers*. He then stated: "It is proposed to publish one of each kind in the above order, so as to show the gradual development of the poem from its briefest into its most elaborate form" (*Parallel Extracts*, 3). Thus the essence of the myth of the poem is assumed from the first: the number and order of the versions and their development over time.

15. Skeat's feeling that the order is so obvious that argument is unnecessary was expressed earlier in his edition of the C-version: "On this point [that C is later than B], the internal evidence is most conclusive; given the B-text, it is not difficult to see how the C-text was formed from it, by various omissions, additions, transpositions, and corrections. But it is hardly possible to turn the C-text into the B-form, without the most improbable and contradictory suppositions. The transition in one direction is simple and natural, but in the other direction is difficult and unlikely. This will appear so clearly upon a careful perusal of the two texts that it is hardly worth while to go into particulars. The only reason for considering the question at all is that Dr Whitaker was of the contrary opinion" (*Text C*, xi).

The shape that the Langland myth took was not inevitable but very much deter-mined by its creator and his times. In his first account of Langland's life, Skeat noted that the great eighteenth-century editor Thomas Tyrwhitt had observed that in passus I Holy Church calls the dreamer Will (see DiMarco, *Reference Guide*, 31). Agreeing with Tyrwhitt's name, Skeat declared that he "would rely yet more" on another line at the beginning of the *vita* (A 9.118), which he quotes as "Oure Wille wolde I-witen yif wit couthe hym techen" (*Text A*, xxxv). He then continues with a remarkably subjective passage: "The phrase 'oure Wille' is exactly the colloquial way of speaking of a friend or relation which may be heard any day in Shropshire still, as I can well testify, having been called 'our Wat' many a time in former days; and it seems to me so utterly unlikely that a man would use a feigned name whilst he was speaking of himself in so familiar a manner" (xxxvi). The autobiographical link between author and narrator ("speaking of himself") is essential to the life of Langland that Skeat constructs from the poem, but the association is asserted rather than proved. Indeed, the textual and philological evidence cited for this crucial move is surprisingly weak for such a learned editor. The reading "our Wille" is found in only a single manuscript and, despite Skeat's assumption, was apparently not used as a form of familiar address in the fourteenth century.[16] The energy driving Skeat's assertion is personal, not scholarly. His own fond memories of being called "our Wat" in Shropshire (the county of Cleobury Mortimer) make it "utterly unlikely" that the poet would use "a feigned name" when speaking of himself. To deny such self-identification by Langland is almost to deny Skeat's own past life. The charm and emotion of the anecdote may disguise its lack of genuine evidence.[17]

Even more determinate of Skeat's theories than personal memories was the histor-ical moment of their creation. At the beginning of the nineteenth century, Whitaker had presented the author of *Piers* as a Romantic poet recalling his experiences in tran-quility, as Bowers and Brewer have noted: "Sometimes I can descry him taking his

16. The reading "oure" at this line is found only in the Vernon manuscript, Skeat's base text for his A-edi-tion. Moreover, the form of familiar address he identifies is apparently anachronistic. Whereas expressions such as "our dame" and "our dog" are common in the fourteenth century, the use of *our* with a first name is not recorded by the *Middle English Dictionary* (*MED*) at all and not until 1847 by the *Oxford English Dictionary*, at about the time when Skeat would have been called "our Wat." No doubt the practice went back further in colloquial speech, but examples of the Middle English use of *our* with a faculty of the soul or mind (*MED*, 1d[c]) suggest that even the unique Vernon reading may be referring to the human will rather than a proper name.

17. So seductive is the biographical myth that it even briefly tempted Skeat into the fanciful kind of anti-quarianism more characteristic of his fellow editor F. J. Furnivall. Skeat made a visit to Malvern in search of the "bourn" next to which the poet first fell asleep, and he announced that he fully believed he had "found the right place," which "goes far to prove that William ascended the hill from Great Malvern, and started from the priory" (*Three Parallel Texts*, 2:xxxiiin).

staff, and roaming far and wide in search of manners and characters; mingling with men of every accessible rank, and storing his memory with hints for future use. I next pursue him to his study, sedate and thoughtful, yet wildly inventive, digesting the first rude drafts of his Visions" (Whitaker, *Visio Willī*, vi; J. M. Bowers, "Editing the Text," 69–71; Brewer, *Editing*, 38–39). Skeat echoed Whitaker's vignette of a perambulating poet, though he placed him in the London district mentioned by the narrator of the C-text: "It requires no great stretch of imagination to picture to ourselves the tall gaunt figure of Long Will, in his long robes and with his shaven head, striding along Cornhill, saluting no man by the way, minutely observant of the gay dresses to which he paid no outward reverence" (*Three Parallel Texts*, 2:xxxv–xxxvi).

If still trailing clouds of Romantic glory, the Langland imagined by Skeat is recognizably Victorian. As T. W. Heyck explains, the Victorian man of letters might be a scathing critic of aspects of contemporary society, like Dickens, but he also shared middle-class values ("order, progress, a more or less orthodox Christian morality, productivity and self-help"), with the result that he preached "social understanding and sympathy but not social revolution" (*Transformation*, 37). The Victorian public expected its writers "to be *useful*, either as entertainers . . . , or most significantly, as moral leaders or guides" (37, his emphasis); they were encouraged to take on "essentially didactic and prophetic functions," though novelists such as Thackery, Trollope, and Eliot were also admired for "accurate observation, or truth to life" (44). Skeat's Langland fits these Victorian requirements well. A keen observer of his time (his poem is "worth volumes of history" in explaining the "true temper and feelings of the English mind in the fourteenth century"), he is an eager moralist (his poem "abounds with his opinions, political and religious") who has a sympathetic concern for his society ("full of love for his fellows, the friend of the poor, the adviser of the rich") (*Text A*, iv, xxxviii). Skeat's Langland is no revolutionary (while "ever craving for the reforms of abuses, he frequently shows a conservative spirit"), and above all, no idle dilettante: the rewriting of *Piers* "not only proved his industry, but has left us an enduring monument of a *useful* life" (*Vision of Piers* [translation], xv; cf. *Vision . . . Notes*, 4:xxxiii, my emphasis).[18]

---

18. Skeat's stress on the poet's usefulness is in response to Jusserand's opposite view discussed later in this chapter. Bowers has noted how Skeat's portrait of a busy, conscientiousness Langland corresponds to the editor's "own standards for Victorian industriousness" (J. M. Bowers, "Editing the Text," 72). Other nineteenth-century influences may be detected in the Langland myth. The claim that the poem evolved from a short, simple A-version through the more complex B- and C-versions seems clearly Darwinian (82–83).

Skeat's work reveals its Victorian origins most clearly in its practicality and self-confidence. Although it was once assumed that better editions of *Piers Plowman* would solve the authorship question, we have come to understand that the editing of *Piers Plowman* can only proceed *after* a decision has already been made about who wrote it (a myth or working theory about the poet) and of the number and order of its versions (a myth or working theory about the poem).[19] Like many another contemporary British explorer into strange lands, Skeat did what he had to do to get where he wanted to go, without worrying too much about the precedents he was setting. His intertwined accounts of poet and poem are enabling myths that allowed him to get on with the difficult task at hand.[20] Absolute proof of these myths was as irrelevant as it was impossible. In a fine English tradition, Skeat became a textual positivist on instinct. He himself always retained a certain skepticism about his own conclusions and frequently insisted that they were speculative and provisional.[21] Thus for a long time he was attracted to the possibility that the poet's surname might have been Langley (it appeared as an alternative name on the title page of his student's text of the B-*visio* and was still there in a 1968 reprinting). Although his parallel-text edition established the ABC texts, the earlier EETS notes identify at least three other authorial versions (4:xvi–xvii).

Skeat's Langland myth of poet and poem were immediately and widely influential. By producing the first complete life of Langland, Skeat rescued the poet from the anonymity of most medieval writing, allowing him to take his place with Chaucer and other named canonical authors. John Hales's article in the *Dictionary of National Biography* (1892), another great Victorian project, gen-

---

19. Donaldson admitted that he and Kane found themselves unable to proceed with their edition of the B-text "until we had committed ourselves to a position on authorship" ("Textual Comparison," 241). More recently, Charlotte Brewer, in "Response," has noted that *Piers* can be edited only after the establishment of "hypothetical notions" of the order in which the various versions were written (94).

20. Originally called to Cambridge as a mathematician, Skeat admired efficiency and practicality. He thought it was silly for the university's public orator to speak in Latin and was famous for giving only a limited amount of time to any one problem before moving on to the next (Sherbo, "Skeat").

21. In an early form of his Langland biography, Skeat qualified his conclusions with phrases such as "the balance of evidence," "the probability," and "hints which we need not suppose untrue" (*Text A*, xxxvi). The fuller formulation of 1871 was still cautious, as we have seen: "[W]e may now piece together the following account of him, which is probably true" ("Section VIII," 247).

In an obituary notice A. J. Wyatt noted that Skeat's "judgment did not appear to be founded upon great principles; he was apt to reverse a decision" (Sherbo, "Skeat" 112). It was those after Skeat who accepted his enabling myth as fact.

erally followed Skeat and accepted the idea of authorial self-portrayal without question: "Langland, as we know from his own testimony, had drifted up to London" (547). The first book-length study of *Piers Plowman*, published in English by J. J. Jusserand in 1894, endorsed Skeat's views of the poem (three versions written in the order ABC) and self-descriptive poet: "[W]hile studying carefully his poem, we can discern the traits of his character, and the outline of his biography, for he has described his person and way of life, and said what he thought of both, in his work" (59).[22] Jusserand developed Skeat's life of the poet, many details of which he repeated, to probe the innermost workings of Langland's psyche. Skeat's useful and hardworking poet became, for Jusserand, an imperfectly educated, disappointed, disorganized, and humiliated soul (80–95). Friendless, thought to be mad, and little more than a beggar, he is assailed by religious doubts, which he tries to assuage with physical pleasure (96–99). Jusserand even offered a diagnosis based on contemporary Continental psychology: Langland suffered from a disease of the will that made him unable to act and produced a split personality, so that in his dialogues "it is always, under various names, Langland's *two selves* that quarrel" (101, his emphasis). Within a generation from Skeat, the elasticity of the biographical myth is clear. If the life he constructed on the assumption that the author reveals himself in *Piers Plowman* can be made to produce both his own industrious poet and Jusserand's neurotic one, what other Langlands could there not be?

Not everyone wholly accepted Skeat's biography, but the few skeptics offered no satisfactory alternative. For example, in his influential *A Short History of English Literature* (1898), George Saintsbury cautioned only that we not necessarily assume that all the details about the narrator of *Piers* (such as the name of his wife and daughter) were those of Langland himself (131). The most substantial early attack on the biographical myth was made by A. S. Jack, who argued in 1901 that the dreamer Will is "merely an ideal picture and not an autobiography" (398). Jack's questions about whether some of the attributes of the first-person narrator were also those of the author led to reformulations of the life of the poet (after him we hear less of Langland wandering

---

22. Cf. "His mode of life, his tastes, his character are clearly indicated in his poem" (73). Jusserand was an extraordinary man and later the French ambassador to the United States. In his autobiography, he records talking with Theodore Roosevelt in the White House about *Piers Plowman* (DiMarco, *Reference Guide*, 139). A presidential topic of conversation that, one assumes, has not often been revisited.

throughout England), but it did little to impede its acceptance. For despite the doubts he raised (usually by suggesting that the evidence for biographical details was improbable though not impossible), Jack provided nothing to replace Skeat's persuasive and, as we have seen with Jusserand, productive narrative life. Moreover, at the end of his article, Jack seems to soften his opposition to the idea of authorial self-description. He agreed that a "rough sketch" of the poet's life could be deduced from the poem (413), as well as conceding the central claim that it indeed recorded his views and inner character: "The opinion, hopes and fears of the author are surely here" (414).

Skeat himself was not doctrinaire about his creation and was always willing to entertain correction. In the notes to his EETS edition of *Piers*, he acknowledges that Jusserand had disputed some points in his Langland biography and magnanimously declared: "I must ask the reader to form his own opinion, setting aside at once any guess of mine that seems to be unlikely. We merely want the truth; it is of no consequence by whose means we arrive at it" (4:xxvii–xxviiin, note the modesty of "guess"). Likewise, in one of his later writings on *Piers*, Skeat phrases statements about Langland's life quite conditionally, and now acknowledges (perhaps in response to Jack) that the biographical myth may rest on an unprovable hypothesis (or what I am calling a myth): "If we may accept as real the various notes which the author has left us concerning himself."[23]

It may come as a surprise that the most fully developed life of Langland, though solidly based on the best available scholarship, was not an academic treatise but a popular novel, *Long Will*, which was written at the beginning of the twentieth century by Florence Converse.[24] Converse introduced an element conspicuously absent from *Piers Plowman*: a romantic love story, in this case between Long Will's daughter, Calote, and an aristocratic squire. Converse also imagined Langland coming into contact with virtually everyone of importance in fourteenth-century England,

---

23. *Vision of Piers* (translation), ix. There are other bibliographical cautions from the introductory essay to Skeat's translation, including "very little is certainly known concerning the author," he "was probably educated at Malvern," he "lived for many years (if we may trust his own account) in Cornhill" (ix), and "if (as he says) he was married" (x). See the two essays on the poet by Edwin Hopkins: in the first, published in 1894, Hopkins talked confidently about the "known facts" of Langland's life ("Character," 234); in the second, published four years later, he was much less definite about the author of *Piers*: "[H]is identity remains, after all efforts to determine it, an unsolved if not an unsolvable problem" ("Notes," 1, cf. 22).

24. Florence Converse was a native of New Orleans and for many years had an association with Wellesley College. *Long Will* was first published in 1903; it was added to the Everyman list in 1908 and frequently reprinted thereafter. It is still rare to go into a secondhand bookshop in a small English town and not find at least one copy.

including Jack Straw, Richard II, Chaucer, and the *Pearl*-poet (who is none other than Brother Owyn of Great Malvern Priory, Long Will's first mentor). Converse is not a great novelist, but her knowledge of the poem and its period is impressive. If her characters tend to be wooden and her style precious ("the long day trembled to latest dusk" [38]), she is no fool, and her portrait of Langland (reformist but not revolutionary; frank, frustrated, and slow to act) carefully follows the interpretations of Skeat and Jusserand.[25] Like them, she derives her Langland from the poem and, by so doing, demonstrates how porous are the borders between scholarship and imaginative recreations in the Langland myth.

THE AUTHORSHIP DEBATE: MANLY AND CHAMBERS

The general acceptance of Skeat's myth of the poet was dramatically challenged in 1906 by John Mathews Manly, a scholar later known for his textual work on the *Canterbury Tales*. Manly's claim that *Piers* was the work of multiple authors and therefore not autobiographical began a spirited debate that, although almost entirely quiescent today, dominated *Piers* scholarship through the middle of the twentieth century.[26] Manly's views produced much commotion and controversy, though the definitive proof he promised for his argument never materialized. In fact, rather than sweeping away Skeat's Langland biography, Manly ultimately reinforced it by provoking a ferocious counterattack, led first by Jusserand and then, more effectively and persistently, by R. W. Chambers.

---

25. The details of the life of Langland in *Long Will* are essentially those first brought together by Skeat: including education at Great Malvern priory, residence in London and marriage that prevented ecclesiastical advancement, and return to the West Country to die. The psychology of Converse's Langland, like his politics, is closer to that of Jusserand, though her poet is somewhat less desperate.

Not all the details in Converse's novel are convincing. Chaucer is shown reciting the *Nun's Priest's Tale* to the young Richard II (255), presumably without the line that tells of Jack Straw and his men killing Flemings, for that bloody event occurs only later in the novel. Nor would the evidence of surviving manuscripts and wills support Converse's implication that the audience for *Piers* was almost entirely made up of common people (Calote's squire buys his copy from a cook's knave [48]), any more than scholars would agree that King Richard would be a very likely reader.

26. Most of Bloomfield's 1939 review article, "Present State of *Piers Plowman* Studies," was a discussion on the debate over authorship and the related question of whether *Piers* is autobiographical. The authorship controversy gradually ran out of steam, and, as Bowers has noted, with the rise of the New Criticism and exegetics, it was "set aside rather than resolved" (J. M. Bowers, "Editing the Text," 74; cf. Brewer, *Editing*, chap. 10). The controversy over multiple authorship did have the effect of discouraging comparison between different versions of *Piers*, however; for a long time critical books tended to deal with only a single version of the poem: Dunning on A in 1939, Donaldson on C in 1949, and Frank on B in 1957. In 1972, Elizabeth Kirk offered one of the first detailed comparisons of different versions in her *Dream Thought*, though she sidestepped the authorship question by referring to the A-author and so on.

Manly opened the controversy with a short article announcing that the various versions of *Piers* were the work of five different authors ("Lost Leaf"). He declared that the first and best poet wrote the *visio* of the A-version (later labeled A1); a second was responsible for passus 9–12 of A (A2), except for the end of passus 12, which was the work of a third writer, John But. The B-version was said to be written by a fourth poet and the C-version by a fifth. These claims, as Manly himself acknowledged, were sensational (360).[27] Although some commentators had previously suggested that *Piers* might have been the work of more than one author, no one had ever presented such a detailed division of responsibility or made an argument for the clear superiority of the A-*visio*.[28] Manly declared that the "materials supporting these conclusions are now well in hand," though they could not be put into book form "until the advent of my vacation, which will occur in the coming spring" (360). Manly's vacation apparently went the way of many scholarly springs, and the promised book never appeared.[29] His views did gain special authority, however, by being restated at length as "*Piers the Plowman* and Its Sequence" in the *Cambridge History of English Literature* (1908).

Manly had no quarrel with Skeat's myth of the poem. He agreed that *Piers* existed in three principal versions written in the order ABC (though he subdivided A), calling Skeat's formulation "undisputed facts" ("Sequence," 1; Brewer, *Editing*, 187).[30] It was instead the related myth of the poet that Manly set out to overturn. If *Piers* was written by several poets, this must "entirely destroy the personality built up for the author"; information about the first-person dreamer in the different versions is thus only fictional and not "to be taken as genuine traits of the author himself" ("Lost Leaf," 359, 360). Instead of seeing one poet gradually revealing his life and personal opinions during successive revisions, Manly insisted

27. The sensation was recognized and indeed promoted by Furnivall, who at first wholly supported Manly and issued special volumes of the Early English Text Society with the major essays of the debate. See Brewer, *Editing*, 186–87.

28. For older suggestions about the multiple authorship of *Piers*, as previously mentioned, see DiMarco, "Eighteenth-Century Suspicions" and his *Reference Guide*, 21–22, 35–36. For suggestions of dual authorship made by Crowley, Hearne, and Wright, see Brewer, *Editing*, 14, 21, 58–59.

29. Although Manly began with a textual argument (the so-called lost leaf), it soon became clear that he himself had not actually studied the manuscripts of *Piers* but relied on Skeat's texts. See Chambers, "Authorship," 21–25 and "Three Texts," 140ff., and Chambers and Grattan, "Text" (1909). Brewer reports private statements in which Chambers claimed that Manly eventually abandoned the theory of multiple authorship (*Editing*, 194n), but see Stroud, "Marginal Notes."

30. Until recently there was almost no dissent from the ABC sequence except in an essay by Howard Meroney ("Life and Death"), whose views had little effect.

on several different authors who variously described an invented dreamer figure, whose attributes had no historical or autobiographical validity.[31]

Manly's hypothesis of multiple authorship not only had the appeal of novelty, but also echoed contemporary scholarly trends. As Middleton has pointed out, "His interpretative strategy resembled that of several nineteenth-century accounts of long, complex, and usually anonymous works from early or traditional societies," such as the Homeric poems, *chansons de gestes*, and *Beowulf* (or the Bible), which were analyzed as "aggregates of separate works, accretions representing stages of construction by several composers" ("*Piers Plowman*," 2225; cf. Kane, *Evidence*, 4–5n). Manly presented himself as the kind of modern scholar who based his arguments on objective textual evidence and logical deduction, in a rationalistic approach later imitated by some who argued against him, especially Kane. His original article cited a "missing leaf" in the A archetype to explain incoherencies not noticed by the author of B, which he would have fixed had he been the original composer. From the first, Manly offered his conclusions as fact: he asserted that his initial suspicions about multiple authorship had become "certainties" and claimed the ability to "prove" it ("Lost Leaf," 359). As Charlotte Brewer has noted, Manly relished his role as the bold herald of what he called a "new truth," one based on the techniques of contemporary research: "I am merely a humble follower in paths of science long known and well charted" (Manly, "Authorship" [1909], 52; Brewer, *Editing*, 192).[32]

Although he associated himself with scientific methods, Manly's interpretation of *Piers Plowman* can be as subjective as Skeat's. His first article opens with this remarkable statement: "Summer before last, in the enforced leisure of a long convalescence, I reread *Piers the Plowman*" ("Lost Leaf," 359). He goes on to say that "fortunately" Skeat's parallel-text edition was not then available to him and thus he read the three texts of *Piers* separately, which brought home to him their sharply different qualities. Manly's autobiographical comments (in the service of denying authorial autobiography) remind us that criticism is always contingent:

31. For example, whereas Skeat had accepted Kitte and Calote as real, Manly insists that "there can be no doubt that both are used as typical names of lewd women, and are, therefore, not to be taken literally as the names of the author's wife and daughter" ("Sequence," 34). Skeat, a gallant Victorian, was deeply offended by such slander of mother and child (see his letter to Chambers quoted in Brewer, *Editing*, 234–35).

32. Manly's most persistent follower, Thomas Knott, makes much of his own up-to-date critical methods in contrast to Skeat's old-fashioned ways, often without real justification (Knott, "Essay").

had Manly not become ill, or not recovered, or not then read the poem in separate volumes, the authorship debate over *Piers Plowman* might never have begun.[33]

Manly's identification of several authors for *Piers Plowman* was fundamentally
an aesthetic judgment. As he read each of the separate versions, he formed "a
definite sense of its style and characteristics" ("Lost Leaf," 359) and became
convinced of their individuality. Neither Skeat nor Jusserand had much to say
about the artistry of *Piers* (as opposed to the opinions and psychology of its
author), but it was what supported Manly's belief in multiple authorship.

Manly's central aesthetic insight is the sharp contrast between the A-*visio* and the
other versions of the poem, especially the B-version. From Crowley through Skeat,
the B-version had generally enjoyed pride of place. Manly proposed instead that A 1
was the poetic masterpiece, and he praised it from the beginning for its "unity of
structure, vividness of conception, and skill of versification" ("Lost Leaf," 360).
Influenced by the literary tastes of his day, Manly valued directness, expressiveness,
and realism, all of which he found only in the first poet, who had the "power of
visualisation and of rapid narration unbroken by explanation or moralisation"
("Sequence," 8): his work achieved "the clear, undisturbed objectivity of excellent
drama, or of life itself" (11). The additions to the confessions of the sins by the
poet who wrote B, however, are dismissed as "confused, vague, and entirely lacking
in the finer qualities of imagination, organization, and diction shown in all A's
work" ("Lost Leaf," 365).[34] Manly's essay in the *Cambridge History* expanded on these
judgments, which remain fundamentally aesthetic: "There are differences in diction, in metre, in sentence structure, in methods of organizing material, in number
and kind of rhetorical devices, in power of visualizing objects and scenes presented, in topics of interest to the author and in views on social, theological and
various miscellaneous questions" ("Sequence," 4). Manly rarely defended or even
provided examples of his impressionistic distinctions but claimed that they were
obvious: the stylistic disparity between the first and second poets of the A-version,

33. The authorship of *Piers* is especially open to subjective views because we have so little external or
objective evidence. Brewer notes Manly's "purely subjective impression" that there was something wrong
with the presentation of the Deadly Sins in the three versions of the poem, though most readers over the
years had been untroubled by these passages (*Evidence*, 191).

34. Manly insisted, "I have never, at any time or in any place, denied the ability of B to write lines as
good as any written by A; on the contrary, B has some passages which—as I think and have always
thought—are entirely out of the range of A's ability" ("Authorship" [1909], 113). But this misrepresents
the tone not only of his earlier views but also of later statements, including that the B-author "had, as we
have seen, no skill in composition, no control of his materials or his thought" ("Sequence," 28)—"a tendency to rambling and vagueness" (23), despite his "sincerity and emotional power" (29).

for example, were said to be "so striking that they cannot be overlooked by any one whose attention has once been directed to them" (17, cf. 31).

Admirers of *Piers Plowman* have always wanted to make this difficult poem more appealing to readers. In the sixteenth century, Crowley promoted it as a pro-Protestant work, and later Skeat provided Langland with the modern edition and biography suitable for a canonical author. Manly's contribution was more drastic, a kind of literary triage. He was willing to sacrifice the two long versions of *Piers* in order to save the favored short work.[35] All that he found diffuse, lifeless, and confusing in *Piers*, Manly attributed to bumbling continuers who obscured the original work of genius, which is "on a level with the best work of the fourteenth century, including Chaucer's" ("Lost Leaf," 360). Derek Pearsall notes that Manly's choice "found a receptive audience among those who were much more willing to read a poem of 2500 than one of 7500 lines" (Pearsall, "Forty Years," 1).[36] Today the *visio*, usually in the B-version, is still more likely to be taught to students than any other part of the poem except passus B 18.[37]

The argument for multiple authorship was difficult even for its adversaries to dismiss entirely (some thirty years after the theory was first proposed, Bloomfield's review article advocated a compromise position), but Manly's challenge ultimately failed—in large part because he never offered an account of poet and poem as coherent and as stimulating as Skeat's.[38] He and his followers were able to cast doubt on the most vulnerable aspects of the Langland biography, as Jack had done previously, and to call attention to differences in the versions of *Piers* without, however, creating an account of *Piers* and its authorship that was able to persuade many readers for long. For instance, few were willing to reject everything in the poem as inferior except

35. In his first article, Manly insisted that his position was not entirely destructive: indeed, because of it, the "poem, as a whole, will gain in interest and significance" ("Lost Leaf," 366).

36. Even Manly's immediate opponents gave implicit support to his argument. Skeat produced a much reprinted school-text of the B-text *visio* alone, and in his summary of the poem in his book, Jusserand gave several times more space to the prologue and first seven passus than to the remaining thirteen (*Piers Plowman*, 23–30 as opposed to 30–31).

37. Manly's position got modern support from Philip Hobsbaum, who argued that the *vita* is much inferior to the *visio*, which he asserts is one of the great English poems ("Through Modern Eyes").

38. Skeat and Manly together demonstrate the way that scholars often approach Chaucer and Langland differently. Just as Skeat, who invented the Langland biography, also undermined the accepted Chaucer biography by showing that some of the poems on which it was based were apocryphal, so Manly, who denied any real person behind the narrator of *Piers*, then wrote *Some New Light on Chaucer*, which claimed to identify historical people behind many of the Canterbury pilgrim-narrators.

A 1. Indeed, the literary qualities Manly most disliked in the longer versions—including digression and wordplay—are what has made *Piers* especially interesting to many modern critics.

Manly ended his essay on *Piers Plowman* in the *Cambridge History* with some
overheated rhetoric echoing Crowley's view of Langland as prematurely
Protestant (thus anticipating David Aers): the poet is linked with Chaucer and
Wyclif as one who was "striving to light the torch of reformation, which, hastily
muffled by those in authority, smouldered and sparkled fitfully a hundred years
before it burst into blaze" ("Sequence," 41). But Manly's peroration also makes a
case that *Piers* contains the voice not just of "one lonely, despised wanderer, but
of many men" (42). The argument that *Piers Plowman* is a social, public text (and
not primarily the autobiographical expression of an individual sensibility) has
been suggested over the years by others (though usually for different reasons
than multiple authorship) and, of course, is the central concern of this book.

Jusserand was the first to respond to Manly's claim for multiple authorship. If
the latter had been willing to give up most of *Piers* in order to save the A-*visio*,
Jusserand felt this was a desecration of what, next to the *Canterbury Tales*, is "the
greatest literary work produced by England during the Middle Ages" ("Work of
One" [1909], 271). The brief but spirited exchange between Manly and Jusserand
during 1909 and 1910, like many polemical debates, revealed the weaknesses of the
opponent's argument more successfully than the strengths of either proponent's.
Manly's assertion that the differences between the versions of *Piers* would be obvious to anyone whose attention was called to them meant that Jusserand needed only
to say that they were not obvious to him (see, for example, Jusserand, "Work of
One" [1909], 299–300, 307–9). Jusserand secured another advantage for himself,
which many later defenders of single authorship would imitate, by insisting that the
myth of the poet is the most natural view. Decrying those who believe that poets
are "always deceitful," Jusserand urges us to be "skeptical about such skepticism"
(326–27). He insists that we are justified "in adhering to our former faith" (329)
of a single autobiographical narrator "so long as no positive text or fact contradicts
the plain statements in the poem" (328). This neatly combines law and religion: the
myth is innocent until proved guilty and a testament to credal loyalty. For all their
learning and intelligence, both Jusserand and Manly are believers, though in separate doctrines. Their debate is not exploratory (their second exchange largely
restates previous positions) but designed to defend an accepted truth. Whatever
points their opponent may seem to score, each in his heart knows that he is right.

During the Jusserand-Manly debate, a new champion emerged on behalf of a single autobiographical poet for *Piers*—the estimable R. W. Chambers.[39] For thirty years he was the most knowledgeable and reasonable voice in the debate (his first publication, with J. H. G. Grattan, appeared in 1909, his last in 1939), as Charlotte Brewer's subtle portrait of him in *Editing "Piers Plowman"* reveals.[40] Like Manly, Chambers accepted Skeat's myth of the poem (three versions in the order ABC) as undeniable fact, but he brought a new sophistication to the related myth of the poet. In his earliest essays, Chambers challenged the missing-leaf theory (which Jusserand had accepted) and showed that some of the textual differences between versions claimed by Manly rested on a naive acceptance of Skeat's editions not supported by the manuscripts (Chambers and Grattan, "Text" [1909]; Chambers, "Authorship"; cf. Brewer, *Editing*, 198). Although Chambers conceded that the theory of multiple authorship might eventually prevail, he, like Jusserand before him, insisted that it was the responsibility of the prosecution to make a case against the traditional view: "It is not argued that A, B, and C are the same man, but only that the arguments so far brought forward are insufficient to prove that they are not" ("Authorship," 29). Perhaps because Chambers had exposed his lack of textual knowledge, Manly soon dropped out of the debate.[41] His place was taken by one of his students, Thomas Knott, who had looked closely at the *Piers* manuscripts and was able to correct Chambers on some points (Knott, "Essay"; see Brewer, *Editing*, 240–45). Knott added little of substance to the debate, however (Brewer, *Editing*, 247–51), and is perhaps best remembered for setting a standard of bad temper and self-righteousness rarely equaled among textual scholars of *Piers*, despite some formidable contenders.

39. Chambers is a pivotal figure who links the generations of modern *Piers* scholarship; he received Skeat's blessing to reedit the A-text for the Early English Text Society (Chambers and Grattan, "Critical Methods," 274–75) and bequeathed what would become the Athlone edition to his student George Kane.

40. Brewer makes clear that Chambers was the driving force in the Chambers-Grattan partnership (e.g., *Editing*, 196). Chambers is the hero of Brewer's book, admirable for what he accomplished and unfortunate for what he failed to do. His editing of *Piers* was never completed, in part because of outside circumstances (including two world wars) and, perhaps most important, because he became overwhelmed by the complexity of the textual issues he found in the manuscripts. If Skeat and Kane are reminiscent of Homeric heroes (the former shrewd and flexible like Odysseus, the latter forceful and uncompromising like Achilles), Chambers is more like Virgil's Aeneas: respectful of his elders, too sensible to go to extremes, and leaving it to others to reach the goal (Rome or new editions of *Piers*) for which he sacrificed so much.

41. Manly's final published work on *Piers Plowman* ended his contribution to the debate with a whimper: a brief note declaring that he was not the first to believe in multiple authorship, for so had the nineteenth-century scholars Thomas Wright and George Marsh (Manly, "Authorship" [1916]). Manly then turned to work on Chaucer.

For all his scrupulousness in argument, Chambers, like Jusserand before him, was a devout believer in Long Will and was shaken by Manly's challenge.[42] Although he may have overestimated how many had deserted the old faith, it clearly needed renewal. Chambers made two major contributions to the myth of the poet, each of which became widely accepted by later scholars.[43]

Chambers's first defense of Langland's self-portrayal in his poem was an appeal to literary history. He classified *Piers Plowman* as a familiar type of medieval allegorical vision (other examples include the *Roman de la Rose* and even Dante's *Commedia*) in which the author deliberately represents himself as the narrator/dreamer, often giving this figure his own name and making him a significant part of the action: "I submit that the view that 'Will' represents the dreamer, but not the writer, is an anachronism" ("Robert," 442; cf. Preface, 17; "Three Texts," 131). Chambers claimed to have shown "how alien to the school of poetry to which *Piers Plowman* belongs is the idea of creating an imaginary dreamer" ("Robert," 444). Conceding that everything we are told about such narrators cannot be literally autobiographical because so many details "are conventional and fictitious" (447), he is nevertheless confident that "we can generally distinguish what may be fiction and what is fact" (449).

Chambers's second contribution was more ingenious. Dismissing Manly's assertions of major aesthetic differences between versions (especially A and B), Chambers argued instead for a development in the thought and beliefs of the same author. Without supplying any additional historical facts to Skeat's life of Langland, Chambers nevertheless produced a dramatic new personal narrative, again revealing the generative potential of Skeat's myth. Chambers insisted that the brief *vita* of A (A 9–11), which Manly thought had been written by a differ- ent poet from that of the A-*visio*, "breaks off sharply" because the first-person narrator raises challenging religious questions to which Langland himself had no satisfactory answers ("Long Will," 53; cf. "Three Texts," 133; "Incoherencies," 31; *Man's Unconquerable Mind*, 129–30). This impasse forced the poet to stop work on *Piers* for fifteen years, the period referred to in the dream-within-a-dream of B 11—though Chambers allows that the confession there of wild profligacy "need not be strictly autobiographical" (*Man's Unconquerable Mind*, 135). What

42. Early in the debate, Chambers rather dramatically wrote that "William Langland is on trial for his life" ("Original Form," 303).

43. He initially sketched out both ideas in 1919 ("Three Texts," 129–33) and developed them in later publications.

frustrated Langland for so long, according to Chambers, were questions of predestination and the efficacy of learning and good works. In particular, the poet
was unable to accept the Church's teaching that even righteous non-Christians
were denied salvation: it is precisely this dissent from orthodox doctrine that
"makes him abandon his work in despair, and which costs him so many years of
struggle and self-reproach" ("Long Will," 67; cf. "Incoherencies," 31; *Man's
Unconquerable Mind*, 148). Rather than a confused continuation of the A-text by
an inferior poet, as Manly thought, the B-text for Chambers is a heroic statement
by an artist who was finally able to triumph over the bigotry of his age: "Not
often has the struggle of a poet's soul during a long series of years been told as
it is in these first two *passus* of the B-continuation" ("Long Will," 68; *Man's
Unconquerable Mind*, 149).[44] Chambers's response to Manly's challenge thus argued
for an even closer identification between poet and poem than had been proposed
by Skeat. The different versions of *Piers* not only sketch the poet's life and record
his opinions, but also, according to Chambers, reveal the depths of his heart and
mind as he undergoes an epic spiritual odyssey.

Chambers's determination to refute Manly's claim of multiple authorship and to
reaffirm the biographical consistency of the different versions of *Piers Plowman* is
shown by the welcome he extended to the most extravagant attempt to discover the
poet's life in the poem: a series of short notes by Allan H. Bright during 1925–26 that
in 1928 were expanded into a slim volume cheekily titled *New Light on "Piers Plowman."*[45]
Like so much else in Langland scholarship, Bright's antiquarian impulse to locate the
actual locations of poetic passages can be traced back to Skeat, who, as noted above,
believed that he had discovered the very spring in the hills above Great Malvern where
the poet had his first vision. Bright announced the discovery of several new sites associated with the poem on the western side of the Malvern Hills, including his own candidate for the poet's spring, Primeswell (*New Light*, 50); a field called Longlands from
which he said the poet took his name (43ff.); and the very Field of Folk itself

44. Chambers's argument can be seen as a development of Skeat's focus on the poet's views and opinions as well as of Jusserand's attention to the poet's mental conflicts; but Chambers went further in
asserting that the poet achieved a remarkably progressive attitude toward non-Christians—a bridge
thrown over the stream of time connecting medieval and modern, as he characterizes it adapting a phrase
of Shelley ("Long Will," 64). For Chambers this was a triumph of man's unconquerable mind, as his
book of that title calls it—a book published at a time (1939) when the world was in crisis and bigotry of
the sort he believed Langland had resisted was dominating Europe. For Chambers, Langland was more
than a premature Protestant, he was a premature modern liberal.

45. Bright's title plays on that of *New Light on Chaucer,* published two years earlier by none other than
Manly himself.

(51ff.).[46] If all interpretation is to some degree personal, Bright's bias is clearer and more extreme than most. Many of the places he identified were on or near land he himself owned at Barton Court in Colwall next to the Malvern Hills.[47]

Bright did not prove or extensively discuss his claims about the poet, but, even more obviously than others, he simply asserted them. Of Langland's birth, he declared: "William, Eustace de Rokayle's son, was illegitimate. His mother is unknown. She may have been some 'serving wench' at Hanley Castle, or, more probably, the daughter of some farmer or tradesman at Ledbury" (*New Light*, 36–37). Nor was Bright given to especially rigorous reasoning. He noted that fields were frequently called Longland in Herefordshire (43), as if this did not undermine his claim to have identified the particular one associated with the poet.[48] Invention is where Bright especially shone. He suggested, for example, that the character Piers might have been based on a maternal relative with whom the poet worked (though "much idealized" [46]), and that the Good Knight of the half acre was James de Brockbury, holder of a manor in Colwall. This same James is then said to reappear in the poem as the character Clergy, Scripture being a portrait of James's second wife, whom the poet had tutored, producing jealousy in her hus-

46. Bright was not the first to identify Longlands and Primeswell as Langland sites; another local antiquarian, Canon Arthur T. Bannister, proposed them in a 7 September 1922 letter to the *TLS* ("Birthplace," 569). Although Bannister is cited in Bright's initial article in the *TLS* (12 March 1925 [Bright, "Birthplace"]), he is barely mentioned in Bright's *New Light*: there Bannister is thanked along with Chambers for "encouragement, suggestions, and assistance" (31), without acknowledgment of the specific ideas that were originally his. Bannister tended to be a good deal more cautious than Bright about his discoveries: "In a matter so obscure as Langland's birthplace one does not dogmatize."

One of Bright's own original claims was that Cleobury, which John Bale had identified as the poet's birthplace, must actually be a reference to Ledbury, a town immediately west of the hills. The evidence he presents in an early article is hardly compelling: he asserts that the distance from Malvern fits Ledbury better than Cleobury and that the two names are "very similar both in sight and sound" ("Birthplace," 172). Evidence is virtually nonexistent in his little book: discussing references to Cleobury in Bale and others, he says, "It is obvious that all these statements come from the same source and that the word 'Clibery' has become substituted for the word 'Lidbery'" (*New Light*, 35). What Bright ignores, of course, is that numbers are more likely to be corrupted and confused than place-names. Ledbury is a pleasant market town whose recent tourist brochure proclaims it to be the birthplace of both Langland and Elizabeth Barrett Browning.

47. In his *TLS* articles, Bright gave his address as "Barton Court, Colwall, Malvern," and, in his first piece on "William Langland's Early Life," he claimed that the poet once worked on the manor of Barton Colwall ("Early Life" [1925], 739). Given the Disneyfication of our world, one might be tempted to imagine that Bright's discovery of places on his own property associated with the poem was part of some mad scheme to create a *Piers Plowman* theme park: Longlands! Featuring dungeons, colorful pub events, and a daily attack by Antichrist. Malvern, a lovely Victorian resort town more suggestive of the world of Skeat than of Langland, today pays little attention, unlike Ledbury, to the poet (though it does have a route honoring the composer Elgar). Malvern's most famous product remains its water, which is still bottled in Colwall.

48. Brian S. Smith also notes that in addition to a "Longlands" at Colwall, there were other fields called by this name in neighboring parishes: Coddington, Sherrards Green, and Malvern Link (*History of Malvern*, 89).

band, "and possibly not altogether without cause" (60–63). Refutation seems beside the point in the face of Bright's enthusiastic and uninhibited imagination.[49]

Chambers contributed a cautious introductory letter to Bright's little study, recommending it to the "very serious consideration" of other scholars (Preface, 26). Although he noted with considerable understatement that Bright's "hypotheses vary very much in probability" (26), he agreed that the view from Primeswell Spring fit the opening description in *Piers* better than any other site on the Malvern Hills or probably than anywhere else in England (11–12). A decade later he again endorsed Primeswell along with the strong possibility that the name Langland was taken from a nearby farm ("Robert," 462). That such a careful scholar as Chambers would encourage such fanciful speculations shows how eager were advocates of single authorship for biographical support.[50] Not that we have reason to feel too superior to *New Light*. Many scholars more brilliant than Bright have believed in the myth of the poet. And even the ideas of an enthusiast can contribute. The possible Langland connection with the Despensers through his supposed father, Stacy de Rokayle, had long been known, but Bright is the first, to my knowledge, to argue that because the Despensers were the lords of Malvern Chase and Hanley Castle, this might explain how a son of one of their retainers came to be associated with the area.[51] Bright also made some intriguing interpretive points, even if they are based on doubtful evidence. His claim that Langland was a bastard has no documentary support, but illegitimacy is certainly a vexed issue in the poem. His further suggestion that Langland's mother was a peasant is equally unattested, but reminds us that the poet has an unusual sympathy for and knowledge of the very poor.[52]

49. Because of its inventive ways, Bright's *New Light* is best taken as a fictional prequel to Florence Converse's *Long Will*, supplying details about the early life of the poet only briefly sketched in the novel.

50. Bright's speculations were also accepted by subsequent writers. In 1935 Stanley James referred to his "true facts" (*Back to Langland*, 9), and a much more serious scholar, Morton Bloomfield, accepted Bright's claim that Langland "was Willelmus de Colewell" ("Benedictine Monk," 57; cf. Bright, *New Light*, 42). In his introduction to a 1969 collection of essays on *Piers*, Hussey agreed with Bright that Langland was probably born in Ledbury (Introduction, 13).

51. *New Light*, 35. In the commentary to his EETS edition of *Piers*, Skeat mentioned in passing the Despenser possession of Malvern and Malvern Chase, but, of course, he believed Langland already had a local connection because he had been born in Cleobury (4:xxvii).

52. Bright thought, unlike Skeat, that Langland's ideas were so politically dangerous that the poet rightly feared to express them openly, a view that has recently come back into favor among some scholars, though we have no evidence that anyone ever got into trouble for reading *Piers Plowman*: "The times were such, and the risks were so great, that it was prudent for Langland to conceal his identity as far as possible, though the name of the author may have been generally, if not openly, known" (*New Light*, 75).

THE ATHLONE EDITION

George Kane's 1960 edition of the A-version of *Piers Plowman* (completing the work begun long before by Chambers and Grattan) proclaimed a new era in the scholarship on the poem. This first volume of the Athlone edition was highly praised and brought a sophistication to the editing of *Piers* that has influenced textual work far beyond the poem itself. The daringly interventionist Athlone B-version by Kane and E. Talbot Donaldson was published in 1975, and the long-announced C-version by George Russell and Kane finally appeared in 1997.[53] The Athlone *Piers* made significant advances in both textual theory and practice, but its core premises remain those first established by Skeat, especially his myth of the poem: three versions written by a single poet in a particular order.[54] Because of this, fundamental questions about the poem and its poet are either avoided or answered preemptively by the Athlone editors without adequate consideration of alternatives.

Skeat's ABC sequence was indispensable to the radical editing practiced in Athlone B. Kane and Donaldson argue that readings found in A and C must once have existed also in B, even if they do not survive in the extant B-manuscripts: "For if the texts of A and C, the earliest and latest versions of the poem, agree in a reading, their agreement sets up a presumption that no revision occurred at that point" (*B Version*, 76).[55] Yet this vital chronological assumption taken over from Skeat rests on very little proof. Kane and Donaldson begin boldly (and I think correctly) by conceding in a footnote that the historical allu-

53. The scholarly reception of the Athlone B-version has always been more mixed than that of its A-version. Admiration for the B-version's conceptual daring and brilliant textual reconstructions, expressed most powerfully by Lee Patterson ("Logic"), coexist with unease about some of its assumptions and specific readings (see, for instance, the review by Turville-Petre). Recently its methods have undergone more systematic and searching critique, most stringently by Charlotte Brewer, many of whose conclusions have been supported by Robert Adams. Ralph Hanna once gave a paper titled "The Mark of Kane(-Donaldson)"; some recent scholarship might be called "The Kane Mutiny."

54. The premise of three (and only three) authentic forms of the poem is declared in the general title of the Athlone edition: *Piers Plowman: The Three Versions*. In a recent statement on the text, Kane continues to assert that Langland permitted his work to be copied on only three occasions, the last perhaps sanctioned by an executor after the poet's death ("Text," 183–84).

55. Kane and Donaldson's "presumption," which they soon take as a given, is an example of the suspect reasoning sometimes used to establish even fundamental points in Athlone. Although the theoretical possibility of authorial revision is mentioned by Kane and Donaldson, it is quickly dismissed in favor of an alternative explanation: corruption of the B-exemplar (76–77). As Brewer has pointed out, the editors "do not *seriously* consider the possibility of whimsical, inconsistent revision" or the "possibility that Langland may have decided against an A reading for his B text, but subsequently have reinstated it in C" (*Editing*, 390, my emphasis; cf. Adams, "Editing *Piers*," 59).

sions often used to date versions of *Piers* cannot establish the order of composition, because such evidence is "equivocal" (71n).[56] Without the support of such allusions, the editors confess, they can defend the traditional sequence only by assertion: "Thus the order of composition of the three versions of *Piers Plowman*, however conceived, must both appear obvious, and be strictly hypothetical" (71). For its obviousness, they cite (again in a footnote) Skeat's one-hundred-year-old appeal to the self-evident discussed above, which now seems outdated amid the modern textual apparatus of the Athlone edition (71n). Because of the importance of the ABC order to their editorial practice, Kane and Donaldson feel obliged to go beyond mere obviousness and "give reasons" for their "opinion" that it is "the best hypothesis" (71). In doing so, they add little of substance. Consider their justification for believing that the A-version was the first form of *Piers*: "In the absence of other considerations a natural presumption that a poem under revision will grow in content, scope and meaning, rather than diminish, must make this seem the earliest form of *Piers Plowman*" (71). A "natural presumption" is not much on which to base a crucial hypothesis, and a central question is not addressed: is *Piers*, in fact, a work under revision? Kane and Donaldson accept Skeat's assumption that it is, without really examining alternatives.[57]

The truisms of the Langland myth often seem to shape Kane and Donaldson's conclusions. Thus they assert that "because in its major features B resembles A more than C does, and also resembles C more than A does, . . . it occupies the medial position. This physical sequence is a fact" (*B Version*, 72). But the resemblances they note would also exist if B had been the author's prin-

---

56. Such topical allusions were very important for Skeat and have been used again recently by Hanna in his *William Langland*, though they remain equivocal. For example, Hanna endorses Skeat's claim that the quotation from Ecclesiastes 10:16 in the fable of the rats and mice about the woe for a realm when its king is young (B pr.193–96) is an allusion to the minority of Richard II (*William Langland*, 13). This may indeed be so (Adam Usk used the verse to refer to the young king in his *Chronicle* [6]), but that assumption is qualified by the use of the same quotation in an early fourteenth-century Anglo-Norman discussion of the requirements for good leadership that appears in a major London municipal collection known as the *Liber Custumarum* (17). The passage in the *Liber*, which (including the quotation) is ultimately derived from Brunetto Latini's *The Book of the Treasure* (*Li livres dou tresor*), seems to be a general argument about the need for wise and mature rule rather than a topical allusion to a particular leader (352).

57. Kane and Donaldson's second reason for believing that A is earliest, which they call "a matter of judgement," is similar to their first: "The basis of our judgement is the general proposition that unless there are contrary indications any authorial version of a poem which both comprises a shorter version and extends its development is likely to be the subsequent one" (*B Version*, 72). They then deal very briefly with the B–C sequence: "[T]he differences between B and C appear as differences between a first, completed poem and a more soberly reflective, but unfinished revision of this" (74).

cipal version, with A and C each separately derived from it. If anything is a fact
about the three versions of *Piers*, it is difference (and the centrality of B), not a
specific sequence. Skeat's myth of the poem has not been tested but has been
taken for granted. Elsewhere in the introduction to the Athlone B-version,
appeals to what Brewer calls "the methodology of the empirical sciences" (*Editing*,
405, cf. 325–26) coexist, sometimes uneasily, with admission by the editors of an
inevitable subjectivity.[58]

Yet the Athlone editors, better than anyone, are aware of the textual complexity of *Piers Plowman* and the pressure this puts on Skeat's tidy myth of
the poem. In grappling with the tangle of the manuscripts, each editor has
had to contend with doubts and enigmas, sometimes concerning basic tenets
upon which Athlone depends. Even George Kane, whose robust confidence
in his methods and judgment allowed him to achieve results that eluded
Chambers, was not without moments of uncertainty. As Charlotte Brewer
has demonstrated, Kane's textual principles have shifted, often without
acknowledgment, over his career (see, especially, "Textual Principles").
Moreover, despite basing the editing of Athlone on the ability to distinguish
between scribal and authorial writing, even in quite minor cases, Kane
admits to uncertainty about a long and especially important passage: he cannot say how much (if any) of passus 12 of the A-version was actually written by the poet.[59]

George Russell's work on the C-version exposed further difficulties with
Skeat's formulations. In an early essay, he noted that the C-author's apparent
use of a corrupt scribal copy of B as his base text, many of whose inauthentic
readings were then incorporated into C, "weakens—or at least calls into question—the proposition of single authorship for all three versions": the very

58. An example of Kane and Donaldson's scientific vocabulary is the reference to their edition as a
"theoretical structure, a complex hypothesis" (*B Version*, 212); for frank acknowledgment of the subjectivity
of their methods, see *B Version*, 75, 191–92, 213. The tension between science and subjectivity in the editing of Athlone B was first noted by Patterson ("Logic") and has been discussed by Brewer ("Authorial vs.
Scribal") and Adams ("Editing *Piers*"), both of whom tend to be more critical than Patterson.

59. Kane declared that A 12.1–98 "may be wholly or partly authentic, representing wholly or partly an
imperfect or abortive continuation of the poem by the author," although he believed it "unlikely" that the
lines were authorial (*A Version*, 51). Compare this with Skeat's certainty about the authenticity of the same
lines: "I have not the slightest doubt of the entire *genuineness* of the new portion. It is Langland's beyond a
doubt, every word of it, from line 1 down to the end of line 100. All these lines are not only in his manner,
but contain his favorite words, phrases, and turns of expression, and have the same changes of rhythm as
we find in his works elsewhere" (143*, his emphasis, in a supplement to A that Skeat published in his 1869
EETS edition of the B-version).

heart of the Langland myth ("Evolution," 44). Despite raising such doubts, Russell supported one author for all versions of *Piers*, but his assumption, shared by Kane, that in writing C the poet had accepted manuscript corruptions into his text had the awkward result of requiring the Athlone edition of C to include as authorial some of the same readings that had been rejected as scribal in Athlone B (see Russell and Kane, *C Version*, 94). The Athlone editors thus suggest that they are able to recognize the author's own words better than he could himself. Russell also long advocated that the final form of the C-version was not the work of Langland himself, but of an editor or literary executor ("Evolution," 45; "Some Aspects," 48; and, especially, "As They Read It," 175–76; cf. Kane's acceptance in "'Good' and 'Bad,'" 144; and with Russell, in *C Version*, 179). Such an origin for the C-version further blurs the Athlone premise of three authorial versions, as well as its attempt to make a sharp distinction between authorial and scribal writing (cf. Galloway, "Uncharacterizable Entities," 75).[60]

But the most subversive questions about the Athlone edition and Skeat's myth of the poem were posed by Kane's other collaborator, Talbot Donaldson. The impersonal, neo-Augustan prose of the introduction to the Athlone *B Version* almost completely muffles Donaldson's distinctively skeptical, idiomatic, and always entertaining voice. Despite what was by every report a harmonious (and exceedingly fruitful) partnership between two great scholars, one might almost imagine that Donaldson had been invited by Kane to join the Athlone project in order to contain his skepticism about the Langland myth. It was Donaldson, before he was Kane's co-editor, who famously suggested that the three canonical versions of *Piers Plowman* might be no more than accidental snapshots of a continuous process: "Indeed, I sometimes wonder whether the C-text, the B-text, and even the A-text are not merely historical accidents, haphazard milestones in the history of a poem that was begun but never finished, photographs that caught a static image of a living organism at a given but not necessarily significant moment of time" ("MSS R and F," 211). In these striking phrases (later formally recanted but still frequently cited

---

60. Russell also questioned whether the poet would have necessarily been much concerned with "the detail of the line," the verbal "minutiae" that, of course, was the point of the deep editing of Athlone (Russell, "Imperative," 242, "Evolution," 43; cf. Adams, "Editing *Piers*," 49n; Brewer, *Editing*, 338).

with approval by others), Donaldson challenged a central tenet of the Skeat-Athlone textual myth: three discrete versions of *Piers*.[61]

The opening sentence of a later essay by Donaldson is less than reverent about an equally major tenet of the myth—single authorship: "The last time that I presented a paper on this ancient and ominous topic I did not try to have it published because the only firm conclusion I was able to reach was that nothing seemed less likely to me than the single authorship of the three texts of *Piers Plowman* unless, perhaps, it was the multiple authorship of *Piers Plowman*" ("Textual Comparison," 241). Donaldson concluded this essay with some provocative statements about Athlone B: he defended its innovative readings not primarily because they were truth, but because they would be "good for intellectuation"; whether or not others approve, at least what he and Kane have done "will make them think" (246, 247).

Despite their recognition of these various difficulties, the Athlone editors all endorse the essence of Skeat's myth of the poem, but their use of the related myth of the poet is more individual. Kane, Athlone's general editor, was the most innovative: he refined Skeat's idea of authorial self-representation and made it more aesthetic. In an important article and short book, both published during 1965 to clear the ground for the Athlone B-edition, Kane managed both to support and to oppose the views of Skeat and of his own teacher Chambers. While reaffirming the single authorship of *Piers Plowman* and celebrating the literary achievement of its poet, he nevertheless denied the possibility of a reliable biography of Langland.

In "The Autobiographical Fallacy in Chaucer and Langland Studies" (significantly given as a Chambers Memorial Lecture), Kane acknowledged the strong desire of readers to discover the personalities of these two poets in their poems, but argued that the results are "attained by inferences both

---

61. Although Donaldson's earlier position that Skeat's three versions were arbitrary representations of the developing poem was disowned in a footnote to the *B Version* (64n), others have since adopted it, including Hanna ("Annotating *Piers Plowman*," 153) and Justice ("Introduction," 5ff.). Derek Pearsall, noting that three distinct versions of *Piers* are not any more likely than intermediate versions, observed that the need to accommodate the manuscripts of R and F within a secure B-tradition produced "some notably ingenious argumentation" in the introduction to Athlone's B-version ("Authorial Revision," 44). Galloway, in "Uncharacterizable Entities," surveys recent arguments for R and F as a separate state of the poem (63–69), and concludes: "Once set forth, the hypothesis finds abundant confirmation and appears likely to constitute a permanent change to the paradigm that Langland scholarship for another period will generally accept" (69).

logically dubious in themselves, and unauthorized by the literary history of the fourteenth century" (2). Such "free biographical inference" has within itself "no element to control its accuracy, and therefore no means by which its logical necessity or even its probability can be checked. It has no rationale. It is essentially imaginative, affective, subjective, pure speculation" (5–6). The accounts of Langland, in particular, thus produced might seem "wise, perceptive, full of insight," but they remain "unverifiable" (6): "[w]e can then, as things are, have no biography of Langland, only speculative 'lives,' without historical necessity" (14).

The essay shows Kane at his most persuasive, without the partisanship of his more polemical writing. He even acknowledged faults in his critical allies. Bright, whom Chambers had endorsed, is called the "worst offender" of "the wilder aberrations of biographical inference" about Langland, and Kane admitted that many believers in single authorship had been guilty of the fallacy, among whom he "shamefacedly" includes himself ("Autobiographical Fallacy," 6).

Kane's essay made no reference, however, to the most influential modern life of the poet, which, twenty years earlier, his co-editor Talbot Donaldson had appended to the end of his pioneering study of the C-version.[62] Donaldson located himself squarely in the biographical tradition established by Skeat, Jusserand, and Chambers ("I shall suggest only the most minor changes in essentials" [*C-Text and Its Poet*, 199]), though, unlike them, he had little to say about the personality, opinions, or inner life of Langland.[63] Donaldson instead described the poet's professional career, if such it can be called, as that of a married clerk in minor orders functioning as a kind of "itinerant handy man" whose "odd jobs were prayers" (218–19). Like his predecessors, Donaldson took much

---

62. In this life, Donaldson seemed almost to anticipate Kane's later charge of speculation and did not shrink from it: "The reader of *Piers Plowman* is almost inevitably seduced into making speculations about its author, so curiously provocative and attractive is the personality that casts its shadow upon every page of the poem" (*C-Text and Its Poet*, 199).

The different histories of Chaucer and Langland scholarship can be striking, as I have already suggested. Skeat discredited the accepted biography of Chaucer after creating a new one for Langland; Manly denied that the poet is describing himself in *Piers Plowman* but later discovered real people behind the pilgrims of the *Canterbury Tales*; and Donaldson, while largely ignoring the difference between poet and narrator in *Piers*, forever changed Chaucer criticism by clearly distinguishing between the two functions in the *General Prologue* ("Chaucer the Pilgrim").

63. His life perhaps most resembles Coulton's account of the poet in *Medieval Panorama* (142–48), which Donaldson cites (199).

of his information about the poet from the beginning of passus 5 of the C-version, arguing that because no one had been able to find a fictional reason for this added "autobiographical passage," "it seems best to assume that Langland was telling the truth about himself and not whimsically devising an elaborate fiction" (220).[64]

Although Kane insisted that no definitive life of the author could be written, he nevertheless believed passionately in that author. His short monograph *Piers Plowman: The Evidence for Authorship* has been widely accepted as settling the authorship question, in part because it often adopts the authoritative, not to say authoritarian, tone also seen in the introductions to the Athlone edition. Calling the debate over authorship "intolerable," Kane insisted that an "unambiguous answer" should be possible, "final at least in the present state of knowledge" (1). Even this concession disappears in the sentence that follows: "If correctly assessed this evidence should point to a single truth" (1). *Truth* is a strong word to use when discussing this work, but Kane means it. "The *Piers Plowman* poems were composed by one man or by several: only one of these alternatives can be true. There is some evidence; it must embody a necessary conclusion, and the truth should be attainable by right thinking" (1–2). Here we see the same robust confidence that enabled Kane to accomplish the heroic labor of editing this textually difficult poem. But, of course, not all answers are unambiguous; moreover, truth, even if it exists and is single, cannot always be recovered even by right thinking. Kane's conclusions are often possible, even probable, but by no means certain. Nor are the unambiguous answers he initially promised actually delivered. As his book proceeds, Kane resorts more and more to less definite statements, such as "how likely would he be," "in what circumstances would he be likely" (30), "hard to conceive" (32), "does not commend itself" (33), "almost certainly," "how likely" (34), "almost certainly," "barely conceivable" (36), "it is even possible to speculate," "more probably" (44), and "the greater likeli-

---

64. Earlier, Skeat made a similar point in response to whether Kitte and Calote were real people: "I can see no reason why we should think that the author is always trying to deceive us about himself" (*A Text*, xxxvi). But a fictional portrait need not be either whimsical or deceitful. Donaldson does seem to allow for the possibility that the "autobiographical passage" is not necessarily about Langland himself, when he says that "though we may deny the existence of any connection between the person described in the preceding paragraph and the author, we can hardly deny that the description was applicable to *some one* living in medieval London" (*C-Text and Its Poet*, 202, my emphasis).

hood" (58). The initial search for truth finally discovers only what might have been.[65]

For all its bark (and despite its wide acceptance), Kane's *Evidence for Authorship* is less conclusive than it proclaims itself to be. John Bowers commented that the book "is astonishing in both the rigor of its argumentation and the narrowness of its three conclusions: a single man wrote all three versions, his name was William Langland, and the title of the poem in all three versions was *Piers Plowman*" ("Editing the Text," 75). The relative attention given to each of these three topics is surprising: the most space in this short work concerns the name of the poet (26–46, 52–70).[66] Yet such an emphasis on establishing the accuracy of "William Langland" had already been implicitly questioned by Donaldson: "Actually, the name is now no more than a point of focus for scholarship. . . . Even if it were possible to prove beyond a shadow of doubt that the author of even one of the texts was William Langland, we should not be much farther along in *Piers Plowman* studies than we are now" (*C-Text and Its Poet*, 200).[67] For all of Kane's efforts to establish the poet's name, he never put it on the title page of the Athlone edition.

The more important issue of single authorship is dealt with only cursorily by Kane. Most attention is given to a negative argument against multiple authorship (*Evidence*, 9–25), in which Kane comes to the rather mild conclusion that the evidence for more than one author "falls short of being compelling" (16), lacks "logical necessity" (22), and has "not yet excluded the possibility that one man wrote the three *Piers Plowman* poems" (26). As we have seen before, the traditional myth is declared true because it has not been proved

---

65. Although he scoffs at J. R. Hulbert's credulity in assuming that the author could not have fallen victim to the same sins of the flesh his poem had denounced ("Autobiographical Fallacy," 6), Kane himself seems guilty of a similar biographical naïveté in giving this reason for believing that the mysterious John But was not lying in reporting the poet's death at the end of some A-manuscripts: "[T]here is, moreover, in all ages a kind of piety which should have restrained even a meddling poetaster from such invention" (*Evidence*, 33).

66. The longest section in Kane's discussion of the name concerns external evidence (26–46), which follows Skeat in giving special value to the Dublin memorandum. Just as Skeat's life of Langland eclectically combined different biographical traditions, as noted previously, so Kane's life resembles his methods in editing the text: faced with a variety of witnesses, he declares one to be authentic (here the Dublin memorandum) and all others the result of scribal corruption (here the colophons that refer to "William W" or the Bale tradition that gives the poet's first name as Robert Langland).

67. Despite the space he gives to it, Kane himself admitted that "the name of the poet is almost a side issue compared with the question whether one man or several wrote the three versions" (*Evidence*, 46, cf. 8).

false.[68] One of the central assumptions of Athlone (the ABC sequence that permits A and C readings to be used to edit B) is never seriously examined in *Evidence for Authorship*, as it is not in the editions themselves. In the opening chapter, Kane can imagine only two explanations for the different versions of *Piers Plowman*: either they are "successive attempts by the same poet to realize an artistic conception" or "three separate works of art" (8, cf. 72). The possibility that the different forms of *Piers* might have been influenced by forces outside the personal artistry of one or more poets is not considered.

In Kane's formalist vision, this artist exists beyond the defacements of readers or history. Skeat's myth of the poet is refined into a name, a literary character, and most important, a supreme writer. The first-person speaker in *Piers* is not the portrait of a real individual living in a particular time and place, as he had been for so many since Skeat; rather he is rarefied into a fictional "construct," one "both more and less than the poet" ("Autobiographical Fallacy," 12). As this construct grows over the three versions of *Piers*, it acquires "temperament," "character," and "personality," but the space it occupies is literary rather than material, in common with other "imaginative creations" (11–12).

The most important manifestation of Kane's poet is in the aesthetic perfection of his poem. In the early nineteenth century, Whitaker had described Langland as a kind of medieval Wordsworth striding along the Malvern Hills, and Patterson has shown how the Athlone editors drew on a tradition of literary thought from the Romantics to New Criticism that valued the literary work of genius (Patterson, "Logic," esp. 102–4). Derek Pearsall points to Athlone's "sublime notion" of a unique author, whose words will always be "ineffably superior" to the scribal variants, and of a unique editor, who will always be able to discern the difference ("Authorial Revision," 43; cf. Edwards, "Observations," 47). Kane's author is so sublime that he escapes from the earthly world to dwell in a realm of pure art.[69] Poet and poem are joined even

---

68. Kane's positive argument for single authorship occupies just a few pages (46–51) and is often unpersuasive. He twice asserts that rubric designations of genre in the manuscripts, such as "book" or "dialogue" or "treatise," were "applied impartially to all versions" of the poem (48, 51), though the evidence he himself supplies here shows that "dialogue" appears only in B-manuscripts, whereas "liber" and "tractus" are found only in A and C manuscripts (46–47).

69. The Athlone editors had so little interest in the historical creation of the poem that, despite their sharp distinction between authorial and scribal writing, the B-manuscript they use as their copy text is not in the poet's own presumed dialect but in that "of a London scribe of about 1400" (Kane and Donaldson, *B Version*, 220; cf. J. M. Bowers, "Editing the Text," 78).

more closely than in Skeat's original formulation as the former becomes impossible to distinguish from the latter.

THE LANGLAND MYTH TODAY

Of course there have always been dissenters from the Langland myth, and despite Athlone's reaffirmation, they have become bolder recently.[70] Nevertheless, Skeat's great Victorian creation, in whole or in part, remains a given for most scholars, however subtle and nuanced their use of it. As for the myth of the poem, one of the announced purposes of the new parallel-text edition of *Piers Plowman* by A. V. C. Schmidt is "to keep the evolution of the poem in the forefront of scholarly attention" (viii), and perhaps the best recent general reading of *Piers*, by James Simpson, reasserts that Langland spent at least two decades "constantly revising his single poem" (*Introduction*, 5). As for the myth of the poet, despite the postmodernist privileging of texts over authors, scholars continue to remain fascinated with what Donaldson called the poet's "curiously provocative and attractive" personality (*C-Text and Its Poet*, 199). Like many since Skeat, the great London historian Caroline Barron accepts the narrator's self-description within the poem as essentially factual with only faint qualification: "But there can be no doubt that this west-country man traveled to London and lived there, if we may accept the autobiographical sections of the poem, in a 'cot' on Cornhill with his wife and daughter" ("William Langland," 104). The linguistic work of M. L. Samuels locates the poet's original dialect in the Malvern area referred to at the beginning of the poem, and others continue to look for surviving records of a historical William Langland (so far in vain).

Two important, if quite different, studies of *Piers Plowman* by Ralph Hanna III and Anne Middleton demonstrate the persistence of Skeat's myths in even the most sophisticated recent work. Hanna's short monograph for the English Writers of the Late Middle Ages series, *William Langland*, clearly and concisely presents information about the poet, his possible family, the manuscripts, and the early printed editions. Hanna here resembles Skeat in his industry, disinterest

---

70. If Manly and his followers are the most famous critics of the myth of the poet, it has recently been challenged in new ways by both John Bowers (*Crisis*) and David Lawton ("Subject"). But it is the myth of the poem that has taken the most battering of late: a new order of composition has been proposed by Jill Mann ("Power"), for example, and Charlotte Brewer and George Rigg have edited what they argue is an earlier authorial version of the poem (the Z-text). The limits of each myth will be the subject of the following two chapters.

(divergent views are fully reported), and good judgment.[71] Hanna also perpetuates Skeat's myths of poet and poem. Although agreeing with the early
Donaldson that the writing of *Piers* was a "process of constant revision" whose
individual forms may not have meant as much to Langland as they do to us (10),
Hanna nevertheless generally accepts the traditional three versions of the poem
(he is doubtful about Z) and, also without much discussion, endorses the standard order of composition.[72] He likewise accepts Kane's work on authorship,
including the name William Langland, though he presents the evidence with due
caution: "[T]here is reason to believe in the accuracy of the Dublin entry" (3).
Aware of the dangers of the autobiographical fallacy, Hanna observes that the
evidence for a life of Langland remains "inferential" and accessed "only through
the poet's representation of himself within his text"—yet he concludes that "at
least some details of Langland's life appear potentially markable and some representations within the poem suggest the parameters of a life" (6).[73]

Despite such careful phrasing, the life of the poet first constructed by Skeat
can still be recognized in Hanna's manual.[74] Hanna declares that "bits of information" can be extracted from the poem, all subject to "scholarly contention" to
be sure, but the most persistent of which "may have their basis in fact" (17). He
then gives a familiar if somewhat sketchy biographical narrative: youth in
Malvern, interrupted education, and eccentric clerical existence on Cornhill. In
contrast to Kane's sublime poet, Hanna wants to historicize Langland: some of
the results are intriguing, if impossible to prove. For example, his hypothesis that
the poet may have been raised at Hanley Castle (near Malvern and held by the
Despensers, whose retainer the poet's father was said to be in the Dublin memo)
makes a nice contrast to Bright's equally fanciful speculation about the poet's

71. Most of what Hanna discusses is not new, but it is presented in detail and carefully assessed. An
example of original research is information about the Somerset Langlands (4–5), whom Hanna suggests
might be the poet's ancestors, perhaps on his mother's side. The association of the Langland name with
Somerset, here and in other documents, would seem to bring Bale's Cleobury Mortimer back into play as
the birthplace of the poet, but Hanna does not find this persuasive (6–7).

72. For Hanna's fullest account of the composition of the poem, which will be discussed in the next
chapter, see his "Versions."

73. This suggests a New Yorker cartoon. Two bored yuppies talking at a fern bar: "I don't have a life,
just the parameters of a life."

74. Kerby-Fulton and Justice cite Hanna as one who seems to believe that the portrait in passus 5 of
the C-version is "autobiographically accurate" ("Reading Circles," 65n). Cf. Hanna's "'Meddling with
Makings'" and "Will's Work."

upbringing among peasants (18).[75] One of the reasons that the Langland myth has been vital for so long is its capacity for adaptation. Thus Hanna proposes that Langland may have found patrons, companions, and audiences in substantial London lay or ecclesiastical households (23–24), presenting a stark contrast to the image of him as an isolated, even crazed figure accepted by so many believers in the biographical myth and based on passages such as B 15.1–10.

Anne Middleton's profound, suggestive, if at times elusive essay "William Langland's 'Kynde Name'" is more highly theorized than Hanna's bibliographical manual, but it too draws on the Langland myth. Like Hanna, Middleton attempts to return *Piers* to its historical context (by looking at the authorial "signatures" within the poem as examples of the politics of self-representation in late medieval vernacular literature), but her approach is more deliberately postmodern: the argument proceeds by implication, association, and pun, deliberately blurs distinctions between external and internal biographical evidence ("'Kynde Name,'" 19–20), and regards the "proof" of even a "far-fetched" claim to lie in "the quality of the readings of this poem that such a hypothesis enables" (44).[76] Many orthodoxies are questioned in this innovative essay, but the Langland myth is not, though Middleton certainly uses it for new ends. She accepts as unproblematic fact the existence of three (and only three) forms of *Piers Plowman* (no mention here of Donaldson's intermediate revisions or the Z-version), as well as their composition in the usual ABC order. This sequence underwrites her assertions about the development of Langland's self-naming: "[H]e signs [his work] in all three of its surviving versions (the A, B, and C texts, representing three successive states of composition), inscribing these signatures more fully, deeply, and indelibly in the fabric of the narrative with each version" (17).

Noting that for most twentieth-century interpreters the "apparently idiosyncratic qualities" of *Piers* have "seemed explicable only by reference to the identity of the author" (19), Middleton also accepts, though recasts, the myth of the poet. She provides no continuous narrative of Langland's life and judges attempts, such as Skeat's and Chambers's, to define his "character and opinions" to be old-fashioned (22). Nevertheless, the poem is still taken to represent the

---

75. Bright, however, was also the first to associate the poet with Hanley Castle, as I noted previously.

76. Middleton's readings in this essay, as throughout her writings on *Piers Plowman*, are always interesting and often strikingly original; many would be equally valid even if the presence of multiple "signatures" by the poet were not accepted.

poet's lived experience. Middleton follows John Burrow in believing that the poet refers to his own age (forty-five years) at B 11.47 and B 12.3 and that Imaginatif's rebuke of Will for writing poetry is meant to be understood as "factual" (53; cf. Burrow, "*Nel Mezzo*"). Yet adjudication between fact or fiction is not what really interests Middleton, who insists that it finally makes "little functional difference": "By the process that Judson Allen calls *assimilatio*, the truth and integrity of an individual life-history is wholly absorbed into the functions of a massively figurative exemplary narrative" ("'Kynde Name,'" 53). Citing Dante and Augustine (54), Middleton goes well beyond the usual Langland biography to treat the narrative self in *Piers* as such an exemplary fiction, but the myth is where she begins.

Middleton accepts that the poet of all versions was named William Langland, though, once again, she complicates the traditional biographical explanation. A variety of possible origins are suggested for the surname: perhaps, as others have claimed, it was a family name of some sort taken from a property holding (63–65); more originally, she proposes a chosen rather than a given name, comparing it at different times to the personal badges of medieval heraldry (28–30) or the pseudonyms used by the leaders of the Rising of 1381 (67–69). From Skeat to Kane, others had called attention to the poet's "signatures" in the poem, especially the supposed anagram in the B-version: "'I have lyved in londe,' quod I, 'my name is Longe Wille'" (B 15.152), but Middleton finds many more self-namings in the poem, including the reference to the "lond of longynge" at the beginning of the first inner dream (B 11.8).[77]

The biographical myth is called upon to shore up what might seem the weakest point in Middleton's argument about the development of authorial signatures in *Piers*: after the apparent naming of himself as Long Will Langland in the B-version (15.152), why does C at this point have the vaguer "Ich have yleved in Londone monye longe yeres" (16.286)? With considerable understatement, Middleton admits that "the anagrammatic character of the latter version of this line is less

77. Middleton admits that the Land of Longing as a signature may at first "seem far-fetched" and says that it had not been previously noticed ("'Kynde Name,'" 44). Yet forty years before, Meroney, a skeptic of the myth, had pointed out that B 11.8 contains all they key words of B 15.152, but ridiculed its significance as a "second cryptic message" ("Life and Death," 4–5).

Middleton also admits that the Langland "signatures" were apparently not understood by the poet's contemporaries and early readers: "[T]hey apparently never functioned culturally as ascriptions"; as "communications and records of authorship" they were "a conspicuous failure" ("'Kynde Name,'" 17, 25).

The punning in *Piers* stressed by Middleton is often matched by her own word play: she asserts that the poet is "inhabitant and heir of the Lond of Longyng" and that as early as the A-version the "ground" of the full signature "already lay dormant, awaiting cultivation" (51).

obvious in isolation," but then asserts that the change of identity from "a fictive rural place to an actual urban one" announces that *Piers* will now be engaged with "contemporary social discourses concerning the grounds of civil identity" (55–56). Supporting the ingenuity and appeal of Middleton's argument is a central element of the biographical myth: Langland's move from rural Malvern to urban London, though it is usually considered to have occurred before or during, not after, the writing of the B-version. The Langland myth is transformed by Middleton into something rich and strange: "The surname—which in B was derived anagrammatically from *longe launde,* a rural holding transformed into the figurative Lond of Longyng, the 'kynde' place of unsatisfied desire that is the author's sole birthright—is rederived in C as an anagram that embodies as part of his name his urban habitation, London, a locus of impropriety that he is here accused of having chosen in order to evade the bond between man and his 'kynde' rural place" (58).[78]

In contrast to Kane, whose Langland is an artist attempting to realize an aesthetic ideal, Middleton sees a more personal and moral connection between poet and poem: "What the name inscribed in the poetic text proclaims is not the author's verbal fabrication, but an ethical fabulation of which he makes himself the center; the value signified is not that of his craft but that of his life" (28, cf. 37, 42, 75). The exemplary life of the poet suggested here is the latest example in a long scholarly tradition of presenting Langland as a principled hero, which includes Jusserand's claim that he was a political progressive and Chambers's that he was an apostle of religious tolerance. The poet's "'making' as a life-consuming and life-defining activity, perpetually running counter to both ecclesiastical and civil dicta," is compared by Middleton to the life and testimony of the Lollard William Thorpe (74). Although conceding that Langland should not be associated only with dissent, Middleton's assertion that his "deepest affinity" was with "reformist or heterodox sentiments and practices" ("'Kynde Name,'" 79) echoes the proto-Protestant Langland of Robert Crowley, the first printer of *Piers* and the first to attempt to provide an identity for its poet.[79] The powerful readings in

78. Middleton here reverse the traditional understanding of the link between versions and biography: the myth's London-based B-version is said by Middleton to describe a countrified poet, whereas the C-version, often believed to have been revised in the West Country, identifies him as a London man.

79. Middleton's Langland may also remind us of the prophetic Christian socialist in Florence Converse's *Long Will.* Like Converse's novel, Middleton's essay puts the life of the poet at its center, while deliberately blurring distinctions between fact and fiction.

Middleton's essay (has anyone ever seen more in the poem?), which have only been suggested here, show the continued appeal of the Langland myth, even as they mark how far we have come from the bluff common sense of Skeat.

One of the most sustained modern attempts to preserve the autobiographical myth, while recognizing its vulnerabilities, is found in the work of John Burrow. In 1981, he resurrected Skeat's view that Imaginatif gives Langland's actual age when he says that he has followed Will for forty-five years (B 12.3; cf. also B 11.47).[80] Burrow went even further than Skeat when he argued that, in addition to offering factual information about how old he was, the poet provides an account of his inner life: "Langland, as I believe, devoted part of B xi–xii to a precise and somewhat painful rendering of his own thoughts and fears at an age which tradition taught him to regard as the threshold of old age" ("*Nel Mezzo*," 41). The following year, in a Gollancz Lecture, Burrow made a more general defense of Middle English autobiographical poetry ("Autobiographical Poetry"). He argued that most critics who claim to be agnostic about the truth claims of such poetry are, in fact, atheists, and he makes the telling point that the presence of conventional elements does not mean that the information is necessarily false: life often follows art.

Burrow's most subtle treatment of the poet myth is found in his recent *Langland's Fictions.* He acknowledges that there is much to prevent us from taking what Will says about himself as a straightforward authorial portrait, including the apparently fictional names of his wife and child and his tendency to blend into other characters, such as the sins (*Langland's Fictions,* 86, 88). He even agrees with David Lawton's argument that Will is not a single consistent character who matures in the course of the poem (90–91). Yet despite the title of his book, the one fiction that Burrow will not accept is the autobiographical. He states frankly what his previous writings had always implied: the myth of the poet is a matter of faith, not reason. A self-proclaimed atheist writing about a Christian poem, Burrow grants that the genuineness of Langland's self-portrayal in *Piers* is not something that can be objectively proved or disproved but is rather a matter of individual "belief" or "disbelief" (83–86). Burrow clearly identifies the subjectivity, at times verging on religious conviction, that from the first has supported the biographical myth.

---

80. "*Nel Mezzo*"; but see Dove's objection to Burrow's biographical reading (*Perfect Age,* 106–9).

Kathryn Kerby-Fulton demonstrates the refusal of many modern scholars to abandon the Langland myth despite the battering it has taken while sailing on increasingly rough seas. In *Reformist Apocalypticism*, Kerby-Fulton notes (and somewhat exaggerates) the current suspicion of autobiography in *Piers* (64), and in a subsequent article she seeks to outflank the claim that Will is only a fictive persona by arguing that this is to read *Piers* as a secular dream vision rather than as a "visionary autobiography," a form often associated with women such as Bridget of Sweden ("Who Has Written This Book"). Such spiritual autobiographies, she maintains, signal real experience, however conventionally (and elusively) presented. As we have seen with others, Kerby-Fulton finds the biographical myth innocent because it has not been proved guilty: she cites Donaldson's challenge to those who reject the autobiographical status of the narrator's apologia at the beginning of passus 5 of the C-version "to show what purpose it was meant to serve if it was fictional (no one has yet been able to do so)" ("Who Has Written This Book," 105). In a more recent essay, Kerby-Fulton borrows the term "bibliographic ego" from Joseph Lowenstein (referring to a poet's explicit discussion of the problems he himself faced in writing and controlling his work) to argue that at least in c 5, Langland is "concerned to present an authorial, rather than a simply fictional 'I'" in order to communicate more directly with his audience ("Bibliographic Ego," 70). She admits that her argument is "based on extrapolation" and is, "in one sense, very speculative"—Kane's designation for any life of Langland—but faced with c 5, she, like Burrow, chooses to believe that Langland "is working with his *own* authorial experience" (her emphasis) and points to "the historical aspect of the *apologia*" ("Bibliographic Ego," 70, 73, 74). Kerby-Fulton's article on Langland in the new *Cambridge History of Medieval English Literature* (1999)—the original edition of which at the beginning of the twentieth century gave prestige to Manly's attack on single authorship—reveals a continued faith in the myths of both poet and poem despite acknowledging detractors. She begins with a nuanced restatement of Skeat's double creation: "The three versions of *Piers Plowman*, as most scholars today believe, were the lifetime labour of a single author named, or at least pen-named, William Langland" ("*Piers*," 513). As for the myth of the poem, Kerby-Fulton recognizes that we can only "dimly perceive the stages of composition of *Piers Plowman*" through the filter of the manuscripts and prints (516), but she continues to advocate the ABC sequence, though as "a *guideline* rather than as the canonical orthodoxy print culture con-

THE HISTORY OF THE LANGLAND MYTH

ditions us to assume" (517, her emphasis).[81] As for the myth of the poet, Kerby-Fulton is fully aware of the "treacherous territory of apparent autobiographical reference within the poem" (513), and yet, once again, she has confidence in the traditional explanation. Echoing Chambers, she too sees a "crisis" over questions of salvation that apparently "led to the breaking off of A" ("*Piers*," 520), and, as suggested by Skeat and Bloomfield (not to mention Converse), insists that "Langland had apparently been part of a monastic literary community at some earlier point in his life" (530). Indeed, so eager is she to find the poet's life in the poem that she is willing to accept that "what *may* be an allusion to the chancel of Little Malvern Priory (c 6.398), *may* suggest that he was schooled in this Benedictine establishment as a boy" (530, my emphasis).[82]

The vigorous persistence in our time of Skeat's venerable myth is directly acknowledged at the opening of Steven Justice's introduction to *Written Work*, an ambitious and innovative 1997 collection of essays on *Piers Plowman*, edited by Justice and Kerby-Fulton.[83] While admitting that the language of Skeat's assertions is no longer available to contemporary scholars and carefully qualifying his claim (or is the use of "seems" in the following quotations having his cake and eating it too?), Justice directly links this new academic collection of essays to what Skeat first invented. Citing the great editor's declaration that *Piers Plowman* "is a true autobiography in the highest sense of the word," Justice notes that all the contributors to his volume "take as a point of departure or of conclusion the single C-version passage [c 5.1–104] in which Langland seems explicitly to offer autobiographical detail" ("Introduction," 1). Having identified the importance of the myth of the poet to contemporary scholars in his first paragraph, Justice invokes the myth of the poem in his second. He states that what Skeat "most famously said about *Piers Plowman* is that Langland wrote it three times," which he glosses as "Langland seems to have refused to create a poem separable

---

81. At other points in this essay Kerby-Fulton seems fully to accept the traditional myth: she ends one section by declaring the need for all three versions, because only together do they show the growth of the poet's mind ("*Piers Plowman*," 526). She also rejects Jill Mann's argument for A as a late rather than early version of *Piers* (to be discussed in the following chapter) because of "historical allusions" (here uncited) of the kind rejected by Kane and Donaldson (Kerby-Fulton, "*Piers Plowman*," 515n).

82. The Little Malvern allusion had been proposed by Robert Kaske in his "*Piers Plowman* and Local Iconography," perhaps the least persuasive work from that great scholar of the poem. Kaske, like Skeat and Bright before him, clearly fell under the powerful antiquarian spell of Malvern.

83. In a separate article, "Reading Circles," Kerby-Fulton and Justice try to imagine the poet's intellectual coterie and link him to many contemporary literary figures (though not, like Converse, to the *Gawain*-poet).

from his continuing labor of authorship" (1).[84] Of course, this is a long way from Skeat's confidence that the number and sequence of versions of *Piers* are obvious or that the narrator's statements are the direct and consistent views of the poet. Like the earlier writings of Burrow, Hanna, and Middleton just discussed, the volume edited by Justice and Kerby-Fulton (which includes new essays by Hanna and Middleton) is anything but naive. But, as Justice so explicitly announces, Skeat's myths of the poet and poem continue to animate some of the most interesting modern work on *Piers Plowman*. As we celebrate their contributions, however, we ought to recognize the fragility of these myths and try to imagine what they might have excluded. That will be the subject of my following two chapters.

84. Later in this essay, Justice himself qualifies the idea that there are only three versions of *Piers*.

2. Beyond the Myth of the Poem

IS THERE A TEXT IN THESE MANUSCRIPTS?

Skeat's Langland myth supports the textual with the biographical. The three established forms of *Piers Plowman* are linked to the stages of a single poet's life: a youthful A-version, mature B-version, and feebler C-version (Skeat, "Section VIII," 245–47). Previous uncertainties about both the form and authorship of *Piers* (how many shapes and by whom?) were resolved by Skeat into a single, convincing narrative, which, as shown in the previous chapter, has been generally accepted by scholars for more than a century, one part of the myth being used to support the other.[1] In the two chapters that now follow, I want to separate the two myths (to the extent that that is possible) in order to highlight some of the limitations of each and to suggest alternative approaches. I begin with the myth of the poem.

The myth of the poem, which Skeat believed was self-evident and whose formulation enabled him to get on with the job of editing *Piers*, has become settled orthodoxy. As noted at the end of the previous chapter, Steven Justice has recently reminded us that what Skeat "most famously said" about *Piers Plowman* was that Langland wrote it three times ("Introduction," 1)—and, as Justice might have added to give Skeat's full formulation, that it was written in a specific chronological sequence. Even Manly, who initiated the authorship debate, endorsed Skeat's ABC order (though he argued for several writers), and most scholars, especially today, assume with Skeat that the writing and rewriting of *Piers* was Langland's life's work. It is taken to be a poem "ever in the making," produced by "a prolonged and continuous act of composition" (Chambers and Grattan, "Text" [1909], 377; Pearsall, "Editing," 99).[2]

Because we are told so often about the rewriting of *Piers Plowman* and the ABC order of its composition, we may forget that both the number and sequence of

---

1. Mann observes that the consensus over the sequence of the versions of *Piers* "contributed to the creation of a biographical picture which, in a kind of hermeneutic circle, helped to support it" ("Power," 22).

2. See also J. M. Bowers, *Crisis*, 188; Hanna, *William Langland*, 10, and "Annotating *Piers Plowman*," 153; Justice, "Genres," 306; Kerby-Fulton, "*Piers*," 515.

versions are conjectures drawn from puzzling manuscript evidence. The poem survives in more than fifty manuscripts representing about a dozen distinct textual forms. For example, there are six A-manuscripts (plus the Z-text) with C-endings, two clear textual traditions of the B-version, and one manuscript (Huntington Library, MS HM 114) blending together passages from all three traditional versions.[3] An even greater variety of presentational and commentary schemes exists. Several *Piers* manuscripts have more than the usual passus initials, others divide the different passus in original ways, and one C-manuscript (Bodleian Library, MS Douce 104) contains an extensive series of illustrations. Most *Piers* manuscripts are also annotated by scribes and readers, but each program is unique (see Benson and Blanchfield, *Manuscripts*; Uhart, "Early Reception").

Skeat's myth of the poem was a powerful tool that made sense to the chaotic manuscript reality of *Piers Plowman*. The desire for such order is understandable, but it may be impossible to satisfy: Derek Pearsall warns us that "very few things are susceptible of proof in matters of textual criticism, and meanwhile scholars might try to hold on to their lack of certainty" ("Authorial Revision," 44). Given the limits of the available information about the writing of *Piers*, we are left to speculate in ways that are not completely different from what Converse does in her novel *Long Will*. Such imaginative conjectures are often necessary and rewarding, as long we recognize that the results obtained are neither fixed nor final. The myth of the poem has contributed much to the editing and understanding of *Piers*, but it does not provide absolute solutions. The very lucidity of the myth can blind us to how little we really know about the construction, reception, or meaning of this great poem.

THE ABC SEQUENCE

The assumption that *Piers Plowman* exists in three and only three versions had become so axiomatic in Langland studies that Rigg and Brewer's claim for an earlier fourth version, the Z-text, caused much excitement, with scholars both supporting and rejecting their arguments.[4] And yet, despite the durability of the

3. For the most recent account of the manuscripts of *Piers Plowman*, see Hanna, *William Langland*. For the two different traditions of B, see especially Donaldson, "MSS R and F"; Justice, "Introduction."

4. Those who support the Z-text as authorial include Hoyt N. Duggan ("Authenticity") and Richard Firth Green ("Lost"). Schmidt included Z in his parallel-text edition, saying that its Langlandian authorship is "overwhelmingly likely" (viii). A strong case against the Z-text as authorial has been made by Hanna ("Studies," 14–22, and "MS. Bodley 851"). Of course, Kane rejected its authenticity ("'Z Version'"); even though Z does not abolish so much as expand the traditional notion of three sequential versions, a fourth version of *Piers* would not only make the Athlone edition incomplete, but also undermine its editors' central claim to be able to distinguish accurately between authorial and scribal writing.

three-text hypothesis, those most familiar with the manuscripts have always been aware of (although they often explain away) the precariousness of its claims. Skeat himself was not dogmatic about the model he had invented (as he was not dogmatic about most things) and noted that *Piers* might be said to exist in at least ten forms, most of them authorial.[5] The Athlone project proclaimed in its general title and practice that there were only three versions of *Piers*, yet each of its editors acknowledged ambiguities in the manuscript history, as mentioned in the previous chapter. Kane, in the course of asserting the integrity of the A-version, recognized the uncertain authorship of the three different forms of passus 12 in A (*A Version*, 51–52). Donaldson originally proposed that the B-manuscripts R and F might represent an intermediate version of the poem ("MSS R and F"), and Russell has long argued that the C-version was probably put into final form by a literary executor and not by Langland himself ("Evolution," 45; Russell and Kane, *C Version*, 179).

Just as important to *Piers* scholarship as the number of versions has been the belief that they were composed in a set chronological sequence—ABC. This assumption was absolutely essential to the editing of Athlone (B is often emended if A and C agree on a reading), and it lies behind most analyses of Langland's literary development, such as in the critical readings of Kirk (*Dream Thought*) and Godden (*Making*) or the historicist work of Middleton (especially "'Kynde Name'") and others.[6] Kane assumes the ABC sequence when he talks of the three versions of *Piers* as "records of a single writer's successive attempts to realize an imaginative and creative experience" (*Evidence*, 72), as does Kerby-Fulton in the new *Cambridge History of Medieval English Literature* when she declares that "together, and only together, can [the three versions] bear witness to the complete growth of a breathtaking poetic mind" ("*Piers*," 526).

Despite its long acceptance by critics and editors, Skeat's assertion that *Piers Plowman* was composed in the ABC order has never been supported by solid evi-

---

5. Skeat, *Vision . . Notes*, 4:xvi–xviii, and *Three Parallel Texts*, 2:xxi–xxiv. Brewer notes that in his summary of Langland's process of composition and revision, Skeat identified "ten forms of the poem of which eight represent different stages of authorial writing" (*Editing*, 174). In addition to the three principal versions, Skeat recognized two other authorial versions of A, a transitional version between A and B, and two transitional versions between B and C.

6. Kane and Donaldson edited on the reasonable, though by no means infallible, assumption that a poet would not write something, change it in a revised version, and then go back to it in a third version (*B Version*, 76). Robert Adams has argued that their practice of voting the readings of two versions against the third is a form of the recension theory they claim to reject ("Editing *Piers*," 59; see also Brewer, *Editing*, 390). Kane and Donaldson's method develops the ideas of Blackman (see "Notes," esp. 518).

dence or detailed argument. The proposition remains, as Kane and Donaldson put it, both "obvious" and "strictly hypothetical" (*B Version*, 71), and its inevitability has recently been challenged. In 1992, after discussing different versions of a Lollard text, Anne Hudson, almost as an afterthought, posed a series of tantalizing questions: "Is it too provocative, in the light of the examples set out here, to wonder whether the usual sequential account of the versions of *Piers Plowman* might be, at least in part, reversible? To ponder whether it is *demonstrably* impossible that A might be an abbreviated version of B, with Z an alternative and more drastic truncation? Or to speculate that perhaps C and B are two independent modifications of a lost hyparchetypal text, rather than members in a chronological sequence?" ("Variable Text," 60, her emphasis).

Tentative as Hudson's suggestions were, they struck at the heart of the myth of the poem and were soon taken up by others. John Bowers pointed out that many problems would be solved (such as the late date of most A-manuscripts) if we assumed that A was written after B ("Editing the Text," 83–87), and Jill Mann, reviving the earlier (but almost wholly neglected) work of Howard Meroney, mounted the most substantial attack ever on the traditional order of *Piers* versions ("Power").[7] Mann has speculated that A was not an early version of the poem but a later adaptation for a nonclerical audience that de-emphasized elements such as Latin quotations, metaphors, and sexual passages. Whether or not Mann's conclusions win general acceptance, they stand as the most detailed effort yet to try to explain (rather than merely to assume) the sequence. As we have seen, from Skeat to the present day, the many supporters of the ABC order have never felt the need to prove it systematically. Those who continue to believe in it must not only refute Mann's arguments, as many believe they can, but also, at last, produce a comprehensive and positive defense of ABC. The traditional order may well be correct, but it has not been firmly established.[8]

Even scholars who still subscribe to the ABC order are beginning to modify the traditional way that they have understood it. In the same year in which Hudson posed her provocative questions, Robert Adams proposed a different

---

7. Charlotte Brewer has endorsed the questioning of Hudson, Mann, and Bowers about whether A precedes B: "Such an enquiry is perfectly reasonable, given that our assumptions about this sequence can be traced to Skeat's commonsense, but quite unargued, assertion that 'the A-text so evidently comes first'" ("Editing *Piers*," 287).

8. For a detailed response to Mann, which reaffirms rather than recasts traditional views, see Lawler, "Reply." I am not here arguing that the ABC order is necessarily false (on the whole, I think it is the most likely sequence), only against the automatic assumption of its inevitability.

order of publication for *Piers,* though not of composition. Adams suggested that B might have been the only version actually released by the poet during his lifetime, with the result that A, though written earlier, was made publicly available by a literary executor only after Langland's death, as Russell had often suggested for C.[9]

Perhaps the most imaginative new thinking about the composition of *Piers* has been by Ralph Hanna. In "On the Versions of *Piers Plowman,*" he proposes that the poem began as a single dream about contemporary conditions, was next extended by the addition of a second symmetrical vision, and was then developed into the full A-version as we now have it. Hanna imagines that instead of releasing this version, the poet immediately went on to write B, which he probably did not consider a new form of the poem. Thus only C qualifies as a distinct revision, Langland's response to the misuse of his work during the Rising of 1381 and rewritten "to insist upon what he meant" (241). Hanna's subtle argument provides fresh ideas about the manuscripts and versions of *Piers.* Of course the appeal of his speculations, like that of Skeat's original myth, comes more from its coherence and creativity than from any clear textual evidence. His narrative of the poem's development cannot be proved, but, to borrow a phrase from Donaldson, to whom Hanna dedicates his essay, it does make us think.

The current rethinking of the ABC sequence suggests that we may be witnessing the end of what Meroney called the "trinitarian dogma of an ABC textual procession, one of the sacred articles in the *Piers Plowman* creed" ("Life and Death," 20). There are advantages to the agnosticism of considering other hypotheses. For instance, putting aside the assumption that A is necessarily a first draft of *Piers* allows us to judge this version on its own merits. Whereas its relative simplicity has often been used to support the view that it is only a preliminary version of the poem, we are now free to explore, with Meroney and Mann, whether this simplicity might have other explanations, such as a less learned audience. Without the presumption that the A-version is an embryo that not did not reach maturity until B and C, we shall be better able to appreciate its special virtues. Manly and his followers thought that the A-*visio* was the one truly

---

9. Adams, "Editing *Piers,*" 59–63. Adams reported that Ian Doyle (in a remark that may have been meant less seriously than it has sometimes been taken) suggested to him that A may have "filled a role as a sort of *Reader's Digest* condensed version of *Piers Plowman,* with much of the dreary exposition and hairsplitting theology left out" (61n). Chambers and Grattan had earlier stated: "It seems highly probable that the A-text was never formally published" ("Text" [1931], 10).

great part of *Piers*. Certainly, it is more narratively coherent than the other versions and concludes just where so many modern (and even medieval?) readers begin to bog down. For many, A is (or should be) *Piers Plowman*.[10] It also contains excellent passages found nowhere else, such as its account of how Do Best grows out of Do Bet: "Right as a rose, that red is and swete, / Out of a raggit rote and rough brere / Springeth and spredith, that spiceris desirith" (A 10.123–25).[11]

If, along with Hudson, Langland scholars further allow themselves to entertain the possibility that B and C are not sequential but instead independently derived from a lost common ancestor, they will be forced to consider the relationship between these two forms of the poem more carefully than they have been accustomed to in the past, no longer presuming a single direction of addition and subtraction. The result would be to consider B and C as genuine versions of *Piers* and not simply revisions. Breaking up the scholarly monopoly of ABC also permits us to consider forces other than the solitary poet in the construction of the poem. How different would our sense of *Piers Plowman* be if we were to conceive of its different forms not as successive attempts by the author to perfect his own personal vision, but as efforts to respond to and reach particular audiences? Thus C need not necessarily be the poet's final statement of what he meant, but instead a version of the poem influenced by the needs, requests, or even collaboration of others.[12]

THE "CRISIS" OF THE A-VERSION

Various theories for the state of the text of *Piers* have been offered over the decades, though they were usually constrained by the orthodoxies of the Langland myth and were presented (and received) as if obvious and not as speculative as they are in fact. A major example is the most common modern explanation for the shape of the A-version: it was abandoned because Langland was stymied by fundamental theological doubts. As Russell puts it, the A-version "seems to have ended in dissatisfaction, even in something approaching despair"

10. Vaughan has recently argued again for A's coherence in "Ending(s)."

11. See also the more visual description of the scene at Meed's wedding in A, which, unlike B or C, suggests a parodic romance setting with references to "a pavyloun proud" and "ten thousand of tentis" (A 2.35–48).

12. Elizabeth Fowler has observed that there is now "no firm consensus" about what the different shapes of *Piers* represent—whether they reflect evolution of the author's opinions as a result of historical events, aesthetic refinement, his response to the reception of the work, or the refitting of the poem for different audiences ("Civil Death," 761).

("Some Aspects," 30; cf. "Evolution," 36). The "crisis" of the A-version was first proposed by Chambers during his defense of the single authorship of *Piers Plowman*. In an early formulation, Chambers asserted that the poem in most A-manuscripts "breaks off suddenly at the end of *Passus XI*, leaving unanswered the problems which the dreamer, in bitter agitation, had raised" ("Three Texts," 129).[13] Although "breaks off suddenly" might be more neutrally expressed, this is otherwise a fair summary. Later in the same essay we see more clearly the influence of the Langland myth, which equates dreamer and poet: the A-version is said to be "abandoned suddenly, after the *author* has raised many difficult problems, to which *he* can find no satisfactory solution" (133, my emphasis).[14]

Although widely accepted today, Chambers's view that the A-version was left unfinished because of the poet's own frustration is by no means self-evident. Many readers, including some medieval scribes, do not recognize the impasse claimed by Chambers, but then and now seem to have accepted A as it stands.[15] But, of course, those in search of artistic or thematic resolution will find only limited satisfaction anywhere in *Piers Plowman*. If A ends inconclusively, the last lines of B and C are also open-ended, with the promise of further pursuit of Piers and grace.

Chambers's argument depends on the presumption in Skeat's myth that the first-person voice who raises difficult questions at the end of the A-version is Langland himself. Yet the closer we look, the harder it is to accept that the speaker must be autobiographical. According to Chambers, Langland's intellectual and spiritual crisis concerned questions of predestination and the salvation

13. Chambers's statement appears in a paragraph that begins: "As to certain facts there should be no doubt" (129). Noting that a short passus 12 has been added to three A-manuscripts, Chambers declared that this supplement "makes no attempt to answer the questions and doubts of the preceding passus" ("Three Texts," 129).

14. Chambers repeated and developed these ideas about the state of A in later writing: see especially "Long Will," and also "Incoherencies," 30–32, and *Man's Unconquerable Mind*, 130–31. A sample of those who have agreed with Chambers that the A-version was abandoned because it raised problems that Langland himself could not then solve includes Donaldson (*C-Text and Its Poet*, 224–25); Pearsall (*Piers: C-Text*, 201n); Godden (*Making*, 62); Burrow (*Langland's Fictions*, 92n); and Kerby-Fulton ("*Piers*," 520).

15. The only crisis explicitly supported by the manuscript evidence indicates a mortal not a spiritual impediment. The so-called John But ending in its fullest form in Bodleian Library, MS Rawlinson Poetry 137, announces that the poet died suddenly, though apparently after the A-version was done—"whan this werk was wrought" (A 12.103). Several manuscripts extend their A-texts with C-endings, suggesting a desire for a longer text but with no indication that the message of the C-addition is in conflict with A. Still other scribes apparently judged the A-version to be complete as is because they add nothing to it. See Vaughan, "Ending(s)."

of worthy non-Christians.[16] The latter topic will be discussed further in Chapter 4, but for now it is enough to note how unsophisticated are the difficulties that supposedly stumped the poet. Debating with Scripture, the first-person voice challenges the value of both works and learning. For who did better "in werk and in woord" (A 11.269), he says, than Solomon and Aristotle, and yet Holy Church considers them both to be in hell. And what is the value of good deeds if the repentant thief at the Crucifixion was saved before John the Baptist or the patriarchs, and if notorious sinners such as Mary Magdalene, King David, and Paul are sovereign in heaven even though they "wroughte wykkidly in world whanne thei were" (A 11.292)? To support his position that learning can be as useless to salvation as works, the speaker cites in Latin "the doughtiest doctour" (A 11.302), Saint Augustine, who laments that the ignorant (*ydiote*) seize heaven while the educated (*sapientes*) are damned (A 11.305).

Predestination and the value of learning and works were the subjects of serious debate in the Middle Ages, but the particular examples given at the conclusion of A, for all their dramatic intensity, would not have disturbed a literate medieval Christian and certainly not the author of *Piers Plowman*. Rather than genuine challenges to orthodox belief, they are more like the sly arguments of Chaucer's Wife of Bath at the beginning of her Prologue. Her reference to Solomon's divine favor, like that to his damnation here in *Piers*, is only part of the story. If the old king was still in hell (an open question), it was not because his good works and words were useless but because they were outweighed by his subsequent fall into lechery and idolatry. Even more unconvincing is the speaker's claim that the salvation of the Magdalene, David, and Paul prove the irrelevance of good works. Any medieval schoolchild, let alone the poet of *Piers*, would have known that all three were in heaven because they so earnestly repented of their sins. Far from proving that good deeds mean nothing, Mary, David, and Paul show that the special favor of God is available even to those who do wrong, as long as they change their ways and do well.[17] Rather than evi-

16. The "A-text breaks off, with a passionate plea for a solution of problems which the greatest authorities had found it difficult to solve—predestination and the fate of the righteous heathen" (Chambers, "Incoherencies," 31, cf. "Long Will," 53, *Man's Unconquerable Mind*, 129). According to Chambers, these problems caused a fifteen-year gap between A and B, which somewhat undercuts the commonly accepted idea of Langland as a compulsive reviser.

17. As I have argued elsewhere, to cite Augustine, one of the four principal Doctors of the Church, as support for anti-intellectualism can only be ironic, especially given that the passage quoted from his *Confessions* occurs just before he is finally converted to Christianity through the act of picking up and reading a book ("Augustinian Irony").

dence of a deep crisis in Langland's faith (so paralyzing that Chambers believed that it caused him to stop writing his poem for years and led him into a life of debauchery), the questions raised here are familiar debating points with obvious answers, some of which are implied as soon as they are posed and some of which Imaginatif supplies in the B-version. There is no reason to assume with so many modern scholars that the speaker's doubts here are in any way the poet's own or to confuse any problems he found in formally concluding A with deep theological perplexity. The agonizing personal crisis in Langland that Chambers detected behind the ending of the A-version is a bold act of the critical imagination but has little support from the text or from what we know of medieval religious thought.

THE AUTHORIAL ATHLONE

The Langland myth encourages readers of *Piers* to approach the poem through its poet. The result is not only biographical explanations for textual riddles, such as Chambers's account of A, but also a desire to recover the true authorial text. The attempt goes back to Crowley's first edition in 1550, which presented a single text as the work of a single poet, one Robert Langland of Cleobury Mortimer, Shropshire—the first of many doubtful editorial claims about the writing of *Piers*. Skeat for a long time thought that he might have discovered an actual autograph copy of the B-version, marked up by the poet himself in the course of producing C (Brewer, *Editing*, 141). Kane and his fellow Athlone editors have perhaps gone the furthest in pursuit of the authorial text, asserting their ability to chip away scribal corruption and reveal the three original poems (or at least their archetypes) imprisoned within the chaos of the manuscripts. Their efforts to rescue and restore these great aesthetic objects is, in McGann's words (*Critique*, 66), a truly "heroic task" (one has only to spend a little time with the *Piers* manuscripts to appreciate how heroic), but it is an adventure somewhat like the last voyage of Dante's Ulysses or the exploits of Don Quixote. The bravery and daring are undoubted, but the value of the results is more open to question.

For all its learned ingenuity, the Athlone edition is only one possible understanding of the text of *Piers Plowman*.[18] As noted in the previous chapter, Kane and Donaldson's principal claim in establishing the B-text was that the poetic style of Langland was radically different from that of his copyists. To arrive at

18. The following discussion on the limitations of Athlone focuses on its *B Version*, the most radically interventionist edition.

the authorial text, the Athlone editors thus set out to distinguish the writing style (*usus scribendi*) of the poet from the writing style of the scribes: "Just as scribal variants tend to flat statement or crude overemphasis, diffuseness in denotation and loss of connotation, dilution of meaning and absence of tension, in general a bald, colourless and prosy expression, so the style of the poet is vigorous, nervous, flexible and relatively compressed, made distinctive by characteristic mannerisms and figures" (*B Version*, 130). Although they acknowledge that such a sharp division depends on choices that are "aesthetic, subjective, and open to question in particular instances" (131), Kane and Donaldson elsewhere proceed as if these differences were capable of conclusive resolution.[19]

Brewer and Adams, especially, have shown that a fundamental problem with the Athlone method is that its definitions of authorial and scribal writing are impressionistic and easily reversible: one editor's scribal overemphasis may be another's authorial vigorousness (Adams, "Editing *Piers*," 40–44; Brewer, "Authorial vs. Scribe," 68–69, and *Editing*, 386ff.).[20] Kane's characterization of scribal practice in his A-edition might also describe the ambitions of a medieval religious poet such as Langland, intent on reaching and influencing a wide audience: "In general scribes set out to produce what seemed to them a more correct, or a more easily intelligible, or a more emphatic, or a more elegant text. Their substitutions seem designed to make the meaning clearer, or to express it more forcibly, or to embellish the form of its expression" (*A Version*, 128; cf. Brewer, "Textual Principles," 85–86; Adams, "Editing and the Limitations," 11n).

Kane and Donaldson's assertion of a sharp divide between the writing of author and scribe often depends on prior assumptions. Consider, for example, their classification of a group of three hundred changes from A in B as scribal. The editors admit that some of these examples might be "the products of ill-judged authorial revision or of the poet himself falling into scribal error": "But by the principle that a major artist's revision should imply general improvement,

19. For instance, in arguing that Corpus Christi College, Oxford, MS 201, is an important witness of the B-version, Kane and Donaldson refer to "the fact of the original readings" in it (*B Version*, 166), which might be more neutrally phrased as "readings we believe to be original."

20. The difficulty, if not impossibility, of making absolute distinctions between scribal and authorial writing was noted in the first reviews of Kane and Donaldson's edition (see those by Burrow, D. C. Fowler, and Stanley). Donaldson himself, not surprisingly given the playful skepticism already noted in the previous chapter, offered one of the earliest and sharpest cautions against what would become a fundamental editorial axiom of Athlone when he denied that there is a clear-cut distinction between the work of poets and scribes: "[T]he terms only describe different functions of the single animal man" ("Texts," 272).

whereas scribal transmission demonstrably implies persistent corruption of identifiable, even predictable kinds, we rule out these explanations" (*B Version*, 83–84). Not only is the question begged of whether B is, in fact, a revision of A, but how, except on the grounds of convenience, can editors rule out what even they admit is possible?

Kane and Donaldson are frank to acknowledge that their editorial method, for all its theoretical sophistication, "encourages an intuitive approach" (*B Version*, 191), but they insist they have "found it indispensable" (131), and they justify it by their long and close association with the poem (cf. 213). But subjective judgments, even by the most experienced readers, remain just that. Ralph Hanna concludes that Kane's assertions of the ability "to recognize intuitively what is Langlandian" are "hyperbole . . . not borne out by practice" ("Producing," 110n; cf. Robinson, "Redefining," 278–79). A famous example, noted by early reviewers (D. C. Fowler, "New Edition," 32; Stanley, "B Version," 445–46), concerns the interpretation of B 10.57 (B 10.58 in Athlone). Dame Study is denouncing those who indulge in presumptuous theological speculation over dinner. They drivel on the dais about the deity, she says, "And gnawen God with the gorge whanne hir guttes fullen": in other words, their throats indulge in both blasphemous speech and gluttony, similar to the later behavior of the Doctor of Divinity at Conscience's feast. At least, this is how the line reads in all the B-manuscripts and in the editions of Skeat and Schmidt.[21] But the Athlone edition, emended from the A-text, reads "And gnawen god [in] the gorge." The editors explain that "*gnawen with the gorge* is actually non-sense," and that what the author in fact wrote was something the scribes "either missed or rejected as outrageous": an "appallingly graphic representation of blasphemy," which they translate as "bite God persistently in the throat" (*B Version*, 103). To my knowledge, no other critic of *Piers* has accepted this astonishing interpretation of the line, and many have given good reasons for following the manuscript reading (see Pearsall, *Piers: C-Text*, 196). Of course Kane and Donaldson may be right about what Langland actually wrote, but the poet they believe capable of producing such an "appallingly graphic" image (in which the deity is not only somehow bitten in the throat but bitten "persistently") is one recognized by few other readers of *Piers*. How far then should we trust the ability of such editors to distinguish unfailingly the poet's own words from scribal rewrit-

---

21. Skeat translates the line as "And gnaw God with their throat (defame him with their words), when their bellies are full," referring the reader to a similar line (unmentioned in Kane-Donaldson) just below at B 10.66: "God is muche in the gorge of thise grete maistres" (EETS edition, 4:236).

ing?[22] The famous challenge that concludes the introduction to Athlone B—
"Whether we have carried out our task efficiently must be assessed by reenacting
it" (*B Version*, 220)—suggests the scientific principle that results are only valid if
they are reproducible by others, but, of course, any reenactment of the editing of
Piers, because it depends on subjective judgments at every point, must necessarily
always produce a different text (see Brewer, *Editing*, 405–6).

As Adams perceptively observes, Kane's defense of his choices in editing the A-
version "sometimes appears to imply that the mere act of explaining how a rejected
[scribal] reading might have arisen is tantamount to establishing that it did arise that
way" (Adams, "Editing *Piers*," 42; cf. Brewer, *Editing*, 323–24). An obvious danger in
this kind of reasoning is that the editor may not have all the information necessary
to make a correct judgment. When Kane and Donaldson reject a manuscript reading
as lacking sense, they may simply not recognize what its sense is. Robert Kaske, John
Alford, and Thomas Hill, among others, have argued persuasively for subtle biblical
and other allegorical echoes in *Piers Plowman*.[23] At B 14.27–28, for example, most of
the surviving manuscripts read, "Ne no mynstrall be moore worth amonges povere
and riche / Than Haukyns wif the wafrer." Kane and Donaldson radically amend
the first half of the second line to "Than Hauky[n] wi[l] the wafrer" because of
what, in the first edition of their B-version, they insist is "the poor sense" of *wif* (*B
Version* [1975], 187). John Alford, however, in his review of Kane-Donaldson, has
shown that the editors not only misunderstood the meaning of the text at this point
(a misunderstanding that has been silently effaced in the revised edition of B), but
also did not consider the possibility that *wif* "makes excellent sense on an allegorical
level" (Review, 1003; cf. Alford, "Quotations," esp. 86n, 89n).[24]

22. Edwards identifies Kane and Donaldson as the kind of editors who feel that they know better than
the texts what the author means: "The role of the editor becomes in this context potentially at least a vatic
one, in which he casts himself as confidante of the author's shade, glossing the mysteries of intentionality"
("Observations," 47). Cf. Pearsall on Athlone practice: "The editor enters into a mystical communion
with its author, from which all others are excluded" ("Theory and Practice," 109).

23. Adams notes that "in editing Langland, one perpetually courts the danger of applying inappropriate standards of originality to unnoticed scriptural allusions" ("Editing and the Limitations," 11).

24. Apparently in direct response to Alford's review, the 1988 revised edition of the Athlone B-version
omits the parenthetical justification for the "poor sense" of *wif* in the 1975 introduction: "(why should her
clothes be compared with those of heralds and harpers?)." Alford pointed out that "there is no mention of
the wife's clothes, nor is she compared with heralds and harpers," for the clothes in the passage are
Haukyn's and the comparison is to him. The emendation of *wil* for *wif* nevertheless stands in the revised
Athlone B text, while an entirely new, and somewhat cryptic, explanatory parenthesis for the "poor sense"
of *wif* is substituted: "(it was Haukyn's own standing that was in question at XIII 227ff.)" (Kane and
Donaldson, *B Version* [1988], 187).

Other kinds of pertinent information may be overlooked by even the most learned and conscientious of modern editors. In a description of the hypocritical Doctor of Divinity at B 13.40 during the feast given by Conscience, most manuscripts read, "this mister ne his man." Kane and Donaldson edit out the Doctor's man, while keeping two apparent references to the pair a few lines later (*B Version*, 42, 43), as Schmidt noted in his first (1978) Everyman edition of B (*Vision*, 286), because "no companion has been mentioned" and "it is not Langland's dramatic practice to introduce unfunctional personages" (Kane and Donaldson, *B Version*, 179). But this explanation ignores the medieval edict that regular clergy, and especially friars like the Doctor, should travel in pairs, as often seen in contemporary images of the life of Saint Francis.

A. E. Houseman bracingly called for the application of thought to textual criticism, but the sometimes brittle logic of the Athlone edition is not always the most appropriate kind of thought. Employing such strict reasoning to the ambiguities and uncertainties of a literary work risks eliminating allusions and other information simply not recognized by the modern editor and depends on too restricted a conception of good sense. What a particular speaker says in a poem as demanding as *Piers Plowman* may be intentionally misleading, incomplete, or even incoherent. Or there may be unrecognized parodies of contemporary discourse. (Imagine editing *Sir Thopas* to make it conform to the sense and style expected of a major poet.) Some readings of the Athlone edition could be described by Kane's own comments about sixteenth-century belief that the poet's first name was Robert: "attained by reasoning sound enough within its limits of available knowledge" (*Evidence*, 45).[25]

As noted in my opening chapter, the playful, questioning voice of Talbot Donaldson is largely absent from the introduction to the Athlone B-version, though he seems to have had a dramatic influence on its actual text. At least I assume that Donaldson had much to do with the frequent and controversial use of readings from Corpus Christi College, Oxford, MS 201 (also known as manu-

The Athlone emendation of *wil* for *wif* may be correct (it is accepted by Schmidt), but the way its justification has been altered is rather sharp practice, as if any explanation would do to rationalize a predetermined reading. The publisher may have insisted that the introduction could not be wholly reset in the 1988 edition (the page begins and ends with the same word, though it is a line shorter), but somewhere a note should have called attention to this and any other such changes in argument otherwise impossible to detect except by chance or a line-by-line comparison between the two editions.

25. Several scholars have suggested that some readings in the Althone B-edition seem to have been chosen primarily to justify decisions previously made in Kane's A-edition (Adams, "Editing and the Limitations," 9, and "Editing *Piers*," 39ff.; Brewer, "Authorial vs. Scribal," 84, and "George Kane's Processes," 84; Hudson, "Variable Text," 50–51).

script F). Before their collaboration, Kane had dismissed this manuscript as one that "has been heavily sophisticated and is of little authority" ("Problems," 19), whereas Donaldson had initially argued for it and another B-manuscript (now found in both British Library, London, MS Lansdowne 398 and Bodleian Library, Oxford, MS Rawlinson poet. 38, and also known as R) as witnesses to an additional authorial stage in the composition of the poem ("MSS R and F"). Kane and Donaldson both recanted their earlier views when they came to edit Athlone B: *Piers* was agreed to exist in only three versions, and Corpus now became an important witness, the work of an "intelligent and critical" scribe, who in addition to many unoriginal readings, produced authentic ones either by correction from lost manuscripts that were better than any now extant or by skillful conjectural emendation (*B Version*, 166–73). The extensive use of Corpus produces just the kind of adventurous, challenging editing that Donaldson enjoyed because it made others think, but it goes against Kane's deep distrust of the scribes. The readings taken from Corpus push editorial subjectivity to its limit, as Kane and Donaldson identify what they assert are genuine authorial readings in a manuscript admittedly full of additions and alterations.[26] The result is that Athlone B is less an authorial text than a postmodern one, as others have noted—in Barthian terms, it is a *sciptible* text (open to rewriting) rather than a closed *lisible* text—with the Athlone editors rewriting the texts they have received as freely as any scribe (see Sturges, "Textual," 126–28; and Greetham, "Reading," esp. 44; cf. Knott, "Essay," 416).[27] I once heard Donaldson jest over a pleasant dinner at the Columbia faculty club that if the multiple-authorship theory were ever revived, he and Kane would have to be included.

BEYOND THE AUTHORIAL TEXT

The editing of *Piers Plowman* has often resulted in detaching the author from his historical setting. This is apparent as early as Crowley's first print, which presented Langland as a visionary able to see beyond the Catholic errors of the

---

26. For Kane and Donaldson's "extraordinary respect" for Corpus and its use in their editing, see, in addition to their own statement, Adams, "Editing *Piers*," 51; and S. Taylor, "F Scribe."

27. Galloway, in "Uncharacterizable Entities," makes the shrewd point that a lasting value of the complete variants in the Athlone edition is not to separate the work of the author from that of the scribes, but the reverse: "Yet, however contradictory and deceptive, [the Athlone] project potentially impels constant labor by the reader to consider the mutual invasions of scribal culture into Langland's poem, and of Langland into scribal culture, the very process that the Athlone theory seeks to put an end to" (85).

Middle Ages. Later scholars have echoed Crowley in identifying a progressive prophet as the author of *Piers*, though usually one who is politically rather than religiously advanced. Others have imagined a different kind of pioneer: a literary genius alienated from his times and listening only to his individual muse as he constantly revised his life's work. The Athlone Langland, as Bowers notes, would seem to be the most solitary figure of all, an artist so removed from the everyday that he resembles a Beckett character: "the writer sealed in an empty room. . . . He is absurdity itself: a voice without an audience" (J. M. Bowers, "Editing the Text," 81–82). According to the Athlone editors, the sublime authorial text they sought was sullied as soon as it came into contact with a copyist.[28]

But *Piers Plowman*, like other literary works, does not belong only to its author: if readers bring corruption to the authorial text, that is the price of its becoming part of the public world.[29] Jerome McGann, especially in *A Critique of Modern Textual Criticism*, has been the most influential voice against Romantic ideas of the individual writer and his pure, and purely personal, work. Arguing for what he calls the "social text," McGann asserts, "Literary production is not an autonomous and self-reflexive activity; it is a social and an institutional event" (*Critique*, 100).[30] Failure to recognize the social nature of writing results in too much attention being paid to the individual author and not enough to the fact that literary works "do not even acquire an artistic form of being until their engagement with an audience has been determined" (44, cf. 122). As McGann and others have made clear, the meaning of any work necessarily extends beyond the intentions of its individual author to include the larger cultural arena in which it is produced and received. The authorial text of *Piers Plowman* and the personal struggles it supposedly reveals are only one way of understanding a poem that also belongs to its medieval (and modern) publics.

Ralph Hanna has recently imagined not merely "[a]n Edition, but a range of use- or interest-driven possible editions," which will "approximate, through diver-

28. Kane has stated that the "essential character of textual criticism" is "the removal of damage, or the identification and signalling of damage, done by scribes to the language and sense of the poem as the author left it" ("Text," 197).

29. This is not to deny that *Piers Plowman* belongs first and foremost to its author. For a recent defense of authorial intention, see Pearsall, "Theory and Practice," esp. 125.

30. Cf. Sturges: "Whether he plans it or not, then, the medieval author tends to dissolve into a literary community, and it is the community as a whole that produces the literary work we now read" ("Textual Scholarship," 116). For the argument that Kane does take the social text into consideration and a discussion of the limits of that concept, see Alford, "Improving."

sity of approach and method, that plurality which is a property of its subject, texts in manuscript" ("Producing," 122). The *Piers Plowman* Electronic Archive, under the direction of Hoyt Duggan, is already making available facsimiles and transcriptions of individual *Piers* manuscripts for use on personal computers. Individual scholars can now access (and electronically manipulate) color facsimiles without traveling to England or settling for the severe limitations of black-and-white microfilm. Eventually, it should be possible to access quickly all the forms of a single line or extended passage in *Piers*, which at present can be reconstructed from the Athlone editions only with the greatest difficulty.

Freed from strict allegiance to the authorial text, we can imagine many new kinds of critical editions of *Piers* for modern readers. One such might be a chrestomathy (or several chrestomathies) of the most frequently discussed episodes from all three or four versions of the poem, such as the tearing of the pardon from the B-version and the "autobiographical" passage from the C-version. This would resemble the text of *Piers* that many readers already carry around in their heads, though its specific contents vary from person to person. Nor would such a compilation be unmedieval. One Huntington Library manuscript (MS HM 114), which I shall discuss below, contains "a carefully edited version of the poem made by one who had before him all three texts of the poem and who sought to produce from their conflation a composite version which would incorporate what he regarded as the best material from all three" (Russell and Nathan, "Manuscript," 119).

As Hanna notes in his suggestion for different kinds of editions of *Piers*, one limitation of the ones we now have is that they often ignore the complex intertextuality that is a striking feature of medieval manuscripts ("Producing," 123–24). Even textual studies of *Piers* ignore or downplay the other works with which it originally appeared. One reason is certainly that in the surviving manuscripts *Piers* generally appears alone or with just a few minor texts. And when *Piers* is found with other major works, the significance of their association is not necessarily obvious. Was a particular miscellany merely a random assembly of available texts or a deliberate selection? If the latter, who made it: the scribe or the patron (who might be an individual or institution), or both, and on what principles? With *Piers* manuscripts we almost never know enough to answer these questions satisfactorily.

Despite uncertainties about the other texts that appear in manuscripts with *Piers Plowman*, they nevertheless offer intriguing suggestions about the discursive contexts in which the poem was originally copied and read. In some manuscripts, *Piers* is found with vernacular religious works, in others with romances, and in one large early collection with a number of Latin histories.[31] These different intertextual settings suggest a range of audiences to which the poem might have appealed, a number of different publics. Each particular manuscript context would have influenced in unique ways a reader's expectations of the poem and sense of its genre.

Modern literary critics regularly compare *Piers* with Chaucer's poetry, seeing a natural affinity, perhaps even direct influence, between two of the greatest Ricardian poets, and the pair is often taught together in university courses. Yet the works of Chaucer and Langland almost never appear in the same manuscript, suggesting that the association might have seemed less inevitable to contemporaries than it does to us. When a Chaucerian work is found with *Piers* (it happens only once, in a B-manuscript), it is the pagan courtly romance *Troilus and Criseyde*, not one of the English *Canterbury Tales*, as we might expect.[32] The work most often found with *Piers* in medieval manuscripts (five times) is one that critics have rarely discussed with the poem: English versions of the prose *Mandeville's Travels*, an association that I shall explore in Chapter 4. The intertextualities created by those who produced the *Piers* manuscripts urge us to go beyond an exclusive focus on the poet. This does not mean that we have to erase the author of *Piers*, but we should try to locate him in a wider social context of public reception.

AUDIENCES

In their quest for the authorial text, the Athlone editors paid little attention to the audiences of *Piers Plowman*, except to deplore contamination by the scribes. The competence of the first readers of *Piers* has also been deprecated by other scholars, who interpret Langland's revisions of the poem as defensive reactions to persistent misunderstanding of his intent (especially during the Rising of

31. The most accessible lists of the contents of individual *Piers* manuscripts appear at the beginning of each Athlone edition. The large early manuscript (late fourteenth century) is University Library, Cambridge, MS Dd.1.17, which includes, among many other works, Ralph Hidgen's *Polychronicon*, Geoffrey of Monmouth's *Historia Regum Britannie*, *Pseudo-Turpin*, Guido delle Colonne's *Historia Destructionis Troiae*, *Gesta Dei per Francos*, *Fides Saracenorum*, Gildas's *De Excidio Britannie*, in addition to *Mandeville's Travels*. For a complete description of the manuscript, see Crick, *Historia Regum*, 67–71. Middleton uses this manuscript to posit an audience concerned with spiritual and temporal governance ("Audience and Public").

32. The B-manuscript in which *Troilus* and *Piers* appear is Huntington Library, MS HM 114; a few stanzas of *Troilus* are now also found with *Piers* in Huntington Library, MS HM 143, but the two works were only later put together (see Hanna, "Emendations," 192).

1381): "Langland's awareness that Piers had found himself in rebel company was one warning, though perhaps the most explicit, that his poem was being read to say what he never meant" (Justice, *Writing*, 233; cf. Hanna, "Versions," 241; Kerby-Fulton, "*Piers*," 524–25; Astell, "Full of Enigmas"). There have been brief studies of those who owned early copies of *Piers* (Burrow, "Audience"; Middleton, "Audience and Public"; Wood, "Fourteenth-Century Owner"), but the sorts of readers (and distinct audiences) Langland might have had in mind when writing his poem, and their response to it, are only just beginning to be explored, and the topic remains limited by the Langland myth.[33] The recent textual work already mentioned by Mann, Hudson, and Bowers, which questions the ABC sequence, suggests a new way of imagining the possible influence of audiences on the construction of the poem. Mann especially urges us to go beyond the unexamined supposition that the different forms of *Piers* are primarily stages of poetic self-expression: Langland's lifetime struggle to perfect a personal artistic vision and make his meaning clear. Whether or not we agree with her argument that the A-version is a late production deliberately designed for younger and less educated readers, Mann challenges us to think seriously about the impact that particular groups of readers might have had on specific versions of the poem. If we do, the surviving shapes of *Piers* (perhaps there were once more than we have now) can be understood as rhetorical as well as subjective, as public as well as personal—particular objects designed for individual groups of users. *Piers* might be considered as something like a piece of scholarly research that any of us might undertake, which would be capable of being variously modified to suit an encyclopedia entry, an essay for a specialized collection, or an undergraduate class. The author remains in charge but is no longer isolated within his locked room; he is writing in the context of the larger social world, listening not only to an inner muse but also to an external public.

The possible audiences for which *Piers Plowman* might have been intended must remain inferential and highly conjectural, not unlike the readers of the poem (including Richard II and Jack Straw) imagined in Converse's novel *Long Will*. There is nothing wrong with this kind of speculation, as long as it is recognized for what it is—and not, as is so often the case with the assumptions of the

33. Kane and Donaldson suggest that Langland "had a patron or group of supporters" (*B Version*, 122). Hanna also speculates about a Langland coterie ("Versions," 236–38; *William Langland*, 23–24). An especially ambitious, and admittedly quite speculative, article by Kathryn Kerby-Fulton and Steven Justice locates Langland's literary coterie within London bureaucratic circles ("Reading Circles"; cf. also Kerby-Fulton, "Professional Readers").

Langland myth, treated as fact. Although little is known about the first patrons and readers of *Piers Plowman,* that need not prevent us from trying to imagine who they might have been.

I shall here only sketch some possible results of including public audiences in our understanding of *Piers.* As noted above, the C-version is usually taken to be Langland's final and most personal statement. But some of its features might also be explained by their being directed to a specific audience: an unfamiliar, non-metropolitan audience suggested by the apparent origin of a number of C-manuscripts in an area near the Malvern Hills (Samuels, "Langland's Dialect" and "Dialect and Grammar"). Perhaps Langland had returned to the West Country in old age, as many have believed, but it is also possible that a request for the poem came from an acquaintance in that area, in reply to which the poet in London found the best copy he could lay his hands on (one that apparently contained much scribal alteration), which he then revised as time and circumstance allowed with this new audience in mind. The poem supplied to such a public would not necessarily be a better or final *Piers,* only a version for a particular group. The long scholastic passage in C distinguishing "mede" from "mercede" (c 3.332–406) implies respect for the learning of these readers, but the poet might also have thought that some things had to be made clearer for them, perhaps worrying that this new audience would be less alert than his usual one to his characteristic ironies and indirections. Such caution could explain the proclamation of some of the poem's central themes at the beginning of C (c pr.10–12), as well as the immediate allegorization of the tower as the dwelling place of Truth and the dale as that of Death and evil spirits (c pr.15–18). Concern for such readers might also explain the absence of the tearing of the pardon at the end of the *visio,* a dramatic episode easily open to misinterpretation. Instead of such puzzles and enigmas, the poet might have concluded that scenes about the poor and the socially marginal were more appropriate for this rural public, including an episode unique to C about needy neighbors and "lunatic lollers" (c 9.71–161): passages that may be less radical poetically but certainly not politically. I make no claim that these suggestions to explain some of the distinctive qualities of C are necessarily true, only that they are possible and no more unlikely than some familiar ones based on the Langland myth. Freed from the limitations of that myth, we shall be able to interpret the poem in light of its potential readers as well as its elusive author.

We might, for example, allow ourselves to wonder whether some of the original audiences of *Piers Plowman* heard the poem recited publicly rather than reading it silently in private—and then go on to consider the implications of such reception. In the Cornhill episode of c 5, the narrator claims that he regularly visits a number of supporters in and outside London, for whom he prays from the primer. The historian Caroline Barron, identifying the poet with the narrator, assumes that, in addition to offering prayers on such occasions, Langland would also have recited from *Piers* ("William Langland," 97; cf. Hanna, *William Langland*, 23–24). Chaucer reading his work in front of listeners is a familiar image (though the makeup of that audience is much disputed), but Langland is only rarely assumed to have done likewise. To imagine contemporary performances of *Piers Plowman*, by the poet or others, begins to suggest a work different from the one with which most of us are familiar (in such readings, which parts would have been featured? which eliminated? in what ways would the poem have been altered for different recitations?). For one thing, the humor in *Piers* would be more evident in dramatic presentation. I have long wondered if snippets of the poem might not have been retailed from the pulpit by parish priests, who seem to have been one of the work's primary reading audiences. *Piers* is full of short alliterative phrases that would have made excellent didactic sound bites, such as "chastise withouten charite worth cheyned in helle" (b 1.188). In light of the many dialogues in the poem, perhaps we should look more closely at the surviving manuscripts (and the text itself) for indications of oral performance (for a beginning, see Scase, "Writing," 127–28).

SCRIBES, EDITORS, AND READERS

Although the actual audiences for whom particular versions of *Piers* may have been intended remain a matter of speculation, the manuscripts do contain traces of the responses of some of the earliest readers of the poem: the scribes who wrote, edited, and annotated them. (I am using the word *scribe* here to include the still imperfectly understood functions of corrector and supervisor). The scribes of *Piers* have received both contempt and compliments from modern scholars: although Kane has dismissed them as "jejune" and "banal" despoilers of the authorial text, they have recently been granted the status of literary critics (I assume this is a compliment) and even co-authors.[34] Such

---

34. Kane, "'Good' and 'Bad,'" 139. For the scribes of the *Piers* manuscripts as critics, see Pearsall, "Texts," 128, and for them as co-authors, see J. M. Bowers, "Editing the Text," 68. Kane has been particularly dismissive of recent scholarly attention to the role of scribes and annotators. Labeling as sentimental claims that scribal response is a kind of early criticism, Kane asserted that on the level of style it is "the response of mediocrity to distinction": "The scribal variant is a deplorable circumstance of the manual transmission of texts. It has value only as evidence for the authorial reading it supplanted" ("Text," 194).

extremes of praise and blame reflect modern conceptions of writing and distort the complex contribution the medieval scribes made to the creation and reception of *Piers Plowman.*

Author is too exalted a title for the *Piers* scribes, whose respect for the text they received apparently prevented the kind of radical recompositions we find in some popular English romances.[35] To compare these scribes with modern literary critics is even more anachronistic. They have little interest in deep or sustained analysis, but respond more practically as hands-on presenters rather than detached literary connoisseurs or theorists. This is not to say that scribal involvement with the poem could not be intense and serious, as Kane, when not indulging his scorn, was one of the first to notice. In the introduction to the Athlone A-version, he observed that *"Piers Plowman* was especially subject to variation as a living text with a content of direct concern to its scribes" (*A Version,* 115).[36]

But if the scribes' participation in the living text of *Piers* does not amount to co-authorship or literary criticism, it can be significant. Saint Bonaventure famously divided the work of medieval writers into four parts: scribe, compiler, commentator, and author (Parkes, "Influences," 127–28; Minnis, *Authorship,* 94ff.). The closer one looks at *Piers Plowman* and its manuscripts, the more these categories tend to blur and overlap for both the author and his copyists. The poet can be seen, even by those who recognize his artistic genius, to undertake all four roles in the making of *Piers Plowman*: he copies biblical and other Latin passages verbatim like the most mechanical scribe, assembles (or compiles) a wide variety of genres and discourses, comments on familiar quotations and images, and is wholly original throughout. But the same quartet of tasks, though producing different results, are also performed by the scribes, erasing any absolute boundaries between their work and his. The author is neither sov-

---

35. Pearsall, "Editing," 100–102. Similar extensive rewriting by scribes is also found in Lollard texts (Hudson, "Middle English," 45–47, and "Variable Text," 58–59) and in such works as the *Simonie* (Embree and Urquhart, *Simonie*).

36. See Pearsall, whom Kane elsewhere sharply attacks ("'Good' and 'Bad,'" 139n) precisely for the value he finds in such scribal contributions: "[T]he processes of amplification, emphasis, and censorship undergone by the *Piers Plowman* manuscripts demonstrate in the liveliest way the reactions of readers and prospective readers to the poem, and provide a sort of history of popular religious ideas in the fifteenth century, as we see the changes that are made in the text of what is still a living poem" ("Texts," 128; cf. "Editing," 104).

ereign nor unique, for others contribute to the creation of the medieval *Piers Plowman*.[37]

Although they do not engage in the extensive rewriting Sylvia Huot has found in some manuscripts of the *Roman de la Rose* (see her *"Romance"*), the scribes of *Piers Plowman* can be found undertaking the loftiest Bonaventurian category, that of original author—at least in particular lines and passages. For example, the three standard versions of *Piers* follow Meed's corrupt request that mayors accept bribes from illegal sellers of foodstuffs with a biblical warning from "Salomon the sage" that fire will destroy the houses of such grafters (B 3.93–100; A 3.82–89; C 3.121–26). To this, one A-manuscript (British Library, MS Harley 875) adds four lines that much more pointedly warn these "maysturs of the lawe" that their souls as well as their dwellings will be at risk if they persist in such corrupt behavior.[38] Scribes often rewrite *Piers* locally with real skill, as in a famous early section of the Ilchester C-manuscript (University of London Library, MS S.L. V.88), which contains material from various textual traditions as well as original lines that are usually attributed to a "Langland enthusiast" or even to Langland himself.[39] Here, as elsewhere, scholars cannot determine exactly where the poet's activity ends and the scribes' begins. Elsewhere, as we have seen, Kane is unable to say how much (if any) of passus 12 of the A-text, the "John But" ending, is the work of the poet (*A Version*, 51), even though the Athlone edi-

---

37. On the overlapping of the work of scribes and the poet of *Piers*, see, for example, Pearsall, "Editing," 104; Machan, "Middle English," 5–6; Adams, "Editing *Piers*," 50. Donaldson, as already noted, observed that the modern terms *poet* and *scribe* describe only "different functions of the single animal man" ("Texts," 272). Skeat also seems to have understood the overlap between the two functions. In a letter to Chambers long after his editing of *Piers* was completed, Skeat imagined Langland's friends borrowing rough drafts of the poem from the poet to copy and "if any of them liked to add lines on his own account, there was nothing to prevent him" (quoted in Brewer, *Editing*, 234). More recently, Galloway has noted that *Piers* has both "its inward absorption, and its constant ability to invite others to feel that they too can add to its idiom and participate in its impulsive spirit" ("Uncharacterizable Entities," 78).

38. After A 3.89 (quoted from Kane, *A Version*, 46):
> Now beoth ye war if ye wole ye maysturs of the lawe
> for the sothe schale be soughte of youre soules so me god helpe
> the suffraunce that ye suffre suche wrongus to be wrought
> while the chaunce is in youre choyse cheose ye the best.
See also Machan, "Editing," 239.

39. For discussion of the "Langland enthusiast," see Pearsall, "'Ilchester,'" 193; in a later essay, Pearsall noted that the changes in Ilchester seem "in a way, the very thing that Langland might himself have done if he had embarked on a D text" ("Editing," 104). For the argument that the Ilchester prologue and interpolations in Huntington Library, MS HM 114 suggest a second tradition of C, see Scase, "Two," although this conclusion is disputed by Hanna ("Versions," 205–12).

torial method is premised on the ability to distinguish between authorial and scribal writing.[40]

The so-called Z-text (Bodleian Library, MS Bodley 851) has recently been the most contentious example of the inability of scholars to agree on what is Langland's work and what is that of the scribes. Bodley 851 was not consulted at all by Kane in his editing of the A-version because he attributed its many original readings to massive scribal corruption, but Rigg and Brewer claim that these differences, often substantial, come from Langland himself and that Z is an early draft of the poem. If the unique passages in the Z-text are not by the poet, as Kane and others so resolutely maintain, then they reveal a scribe capable not only of active engagement with the text of *Piers* but also of imitating the Langlandian style so well that it has been accepted as genuine by modern scholars (see note 4 in this chapter). Rather than attempting to make absolute verdicts about what in the *Piers* manuscripts is by the author and what is not, it might be more useful to adopt the practice of art history and use such phrases as *the workshop of William Langland* or *the school of Langland.*

Recognition that scribes could act as authors, however intermittently, should make us more cautious about literary interpretation of *Piers* that depend on a single line or phrase. Much of the best Langland criticism is based on the close reading of the poem, but medieval authors and readers knew how easily a piece of writing could disappear or be altered in even a good manuscript. For example, after the sharp denunciation of Meed by Holy Church, we get a new and more positive view of the character when Theology suddenly appears in all versions to object to her proposed marriage to False and announce that the bride is a proper lady whose mother is none other than Amends (B 2.119; A 2.83; C 2.120). The Athlone B-version prints this crucial line as "For Mede is muliere of Amendes engendred." The corresponding line in the Athlone A-version, as amended (also in Schmidt), is very similar to that in B; "For mede is molere of [m]endis engendrit"; but many A-manuscripts, as recorded in the Athlone variants, have quite different readings. Instead of characterizing Meed as a respectable woman ("molere," i.e., *mulier*), British Library, MS Harley 875 calls her "a medeler," and

---

40. In another example of the potential interrelations between the roles of author and scribe, Bowers says that he is tempted to "imagine" (the wholly appropriate word is his) a narrative of reception and composition that extends beyond *Piers* itself: John But, after completing A as a tribute to Langland, goes on to write *Richard the Redeless* and *Mum and the Sothsegger* in imitation of his master (J. M. Bowers, "Editing the Text," 88–89). The Athlone editors, as previously noted, posit that the C-version contains the unspecifiable contributions of a literary executor.

the important Vernon manuscript, Bodleian Library, MS English poetry A 1, reads "a Iuweler," suggesting her wealth and vanity rather than her virtue (the same variants appear in these manuscripts at A 2.96). Moreover, instead of having Meed engendered by "mendis" (Amends), Kane's copy text, Trinity College, Cambridge, MS R.3.14, and four other manuscripts say the act was performed by "frendis." Another manuscript, University College, Oxford, MS 45, has "frendis of frendis," and still another, Trinity College, Dublin, MS 213 (D.4.12), "fendes," all of which imply irregular parentage indeed. In contrast, National Library of Wales, MS 733B, inserts several lines from the C-tradition after 2.83 that say Meed should be wed to Truth because she represents heavenly reward (see Kane, *A Version*, 213 and 30; Chambers and Grattan, "Text" [1909], 368–69). Thus the single line (and especially a couple of nouns) that has been crucial to modern arguments that Meed is a morally complex figure would have been unavailable or even contradicted in several A-manuscripts, including the base manuscript for the Athlone edition. This does not mean that we should abandon close readings of *Piers*, only that we must be alert to the variance of medieval texts. Every manuscript is unique, with the author's words transmitted through and transformed by the activity of individual scribes.[41]

If the scribes of *Piers Plowman* on occasion function as authors, they are more commonly found in the role of compiler (the modern term might be *editor*), in the sense that Malcolm Parkes defines him: "The compiler adds no matter of his own . . . but . . . is free to rearrange. . . . What he imposed was a new *ordinatio* on the materials he extracted from others" (Parkes, "Influence," 128).[42] In contrast to the several manuscripts that contain selections from the *Canterbury Tales*, almost no miscellanies survive with excerpts from *Piers*, which is admittedly a harder poem to anthologize.[43] Nevertheless, many manuscripts are compilations

---

41. Textual variants that are scribal rather than authorial are valuable witnesses to how the poem was first understood. A detailed study is still needed of such contemporary editing and rewriting of *Piers*, as Barry Windeatt has provided for Chaucer's *Troilus and Criseyde*, to reveal what Anne Hudson has called the "fascinating light shed upon contemporary reactions to *Piers Plowman* by the variants disparagingly swept away by Kane and Donaldson as unauthorized modifications" ("Middle English," 49).

42. Cf. Chambers and Grattan, who call the scribes of *Piers* "not exact copyists, but editors, although working without an editor's sense of responsibility" ("Text" [1909], 368).

43. An exception is the twenty-line passage on free will from a C-text that John Cok copied into the anthology that is now Gonville and Caius College, Cambridge, MS 669*/646 (see Russell, "As They Read It," 183–84; Russell and Kane, *C Version*, 2). For a copy of the opening few lines of the C-prologue in another manuscript, see Hanna, "Emendations," 194.

of different versions of *Piers,* perhaps made with no other motive than to produce a fuller text: these include the seven manuscripts that add C-endings to fill out their A-texts and three largely B-texts that begin with material from A and C.[44]

Two B-compilations demonstrate how often the activities of authors and scribes overlap. The first has already been mentioned: the early and quite elegant Corpus Christi College, Oxford, manuscript (also known as F), one of a pair that forms an alternate textual tradition to the majority of B-manuscripts.[45] The Corpus manuscript contains many examples of local scribal rewriting, including numerous unique readings that so impressed the Athlone editors that they adopted them as authorial. But it is as a compiler that the scribe of Corpus is most active. For example, without changing the content of the text itself, he adds nine extra-large initials (or spaces for initials) of the kind also found at his passus divisions, most of which mark the beginning of a significant speech or the introduction of a significant character, especially the sins (3.170, 3.228, 4.1, 5.60, 5.133, 5.186, 5.297, 5.386, and 10.137).[46] The scribe of Corpus also reorders the usual passus divisions to give a new emphasis and organization to some of the most important episodes in the poem. Thus passus 3 and 4 are joined to make Meed's adventures at Westminster into a single continuous narrative. Haukyn's story is also unified into a single passus (instead of having it spread over passus 13 and 14), as are the three passus that tell of the confession of the folk, their plowing of the half acre, and the

---

44. The A-texts with C-endings are Liverpool University Library, MS F.4.8; British Library, MS Harley 6041; Bodleian Library, MS Digby 145; National Library of Wales, MS no. 733B; Trinity College, Cambridge, MS R.3.14; *olim* Duke of Westminster's Manuscript; Bodleian Library, MS Bodley 851. The B-manuscripts are British Library, MS Additional 10574; Bodleian Library, MS Bodley 814; British Library, MS Cotton Caligula A.xi.

45. For the Corpus manuscript, see Weldon, *"Ordinatio"*; S. Taylor, "F Scribe." Hanna says about Corpus: "[F]rom the standpoint of the scribe's enthusiastic reception of the poem, it may be the most interesting copy of any version except Bodley 851" ("Versions," 216). The other manuscript in this tradition (also known as R) is Bodleian Library, MS Rawlinson Poetry 38, with some folios now in British Library, MS Lansdowne 398.

46. The first two (3.170 and 3.228) mark dialogues that precede key speeches in the Meed episode, and the third occurs at 4.1, which is not identified as a passus division with a heading in this manuscript. The fourth initial occurs at the entrance of Repentance (5.60), and the following four, including two spaces for initials that were not executed, mark the introduction of individual sins (5.133, 5.186, 5.297, and 5.386). The last appears at the silencing of Wit (10.137). Two other B-manuscripts, University Library, Cambridge, MS Gg.iv.31, and Trinity College, Cambridge, MS B.15.17, also have extra initials. See Benson and Blanchfield, *Manuscripts.*

pardon sent to them from Truth.[47] Although the changes in the Corpus affect the presentation and not the substance of *Piers,* they are intelligent and original reorganizations that would influence all who read the poem in this manuscript. The scribe edits the authorial product.

The most complex compilation of *Piers Plowman* is Huntington Library, MS HM 114. HM 114 is primarily a B-text, but it also contains many lines and sometimes extended passages from A and C, all blended into a new whole. Because of this conflation, Kane and Donaldson rejected the manuscript as a witness to the authorial B-version, but, like the Corpus manuscript, it is an invaluable witness to *Piers* as a social or public text.[48] Huntington 114 offers an astute selection of what an experienced London scribe apparently considered to be the best material from the different versions of the poem available to him, including the so-called autobiographical Cornhill episode and the passage on the needy who are our neighbors from the C-version. Such a discerning compilation might be thought of as the ultimate critical edition (taking into account different versions as well as different manuscripts)—an omnibus *Piers* with all the best parts regardless of textual origin.[49] This manuscript demonstrates that a purely authorial text, even if it could be achieved, would run the risk of misrepresenting the experience of medieval writing and reading. The question is not, as Manly and his opponents once debated, whether *Piers* is the work of one or five, but whether it exists in three forms or fifty. Modern editors and literary interpreters necessarily, if quixotically, try to stabilize what

---

47. Corpus labels the prologue passus 1, then combines passus 3 and 4 as "Passus Quartus" and combines 5, 6, and 7 as "Passus Quintus" (a later hand writes "passus sextus" at 6.1). Passus 13 and 14 are also combined as "Passus Decimus."

British Library, MS Harley 3954, which is a B-version only into passus 5, begins its third "part" not at 3.1 but at 3.101, when the king calls for Meed and asks her to marry Conscience, and then begins its fourth part at 5.1. Thus the entire Meed episode is divided logically into two sections rather than the three sections of other manuscripts.

48. For an early description of this manuscript, see Russell and Nathan, "Manuscript"; for a more recent one, see Dutschke, *Guide,* 150–52; see also Doyle, "Remarks," 41.

49. In his full study of the scribe of Huntington HM 114 (who also copied the beginning of British Library, London, MS Harley 3943 and Lambeth Palace, London, MS 491, part 1), Hanna classifies him as the kind of scribe "who arrogates to himself the powers of a modern eclectic editor" ("Scribe," 121). Pearsall, commenting on the freedom of the scribes of Bodley 851 (the Z-text) and HM 114, notes: "The precise difference between this kind of enterprising editorial activity and the original activity of the author engaged in the processes of revision and recomposition is a legitimate matter of debate" ("Editing," 104).

was still an open, collaborative text in the later Middle Ages and is still unsettled today.[50]

As well as being authors, copyists, and compilers, the medieval scribes of the *Piers Plowman* manuscripts were also, and perhaps most significantly, commentators. They supplied their texts with editorial annotations, further complicating any absolute distinction between them and the poet. We have already noted extra initials in some manuscripts. More common are the rubrics that introduce, conclude, and number or even describe individual passus of the poem. These rubrics, which exist in a number of different forms in the manuscripts of all three versions, are not included in the Athlone editions, apparently because they were judged to be scribal. Indeed, Robert Adams has argued that they are "the wrong-headed offspring of some mediaeval editor rather than of the author himself" ("Reliability," 209), though others have asserted that they derive ultimately from Langland.[51] Whether wrongheaded or authorial, they were an essential (and undoubtedly helpful) part of the poem for medieval readers, as they have been for moderns. If Adams is right, they again show the scribes trying to make sense of the poem by taking on an editorial function that elsewhere might be performed by the author himself.

In addition to passus rubrics and extra initials, three other kinds of annotations are found in the manuscripts of *Piers Plowman*, though they are generally ignored by scholars of the poem: they are (*a*) marginal notes (written both during the original production and later readings of the manuscripts), (*b*) words emphasized in the text, and (*c*) paragraphing.[52] None of these categories of annotations appear to be the work of the author, nor do they develop into a

50. See Machan: "But perhaps the most important determinant of editorial procedure for medieval literature, I would argue, is not the work, nor the transmitter, nor the original writer, if we have his or her name. It is the manuscript, for to a medieval reader, in contradistinction to a modern one, the individual manuscript typically determined the reader's view of the text and writer he was reading; and, in turn, the manuscript may tell the editor about the nature of the work he is editing" ("Middle English," 16).

51. See also Adams, "Langland's *Ordinatio.*" For claims that the rubrics may be authorial, see especially Clopper, "Contemplative Matrix," "Langland's Markings," and "Response"; see also Burrow, *Langland's Fictions*, 20n.

52. The following discussion of scribal annotations is based on the practice of the B-manuscripts of *Piers* and draws on my introduction to Benson and Blanchfield, *Manuscripts*. The three kinds of annotations identified here are often hard to separate in practice. For example, it is not clear to me how one can make a meaningful distinction between a word emphasized in the text and a note that copies the same word in the margin. An individual manuscript will often employ different forms of annotation to similar effect, using either notes or paragraph marks to call attention to the items in a list, for example.

standard *scholia* for *Piers:* the program for each manuscript is unique. None, not even the marginal notes, display much learning or intellectual analysis, and they are frequently hard to interpret: a *nota* next to a line does not obviously tell us what it was that the scribe found so notable. Nevertheless, the *Piers* annotations are almost never merely random or automatic, but, once again, reveal early readers responding alertly to the poem as a living text.

Some scholarly attention has previously been paid to the original marginal notes of *Piers*. George Russell ("Some Early Responses") first printed selections from two early programs of notes (Huntington Library, MS HM 143, and Bodleian Library, MS Douce 104) and one late one (British Library, MS Additional 35157); Carl Grindley has transcribed all the marginal notes from Additional 35157 and Huntington HM 143; Kathryn Kerby-Fulton and Denise Despres have written a book on the annotations and illustrations in Douce 104; and Marie-Claire Uhart produced a provisional list of the marginal notes in all *Piers* manuscripts. Yet this valuable work may leave a misleading impression. Russell, Grindley, and Kerby-Fulton and Despres deal with the marginal notes in only a few C-manuscripts that have unusually full and frequent annotations. Although most B-manuscripts also have marginal notes of some kind, only one A-manuscript, a late one written by Adrian Fortescue (see Turville-Petre, "Sir Adrian"), has many (Bodleian Library, MS Digby 145). Moreover, even when they are plentiful, the notes in *Piers* manuscripts are generally terse (often consisting of only a single word or phrase). No *Piers* manuscript contains anything like the extensive commentaries (frequently longer than the original text) so familiar from medieval academic manuscripts. The marginal annotations in *Piers* are indeed notes, not true glosses.[53]

Despite the limitations of the marginal notes, they do reveal areas of scribal interest that illuminate the early reception of *Piers Plowman*. The notes pay special attention to lists of the Deadly Sins, for instance, suggesting the importance of this schema to medieval audiences, however mechanical it may seem to many today. Although the annotators show little theoretical sophistication, they are sensitive to the range of genres, registers, and nonnarrative elements that are

---

53. Russell observes that the annotation in two of the C-manuscripts he studied contains "nothing esoteric or pretentious," but is "essentially an unambitious attempt to make the text more accessible to an undemanding but earnest reader" ("Some Early Responses," 280). The discussion of the *Piers* marginal notes that follows concentrates almost entirely on those annotations that were part of the original production of the B-manuscripts, though the annotations by later readers are often similar.

embedded in the poem. For example, they mark such things as Latin verses, Meed's marriage charter, Piers's testament, and the many prophecies in the poem. The notes also show real interest in clerical abuse and reform, although their objectivity often makes it hard to be sure of the scribes' exact views on this issue. Characteristically, the marginal notes reflect and index what is already in *Piers* rather than developing, commenting on, or challenging the text.

The two final categories of annotations in *Piers* manuscripts (emphasized words and paragraphing) are even more laconic and have received almost no scholarly notice until very recently.[54] Modern editions of *Piers* emphasize the formal Latin quotations in *Piers*, usually by setting them in italic type (our equivalent of rubrication), but important individual words in English and Latin that are also frequently marked in the manuscripts by means of underlining, boxing, highlighting, or actually writing the words in red are almost never so distinguished in the texts we use.[55] The rubrication of words in *Piers* B-manuscripts is not careless or random, but clearly done with attention. The general categories of words annotated include proper names (such as Meed or Piers and biblical figures), places (such as Jerusalem), and abstract or allegorical concepts (for example, any of the three do's or *Spiritus Prudencie*). Rubricated words, like other kinds of annotations, reveal not only general scribal responses to the poem but also the particular interests of individual readers. For example, the Corpus scribe constantly rubricates the word "quad" (i.e., "quod"), many examples of which he has added to the text, as well as the names of different speakers. These markings emphasize what many modern critics sometimes forget: the number of different voices that occur in *Piers*, which was apparently recognized by the scribes of several B-manuscripts who label the work a "dialogue."

The most overlooked contemporary annotation in the manuscripts of *Piers Plowman* is paragraphing, which is indicated by paraph signs or guides for signs, spacing, or both. Almost all the B-manuscripts have paragraphing of some kind, often extensive. Unlike the signs that mechanically indicate stanza divisions (as in the manuscripts of Chaucer's *Troilus and Criseyde*) or modern paragraphing, the paraphs in the *Piers* manuscripts are employed for a range of different purposes

54. An exception is a passing mention in Russell, "Some Early Responses," 284. See my introduction to and lists of both words and paraphs in Benson and Blanchfield, *Manuscripts.*

55. Rubrication of this kind occurs to some extent in twelve of the eighteen B-manuscripts, four of which are heavily annotated. Such manuscript rubrication may have been more commonly applied to medieval prose than poetry and cannot be authorial in *Piers* because it varies so much from manuscript to manuscript.

and work in concert with other forms of annotation. In addition to marking off units of the text (often into smaller subdivisions than those found in modern editions), and signaling the appearance of new speakers, paraphs are used in *Piers* manuscripts to call attention to important or vivid lines in the text, functioning very much like a *nota*. Examples of this last kind of emphasis in many of the B-manuscripts are the paraphs placed at Meed's request to the friar to have mercy on lechers (3.59), at Conscience's warning to Reason that Waryn Wisdom and Witty love covetousness (4.32), and at Haukyn's confession that he could not keep his baptismal coat clean for an hour (14.12). Whether few or many, paragraphing is almost always deliberate. For example, paraph guides in Oriel College, Oxford, MS 79 drop off sharply after passus 5 (none is found after 10.149), but one of the last occurs at Wit's dramatic statement that no Christian would be forced to cry for help in public if prelates behaved correctly (9.80), indicating that though the scribe's paragraphing may be sporadic, it is not casual.

The different kinds of annotations in *Piers* manuscripts tend to be brief and sometimes opaque responses to the literal level of the text. Rather than the deep analysis we expect from modern literary critics, the medieval scribes are engaged in the more humble task of making the text manageable. In this they resemble a college instructor marking up a text for classroom teaching with underlining, symbols, and brief comments. The *Piers* annotations range all the way from isolated paraph guides and single words rubricated in the text to one expansive and comically misguided late note next to the dreamer's account in c 5 of his family life on Cornhill that suggests remarkable new biographical vistas: "Pers dwelled in cornewell with his frind christofor or his wyf Catte—in there beds had a vision" (British Library, MS Additional 35157, fol. 28b).

For all their elusiveness, the manuscript annotations are by far the best early records we have of the public reception of *Piers Plowman*. They indicate some of the general concerns of its medieval readers, as well as revealing individual responses. Each manuscript has its own set of annotations, so that even closely affiliated copies differ. Annotation varies greatly from one manuscript to another, but whether light or heavy, again and again it shows an alert response to the text.[56]

---

56. The annotations in these manuscripts, whether by the original scribes or early readers, are modest predecessors of the scholarly apparatus that has distinguished the editions of *Piers Plowman* by Skeat, Pearsall, and Schmidt, and further evidence of the editorial function of the scribes and later readers of the poem.

Because the annotations are difficult to recover, multilayered, and nonauthorial, they have been largely excluded from the editing of *Piers Plowman* since Crowley, who provided his own set of notes. Skeat ignored them altogether, though the commentary to his later edition of Chaucer listed manuscript glosses, which he may have considered authorial. The Athlone edition contains the most extensive information yet about the manuscripts of *Piers*, but it says almost nothing about annotation. An occasional marginal note is mentioned in the variants, but rubricated words are not indicated in any way except for formal Latin quotations, and paragraphing is wholly unmarked, even though this is the most common form of annotation in the original manuscripts. The absence of any record or even acknowledgment of such scribal activity misrepresents the text of *Piers* as it would have been known to most medieval readers.[57]

THE PUBLIC TEXT OF PIERS PLOWMAN

Whoever originally wrote it and for whomever its original versions were designed, *Piers Plowman* was quickly appropriated by a public audience—or, to be more accurate, by multiple, overlapping public audiences.[58] As we have seen, the poem appeared in medieval manuscripts along with learned Latin historical prose treatises, but also with more popular vernacular religious works and romances. In the fourteenth and fifteenth centuries, copies of *Piers* were owned by both clergy and laypeople as well as by both men and women: a Speaker of the House of Commons had one, and phrases from it were also used by the rebels of 1381 (see Wood, "Fourteenth-Century Owner"; Burrow, "Audience"; Middleton, "Audience and Public"). It has been plausibly argued that *Piers* influenced the court poet Chaucer, and it certainly inspired a lively tradition of dissident alliterative social criticism (see, especially, Hudson, "Legacy"; Barr, *Signes and Sothe*). The poem was subsequently adapted to appeal to a variety of later public audiences:

57. The Athlone pursuit of the authorial text may have precluded much attention to scribal annotation. Kane's first editorial project was the A-version, whose manuscripts are lightly annotated. His base manuscript (Trinity College, Cambridge, MS R.3.14) is especially virginal, with no emphasized words, no paragraph marks, and virtually no original or later marginal notes. As others have noted, Kane's initial decisions with A often determined his later practice even in the face of contrary evidence.

58. These different audiences are anticipated within the text of *Piers* itself, which explicitly addresses a number of disparate groups. Often the poem speaks to a general "you" (as at B pr.76; A pr.73; C pr.74), but at other times to "lords" (B 3.69; A 3.60; C 3.73) or to "werkmen" (B 6.319; A 7.302; C 8.342). The rich, the learned, and clerics are frequently addressed (sometimes rich, learned clerics), often unexpectedly: Holy Church calls on "yow rich" (B 1.175; A 1.149; C 1.170) in the midst of what is ostensibly a speech to the humble dreamer/seeker.

Crowley's first printed edition was addressed to Protestant readers; Skeat and more recently Schmidt have produced scholarly parallel-text compilations; and Florence Converse used the poem as the basis for a popular historical novel.

Middle English authors expected, even welcomed, such modifications of their works. The author of *Ancrene Wisse* urged readers to change what he had written to suit their individual needs, and subsequent scribes altered that work to fit different audiences (Hudson, "Middle English," 34). The original Middle English prologue to the *Orcherd of Syon*, a translation of *The Dialogue* of Catherine of Siena for the Bridgetine nunnery at Syon near London, is explicit about such customizing; it does not envision actual rewriting, but the effect is similar as it urges individual readers to decide for themselves which parts of the work are worthy of interest or in what order they should be read:

> [I]n this goostli orcherd [the work itself], . . . I wole that ye dis-
> porte you & walke aboute where ye wolen with youre mynde &
> resoun, in what aleye you lyke, and namely there ye savouren best, as
> ye ben disposid. Ye mowe chese if ye wole of xxxv aleyes where ye
> wolen walke, that is to seye, of xxxv chapitres, o tyme in oon,
> anothir tyme in anothir. But first my counceil is clerely to assaye &
> serche the hool orcherd, and taste of sich fruyt and herbis resonably
> aftir youre affeccioun, & what you liketh best, afirward chewe it wel
> & ete thereof for heelthe of youre soule. (1)

Each reader is to make her own compilation.

The scribal rewriting deplored by the Athlone editors, as well as the recon-structions that others have questioned in Athlone itself, are similar, even inevitable responses to *Piers Plowman*. The work not only allows such involve-ment; it demands it. *Piers* is an interactive text meant to be applied to its readers' lives. As such, it somewhat resembles a modern newspaper, which different read-ers will use differently, each one finding information or advice to suit his or her own needs. In form as well as direct injunction, the poem constantly insists upon interpretation (not that it is unaware that the lessons drawn may be erroneous).[59]

---

59. Examples of faulty interpretation in *Piers Plowman* include Meed's selective quotation of a biblical text (B 3.331–52; C 3.483–99) as well as clerics and other lewed men driveling on blasphemously about cen-tral Christian doctrines such as the Trinity or the Fall. In B 18 (C 20), even Truth and Righteousness do not at first understand the meaning of the Redemption that unfolds before them.

The pardon scene at the end of the *visio* is all about the need to evaluate an unstable text. The pardon is at once two lines of Latin and an extended English gloss on the various occupational groups, and the dispute between Piers and the priest over its meaning and genre (is it really a pardon?) is a practical demonstration of the inevitability and complexity of interpretation, which is further emphasized by the dreamer's own attempts to understand the significance of what he has seen when he wakes up. But analysis, however subtle, is not enough; the reader must also act. The Plowman demonstrates this when he tears up the text of the pardon and changes his life. As Julian of Norwich says at the end of her book of showings, *Piers* may be written but it is not yet performed. Or as Holy Church puts it, "feith withouten feet" (words without deeds) are "as deed as a dorenail" (B 1.186–87; A 1.160–61; C 1.181–82). Only by adapting the complex narrative strategies and thought of *Piers* to themselves can readers achieve anything like the "kynde knowing" the poem demands.[60] Clearly, William Langland (if that was his name) did best in originally writing the poem, and the many anonymous scribes did better than they might have in producing so many individual and annotated texts, but modern audiences will do well to make *Piers Plowman* their own, if the poem is to continue to be a living text and not a document of merely antiquarian interest.

60. See Middleton: "His poem was itself a mirror in the marketplace, for whose personal and public use every reader was made fully responsible—not only for understanding what he saw there, but for turning all of it to profit in his own time" ("Audience and Public," 123).

3. Beyond the Myth of the Poet

LOOKING FOR LANGLAND IN ALL THE WRONG PLACES

The identity of the poet of *Piers Plowman* has always intrigued readers of the poem. That interest is seen in medieval manuscript annotations and in Crowley's first print; it shapes Skeat's editorial work and much modern criticism. Curiosity has been sharpened by the paradox that whereas *Piers Plowman* often seems highly personal and was widely popular in its day, nothing certain is known about its creator or the conditions under which it was composed. As John Bowers puts it, "[T]he author of *Piers Plowman* remains a man of absolute mystery" (*Crisis*, 167).[1] Scholars have attempted to solve the authorship puzzle in two ways: by searching for information about the historical poet or by constructing an autobiographical account from within the poem itself. The second approach especially has produced powerful critical readings, but, like the first, it relies heavily on assumption and speculation. External information about the poet is both limited and disputed, whereas the figure of the poet within the poem is dispersed, elusive, and unstable. Before we can move beyond the limitations of the myth of the poet, its fragility must be recognized and alternatives to it examined. In this chapter I shall discuss the difficulty of establishing the name, life, and views of the historical poet and argue that his fictional image in the poem is less unified and more general than allowed by the Langland myth.

WHAT'S IN A NAME? THE EXTERNAL EVIDENCE FOR WILLIAM LANGLAND

Although the search for the author of *Piers Plowman* has a long history, it has made little progress. Among the major Ricardian writers, only the identity of the *Gawain*-poet is more obscure, and his work lacks the wide distribution and

---

1. More recently, Fiona Somerset has observed: "*Piers Plowman* gives us no definite specification of its author's or even its narrator's rank, status as clerical or lay, level and source of education, immediate or projected audience, or source of support during the writing of his poem" (*Clerical Discourse*, 22).

clear metropolitan connections of *Piers*.[2] The medieval manuscript annotators apparently knew nothing more about the poet than that the narratorial "I" identifies himself as "Long Will" in the B-manuscripts (15.152), the same first name by which, in his ending to some A-manuscripts, "John But," whoever he was, called the poet, which he may also have derived from the poem.[3] More details about the author were provided by the Protestant tradition associated with Bale and used by Crowley: it supplied a birthplace—Cleobury Mortimer—in addition to a name (Robert Langland) and, in some redactions, the information that Langland was a priest, attended university, and was a follower of Wyclif. Even if this information drew on older sources, as Clopper suggests ("Need Men," 111), its validity, if any, is hard to assess because some details were apparently taken from the poem itself and others are inaccurate. Thus the name Robert was probably deduced from a manuscript variation of "yrobed" at the opening of the *vita*, and Cleobury Mortimer is farther from the Malvern Hills than the eight miles claimed by Crowley.[4] That the author of *Piers* was a cleric and follower of Wyclif would have been natural assumptions in the sixteenth century about a didactic reformer of the fourteenth. Other identities were occasionally given to the poet between the time of Crowley and Skeat, as noted in Chapter 1, ranging from the fanciful (John Lydgate) to still others suggested by the poem (John Malvern and Piers Plowman himself).

The most convincing piece of medieval external information about the poet, whose importance was not recognized until the nineteenth century, is the memorandum added in about 1412 to a C-text (Trinity College, Dublin,

2. A. S. Jack long ago noted this odd ignorance: "[T]here is no parallel to be found in English Literature of such a well-known poem going begging for an author for so long a time and this is hard to explain, if while living the author was a well-known figure in London" ("Autobiographical Elements," 413). In their recent article ("Reading Circles"), Kerby-Fulton and Justice associate Langland with London reading circles that may have included Chaucer, Gower, and Hoccleve, which would seem to make the lack of evidence about the poet all the more surprising.

3. B 15.152 is marked in some way in ten of the surviving B-manuscripts, including the note "Nomen auctoris huius libri est longe wille" in British Library, MS Additional 10574, fol. 62v. A later marginal note to Bodleian Library, MS Laud Misc. 581, fol. 64r reads: "nota the name of thauctour." But no manuscript includes any additional evidence about who the author might be. See Benson and Blanchfield, *Manuscripts*.

Hanna suggests that the surname But is derived from *butts*, the short strips at the end of a row in a field (*William Langland*, 8n).

4. Skeat first suggested that some manuscript may have read "I Robert" instead of "yrobed" (*Three Parallel Texts*, 2:xxviii), and a manuscript with such a reading ("Roberd") was subsequently identified (Society of Antiquaries of London, MS 687). In Cleobury there is still a plaque in the church attesting to the poet's birthplace, as well as a nineteenth-century window showing him dreaming his vision.

MS 212 [D.4.1]) that states that the poet of *Piers Plowman* was William Langland (see pages 6–7 above). The author of the memorandum seems generally well informed and there is no reason to assume that he was being deceitful, but writing as long as a generation after the presumed death of the poet, he could have been confused or simply misinformed. Even if we accept the memorandum as true, it tells us frustratingly little. Almost all its details are about the poet's father, Stacy de Rokayle (his social status and feudal associations), with nothing else about the poet except his name (and no explanation of why a son of Rokayle is called Langland).[5] The most important questions about the poet (his education, occupation, associations with London and Malvern) are left unanswered by the memorandum.[6] In unpublished papers, Lister Matheson, alone and with M. Teresa Tavormina, has provided additional information about the Rokayle family and, believing that Langland was probably a name adopted by the poet for his writing, offers the intriguing, but unverifiable, identification of him as a certain "William Rokayle," who was ordained to the first tonsure by the bishop of Worcester

5. The memorandum did cast doubt on the Bale tradition, which identified the poet's birthplace as Cleobury Mortimer. As its name proclaims, Cleobury was controlled by the Mortimers, the great rivals of the Despensers from whom Rokayle was said in the memorandum to hold lands.

Skeat used the memorandum for the name of the poet, but in his characteristically inclusive way incorporated details from the Crowley-Bale tradition that were not directly contradictory: thus for Skeat the poet became William rather than Robert Langland, yet his birthplace remained Cleobury Mortimer.

6. Defenders of the biographical myth have recently seized on one additional piece of evidence: M. L. Samuels's argument, based on the work of the Edinburgh Middle English Dialect Project, that Langland's native dialect can be located to an area of Southwest Worcestershire near Malvern (Samuels, "Langland's Dialect" and "Dialect and Grammar"; cf. Kerby-Fulton, "'Who Has Written This Book,'" 105). Despite the immense labors of Samuels and his colleagues, the possibility of circular reasoning is always present in such work. We might feel more confidence in his conclusion if the Malvern locale were not already so well established.

In fact, like many other supporters of the biographical myth, Samuels depends on something like faith to reach his conclusion. In "Dialect and Grammar," he admitted that "the skeptic" might discount the circumstantial "indications" he has cited (setting, distribution of the extant manuscripts, and dialectically significant alliterations), even though they all point to Malvern. But rather than "give up and decline to follow the trail any further," Samuels urges us to "accept the challenge and attempt to deal with the mass of seemingly inconclusive evidence" (209–10). He then offers "a clue" to get out of this morass: relict spellings from Southwest Worcestershire in two eastern B-manuscripts (210). How Samuels knows these are relict authorial forms and not scribal or contamination from Western manuscripts, I am not certain, but even if we choose to accept his findings about the dialect of *Piers*, we are left knowing nothing about the poet except that his birth (or at least a significant part of his childhood) occurred in the West Country, which was first claimed by Crowley (but not mentioned in the Dublin memorandum). For some questions about Samuel's argument, by one who generally accepts his conclusions, see Hanna, "Studies," esp. 5–7.

before 1341 (Hanna, "Emendations," 186–87; cf. the review of Hanna's earlier work by Matheson).[7]

Such is the sum of the contradictory, anonymous, and above all, scant external evidence about the name and life of the author of *Piers Plowman*. The rest is silence—and speculation. No further reliable data exterior to the poem itself has yet been discovered about the poet, despite the best efforts of many scholars: Clopper has ruefully described the frustration of searching for documentary records of him in likely medieval archives only to come up empty ("Need Men," 111–14). Even if we believe with many that B 15.152 ("'I have lyved in lond,' quod I, 'my name is Longe Wille'") contains an anagram of the poet's first and last names and that there are other, even more hidden, "signatures" in the poem, we must still deal with Middleton's conclusion that this extensive self-naming was apparently not recognized by Langland's contemporaries and early readers ("'Kynde Name,'" 17, 25). Except for the obscure Dublin memorandum, there is no indication that anyone in the fourteenth or fifteenth century knew (or even thought he or she knew) the full name of the poet of *Piers Plowman*.[8]

The putative first name of the poet, Will, is especially volatile. Whether or not the poet was in fact called this, the word could also always be read

7. Matheson's William Rokayle is not obviously a stronger candidate for "Langland" than Bright's William of Colewell (Colwall, near Ledbury, was the parish where Bright believed the poet lived), who was ordained as acolyte in 1348 by the bishop of Hereford (Bright, *New Light*, 42).

Samuel Moore first cited records concerning Stacy de Rokayle ("Studies" [1914], 44–49), which has been supplemented by unpublished research by Matheson and John Alford (see Hanna, *William Langland*, 26). For the Rokayles in East Anglia, see Cargill, "Langland Myth."

8. See Machan: "[T]here is certainly no evidence that the author of the poem(s), vernacular writer that he was, made much effort to identify himself, to claim responsibility for his composition(s), or to preserve the particular lexical construct(s) he produced" ("Middle English," 14). Kerby-Fulton, a strong modern supporter of the bibliographic myth, makes the somewhat circular argument that the supposed anagrammatic signatures in *Piers* suggest that Langland was writing for "a known and knowing audience—at least, it is unlikely that he would have used these anagrams if he were unknown to those to whom he *wanted* to identify himself" ("Bibliographic Ego," 72). Kerby-Fulton has also revived the old idea that the author of *Piers* suppressed his name because of his dangerous views (Kerby-Fulton, "Piers," 514), though there is no evidence to support this, and the supposed subversiveness of the poem seems belied by the number of respectable, even eminent, readers (including clerics and a Speaker of the Commons) who owned a copy.

As noted before, Donaldson has suggested that even if we could be confident that the poet was indeed called William Langland (which is not unreasonable and solid evidence for which may some day be discovered), we will have satisfied little more than an antiquarian curiosity. The name alone tells us nothing significant about him or his poem (*C-Text and Its Poet*, 200).

allegorically as the human faculty so central to medieval theological thought.[9] Willfulness is a central characteristic of the dreamer/narrator, and so the name, as Elizabeth Kirk has noted, is "almost too appropriate to be autobiographical" (*Dream Thought*, 49n). In a powerful recent essay, James Simpson argues that both traditional names for the poet ultimately take on a public rather than a personal significance: instead of just a proper name, *Will* points to a more general "common will," which occupies "increasingly inclusive and anonymous discursive spaces, whereby the poem's authorship ideally becomes its readership" ("Power," 154). According to Simpson, a similar significance may also be true for "longland": he sees the word standing for a long-suffering (*longanimis*) common will, a voice "who speaks for the whole land" (163).[10]

The character Will caused uncertainty in early readers of the poem. Both Crowley and Warton confused him with Piers on occasion (Brewer, *Editing*, 16n and 29; see also Thorne, "Piers or Will"; Middleton, "Audience," 119), and each name is still sometimes used for the other—and not only by undergraduates. This persistent misunderstanding is another illustration of the instability of the name Will, which at times seems to refer directly to the author (and may have been given to him at baptism), but, more important, expands beyond any merely private autobiographical designation to suggest the human will in general.

A vexing question is deciding what to call the first-person narrator of *Piers Plowman*. As already noted, this "I" is frequently referred to familiarly as Will,

9. The best and most extensive discussion of the concept of will/Will in *Piers* is Bowers, *Crisis*; see also Dillon, "Margery Kempe's Sharp Confessor/s." Brewer notes that Ritson in the late eighteenth century suggested that the name Will might have been chosen by the author as a personification of the mental faculty and then mistakenly applied to the poet (Brewer, *Editing*, 34).

There are other complications with the supposed first name. For example, the sudden mention of a Will weeping at B 5.61 (A 5.44; C 6.2) does not seem to refer to the dreamer/narrator, since he is the one speaking at this point (see Kirk, *Dream Thought*, 47ff.). Will is never directly given a full name, the way Amans is identified as John Gower at the end of the *Confessio Amantis*, despite the efforts of scholars to find one hidden at 15.152 of the B-text.

10. Simpson ("Power," 163n) cites Meroney ("Life and Death," 4) as the first to suggest that Long Will might be translated as *longanimis* ("long suffering") based on I Corinthians 13:4 and other Pauline epistles. Cf. D. C. Fowler, *Bible*, 277.

Simpson's study of the name William Langland may cause us to wonder if there are any genuine autobiographical names in the poem. The narrator's passing reference to "Kytte my wif and Calote my doghter" (B 18.428; C 20.472; "Kytte" is also named as the narrator's companion at C 5.2) is often taken to refer to the poet's actual nuclear family, but *wife* in Middle English does not necessarily mean a married woman, and Kitte and Calote may be no more than general (and not necessarily complimentary) female names. Actif's "wyf" is called "a Kitte" at C 7.303. See Hanna, *William Langland*, 22, and "Will's Work," 33; Raw, "Piers," 170; Godden, *Making*, 9–10; and Burrow, *Langland's Fictions*, 86.

although the name itself actually appears sparingly in all versions of the poem (not clearly as a proper name until 8.126 in B and 9.118 in A, though at 1.5 in C), and it is far from obvious that the speaking subject is always meant to be the same figure. The "I" in *Piers* certainly adopts a range of roles and tones. The voice speaks as the dreamer of the poem's visions, but also in and out of those visions as a preacher, a pilgrim, a reader, and a fool. Sometimes the "I" is prophetic, sometimes clueless; sometimes learned, sometimes *lewed*; sometimes reasonable, sometimes crazed. It is not even clear whether the "I" should be referred to as "he" or "it" (or perhaps even "they"). The dialogic multiplicity of the "I" will be discussed in detail below, but, for now, it is enough to recognize the problem. I shall not use the name Will much in what follows in order to resist too easy a homogenizing or anthropomorphizing of the subject in *Piers*. I shall instead resort to such phrases as the *narratorial "I"* and the *narrator/seeker*, using punctuation (quotation marks or slash) and occasionally even the pronoun *it* to defamiliarize the subject and point to its discursive function.

WHOSE LIFE IS THIS? BEYOND AUTHORIAL BIOGRAPHY

Of course, the scholarly quest for the author of *Piers Plowman* has always been about more than what he was called. Skeat's great achievement in his myth of the poet was to go beyond a name and local habitation and provide instead a plausible life story.[11] An identifiable creator offered the promise of unity and clarity for *Piers*, because, as Foucault famously noted for literature in general, "The author is the principle of thrift in the proliferation of meaning" ("What Is an Author," 221). The lasting utility of Skeat's bibliographical myth testifies not only to the persuasiveness of his narrative, but also to the desire of modern and postmodern readers, no less than Victorians, to rely on the life and personality of the author to make sense of a difficult and often confusing work. As Middleton has observed, modern interpreters of *Piers* have often found its idiosyncratic qualities "explicable only by reference to the identity of the author" ("Kynde Name," 19).[12]

11. In his pragmatic way, Skeat assumed that Langland provided a self-portrait of himself in *Piers* that was deliberate, accurate, and unproblematic: "[T]he internal evidence of his poem really reveals much more, quite enough, in fact, to give us a clear conception of him" ("Section VIII," 245). Dahl calls Skeat's account of the author's life "a tour de force in the construction of literary biography out of every possible fragmentary reference" ("*Diuerse Copies*," 73).

12. Middleton herself continues this tradition by arguing that the internal signatures of *Piers* (like parallel elements in Chaucer's works) point to a historical poet whose personal example validates his literary work: "The ultimate referent of the written text, these gestures imply, is the life lived, and the specific finite body becomes the guarantor of the general truth of the discourse" ("'Kynde Name,'" 37).

This approach has produced many useful readings, but it has too narrowly chan-neled the critical discussion of *Piers Plowman*.

Until recently, the only sustained dissent to the myth of the poet was the multiple-authorship theory of Manly and his followers. A counterpart to the growing awareness during the twentieth century of the complexity of Chaucer's representation of himself in his poetry is rarely found in *Piers* criticism. Long after the mythical life of Chaucer was abandoned, the mythical life of Langland continued to flourish.[13] Donaldson produced the most influential modern ver-sion of Langland's life in the tradition of Skeat, even though he subsequently taught readers to separate Chaucer the poet from Chaucer the narrator and also warned that "the business of talking in terms of poets when one is really think-ing in terms of poetry is potentially very dangerous, capable of deceiving both the critic and his audience" ("Textual Comparison," 245).[14]

The myth of the poet is all the more deceptive because the shape of Langland's life is routinely taken for granted rather than argued. A geographical detail suggests how cautiously we need to handle apparent biographical evidence. Malvern and London are significant locales in *Piers Plowman*, which I shall discuss further in the final chapter, but the poet's actual relationship with each is far from clear, though scholars often write as if it were certain. Consider Malvern. Because its famous hills are mentioned in the first few lines of all versions, it has often been assumed that the poet was born in the vicinity and perhaps even educated at Great Malvern Priory. It may be so. Samuel's dialectical studies support the hypothesis, as does, more indirectly, the Dublin memorandum, which suggests a possible connection between the poet's father and Hanley Castle, held by the Despensers and located near the Malvern Hills. But the three mentions of Malvern in the *visio* (and only in the *visio*) made by A and B (four by C) are neither all that important nor very detailed (Barron, "William Langland," 93). The first (B pr.5; A pr.5; C pr.6) and last (B 7.142; A 8.129; C 9.295) examples—and the additional one in C (5.110)—

13. Bowers: "Much of the best twentieth-century criticism of the poem [*Piers*] is likewise based on the assumption that the seemingly autobiographical references are true and factually undistorted" (J. M. Bowers, *Crisis*, 165). Muscatine likewise noted the familiar critical approach to *Piers* in which "the author himself becomes the unifying feature of the work": in such a reading the poem "becomes, rather than a self-contained consciously wrought work of art, an intensely moving record of a man who wrote a lot of poetry in the midst of a prolonged spiritual struggle" (*Poetry and Crisis*, 92).

14. Not, of course, that the myth has been central to all writing about *Piers Plowman*: it plays little part in the important studies of Mary Carruthers and Elizabeth Kirk, for example (though Kirk does assume that B is a later revision of A), or, to choose a prominent recent example, in the work of Wendy Scase.

do not claim that the first-person dreamer was born or grew up in Malvern, only that this is where he had a vision after wandering widely. The other reference to Malvern (B pr.215; A pr.88; C pr.163) has nothing at all to do with the dreamer. Certainly, Malvern is a sufficiently remote locale to suggest that the poet had some personal association with it, but the nature and extent of that association remains unknown.[15]

A later Malvern period in the poet's life is suggested by Schmidt's comment in the preface to his Everyman edition that Langland "possibly return[ed] to the West Country in his last years," which Hanna endorses by noting that the apparent origin of most C-manuscripts in the Worcestershire area "support[s] the theory that Langland returned late in life to Malvern" (Schmidt, *Vision*, vii; Hanna, *William Langland*, 17). But *theory* is too grand a word for this distant echo of Shakespeare's retirement to Stratford. As far as I know, the origin and only support for such a return to the west is Skeat's long-discredited belief that Langland was also the author of *Richard the Redeless*, which announces that it was written at Bristol (Skeat, *Three Parallel Texts*, 2:xxxv, lxxxii–lxxxvi). Thus the biographical myth perpetuates itself.

Skeat's life of Langland, which he made so compelling and which so many have subsequently accepted in whole or in part, is a patchwork of isolated moments taken from all three versions of the poem. The narrator who introduces himself as "an hermite unholy of werkes" (B pr.3; A pr.3; C pr.3), without further personal detail, at the beginning of the poem appears only rarely in the first two visions, except when he questions Holy Church. Nor is the simple-minded but earnest ignorance she exposes in him about the basic teachings of the Church obviously consistent with his later displays of clerical learning. The person behind the narratorial "I" remains shadowy during his more consistent appearances in the second half of the poem, for the primary function of this voice is to listen to others talk. The "I" is not as vividly characterized or clearly located in time and place as, say, Piers, Haukyn, or even Trajan.

We never learn enough about the "I" in *Piers Plowman* to generate a coherent life, let alone a spiritual autobiography, and much of what we do know is the

---

15. That the poet lived primarily in London is also often rather too easily assumed by critics, even if the "I" of the C-text says that he dwells in Cornhill (C 5.1) and, later, "Ich have yleved in Londone monye longe yeres" (C 16.286). Obviously the poet knows London well, but whether he lived most of his mature life there, resided there during certain periods, or only made extensive visits is unclear. An irregular connection with the city might help to explain the lack of records and other information about this popular writer.

reworking of traditional material, just as the portraits in Chaucer's *General Prologue* are not primarily sketches from life (though they may contain factual details of historical persons) but largely derived from estates satire (Mann, *Estates*). John Burrow has shown that the conventional can also be historical, of course, for real human beings construct their lives, and especially the stories of their lives, in imitation of traditional narratives ("Autobiographical Poetry"). Nevertheless, the life of Will (even if that name is assigned to all the "I" statements in the poem) lacks the network of particular details that convince us of the historicity of a Hoccleve or Margery Kempe. Apparently personal passages in *Piers* may be no such thing. The first-person praise of monastic life as a heaven on earth (B 10.299–302; C 5.152–55) has been taken to reflect the poet's own experience of the cloister, perhaps at Great Malvern, but Kaske has shown that the source of the passage may well be Benvenuto da Imola's commentary on Dante's *Divina commedia* and that such praise was a common topos ("*Paradisus*").

The function of the various traits given to the "I" in *Piers Plowman* often seems less biographical than literary or thematic, frequently for local effect. The fervent declaration by the "I" that it wishes to know "Alle the sciences under sonne and alle the sotile craftes" (B 15.48; C 16.208) is probably less a self-revealing confession (though the poet may well have worried about such ambitions in himself) than a striking expression of the intellectual pride so frequently denounced in clerics during this section of the poem. At the beginning of the same passus in B, the "I" describes himself as one considered a fool because he will not salute "Lordes or ladies or any lif ellis" (B 15.6). Instead of presenting an accurate portrait of the alienated poet, as is regularly assumed, these lines are a continuation of the mood of despair created by Haukyn at the end of the previous passus (missing in the C-version), which leads to the introduction of Anima. The supposed forty-five-year pursuit of women and land described in the poem's first dream within a dream (B 11.6ff.; C 11.167ff.) has been accepted as genuine self-description by many, but it does not accord very well with the wandering hermit and poor friendless loller described elsewhere. The thematic purpose of such a passage at this point in the poem is more obvious than any possible personal revelation.[16] At the end of the poem, the narratorial "I," who has been largely absent in this section, suddenly presents himself as one who has

---

16. It somewhat anticipates, by contrast, the Franciscan image of elective poverty set out at B 14.262–72 (C 16.101–12).

become bald, deaf, toothless, gouty, and impotent (B 20.183–98; C 22.183–98). This is too much like a standard catalogue of all the frailties to which aged male flesh is heir to be taken as a reliable medical diagnosis of the poet's individual infirmities (though the lines are narrated with great energy, especially the account of Elde's moving over the narrator/dreamer's hair like a lawnmower and his wife's wishing he were in heaven now that he can no longer use "the lyme that she loved me fore").[17] The poet's skill creates striking scenes, yet their relationship to his own life is unknowable and not apparently the narrative point.

The obvious exception to the usually brief appearances of the "I" in or out of dreams is the unique passage that begins passus 5 in the C-text, which Pearsall (following Donaldson) calls the poet's *apologia pro sua vita*.[18] Ever since Skeat, these hundred lines have shaped the biographical myth, even though some of the details that became central to the standard life of Langland (such as an interrupted education, residence on Cornhill, and providing an itinerant prayer service) have little or no corroboration elsewhere in the poem.[19] The appearance of the important allegorical characters Conscience and Reason in C 5 should prevent us from too realistic an interpretation, just as echoes in the passage of major political topics, such as the

17. In contrast, Chessell calls this description of old age "probably the most personal moment in the poem" ("Word Made Flesh," 123). Although Alice Nitecki finds the passage "psychologically astute," she also notes how many of its details, such as impotence, are conventional ("Figures," 111–12), and Salter detects reminiscences of "the most popular and ordinary reading-matter," such as the *Poema Morale* ("Langland and the Contexts," 23).

18. Donaldson's influential life of Langland was based almost entirely on this passage. The greater detail of C 5 accords with the widespread assumption that the poet increasingly came to reveal himself as he rewrote his poem (Chambers, *Man's Unconquerable Mind*, 98; Kane, *Evidence*, 65) and is another way in which the myth of the poem (the ABC order) is used to support the myth of the poet.

19. Bowers notes that the narrator's stress in C 5 on his religious vocation is absent from other brief moments of self-description, in which he presents himself as a wanderer and lunatic or as going to church with wife and child, presumably as a layman (J. M. Bowers, *Crisis*, 169–70). Galloway reminds us that the texts the "I" says he read to others, such as the *primer*, are "undistinguished by any vocational specificity" and contained devotions that could have been performed by any literate person ("Schools," 96).

Confidence in the bibliographical truth of C 5 remains strong. Kerby-Fulton declares that Donaldson "threw down a challenge to anyone who rejected [C 5's] autobiographical status to show what purpose it was meant to serve if it was fictional (no one has yet been able to do so)" ("Who Has Written This Book," 105). Of course, not being able to identify a purpose does not mean that none exists, and, in fact, several have been suggested. Kerby-Fulton herself links the passage to other "visionary autobiographies," a genre that she admits moves in the direction of what might be called fiction by shaping experience to fit conventional expectation. Others, as though accepting the challenge of Donaldson and Kerby-Fulton, have found thematic reasons for C.5 that have nothing to do with the author's own life, including Bowers, who argues that the passage is a debate between Wit and Will (J. M. Bowers, *Crisis*, 167, 176ff.) and Wendy Scase, who reads it as a contribution to the poem's vein of *gyrovague* satire against wandering mendicants (*Anticlericalism*, 125ff., 139–40, 170).

regulation of wandering clerics and enforcement of the labor laws, warn us against reading it as wholly personal. In many ways the passage reveals not so much who the "I" figure is, but who he is not. Conscience and Reason attempt to categorize him as a member of one of the traditional three medieval estates (those who pray, those who labor, and those who fight): does he sing or serve in a church (c 5.12), does he work the land for others (c 5.13–21), or is he supported by lands and lineage of his own (c 5.26–27)? Because the "I" fits none of these classifications, Reason concludes the figure must be an idle waster (c 5.27–32)—unless he is disabled (c 5.33–34). Whatever autobiographical truth these lines contain, their primary purpose appears to be a preview of the social concerns about work and communal obligation that will soon be explored in the plowing of the half acre.

When the "I" eventually defends himself, he does not offer a full account of his life, but a series of excuses, evasions, and empty boasts that do not add up to a biography or even a résumé. First, he describes his youth and introduction to the clerical life:

> "When I yong was, many yer hennes,
> My fader and my frendes foende me to scole,
> Tyl I wyste witterly what Holy Writ menede,
> And what is best for the body, as the Boek telleth,
> And sykerost for the soule, by so I wol contenue.
> And foend I nere, in fayth, seth my frendes deyede,
> Lyf that me lykede but in this longe clothes."
>
> (c 5.35–41)

Andrew Galloway has noted "a series of ambiguities" here and in the following lines that discuss praying for others, including questions about the figure's training and occupation ("Schools," 94–96). The speaking "I" mentions an education supported by father and friends, the nature of which is left undefined— "scole" could refer to either a cathedral school or a university (see Orme, "Education," esp. 258–59; J. M. Bowers, Crisis, 19–23; Galloway, "Schools"). He then implies, but does not directly state (despite the assumption of many scholars), that the death of his friends interrupted this education.[20] Nothing is said

---

20. The language of the passage is very slippery. The "I" says that his father and friends sent him to school, and that he never found a life that he liked better since his friends died. No direct cause and effect between the death of his benefactors and his leaving school is made, though it is certainly suggested.

about any precise ecclesiastical rank he might have achieved, though many have concluded that he must be in minor orders. For reasons not specified, but often thought to involve marriage to Kitte (though marriage is not actually mentioned here), the figure has no regular ecclesiastical appointment but depends on the support of others, for whose souls he says various prayers (c 5.42–52).

Faced with this record of nonaccomplishment, the narratorial "I" mounts a number of evasive and irrelevant defenses. He asserts to Reason that clerks should not have to do the physical labor appropriate to knaves, though exactly what right he has to such status is left unclear (c 5.53–62). Then, as if to deflect Reason's accusations by shifting attention from himself, the "I" begins a digressive denunciation on the appointment to high church office (and to knighthood) of peasants and those born illegitimate (c 5.63–81). Perhaps believing that he has achieved a measure of self-respect as a result of these stern attacks on the abuses of the times, he declares that Reason should not rebuke him because in his "consience" he knows what Christ wants him to do (c 5.82–83). In a flurry of learned Latin (to justify his clerical status?), he concludes with the ringing declaration that the "Preyers of a parfit man and penaunce discrete / Is the levest labour that Oure Lord pleseth" (c 5.84–85). The implicit comedy of someone invoking his conscience in response to Conscience is fully realized when the latter laconically observes that he fails to understand how perfection applies to the one who stands before him:

> "By Crist, I can nat se this lyeth;
> Ac it semeth no sad parfitnesse in citees to begge,
> But he be obediencer to prior or mynstre."
>
> (c 5.89–91)

The "I" is now properly deflated, his evasions and self-justifications at an end, and it is time to sue for mercy. He admits that he has misspent and wasted his time (possibly while he was in school or in not striving for a normal clerical appointment), but insists that he still hopes through grace to begin a time that will be more profitable than the past. Reason urges him to start quickly a "lyif that is lovable and leele to thy soule" (c 5.103), and Conscience encourages him to continue in it. What we have in this extraordinary passage is not much like either modern autobiography (we learn few details about the "I" except his waste of a number of opportunities) or genuine medieval apologia (his final acknowledgment of fault resembles the reluctant confessions of the sins that immediately follow rather than a sincere self-examination). To expect reliable details of Langland's life here is to mistake the thrust of the episode, which, as Reason makes plain, reveals that for this unfulfilled, irregular figure no life worth the name has yet begun. Thus even the single passage that has contributed most to the traditional Langland biography tells us less about the individual poet than about the general themes of his poem.

Human subjectivity has become one of the central topics in contemporary thought, explored and redefined by Marxists, feminists, psychoanalytic critics, poststructuralists, and others.[21] Whatever the differences between these approaches, each to some degree questions the established Western belief in human beings as free, autonomous, coherent individuals—what is sometimes called the bourgeois self and is often traced to Descartes. The use of the term *subject* instead of *self* or *person* in such studies indicates both the dependence on a linguistic model (the subject position in discourse) and, more woundingly for human dignity, the view that, far from being the author of our own ideas, feelings, and actions, we are subjected to structures and ideologies beyond our control. Rather than a center or presence, the subject is seen to be a site on which powerful, impersonal forces contend. In the introduction to their *Mapping the Subject,* Steve Pile and Nigel Thrift note both the "forests of literature on the subject" (1) and the lack of agreement about it, except that "the subject is a primary element of being and that the Cartesian notion of the subject as a unitary being made up of disparate parts, mind and body, which is universal, neutral and gender-free, is in error" (11). Modern structuralist thought at its most extreme seemed utterly to deny human freedom and individuality, but a reaction against this, allowing the possibility of political resistance, has recently been mounted by such as Pierre Bourdieu, Michel de Certeau, Paul Smith, and Slavoj Žižak, who explore how humans, though shaped by outside forces, may nevertheless still exercise agency, however limited and contingent. The broad topic of subjectivity is much too complex to treat adequately here, but some of the issues it

21. The subject has also been a popular topic in recent Middle English criticism, especially Chaucer studies, as seen in the titles of two influential books: H. Marshall Leicester's *The Disenchanted Self: Representing the Subject in the Canterbury Tales* and Lee Patterson's *Chaucer and the Subject of History.*

raises can suggest ways to go beyond the Langland biographical myth and look again at how subjects, especially the narratorial "I," function in *Piers Plowman*.

Because the Langland myth was created in Victorian England, in a time that valued bourgeois individualism, there is nothing surprising about its assumption that the narratorial "I" in *Piers* represents a particular human being who is identical with the poet. But literary history suggests a more general figure. In an influential essay, Leo Spitzer argued that "in the Middle Ages, the 'poetic I' had more freedom and more breadth than it has today" because literature then "dealt not with the individual but with mankind" ("Note," 415). As I have already shown, the "I" of *Piers Plowman*, if not exactly an everyman, is often generic and various rather than individual and personal—representing a range of collective types (including an arrogant intellectual and senile old man) to produce effects that are thematic rather than biographical. This flexible and universalizing sense of the first person in medieval literature means that apparently autobiographical details need not refer to the author at all. In the works of both Juan Ruiz and Marie de France, for instance, we find "the appropriation of narrative material from other sources, presented as a personal experience" (Spitzer, "Note," 419; cf. De Looze, *Pseudo-Autobiography*; Vance, "*Confessions*"; Zink, *Invention*; Zumthor, "Autobiography"). Of more immediate relevance, in the *Pèlerinage de la vie humaine*, often thought to be a direct or indirect source of *Piers*, Guillaume de Deguileville represents himself as a layman, even though he was, in fact, a monk (Godden, *Making*, 10).

The great English Ricardian poets, although they may tease us with hints about themselves through their first-person narratorial voices, never provide anything like a full or accurate biography. The *Gawain*-poet is almost a complete cipher: we know nothing for certain about his name, profession, or associations. The first-person narrator is the central character in *Pearl* (despite being almost wholly absent from *Gawain*), but he tells us little about the poet, who certainly did not share his theological ignorance and perhaps not the actual loss of a daughter (if that is who the maiden in the poem is supposed to be).[22] Middle English poems may contain genuine autobiographical details without attempting to represent a life. Jack Benny and Burns and Allen used to play "themselves" on radio and television, using their own names and professions, without telling

---

22. See especially Spearing, "Poetic Identity," in which Spearing notes that the "I" of narration is not consistent in the poems of Cotton Nero A.x: in *Sir Gawain* he is "a storyteller," in *Cleanness* and *Patience* "an expositor," in *Pearl* both "a storyteller and the experiential focus of his story" (42).

us very much about their real selves.[23] The senile amorist of the *Confessio Amantis* is not a reliable portrait of Gower, even if he is given the poet's name, any more than Chaucer, the successful bureaucrat and diplomat, is likely to have been as antisocial, abstracted, or genial as he represents himself in his poetry. As Kane has shown, we can only speculate about the resemblance between late medieval English narrators and their authors ("Autobiographical Fallacy").[24]

It was once believed that Middle English poets spoke clearly to their readers. Great critics like Kittredge assumed that the Chaucerian "I" was the voice of the man himself. The discovery of the narrator (as opposed to the poet) in the *Canterbury Tales* and *Troilus* is a relatively recent development (Spearing, "Ricardian 'I,'" 1). But if scholars now automatically separate Chaucer the poet from Chaucer the pilgrim (sometimes perhaps too confidently), the same distinction is less often made in discussions of *Piers Plowman*. Whatever personal commitment we sense in the writing of *Piers*, the historical poet cannot be recovered through the poem's narrator. Spearing has shown that in the English literature of the period this first-person device lacks a "unitary psychic substance": instead, Ricardian writers "construct for themselves an 'I' very different from this conception of self—an 'I' that is shifting, divided, transient, and always liable to dissolve into the very forces at whose intersection it is formed" ("Poetic Subject," 13).

The complexity of the poetic subject in *Piers Plowman* has been most thoroughly explored by David Lawton. In contrast to those who want to use the first-person figure in *Piers* as "the fixed center of a turning work" ("Subject," 2), Lawton, drawing on recent French theoretical ideas of consciousness, proposes (not unlike Spearing) that we apply to medieval writers such as Langland current ideas about the subject that view it as "the site of contradictory discourses" rather than a "whole or united" self ("Subject," 6). More specifically, Lawton

23. Spearing, who has written some of the most useful essays about the subject in Middle English literature, compares the lack of personal unity in the medieval textual "I" to a modern stand-up comedian or talk-show host who "utters words spoken inconsistently from a wide variety of imaginary positions; they issue from a single mouth, but not from a single identity or even a single fixed persona" ("Ricardian 'I,'" 19).

24. Kane accepted that there was some relationship between poet and narrator but properly insisted that its exact nature must always remain in doubt. Indeed, a reader may observe that the narrative "I" in *Piers* shows great interest in and knowledge about peasants, aristocrats, and ecclesiastics. But does that necessarily mean that the author was a peasant who became a cleric, as Bright maintained, or that he was of gentle birth, though poor, with "aristocratic sympathies," as Bright's sometime sponsor Chambers thought (*Man's Unconquerable Mind*, 100)?

demonstrates that the first-person in *Piers* speaks with multiple voices—sometimes seemingly as the authoritative poet, sometimes as the dreamer making immediate observations, sometimes as a blend of the two, and sometimes as neither (8–9).[25] Lawton, following Lavinia Griffiths, asserts that the subject in *Piers* is "laden with a bewildering number of attributes," too many to make a single coherent personality—it is, in fact, an "open persona" (11). More than an individual, this subject encompasses a variety of types (idler, beggar, minstrel, and false religious) that together make a common, public figure: "the anxieties and faults of the dreamer and his society are identical" (12). As a depersonalized subject, the first-person voice is not consistent but "responds differently in different discourses" (14; cf. Spearing, "Poetic Identity," 45; Zumthor, "Autobiography," 32). The "I" in *Piers* is regarded by Lawton as a literary device rather than a consciousness (he prefers the structuralist term *actant*), whose function is not to reveal a personal self but to produce "disjuncture and deferment, the sudden substitution of one sort of discourse for another" so as to prevent thematic closure (15). *Piers* is not, according to Lawton, any more personal or less social in its second half: "The poem's values are collective throughout: they frustrate the distinction between private and public, between personality and 'al maner of men'" (21).

Lawton's essay freed *Piers* criticism from the biographical literalness that had stifled much past discussion of the poem's subject. Rather than a reliable authorial self-portrait, the "I" in *Piers* can now be seen as constantly fracturing and reforming, lacking both the centrality and consistency assumed by the myth of the poet. For large parts of the poem, such as the Meed episode or most of the last two passus, the "I" is barely heard at all. Sometimes it is an active participant in the action, at other times only an onlooker. Occasionally it pops up from nowhere, as during the dispute between Piers and the priest over the pardon (B 7.108; A 8.92; C 9.283). When the "I" reappears in the poem after a long absence, are we to assume that it is the same figure last seen or, as Lawton suggests, one playing a number of roles, as Piers so clearly does?[26] The poetic sub-

25. More than one narrative voice had been recognized by other critics, as in Barbara Nolan's distinction between the speech of the "sleepy wanderer" and that of the "doomsday preacher" (Nolan, *Gothic Visionary Perspective*, 217; cf. Mann, *Chaucer*, 209; Raabe, *Imitating God*, 82). Spearing cites Minnis on Bonaventure's recognition that the "I" of Ecclesiastes expresses the opinions of various people, and he concludes that "commentators long before Chaucer had clearly grasped that the 'I' of a single text need not refer to a single narratorial persona" ("Ricardian 'I,'" 20).

26. Even Burrow, a strong supporter of the biographical myth, observed that in Langland's "discontinuous dream-world," figures such as Piers and Long Will are not "characters in a continuous narrative" (*Langland's Fictions*, 10).

ject of *Piers* speaks everything from revealed truth to errant nonsense in a range of tones from many ideological perspectives to a number of audiences.

Such a slippery, polymorphous "I," who is both baffled dreamer and authoritative prophet, resident of a particular cot in Cornhill and the voice of common experience, marginal outsider and institutional representative, is not so much a single subject as one who occupies a variety of positions. As such, the dreamer/seeker cannot really be said to develop in the course of the poem like a novelistic character, though such growth has frequently been claimed.[27] The first-person does have moments of apparent enlightenment, such as in its definition of Dowell as "To se muche and suffre more" (B 11.410; C 13.221), but it is not clear that these insights are permanent or cumulative. Moreover, in a poem that recommends deeds, the dreamer/seeker accomplishes almost nothing. The climactic moment of the poem is the account of the Crucifixion and Harrowing of Hell (B 18; C 20), but the narratorial "I" remains an observer throughout, without saying what it has understood. At the end of the episode, this figure does materialize outside the dreamworld in a rare public moment, taking Kitte and Calote with him to church to reverence the cross (B 18.426–33; C 20.470–78), but when he sets off to Mass at the beginning of the following passus there is no mention of his family, and he promptly falls asleep. The "I" is heard only briefly in the rest of the poem.

The differing views of Catherine Belsey and David Aers reveal how hard it is to come to grips with subjectivity in medieval literature. In her *Subject of Tragedy*, Belsey argues that the subject as understood by modern liberal humanism, the "free, unconstrained author of meaning and action, the origin of history" (8), does not exist in the drama of the late Middle Ages. The true agents in such plays, according to Belsey, are good and evil or God and the Devil, for man is only the "temporary location of a conflict which exists before he is born and continues after his death" (15). Lacking a "unifying essence," but instead presenting an unstable alliance of immortal soul and transient body, "the hero of the moralities is not the origin of action; he has no single subjectivity which

27. For the concept of subject position, see especially Paul Smith, *Discerning the Subject*. For examples of those who, from a variety of perspectives, have seen some kind of growth and development in the dreamer, see Arn, "Characterization"; Blythe, "*Transitio*"; Clopper, "Life"; Coleman, *Moderni*, 193; Longo, "Tropological Matrix"; St.-Jacques, "*Christus Medicus*"; see also generally Robertson and Huppé, *Piers Plowman*; Simpson, *Introduction*.

could constitute such an origin; he is not a subject" (18).[28] In response to Belsey, Aers, in his influential essay, "A Whisper in the Ear of Early Modernists," argues that there are multiple examples in medieval writing of complex figures with inner lives, including those in courtly romance, in Chaucer's works, in the *Book of Margery Kempe*, and in *Piers Plowman*.[29] Aers insists that there "is no reason to think that languages and experiences of inwardness, of interiority, of divided selves, of splits between outer realities and inner forms of being, were unknown before the seventeenth century" ("Whisper," 186).

The disagreement between Belsey and Aers is partly a result of their not talking about the same thing (her focus is on agency, which he largely ignores), and both tend to blur distinctions between the related but by no means identical concepts of interiority, subjectivity, and the self. The inwardness that undoubtedly exists in the Middle Ages does not indicate that the period had anything like the modern sense of a unified subject with agency. Julian of Norwich has a rich inner life of vision and meditation but lacks much interest in herself as an individual. Augustine, whom Aers appropriately cites as crucial here, does advise us to look within; but what is to be discovered there is not an independent self, but instead God, who is above and beyond humans and alone the origin of meaning.[30] Aers is right to stress the continuity of interiority across the medieval-Renaissance divide, just as Belsey correctly notes how older concepts of subjectivity differ from those of liberal humanism (which, despite recent challenges, still seems to be used by most people today, scholars and others, to express their sense of themselves).

The myth of the poet encourages us to read current ideas of the self back into the "I" of *Piers Plowman*. The dispute over the Langlandian subject should

28. Belsey does note some complexity in the subjectivity of the Middle English play *Mankind:* "As analysis it shows human beings dispersed, unfixed, not in control; as exhortation it requires the spectators to make choices, precisely as if they were unified agents of their own actions" (*Subject of Tragedy*, 23). But she insists that only in the Renaissance do we begin to see indications of the authentic inner reality that will develop in the later seventeenth century into the unified subject of modern liberal humanism.

29. Aers accuses Belsey of joining with other Cultural Materialists and New Historicists in reinforcing idealistic, conservative interpretations that turn "the Middle Ages into a homogeneous and mythical field which is defined in terms of the scholars' needs for a figure against which 'Renaissance' concerns with inwardness and the fashioning of identities can be defined as new" ("Whisper," 192). He also tellingly notes the narrowness of such scholars' medieval examples.

30. On Augustine and the self, see Charles Taylor's *Sources of the Self* (esp. 127–43), which is also cited by Aers. Taylor notes that for Augustine the healing from sin that humans need comes from within: "But it does not come from a power which is ours. On the contrary, we turn to the path within only to accede beyond, to God" (143).

not be between medieval and Renaissance but between both of them and us. *Piers* criticism needs a surer recognition of how historically determined are notions of the self. In a short article and a long book, respectively, Marcel Mauss and Charles Taylor have stressed the gradual evolution of this topic in Western thought (see also Balibar, "Subjection"; Porter, "Introduction"; Sawday, "Self"). According to Mauss, person and self are not innate human concepts but were "slowly born and grew through many centuries and many vicissitudes" ("Subject," 59). Despite the contributions of Roman and medieval thought, the category of the modern self is relatively recent and still capable of change.[31] Taylor likewise traces the "rise and development" of the modern sense of inwardness, one that "had a beginning in time and space and may have an end" (C. Taylor, *Sources*, 111). Although Taylor identifies Saint Augustine as the one "who introduced the inwardness of radically reflexivity" to the West (131), the saint's views are said to be but an intermediate stage in the progression from Plato to later philosophers, who only in the eighteenth century began to construct "something recognizably like the modern self" (185).[32]

Piers Plowman recognizes human inwardness but not the individual coherence of the modern self. The narrative "I" of the poem occupies a range of subject positions in the poem and is so lacking in fixed identity that it often seems to metamorphose into other figures. The Seven Deadly Sins who appear in the *visio* have been seen as aspects of this "I" (Burrow, *Langland's Fictions*, 88–89), and their desire to confess is indeed linked to an apparently personified Will: "Thanne ran Repentaunce and reherced his teme / And garte Wille to wepe water with hise eighen" (B 5.60–61; A 5.43–44; C 6.1–2). At the end of the confession of Wrath in the B-version, the "I" is further implicated when Repentance's injunction turns insistently personal: "*Esto sobrius!* he seide, and assoiled *me* aftur, / And bad *me* wilne to wepe *my* wikkednesse to amende" (B 5.184–85, my emphasis).[33] The long speech at the end of passus 10 in B during which the narrative "I" pessimistically raises questions of

---

31. "It was formed only for us, among us. Even its moral power—the sacred character of the human person—is questioned, not only everywhere in the East, where they have not attained our science, but even in some of the countries where the principle was discovered" (Mauss, "Subject," 90, cf. 62); in an anticipation of Foucault, Mauss also notes that "with us the Idea may disappear."

32. Taylor argues that, unlike Augustine, for whom the path inward is a step upward to the transcendent God, Descartes firmly "situates the moral sources within us" (143), whereas Montaigne, even more our contemporary, is in search of "each person's originality" (182).

33. The confession of Wrath is missing from A, and the corresponding passage at C 6.168–69 puts the pronouns in the third person and omits the word *wilne*.

learning and salvation that many have thought were the poet's own is given to a greatly expanded and more general figure in C—Rechlessness (C 11.195ff.).

In the B-version, the character that most resembles the first-person speaker is Haukyn (see Carruthers, *Search*, 115). Haukyn introduces himself as a kind of poet—"I am a mynstrall" (B 13.225)—and like the dreamer at the beginning of the poem, dresses as "an heremyte, an ordre by hymselve" (B 13.285). He too has a wife and is generally critical of others: "Lakkynge lettrede men and lewed men bothe" (B 13.287). When Haukyn asks, "Where wonyeth Charite?" and observes, "I wiste nevere in my lyve / Man that with hym spak, as wide as I have passed" (B 14.97–98), he sounds very much like the "I" who is in search of the literal dwelling of Dowel at the beginning of the *vita*, even as he anticipates the dreamer/seeker's abrupt and significant question in the next passus: "What is charite?" (B 15.149). The similarities between the poetic "I" and Haukyn suggest that though both are given biographical particularities, neither portrays an individual person. Indeed, Haukyn loses his human name in the C-version and becomes the more obviously allegorical Activa Vita, and examples of his misdeeds, which are specific to him in the B-version, are transferred without change to the general confession of the sins in C. Haukyn, like Will, is not an independent, autonomous self but an amorphous, collective subject whose functions are more aesthetic and thematic than autobiographical.

Some of the difficulty for modern interpreters of subjectivity in *Piers Plowman* can be seen at the beginning of B 11 and the parallel episode in C. Scripture scorns the first-person figure and makes him weep by saying that "*Multi multa sciunt et seipsos nesciunt*" (B 11.3; C 11.165).[34] Despite both this injunction to self-knowledge and the inner dream that immediately follows, the resulting action is far from the private introspection we might expect. Instead, Fortune makes the dreamer/seeker look into "a mirour that highte Middelerthe" in which he will see "wondres" (B 11.9–10; C 11.170–71). Rather than discovering individuality, the figure recognizes that his life has imitated a depressingly conventional pattern of sinful desire, represented by the familiar trio of "*Concupiscenia Carnis*," "Coveitise of Eighes," and "Pride of Parfit Lyvyng" (B 11.13–15; C 11.174–76).

A seemingly more personal mirror is mentioned later in B, just after the "I" has identified himself as Long Will, which many consider one of the clearest moments of self-identification in the poem:

34. This passage is important to studies of the dreamer's psyche by Middleton ("'Kynde Name,'" 46), and, especially, by Wittig ("Elements").

"Clerkes kenne me that Crist is in alle places;
Ac I seigh hym nevere soothly but as myself in a mirour:
Hic in enigmate, tunc facie ad faciem."

(B 15.161–62b)

Yet, once again, what the "I" beholds in the mirror is not a unique self, but instead an ideal and universal figure: the way in which he, like all other humans, has been made in the image of God. He does not see who he is, but rather who he might be (cf. E. Fowler, "Civil," esp. 762–63).

The kind of subjectivity expressed by these mirrors has been analyzed by Deborah Shuger, who argues that in the Renaissance (and Middle Ages) people do not see their literal selves in literary mirrors but instead see a model of what to do or what to avoid, "an exemplary image, either positive or negative," as revealed in such titles as *A Mirror for Magistrates* ("'I' of the Beholder," 22; cf. Kruger, "Mirrors," esp. 74–75).[35] Selfhood in this period "was not experienced reflexively but, as it were, relationally" (Shuger, "'I' of the Beholder," 37), by means of exemplars, other people, and God.[36] The "I" of *Piers Plowman* exhibits exactly this relational rather than reflexive sense of self: it recognizes itself by looking outward. The poem offers a number of different figures for the dreamer/seeker (and, more important, the reader) to avoid or imitate, from those on the Field of Folk to Christ. Subjectivity is important to the author of *Piers Plowman*, as it is to that postmodern theorist of the mirror, Jacques Lacan, but in both cases it is a much more unstable and less autobiographical subjectivity than that claimed by the myth of the poet: the "I" of *Piers* is at once more fractured and more universal than the autonomous selves of modern tradition.[37]

Other subjects in *Piers Plowman* besides the narratorial "I" also fall far short of being modern humanistic selves. They lack life histories and rarely exist in any sustained narration. Many of these figures are personification allegories (Meed,

35. "One would be hard-pressed to find any early modern English instance of mirroring used as a paradigm for reflexive self-consciousness" (Shuger, "'I' of the Beholder," 31).

36. Shuger suggests that before the seventeenth century "most people seem rather to have encountered their image reflected in another" rather than directly (38), just as people today recognize they are funny not by inner reflection but from the laughter of others.

37. Although it would be pointless to push the comparison between these passages and the "mirror stage" too far, the premodern subjectivity of *Piers Plowman* and the postmodern subjectivity of Lacan do both stress a desiring and a split subject, each trying to make coherent sense of itself through images of the other and unable, at least in this world, to achieve full satisfaction.

Conscience, Study, Imaginatif), which reveal not themselves but their definitions (see, for example, Schroeder [Carruthers], "Character of Conscience"; Simpson, *Introduction*, e.g., 40–49). When complexity is found in them, as it is most clearly in the case of Meed, it is not a result of their human qualities but because the ideas they embody are not simple. What may appear to be personal details— Meed's parents or Study's marriage and testiness—do not describe an individual so much as elucidate an intellectual abstraction. Hunger is an important figure in the *visio* (he concludes the scene of the half acre and leads to Truth's pardon), but he has no independent and unified self. Instead, he is a device through which to present a variety of discourses about both physical and spiritual hunger, as I shall briefly discuss in the following chapter.

Similarly, the sins who confess so dramatically in the *visio* are not coherent selves but manifestations of particular desires and appetites. Their portraits often do not even pretend to describe individual lives, thus sexes and professions are mixed together: Wrath, for example, is both male and female, lay and religious. Like other personification allegories, the sins are not reflective or capable of change, for each is no more nor less than its name. What may be taken as indications of individuality by modern readers—Envy's anguish over a neighbor's new coat (B 5.109–10; A 5.91–92) or Covetise and his wife's fraudulent selling of ale (B 5.215–23; A 5.133–41; C 6.225–33)—are examples of their particular sin and thus their inability to have genuine relationships with other humans or with God. Gluttony is the sin that most resembles a believable human figure or modern literary character: like the narrator/dreamer he has a wife and child and is the only one of the seven vices presented in a single continuous narrative. For all the vividness and specificity of his story, however, Gluttony exactly follows a traditional pattern already defined in the poem's prologue: this sin leads directly to sleep and then sloth (B pr.43–45; A pr.43–45; C pr.44–46). Even "historical" figures in *Piers* are universalized into abstractions: Abraham is Faith, Moses Hope, and the Samaritan Charity.

Only one figure in *Piers Plowman* has something like the independent agency and individuality claimed for the self in the modern Western tradition—Jesus Christ. He, and certainly not the narrator/dreamer, is given the one full biography in the poem. The life of Jesus is described repeatedly and in detail in the longer versions of the poem. He alone acts and enforces his will, as he shows in the climactic passus of the poem when he triumphs over death at the Crucifixion and over the Devil to bring about the salvation of humankind during the

Harrowing of Hell. Rather than striving to copy someone else, he is the model that all humans are enjoined to imitate and whom the admirable figures in the poem, such as Piers and Samaritan, try to follow. Christ promises eternal life and the realization of human potential. True selfhood and salvation are only possible to the degree that humans resemble him.[38]

WHAT THEN DOES LANGLAND MEAN? BEYOND THE AUTHORIAL VOICE

Whatever the complexities of subjectivity in *Piers Plowman*, readers have long believed that they could detect the authentic voice of the author. Crowley, for instance, had no doubt that he was a prophet of Protestant truth. The most influential presentation of *Piers* as authorial statement was by Skeat, who in addition to constructing a life of Langland also asserted a more fundamental kind of self-revelation. Insisting that it is "of little moment" that we have so few historical facts about the poet, he declared that *Piers* "is a true *autobiography* in the highest sense of the word" because it "abounds with [Langland's] opinions, political and religious, from end to end, all expressed in the most decided language and evidently the result of much thought." When Skeat enumerated these opinions, however, they turn out to be rather unexceptional: "On two points he is especially clear, viz. on the duty of every man to use his own common sense, and on the simplicity which should characterize a plain Christian man's religion." Skeat's Langland is as admirable as he is indistinct: "I le shews himself to us as a man of simple, noble, and pure faith, strong in saving common sense, full of love for his fellows, the friend of the poor, the adviser of the rich" (*Vision . . . A-Text*, xxxviii). Aware that the poem is stuffed with opinions and lessons "from end to end," Skeat believed (wrongly in my view) that they can be linked directly to Langland, but he is sensible enough not to claim that the author's views are more than generalities: "common sense," "simplicity," "the friend of the poor, the adviser of the rich."

Piers is indeed saturated with didactic passages, but they are far from consistent, and what the poet himself wants to teach his readers is much less clear than Skeat assumed. In saying this I am hardly being original, for it has been argued by some of the best modern readers of the poem, such as Mary Carruthers and Elizabeth Kirk, the latter of whom noted how our demands to recover the clear

---

38. As Spitzer noted, "[A]ccording to Augustine, it is the personality of God which determines the personal soul of man: only through God's personality has man a personal soul—whose characteristic is its God-seeking quality" ("Notes," 417).

sense of *Piers* go unsatisfied: "We seek continually in the argument for a stability and satisfaction it does not provide" (*Dream Thought*, 200). Spearing suggests that if *Piers* is often obscure, it is not because the poet deliberately sought to veil the truth but because "the truth itself was to him obscure and uncertain" (*Medieval to Renaissance*, 249). Hanna has claimed that "the text more nearly resembles the deconstruction than the fulfillment of any instructional program" ("Versions," 318n). If many readers nevertheless persist in trying to identify such a program, one reason is that the pressure to find meaning is so constant in the poem, as in the dreamer's first question to Holy Church about his vision: "Mercy, madame, what may this be to meene?" (B 1.11, A 1.11, C 1.11).

Because *Piers* is so full of strong opinions, critics sometimes assume that they know which are the poet's own. Surely we are on safe ground when we say that he is sympathetic to the poor and suspicious of the rich or on the side of truth and against wrong. But if we try to go much beyond this (and most of us do), we soon get into trouble. For example, does sympathy for the poor include the undeserving poor? And how exactly should that sympathy be shown? By means of unrestricted alms or by setting the poor to productive work? Any final answers to these questions usually involve ignoring the actual speakers and context of the statement we choose to privilege and smoothing over any contradictions elsewhere in the poem. The result too often is to homogenize a dynamic text. The most successful interpretations of single versions of *Piers*, such as those by Dunning, Frank, and Simpson, though they may recognize discursive complexity, are forced by the need to produce a coherent account of an unruly work to make crooked places straight and rough places plain. But it is what is crooked and rough that gives *Piers Plowman* its peculiar greatness.

Those most certain about the poet's views cannot agree on what they are. Langland has been called "the most Catholic of English poets" (Dawson, *Medieval Essays*, 213), even though Crowley published him to support the Protestant cause, and, more recently, David Aers has argued that the poem finally abandons "the visible Catholic Church" ("Reflections," 71). Langland has long been judged a social conservative, but he has also been seen as a radical (not least apparently by the rebels in 1381), even a prophet of democracy, or at least of the English Parliament (Whitaker, *Visio Willi*, xix; Jusserand, "Work of One" [1909], 272).[39] *Piers Plowman* at times expresses all these competing positions (and

---

39. Salter noted that "Langland criticism has found it possible to move between opposed, and not unreasonable conclusions—that he is at heart a reactionary, a heart a revolutionary" ("Alliterative Verse," 108).

more), but which (if any) represent the poet's own is as uncertain as whether any of the Canterbury tellers speak for Chaucer.

As previously noted, we cannot be confident that we are hearing Langland when *Piers* addresses us in the first person. Even a quick glance at the prologue suggests the protean permutations of the "I" in *Piers*. This voice first identifies itself as issuing from "an heremite unholy of werkes" (B pr.3; A pr.3; C pr.3), which would seem to compromise its authority, but then does not hesitate to pronounce summary judgment on pilgrims, beggars, friars, and even other hermits. One moment the "I" is slyly ironic about merchants (B pr.31; A pr.31; C pr.33), the next earnestly supporting the innocence of good minstrels (B pr.34; A pr.34; not in C), and the very next damning "japers and jangeleres" (B pr.35ff.; A pr.35ff.; C pr.36ff., much rewritten). The "I" veers from direct rebuke of the audience (B pr.76 [less direct in the B manuscripts]; A pr.73; C pr.74) to a seeming reluctance to criticize cardinals (B pr.109; C pr.136; not in A), from a claim of ignorance about what his dream might mean (B pr.209–10; C pr.217–18; not in A) to an assertion of literary control over the poem's structure (B pr.218; A pr.97; C pr.221). The "I" is no more coherent later in the poem, ranging from meek deference (as toward Study) to stinging attack (as toward the Doctor of Divinity at Clergy's feast), from detailed criticism of particular social abuses (such as solitary dining by the nobility) to millennial prophecy. One could easily compile a number of separate anthologies of selections from the poem, each volume containing radically different views and tones of voice, all expressed by the "I." It is no wonder that individual scholars have been able to conclude that "Langland" is conservative or revolutionary, orthodox or heretical, friend of the poor or supporter of aristocracy, learned university man or seedy autodidact.

If the "I" of *Piers* does not represent a single authorial voice, still less do other characters necessarily speak for the poet. Yet critics of all schools claim to be able to recognize when Langland himself is addressing us through his creations. One of the very best readers, Talbot Donaldson, argued that the rat parliament in the prologue to B and C means that the poet "seems to have thought" that the people should endure unjust rulers, however acute their suffering (*C-Text and Its Poet*, 94). He assumes, as do others, that Langland agrees with the defeatist position of a "mous that muche goode kouthe" (B pr.182, C pr.196), though this is not the inevitable interpretation of the fable. Indeed, the narrative voice ends the episode by insisting, with whatever degree of seriousness, that his readers must themselves determine what "this metels bymeneth (B pr.209–10;

c pr.217–18), and the same fable was used by Bishop Thomas Brinton in 1376 to draw a very different political lesson: the need for humans *not* to act like rodents (Pearsall, *Piers: C-Text*, 38, note to pr.165–215; see Orsten, "Ambiguities").

The full dramatic quality of *Piers Plowman* is often overlooked; that is, its parliament of different voices lacking a central authoritative speaker. Crowley's practice in his first printing of *Piers*, as Anne Middleton has explained, was to take "what is said by the poem's several personifications" and resolve it "into the utterance of a single voice, loosely identified with that of the poet" ("Introduction," 5). Critics still do this today, attributing to Langland what is said by various characters in the poem. I know that in teaching *Piers* I have been guilty of ignoring the actual speaker of a passage and instead slipping into such careless formulas as "Langland says X" or "Langland believes Y," which is the equivalent of saying, "As Shakespeare teaches us, 'To thine own self be true.'" This practice may be innocent enough, as when Spearing, whom I previously quoted warning against clear authorial meaning in *Piers*, prefaces a statement in praise of the monastic life spoken by Clergy with the phrase "as Langland put it" (*Medieval to Renaissance*, 309). We may assume that by this Spearing means something like "as Langland wrote in the voice of Clergy," but even such a formulation leaves unclear who precisely is speaking and with what authority. In her splendid book on marriage in *Piers Plowman*, M. Teresa Tavormina writes, "Speaking through Wit, Langland describes marriage as it can be rightly used and as it is all too often abused" (*Kindly*, 79), implying that Wit's views on marriage are identical to Langland's. Similarly, Anima's anticlerical statements were assumed by George Kane to be the poet's own (*Middle English*, 194–95), and recent critics are even more explicit: Schmidt says that Anima's "long, unbroken tirade against moral and spiritual and cultural decline in Christendom may be safely taken as expressive of Langland's own convictions" (*Clerkly Maker* 21), and Steven Justice calls Anima "one of [Langland's] mouthpieces" ("Introduction," 8).[40]

The poet is at least partially at fault when readers conclude that he is the one speaking behind the masks of his creations, for his characters are not always given

---

40. See also Aers, "Christ's Humanity," 119–20. There is some justification in thinking that Anima speaks for the poet, as James Simpson has suggested to me, because the figure represents the whole soul as opposed to partial mental faculties like Thought and Wit. But Justice's remark, especially, implies that Anima is but one of many puppets through whom Langland ventriloquises. Skeat ("Langland," 286) and Manly ("Sequence," 24) also both insisted that the allegorical characters in *Piers* may become little more than "mouthpieces of the author." Even if Anima is taken to be more persuasive than other personifications, he by no means has the final word in the poem.

distinct voices. In this, as in other things, Langland suffers by comparison with Chaucer. The unique accents of the Wife of Bath or Canon's Yeoman are clearly heard even when they discuss the most traditional and technical material. Speeches in *Piers*, by contrast, may start dramatically enough, but they often lose individualizing traits as they go on, allowing the reader to forget that a specific figure is doing the talking. Perhaps the most extreme example of this is Trajan. His entrance is unforgettable: "'Ye, baw for bokes!' quod oon was broken out of helle" (B 11.140; C 12.76); and it shows the poet's skill at personalized dialogue when he wishes to exercise it. But the Trajan episode does not long maintain this vivacity, and scholars have been uncertain about when he actually stops speaking and who is responsible for the many challenging and argumentative lines that follow.[41] Too often in such cases we assume that obsessive, dogmatic Langland has commandeered the stage, elbowing his pale characters aside to address us directly.

No voice can be accepted uncritically in *Piers*. This apparently most preachy of Ricardian poems offers only elusive and unsatisfying instruction. For, to adapt Meir Sternberg's useful observation about the Hebrew Bible, *Piers* may indeed be "ideological," but it is not "didactic." By this Sternberg means that the Bible, like all narratives, contains an ideological worldview, but, instead of direct preaching, its stories constantly generate ambivalence and discordance (*Poetics*, 36–38). Holy Church, for example, is sometimes treated as if she expressed what Bloomfield called "the 'message' that Langland is bringing to his age and perhaps ours" (*Apocalypse*, 152). This would be true if Holy Church were a figure like Lady Philosophy in Boethius's *Consolation of Philosophy*, but she is not. Her answers produce no clear "kynde knowing" and force the dreamer to search on. Other apparent authority figures are equally unsatisfactory. Although Conscience in opposing Meed is said by Aers to express "Langland's conscious views" (*Chaucer*, 8), both he and Reason, for all their virtue, are too certain and self-righteous to address the real problems of humans.[42] Imaginatif will later

---

41. Godden notes that the speaker of B 11.153–318 is in doubt ("Making," 99n): different editors have identified the speaker as Lewte, Trajan, or the narrator. Similarly, Pearsall observed that it is not entirely clear when Rechlessness stops talking in C ("Theory and Practice," 122).

42. For example, Conscience's initial lofty dismissal of Meed as a faithless and destructive whore (B 3.120–69; A 3.109–56; C 3.155–214) changes in both tone and substance in response to her effective rebuttal. Not longer able to win the argument by condescending personal abuse, Conscience is forced to acknowledge that there are at least two kinds of Meed and calls on a number of biblical quotations, not used in his first speech, to bolster his argument with authoritative learning. For the limitations and development of Conscience, see especially Schroeder (Carruthers), "Character of Conscience."

answer some of Will's most vexing questions, but he concludes his statements by stressing the limits of his knowledge and admitting that there are things he is unable to resolve. Even the admirable Piers is compromised by resorting to the murderous Hunger to solve the labor problems on the half acre. In *Piers Plowman* no single voice offers a final answer. A fundamental achievement of the poem is its open and public debate.

And yet surely there is one figure in *Piers Plowman* whose words and actions must be wholly authoritative and whom the poet fully endorses: Jesus Christ, the only character in the poem, as previously noted, with independent agency. The poem often suggests him as the remedy for the human condition: Holy Church early invokes his Incarnation in the magnificent "plant of peace" passage (B 1.148–58; C 1.145–53; not in A); and Abraham, Moses, and the Samaritan look forward to the Redemption he will offer at the joust in Jerusalem. The story of Christ's fight with death on the cross and his Harrowing of Hell are regarded by many readers as the true climax of the poem and perhaps its only resolved narrative. *Piers Plowman*, as has often been noted, is indeed a Christ-centered work.

Why then should we not assume that the Son of God's words are endorsed by the author? They certainly contain some of the most powerful and sublime poetry in *Piers*, as when Christ explains his rescue of humans from their demonic captivity in the majestic passage that begins, "For I that am lord of lif, love is my drynke" (B 18.366; C 20.403). Here indeed is the king of kings and the remedy for human damnation. In his masterly summary of the poem, John Alford sees Christ's words as answering Truth's pardon by reconciling justice and mercy: "[D]ivine pardon is linked inextricably to a penitential system through which sinners can pay what they owe" ("Design," 57). In support of such penance, he quotes the lines from B in which Christ says that those "that diden ille" will be clensed in "my prisone Purgatorie" (18.391–93).

As reasonable as Alford's argument is, other critics have pointed to a more radical element in Christ's speech: its promise of general salvation. Thomas Hill ("Universal Salvation") calls attention to Christ's sweeping claim about the Last Judgment: "thanne shal I come as a kyng, crouned, with aungeles, / And have out of helle alle mennes soules" (B 18.372–73; C 20.413–14). All men—presumably even sinners, heretics, and the unbaptized. Christ goes on to explain that as king he has the right to pardon anyone condemned to death, and that he is forced to so reprieve humans because they are of his blood: "Ac blood may noght se blood blede, but hym rewe" (B 18.396; C 20.438). Joseph Wittig observes that the "possibility of universal salvation dominates here. . . . Conditions and limitations practically disappear: for example, the penitential requirements of restitution and satisfaction become muted to mere whispers" (*William Langland*, 136). Indeed, even in the lines quoted by Alford, punishment is now only a temporary Purgatory, not eternal damnation. Like Wittig, Nicholas Watson, in an important essay, sees the poet as fully endorsing the most optimistic interpretation of Christ's words: "Langland can thus at last set out explicitly his hope that all will finally be saved" ("Visions of Inclusion," 158).

The problem with taking Christ's promise of universal salvation as the author's final word is that it conflicts so sharply with what we find in the rest of the poem, including the echo of the Athanasian Creed in the pardon from Truth: "*Qui vero malo [egerunt ibunt] in ignem eternum*" ("those who do evil will go into the eternal fire," B 7.110B; A 8.96; C 9.287). As Wittig notes earlier in his book, "Langland challenges all presumption of grace without human effort, of salvation without amendment" (*William Langland*, 30).[43] In contrast, Christ's words during the Harrowing reduce humans to mere passive spectators. As he disputes with the devils and declares his royal pardon for his subjects and blood brothers, only he is active. His exercise of absolute power eliminates any need for good works or even the most minimal gesture of human repentance. I am not suggesting that Christ's words here are false or deceptive, only that they cannot be taken as the direct authorial message of the poem. What Christ says is wonderfully hopeful, but it is also as mysterious (at least to us humans) as his promise to Julian of Norwich that somehow all shall be well.

To question whether *Piers* can be read autobiographically as a clear expression of Langland's own beliefs does not deny that the poem has an intensity, commitment, and even desperation that makes it unique among Ricardian poems. Yet the powerful involvement of *Piers* with its culture does not provide direct access to the poet behind the text or allow us to conclude that he expresses himself through the narratorial "I" or any other single character. But if we are unable to recover the life of the author or be sure of his personal opinions, there still was a shaping hand behind this most idiosyncratic (in structure and development) of great Ricardian poems, however much others later contributed to its

43. Even Lawler, who agrees with Alford that Christ's words in hell mean that mercy depends on repentance, admits, in an odd metaphor, "These lines go overboard to emphasize divine freedom" ("Pardon Formula," 151).

shape and presentation. *Piers Plowman* is an intentional work of art that uniquely employs the discourses of its time: some of which will be discussed in the following chapters. But an original engagement with the culture of late medieval England does not mean that the poet of *Piers* is necessarily dramatizing his own private experiences or that he believes he has any final answers to the public questions that preoccupy him and his world.

THE PUBLIC POET OF PIERS PLOWMAN

Piers Plowman in all versions opens with a pair of striking images: first, the solitary wanderer falling into a dream on the Malvern Hills, and then, second, located between the high tower and deep dale, a field full of folk, "Werching and wandrynge as the world asketh" (b pr.19; a pr.19; c pr.21). Under the influence of Skeat's myth of the poet, Langland criticism has often emphasized the private experience of the dreamer (regularly conflated with the poet) over the public actions of the folk—or, to be more precise, understood the public by means of the private. But life on the field of folk, which is never forgotten in *Piers*, is more than the subjective vision of one man. The work offers the most comprehensive poetic account we have of late medieval English society and culture, which is why *Piers* tends to be read (albeit in translation) more often in history in than literature classes. Despite the (intermittent but central) presence of the narrative "I" and the psychological functions that dominate the *vita* in particular, *Piers* looks outward as much as it looks inward. In addition to the confused and often contradictory notions of the first-person narrator are the varied expressions of the many other figures in the poem. Diversity of utterance has long been recognized in the work of Chaucer, especially in his *Parliament of Foules* and *Canterbury Tales*, but it is regularly obscured by critics of *Piers* in their pursuit of the poet and his opinions.

Despite its didactic tone, *Piers Plowman* is a dialogue (as so many of the B-version manuscripts label it) or public forum rather than direct authorial statement. The narrative "I" is neither individual nor stable, and the other characters in the poem, however admirable, lack the teaching authority of Virgil in Dante's *Inferno*, let alone Beatrice. Even Christ's thrilling words to humans at the Harrowing do not answer all our questions. The method of *Piers* is dispute and debate, which permits no final resolution to the poem's central issues: including the relationship of the three lives to one another or of faith to works and of justice to mercy. The illusiveness of the poet in *Piers* is demonstrated by the many contradictory portraits of him by critics from the sixteenth century to the present: Protestant Langland, commonsensical Langland; liberal Langland, mad Langland, aesthetic Langland, anticlerical Langland, orthodox Langland, prophetic Langland, scholastic Langland, radical Langland, Franciscan Langland, apocalyptic Langland—the list could be multiplied. But Langland (if that was his name and whatever the story of his life) is not to be found in the narrative "I" or in any other single voice in *Piers*. Rather than the characters and personifications of *Piers* serving as mouthpieces for the poet, as is so often assumed, it may be more accurate to say that the poet is the mouthpiece of a range of late medieval discourses. Of course he dramatizes, complicates, and puts under stress these discourses—by means of figures as different as Haukyn, the Doctor of Divinity, Study, and Holy Church and by places that range from a sordid tavern to a garden in which grows the tree of Charity. The various voices and settings in *Piers* express aspects of an elite learning that was available only to the few, but also the more general, common culture of contemporary England: the public world that is the subject of the rest of this book.

PART TWO

Piers Plowman *and Public Culture of Late Medieval England*

PREFATORY NOTE: MAKING IT PUBLIC

Having asked questions about the traditional Langland myth of poet and poem and suggested ways that scholarship might go beyond each, I now want to offer a new historical approach to *Piers Plowman* to replace or at least to supplement the traditional myth. Instead of treating *Piers* as self-portraiture or as the obsessive product of an eccentric intellectual, in the second part of this book I explore the poem's relationship to aspects of the common culture of late medieval England—I attempt to understand *Piers* as a public poem. The public discourses and practices I discuss in the following three chapters may not have been accessible to all in late medieval England, but they were available to the many rather than just the few. This is not to deny the existence of individual or learned elements in *Piers* (nor the past and future value of their study), only to recognize that scholarly attention has tended to emphasize the personal and elite in the poem at the expense of the general and public.

For all its uniqueness as a poetic masterpiece, *Piers Plowman* shares much with the broad cultural environment of its time and place. In examining these public contexts, I make no attempt to identify direct influences on the poem or the specific influences it had on later writing. Much of what can be discovered about the sources of *Piers* as well as about the so-called *Piers Plowman* tradition (often not a great deal) has been done (and done well) by others. My interest here is in more indirect relations that help to describe the world in which *Piers Plowman* was produced and received. Each chapter deals with a different aspect of contemporary culture not ordinarily discussed with the poem: the first, on public writing, reads *Piers* through *Mandeville's Travels* and the *Book of Margery Kempe*; the second, on public art, reads the poem through the images that once covered the walls of English parish churches; and the third, on public life, reads it through the civic institutions and practices of London, especially those associated with the Cornhill area.

My attempt to present a public *Piers Plowman* is necessarily preliminary. A single study can do little more than sketch out some possible ways to deal with such a complex subject. Moreover, even if my work were more complete, it would remain only one approach among many. The most I can hope for (a bold hope indeed) is to offer new perspectives on this most challenging of major Middle English poems.

4. Public Writing

The natural place to begin a study of the public contexts of *Piers Plowman* is with other late medieval writing. The examples that I shall use here, however, are not the poetry usually associated with the work: French allegorical dream visions such as the *Pélerinage de la vie humaine,* English alliterative satires such as *Winner and Waster,* or contemporary English masterworks such as Chaucer's *Canterbury Tales.* Nor do I discuss *Piers* in the context of exegetical and scholastic thought by such as Hugh of St. Cher, Aquinas, or the *moderni. Piers* does indeed resemble these works in many ways: the complexity and comprehensiveness of its allegory is the equal of its French predecessors, its artistry rivals that of the best Ricardian poems, and the daring of its religious speculation is shared by advanced academic thought. I do not question the importance to *Piers* of these literary and intellectual texts, but I want to augment them with a less familiar and more ordinary context, what I am calling public writing.

I use *public writing* as a flexible rather than a prescriptive term, one that does not follow a fixed set of rules, either medieval or modern, but rather describes a series of associated and overlapping qualities. If it were a genre, public writing would be more like medieval romance or the modern novel, neither of which can be defined with absolute precision, rather than the sonnet or classical epic with their clear formal expectations. Public writing in late medieval England, as I employ the concept, shares a group of affiliated or, as Wittgenstein might put it, family resemblances. Such writing was public in respect to its audience, form, and content. First of all, public writing aimed for a general readership. It was not addressed to a coterie or narrow group, but to a diverse public, women as well as well as men, the humble as well as the powerful, the laity as well as clerics. If it was not meant for the most lewed, it was also not restricted to the most learned. In the Middle Ages, writing was always a medium of privilege, of course, but public writing sought to extend its reach, as indicated by its form, which, though it may occasionally employ Latin, was fundamentally vernacular in order to be understood by a large audience (see Wogan-Brown et al., *Idea of Vernacular*). Indeed, a central concern of public writing was to make more widely available information that had been the province of educated elites. It publicized learning. The questions raised by public writing went beyond the concerns of individuals or particular classes to general matters of faith and society.

Some contemporary writing that fits my definition of *public* has previously been compared to *Piers Plowman*, perhaps the most important being sermons and mystery plays, which have obvious connections to the poem's homiletic and dramatic elements. But I want here to read *Piers* with two less expected examples of public writing that at first appear to be as different from the poem as they are from each other: *Mandeville's Travels* and *The Book of Margery Kempe*. Indeed, this trio could reasonably be the answer to a question: which Middle English works have the *least* in common? The English *Mandeville's Travels* (the title is modern but will be used here for convenience) is a collection of adventures attributed to a knight from St. Albans, Sir John Mandeville, recounting his journeys to Jerusalem and then into the remote East. In contrast to the worldly *Travels*, Kempe's *Book* is mystical and provincial. Its protagonist is also often on the move, but in pursuit of Christian holiness rather than exotic marvels. Whereas the knight has conversations with the sultan and the khan, she speaks often with Jesus. The *Travels* became an authority for genuine explorers and entertained generations of armchair voyagers, but the self-absorption and extravagant religiosity of Kempe's *Book* often irritate modern readers as much as she herself did contemporaries.[1]

The *Travels* and Kempe's *Book* are only occasionally discussed together by scholars, and neither is much mentioned with Langland.[2] But connections do

1. Because the *Travels* differs significantly from text to text, as discussed below, my citations are to several major English versions. I generally use M. C. Seymour's recent EETS edition of the Defective version as my default text, because Defective was the version of the *Travels* most widely known to medieval English readers, but I also cite the two versions most often used by modern scholars, Cotton (from Seymour's Oxford edition), and Egerton (from George Warner's Roxburgh Club edition with reference to Moseley's Penguin translation in square brackets), as well as the Bodley version (in Seymour's EETS edition) when appropriate. The first English print of the *Travels* by Pynson (1496?), a version of Defective, has recently been edited by Tamarah Kohanski.

Quotations from *The Book of Margery Kempe*, cited by page and line number, are from the EETS edition of Sanford B. Meech and Hope Emily Allen; as with *Piers* I have modernized the text slightly for easier reading, similar to the form of Lynn Staley's TEAMS edition, which I also cite in square brackets by book and line number.

2. Although these works are undoubtedly often taught with one another, there are a limited number of published comparisons between any two of the three; the most common of these comparisons are between Langland (and/or the dreamer Will) and Kempe. Hanna notes that Will and Kempe similarly

exist between *Piers* and each of these prose works. The most intriguing is the appearance together of *Piers* and the English *Travels* in five medieval manuscripts.[3] No other text occurs anything like as often with either work in the surviving manuscripts, suggesting that contemporary scribes or patrons recognized some sort of compatibility between the two. The connections between *Piers* and the later *Book of Margery Kempe* are thematic and tonal rather than textual.[4] Each work contains a marginal central character who, though secular, is on a passionate, often bumptious, religious quest for salvation in an England where Christian devotion has to compete with more worldly concerns.

Because of their obvious contrasts to one another, the *Travels* and Margery's *Book* suggest something of the spectrum of public writing in late medieval England during the time when *Piers Plowman* was written and first read. For despite their differences in subject and mood, both are public in important ways. To begin with the most literal, the events in both work tend to take place in public spaces before witnesses. The *Travels* and the *Book* also both display some of the more metaphorical qualities of public writing that I have already mentioned. They each in their own way use the vernacular to bring to a broad general audience information and learning usually restricted to a select few. The formal structure of both is also public in its looseness and ability to accommodate diverse materials and genres. Each creates something like Habermas's public forum in which different voices are able to be expressed and to contest one another. Moreover, the two texts, and especially the *Travels*, were open to rewriting by others. Finally, both works see a crisis in Western Christianity and

---

combine contemplation and wandering and that both justify their ways of life before authorities ("Will's Work," 32, 43, 66n). Middleton compares Will both to the Wife of Bath and to Margery Kempe with her "theatrical sincerity" ("Narration," 109). Spearing identifies Langland and Kempe as examples of "writers struggling to find means of centring their works in their personal histories rather than in abstract intellectual schemes" (*Medieval to Renaissance*, 113). Frank Grady says that *Piers* and the *Travels* are two of the medieval works in which virtuous pagans are permitted to speak in their own voices ("Rule of Exceptional Salvation," 86). Nicholas Watson has argued that *Piers Plowman*, the *Book of Margery Kempe*, and *Mandeville's Travels*, among other contemporary works, express a kind of vernacular theology of universal salvation ("Visions of Inclusion").

3. See Seymour, "English Manuscripts," 172; the manuscript association of *Piers* and the *Travels* has also been mentioned by Middleton ("Audience and Public," 105) and J. M. Bowers ("Police," 23). The manuscripts in which both appear are British Library, London, MS Harley 3954; University Library, Cambridge, MS Dd.1.17; University Library, Cambridge, MS Ff.v.35; Huntington Library, San Marino, MS HM 114; and Princeton University Library, MS Taylor 10, once part of University of London, MS Sterling Library v.17.

4. The best, albeit brief, previous account of their similarities is by David Lawton, who refers to both Will and Kempe as "preposterous vessels of unmediated divine grace" ("Subject," 26–28, esp. 27).

describe a kind of public religion, which is available to the laity and even to non-Christians.

I. PUBLIC PLACES, AUDIENCES, AND STRUCTURES
In Public

Mandeville's Travels, the *Book of Margery Kempe,* and *Piers Plowman* are full of public places and events. This is most obvious in the *Travels,* which recounts a variety of remarkable sights, including strange flora and fauna, the buildings and stones of Jerusalem, and the social customs of foreign peoples. The book consists largely of what is publicly visible to a visitor. Sir John rarely says anything about how he is affected psychologically by his travels, nor does he describe his personal life. He does not mention family, lovers, or particular friends, but rather details the routes he takes and what he has observed along them. His human characters are also portrayed from the outside, as they show themselves to others. We are told that in the land of the Great Khan a man may have as many wives as he wants (some have forty or a hundred), but we learn nothing about the private experience of such relationships. When Sir John has a tête-à-tête with the sultan, they talk about the condition of Christendom, not about their own individual religious faiths.

Kempe's *Book* at first seems much more personal, for it does mention family, lovers, and friends. Moreover, her central conversations with Jesus take place in secret (often in her bed), though even here the Virgin and other saints are sometimes witnesses and public events are frequently discussed: how Kempe should dress and act in the community, who among those she knows will prosper and who will not, when it will rain or storm at sea. Comparison with her fellow English female mystic, Julian of Norwich, shows the difference. Julian indicates that her mature life was spent in private meditation on the meaning of her revelations, and she says nothing about any activity in the world after those visions. But Margery will not be confined to any one place, far less a cell (though some wanted to put her in one), and her most distinctive and emotional devotions are regularly described as occurring in public venues such as parish churches, city streets, and fields.[5]

The *Book* reports that Kempe often sought public regard. Before her religious vocation, she dressed extravagantly to attract attention and started two retail

---

5. Susan Dickman notes that to "a much greater degree than any other pious woman, Margery was inclined to interpret her spiritual experience in social terms," such as the "public ceremony" of her mystical marriage to God, in contrast to the private pledges by such as Catherine and Dorothy ("Margery Kempe," 161; cf. Fredell, "Margery Kempe").

businesses. She more than once reminds others of the high civic offices held by her father. A remarkable number of the most important moments in the *Book* take place in public, one reason it has been dismissed by some as not truly mystical: these scenes include visits to famous holy sites, disputes with fellow travelers at meals, and civic and ecclesiastic trials. Even the agreement she reaches with her husband about a chaste marriage occurs not at home but in the open: by a cross on the road from York. Kempe was a public witness to God's grace, as she would have it, or, in the view of some contemporaries, a public nuisance.

Although often read as an eccentric work written by something of a recluse, *Piers Plowman*, like the *Travels* and Kempe's *Book*, is largely set in public spaces. Portraying a range of disparate groups, *Piers* provides the fullest poetic account we have of the ordinary life of late medieval England. The poem opens with a diorama of the Field of Folk: "Of alle manere of men, the meene and the riche, / Werchynge and wandrynge as the world asketh" (B pr.18–19; A pr.18–19; C pr.20–21). The first two visions contain numerous social events: the marriage and trial of Meed, the confession of the sins (apparently made jointly before Repentance and emphasizing transgressions against others), the plowing of the half acre, and the pardon from Truth. The *vita* is more of a psychological journey, especially during its inner dreams, and yet it never abandons the communal world: there is little resemblance here to Gawain's solitary journey in search of the Green Knight or the secrecy of the love between Troilus and Criseyde. In the *vita*, the way to know oneself is through others. The narrator/dreamer proceeds by seeking and interacting with a range of authority figures, some of whom are historical beings or represent public institutions such as the university. A major theme throughout is the obligation of Christians toward their fellows. Perhaps the ideal human figure in the *vita* is that quintessential social worker, the Good Samaritan. *Piers* becomes increasingly public as it nears its end. The Crucifixion and Harrowing occur amid spectators (including the narrative "I"), and when the seeker/dreamer finally mentions a wife and daughter, it is not to describe intimate domestic life but rather worship in church at Easter. The poem concludes, as it began, with a broad social perspective: the founding of the Church and its subsequent history.

Public Address

Mandeville's Travels, the *Book of Margery Kempe*, and *Piers Plowman* are never more public than in their shared desire, though realized differently, to address a general audience. The *Travels* was the most successful in achieving this, for it became a medieval best-seller. Quickly translated from its French original into at least nine European languages (sometimes more than once in the same language), it still survives in an astonishing 250–300 medieval manuscripts.[6] My concern is with the English versions, of which there were several (including one in verse), making the *Travels* the "most popular piece of nonreligious Middle English prose" (Hanna, "Mandeville," 121). The *Book of Margery Kempe* never achieved anything like the popular reception of the *Travels* (only a single manuscript survives from the Carthusian monastery at Mount Grace in Yorkshire along with a few early prints of extracts), but its heroine clearly imagined that her mystical experiences would be of general interest. We read of Margery's constant conversations about them with a wide variety of clerics and laypeople. The scribal preface that introduces the *Book* notes that Kempe had long been urged by others to write an account of her life, but resisted until finally ordered to do so by Jesus, who states that her future readership will be without limit, a prophecy that only began to come true at the end of the twentieth century: "he comawnded hyr and chargyd hir that sche shuld don wryten hyr felyngys and revelacyons and the forme of her levyng, that hys goodnesse myth be knowyn to *alle the world*" (3.31–4.2 [1.64–66], my emphasis).

Piers, too, was addressed to the larger world, though we may underestimate the breadth of its original appeal because it is such a specialist academic text today. *Piers* survives in more manuscripts than any other Middle English poem except the *Prick of Conscience* and the *Canterbury Tales.* It should probably be considered the first truly national poem in Middle English because, although written in a western dialect and in the alliterative verse form, its language (unlike that of the *Gawain*-poet) was easily comprehensible to readers throughout England. It was known and copied in the greater London area and in the North as well as in the West. As mentioned in my second chapter, manuscripts were owned by men and women, merchants and ecclesiastics.

All three works were also public in bringing to their readers information usually reserved for the select few. Iain Higgins links the author of the *Travels* with those, such as Brunetto Latini, John Trevisa, and Christine de Pisan, "who sought to enlarge the domain of the vernacular by adapting into it the

---

6. Seymour cites the survival of "over 250 manuscripts" in several European languages (*Sir John Mandeville,* 3), and Iain Higgins refers to some three hundred extant manuscripts and multiple translations (*Writing East,* vii). There were at least four separate translations of the *Travels* into German/Dutch, for example.

concerns of Latin learning" (*Writing East*, 9–10). Whatever the original author's personal experience of foreign lands (it is now believed that he was more of a reader than a traveler), the writer of the *Travels* drew on a range of erudite authorities (whom he knew either in Latin or in translation), such as Vincent of Beauvais and Jacobus de Voragine, including his two principal sources, William of Boldensele's *Liber de Quibusdam Ultramarinis Partibus* and Odoric of Pordenone's *Relatio* (Higgins, *Writing East*, 9). The achievement of the *Travels* was in making this varied and sometimes esoteric material appealing to a large public.

Although most of its matter is more local than that in the *Travels* (and presumably more authentic), Kempe's *Book* also draws on Latin or Latin-derived sources: we are told that the Bible and, perhaps more important, its commentaries, were read to her, as well as "Seynt Brydys boke, Hyltons boke, Boneventur, Stimulus Amoris, Incendium Amoris, and swech other" (143.27–29 [1.3390–92]). Given her claim to be ignorant of Latin, the implication is that these works were translated for her use by her clerical supporters. In turn, Kempe translated these written sources along with her meditations into public acts that were later recorded for all in her book. The persecutions of the saints are reenacted in her trials before English secular and ecclesiastical authorities, the life of Saint Bridget becomes a model for her own behavior, and affective identification with Christ's Passion is expressed on the streets of Lynn.

Like the *Travels* and Kempe's *Book*, *Piers* publicizes elite thought. Only a few Latin phrases are found in the two prose works, but they occur often in the poem, providing, according to some, its basic framework (Alford, "Quotations"). These direct quotations begin to suggest the extensive Latin sources behind the poem, which includes legal maxims, biblical exegesis, monastic treatises, grammatical theory, antifraternal tracts, bestiaries, faculty psychology, and the liturgy. *Piers* is much more learned than either the *Travels* or the *Book*, but it is equally committed to conveying its knowledge to a large audience. Latin quotations are almost always translated into English and often analyzed. Although the work of an intellectual, *Piers* is not just for or about intellectuals. The poem begins with a common field of folk and never thereafter forgets ordinary people. It pays little heed to the sophistries of the exalted Doctor of Divinity at Conscience's feast except to mock them, but gives the most detailed and sympathetic attention to Haukyn's mundane failures to keep his baptismal coat clean while practicing an active life in the world.

The Form of Travel

The public accessibility that *Piers Plowman* shares with *Mandeville's Travels* and the *Book of Margery Kempe* is echoed in their structures. The variety, even jumble, of the poem's form has often been recognized. *Piers* follows no single genre for long: Morton Bloomfield (*Apocalypse*, 10) suggested that, in some form, it contained no less than seven (allegorical dream, dialogue or debate, encyclopedic satire, complaint, commentary, sermon, and apocalypse), and Geoffrey Shepherd ("Alliterative Poetry," 64) listed nine (satire, complaint, preachment, dream allegory, meditation, apocalypse, debate, moral tract, and epic). According to Middleton, *Piers* lacks the "clarity, explicit organization, and comprehensiveness of form" found in other English didactic works such as Robert Mannyng's *Handling Sin*, Dan Michel's *Ayenbite of Inwit*, or *Cursor Mundi* ("Audience and Public," 112). Instead, *Piers* has been compared to a madcap vaudeville film (Brooke-Rose, "Ezra Pound," 78), and Rosemary Woolf asserted that "there can be few Medieval poems in which the literal level is so tenuous and confused" ("Non-Medieval Qualities," 112). The frustration that many modern readers feel about the poem's incoherence echoes the complaint of the folk over Piers's elaborate directions to Truth: "This were a wikkede wey but whoso hadde a gyde" (B 6.1; A 7.1; C 7.306).[7]

Two quite useful guides to the structural disunity of *Piers* are *Mandeville's Travels* and the *Book of Margery Kempe*. They suggest that medieval readers would have been accustomed to amalgams of diverse elements and genres. In his innovative book on *Mandeville's Travels*, Higgins takes note of what he calls its "accumulative style," which results in "a fascinating geographical grabbag of objects, events, and persons" (*Writing East*, 66).[8] Kempe's *Book* is an equally rich and diverse mixture, with incidents that range from the sublime (her marriage to God

---

7. Complaint about the formlessness of *Piers* is not recent: in 1819 Thomas Campbell declared that "if it has any design, it is the most vague and ill constructed that every entered into the brain of a waking dreamer" (*Specimens*, 67). See also DiMarco, "Godwin," esp. 130.

8. For example, an account of nudity, communal sex, and cannibalism on the island of Lamory is followed by a long discussion of the Pole Star and the rotundity and size of the earth in many versions (Defective, 77.26–82.13; Cotton, 131.5–137.13; Egerton, 89–93 [trans., 127–31]; not in Bodley). Similarly, the Cotton version of the *Travels* places a description of Mary Magdalene's and Mary Cleophas's tearing their hair at the Crucifixion (one of the most powerful images in medieval art) just after the mundane architectural details of a Jerusalem hospital (Cotton, 59.12–20; cf. Egerton, 41 [trans., 80], in opposite order and with fewer details; the architectural details are not in Defective or Bodley).

Such rapid changes of character, incident, and tone in the *Travels* has been associated by Mary Campbell with polyphonic music (*Witness*, 130n, see also 151–52), though that seems to grant it too much art. The view that the *Travels* should be treated as a work of fiction, especially argued by Josephine Bennett,

the Father) to the banal (a divine revelation that the prior of Lynn would be recalled home to Norwich, though later return to Lynn). Nor, as with *Piers*, does either prose work follow for long a single, recognizable literary type. Higgins comments on the striking "discursive and generic variety" of the *Travels* (*Writing East*, 11).[9] The *Book of Margery Kempe* also resists generic classification (is it a tract, an autobiography, a saint's life?), as Lynn Staley Johnson ("Margery Kempe," 160) and Douglas Gray ("Popular Religion," 12) have observed. Both works thus establish an important formalistic context for *Piers*. Instead of the careful structures of elite writing, they embrace a diversity of materials to produce a forum of competing discourses, a kind of dialogic bazaar.

The one principle of organization shared by all three works is the journey. The *Travels* most obviously, but also the *Book* and *Piers*, in their own way, are travel books, reporting on the strange worlds through which they move.[10] A travel book tends to lack coherent form because of its constant serendipity (see Kohanski, "'What Is a "Travel Book"'"). Movement is both a stimulant and an impediment to its shape, producing new things to write about, even as it prevents the development of a single, unified story. The centrality of travel in all three works may help to explain their loose structure, as well as their miscellaneous materials. In each case, a series of apparently unrelated and unhomogenized elements are hung on a picaresque frame, not wholly different from the structure of Chaucer's *Canterbury Tales*.[11] No definite narrative route is mandated, for many potential paths appear within each work, allowing readers to undertake

is an attempt (mistaken in my view) to locate a guiding purpose behind its assortment of details: see, for example, Bennett's claim that Mandeville uses his materials "like a creative artist" (*Rediscovery*, 9) or her comparison: "Odoric piles on his marvels indiscriminately, the bad with the good, without proportion or arrangement, Mandeville, like a careful gardener, weeds, prunes, transplants, and arranges his materials to insure variety, harmony, and continued interest" (48). See also Butturff, who seeks to discover a "formal principle" in the *Travels* (*Satire*, 164).

9. See also Seymour, who argues that the *Travels* has "no intense preoccupation with the form of the book" (*Mandeville's Travels*, Cotton ed., xvii), and Donald Howard, who notes the work's "helter-skelter" and "disjunctive" perspective ("World," 9, *Writers*, 71). Failure to recognize its generic variety "tends to "reduce the *Travels* to the barest skeleton of itself, sacrificing the work's variety to the goal of coherence" (Kohanski, "'What Is a "Travel Book,"'" 120).

10. Terence Bowers describes Kempe as "a virtuoso traveler" ("Margery Kempe," 2), whose movement "is perhaps her most important and distinctive activity" (1).

11. Higgins refers to the "composite world" of the *Travels* in which "charity, prejudice, hatred, piety, and tolerance—no less than entertainment, instruction, self-criticism, and propaganda—are perfectly compatible with each other" (*Writing East*, 81). He goes on to observe that these "apparent contradictions" did not seem to bother most of the work's translators (82).

their own individual journeys. This open, inclusive form was valued in late medieval England, as evidenced by the number of surviving manuscripts of the *Travels* and *Piers* and by the respect with which the single manuscript of Kempe's *Book* was annotated at Mount Grace.

The original author of the *Travels* may never have moved very far from a well-stocked library, but that only reinforces the ceaseless journeying that makes his work a "hymn to mobility" (Greenblatt, "Dome," 38). Rather than the historical record of one man's travels, it is "a *summa* of travel lore" (Howard, "World," 2, *Writers*, 58; cf. Higgins, *Writing East*, 14, 265). Likewise, Kempe, far from being a cloistered mystic, was "mevyd in hir sowle to go vysyten certeyn places for gostly helth" (22.26–27 [1.505–6]). Her travels are extensive, even compulsive, taking her not only throughout England but also to Europe and the Holy Land. *Piers Plowman* also, though it has been rarely noted, begins as if it were a book of travels: the narrative "I" announces itself in all versions as a wanderer who "Wente wide in this world wondres to here" (B pr.4; A pr.4; C pr.4). Could one find a better short description of the reported experience of Mandeville?[12] No other motive for Will's journeys except the desire for such worldly wonders is given, nothing to compare with the inner spiritual crisis at the beginning of more conventional religious quests such as those in Dante's *Commedia* or in the Middle English *Pearl*. Other travels are undertaken in the poem, sometimes along allegorical routes, such as the way to Truth or to Clergy (B 10.159–69; A 11.114–24; rewritten in C 11.106–12). As one critic puts it, the many journeys and verbs of motion in *Piers* convey "a feeling of persistent exploration" (Elliott, "Langland Country," 233; cf. Kirk, *Dream Thought*, 198–99). A possible alternative title for the poem might be *Will's Travels*.

If the organization (or disorganization) of all three public works can be explained in part by their resemblance to travel writing, *Piers* reveals its characteristic complexity by also expressing a suspicion of travel, which it finds much more problematic than do the two prose pieces. Sir John is proud of his English disposition to wander (*Defective*, 72.9–14; *Cotton*, 119.20–120.6; *Egerton*, 81 [trans., 120]), which he exercises until laid low by old age; and Kempe travels

---

12. As well as "wonders," the Rawlinson text of the Bodley version of *Mandeville's Travels* announces that it will also tell of "ferlies" (45 n. 9) and then later of "wondris and ferlies" (79 n. 23); "a ferly" is what the dreamer in A and B calls his initial vision on the Malvern Hills (B pr.6; A pr.6). Instead of mentioning ferlies, C uses other, related terms: "And say many sellies and selkouthe thynges" (C pr.5). A similar line is in the Z-text: "Ant sey many sellys, I can nat sey alle" (Z pr.5).

with divine authorization, despite familial, societal, and ecclesiastical opposition. Journeys in *Piers*, by contrast, are often shown to be unnecessary or even wicked, such as those undertaken by priests who leave their poor parishes for the easy money of London (B pr.83–86; A pr.80–83; C pr.81–84). The fear of wandering clergy that *Piers* shares with so many other reforming voices in the Middle Ages is expressed most clearly in the attention the poem gives to the restless, unregulated friars (see Scase, *Anticlericism*, 125ff.).[13]

At the center of all three works is the most distinctive and public kind of medieval travel—pilgrimage—though each redefines that activity in a unique way. Once again *Piers* has the strongest doubts about the practice, without wholly rejecting it. In contrast, Kempe's enthusiasm is unambiguous (going on pilgrimage is an important way in which Kempe distinguishes herself from the Lollards), and she visits most of the important shrines in England, on the Continent, and in the Holy Land. The *Travels* initially presents itself as a pilgrimage guide to Jerusalem, with the narrator promising potential travelers that "I schal telle the way that thei schul holde thidere" (Defective, 5.21–22; Cotton, 3.32–33; Egerton, 3.9 [trans., 45]).

But pilgrimage in neither the *Travels* nor Kempe's *Book* is simply conventional. Although Sir John, in accord with contemporary geography, says that Jerusalem is the center of the world, it cannot hold him. He expresses no personal spiritual response to the shrines he finds there, and soon he is ready to move on to seek Eastern marvels. The interest of the *Travels* in non-Christian practices such as cannibalism and rule by pagan leaders makes it seem more a work of cultural anthropology than a standard pilgrim's guide (see Zacher, *Curiosity*, 131). In contrast to the spiritual tepidness of Sir John, Kempe's pilgrimage to Jerusalem is

---

13. The traveler's curiosity that impels both Kempe and Sir John (in the former a curiosity for holy conversation and sites, in the latter for new peoples and places) is explicitly questioned in *Piers Plowman*. Imaginatif, noting that Adam was safe in Paradise until he "entremetede to knowe / The wisedom and the wit of God" (B 11.415–17; C 13.226–28, somewhat rewritten), scorns the dreamer/seeker's Mandevillian inquiry into the habits of birds and the beasts as nothing more than "selkouthes" derived from "diverse sightes" that "nevere no soule ysaved" (B 12.128–36; C 14.72–80, somewhat rewritten). Earlier in A and B, Study memorably declares that anyone wanting to know "the whyes of God almyghty" should have his eye "in his ers and his fynger after" (B 10.124–25; A 11.80–81). The depth of the seeker's curiosity is revealed when he says, "Alle the sciences under sonne and alle the sotile craftes / I wolde I knewe and kouthe kyndely in myn herte" (B 15.48–49; C 16.208–9), prompting Anima to rebuke him as "oon of Prides knyghtes" (B 15.50; C 16.210).

And yet such is the complexity of the poem that criticism of curiosity is not all; the desire to know about sin, salvation, and society (to mention only three alliterative topics among many) drives *Piers* as surely as do the different kinds of curiosity in the *Travels* and Kempe's *Book*, offering the best hope of heaven for the "I" and, perhaps, the reader. How can one find if one does not seek?

extreme in its fervor. At the site of the Crucifixion she responds as if present at
the original event: "And the forseyd creatur wept and sobbyd so plentyuowsly as
thow sche had seyn owyr Lord wyth hir bodyly ey sufferyng hys Passyon at that
tyme" (68.7–10 [1.1568–70]). In fact, Kempe does not really need to trek to
sacred places (though she reaches many of them), for she can achieve the devotional purposes of pilgrimage anywhere. Christ's suffering in Jerusalem comes
alive to her from the most mundane and local of physical prompts: an animal
being beaten or even the sight of a handsome young man. Wherever she is,
Kempe is always on her own unique pilgrimage.

Piers Plowman is more skeptical of pilgrimage than either the *Travels* or the
Book. Sir John himself is a clear analogue to the poem's most negative example of
a pilgrim, the palmer encountered by the folk who is "apparailled as a paynym in
pilgrymes wise" (B 5.516; A 6.4; C 7.160). This outlandish figure has gone everywhere (and wears the badges to prove it), but he has learned nothing spiritually
significant.[14] Similarly, the foreign travels in Kempe's *Book* illustrate Reason's earlier admonition to seek a more abstract and less physical pilgrimage than that
which Margery achieves: "And ye that seke Seynt James and seyntes of Rome, /
Seketh Seynt Truthe, for he may save yow alle" (B 5.56–57; A 5.40–41;
C 5.197–98).

Nevertheless, despite these attacks, *Piers* never entirely abandons pilgrimage.
As Burrow has pointed out, the concept is redefined by Piers as communal
work on the half acre ("Action," esp. 216–18): "I wol worshipe therwith Truthe
by my lyve, / And ben His pilgrym atte plow for povere mennes sake"
(B 6.101–2; A 7.93–94; C 8.110–11). The effort by "Perkeyn and thise pil-
grimes" (B 6.105; A 7.97; C 8.112) to create an ideal commonwealth fails
because of human self-interest, but the social pilgrimage of doing well for others (rather than going on individual journeys as do Sir John and Margery)
becomes a goal in the rest of the poem. Nor is the concept of pilgrimage or its
implications forgotten later in the poem. In a discussion of poverty, we hear
that "pilgrymes are we alle" (B 11.240; C 12.132), and Conscience identifies his
bold decision to leave Clergy and go with Patience, a figure who is described as

14. See Pearsall, *Piers: C-Text*, 138, note to 7.171–73, in which he observes that this palmer has visited
many of the same places supposedly visited by Sir John.
    As Zacher observes, pilgrims were traditionally associated with false tale-telling (*Curiosity*, 144–45).
The lies of pilgrims are mentioned especially in the B-version, by the narrative "I" (B pr.48–52; more
briefly in A pr.48 and C pr.49–50) and by the Doctor of Divinity (B 13.179).

dressed "in pilgrymes clothes" (B 13.29; see C 15.34, where he is compared to a "palmere"), as becoming a "pilgrym" (B 13.183; cf. B 13.216; C 15.187). Anima describes Charity's custom "to wende on pilgrymages / Ther poore men and prisons liggeth" (B 15.182–83; C 16.322–23). When Conscience sets out again at the very end of the poem, he says,

> "I wol bicome a pilgrym,
> And walken as wide as the world lasteth,
> To seke Piers the Plowman . . ."
>
> (B 20.381–83, C 22.381–83)

This final journey does not occur within the poem, for it is a pilgrimage back into the wide public world, echoing the beginning of the poem, and a pilgrimage that must be undertaken by the poem's readers themselves.[15]

II. PUBLIC TEXTS AND VOICES

Multiple Texts

Mandeville's Travels and the Book of Margery Kempe offer a contemporary context for the varied texts and voices of Piers Plowman already discussed in my second and third chapters. The work we know as the Travels was a thoroughly unstable work. Originally written in French (three different versions survive), it was translated into a number of Continental languages and often extensively

---

15. Pilgrimage is often presented in Piers as a traveling inward rather than outward. Perhaps the most exotic locale reached in the poem is the Land of Longing, which is apparently to be associated with the land distant from God, terra longinqua, of the prodigal son and with Augustine's land of unlikeness, regio dissimilitudinis (see Wittig, "Passus IX–XII," 232–34), a moral and psychological realm that the seeker reaches by way of his first dream within a dream (B 11.6ff.; C 11.167ff.). Fortune describes this land in terms that would fully satisfy the curious Sir John (or the dreamer at the beginning of the poem): "Here myghtow se wondres, / And knowe that thow coveitest" (B 11.10–11; C 11.171–72). What Will finds in this strange land is not a distant people but himself.

The anthropological journeys in the Travels discover a number of bizarre human creatures, including those with eyes in their shoulders and mouths in their chests. Piers is not without its own grotesques, but, in keeping with the nature of its travels, they tend to represent spiritual rather than physical states, such as Anima in the B-text: "a sotil thyng withalle— / Oon withouten tonge and teeth" (B 15.12–13). Covetise, repulsive in body and dress (B 5.186–95; A 5.107–13; C 6.196–205), outwardly is no more than an especially ugly human being ("He was bitelbrowed and baberlipped, with two blered eighen"), and not as strange as Sir John's people with dog heads. That is because Covetise's most frightening transformation has occurred within and affects his relationship with others: when asked by Repentance in the B-text if he is charitable to his neighbors, Covetise replies, "I am holden . . . as hende as hounde is in kichene" (B 5.257). More monstrous than a dog's head is this stray dog's heart.

altered.[16] The Middle English *Travels,* our chief concern here, is no less diverse. Although it survives in approximately forty manuscripts, modern literary criticism has often cited only a single text (usually Egerton or Cotton because they have been the most accessible in modern editions) as if it fully represented the work as a whole. But the *Travels* exists in five distinct Middle English versions: four in prose (Bodley, Cotton, Defective, and Egerton) and one in verse (Metrical), not to mention shorter extracts and epitomes.[17] Even though most English versions descend directly or indirectly from a single French tradition (Insular), they nevertheless differ, sometimes radically, from one another.[18] For instance, Cotton and Egerton, each extant in a single manuscript, are generally similar in organization and incident, but even they have significant inconsistencies, such as unique passages or chapter headings.[19]

16. For recent surveys of the theories about who might have first written the *Travels,* and where, when, and how, see Seymour, *Sir John Mandeville,* 5–24, and Higgins, *Writing East,* 8–13.

The principal French versions of the *Travels* are the Continental (more that thirty manuscripts survive), the Liège (seven manuscripts), and the Insular (more than twenty manuscripts). See Seymour, *Sir John Mandeville,* 3–5, 38–39, 42–43, 46.

The original form of the *Travels* established but did not fix the work, for as Seymour puts it, "The book was much given to interpolation" (*Sir John Mandeville,* 25). He has counted one hundred such interpolations in French, Latin, English, and Irish manuscripts of the Insular version alone. Higgins's book repeated calls attention to striking differences between versions. For example, of the four German/Dutch translations, the two most popular were written in the late fourteenth century by Michel Velser (forty surviving manuscripts) and Otto von Diemeringen (forty-five manuscripts). The former adapts his primary source (Continental) by adding personal testimony to enhance the credibility of certain episodes; the latter changes his source (Liège) by postponing the central account of the Saracens and passages about other religions until the end (Higgins, *Writing East,* 22, 24–25; see also Letts, "German Manuscripts," and Morrall, "Michel Velser").

17. See Seymour, "English Editions," "English Manuscripts," and *Sir John Mandeville;* Moseley, "Metamorphosis," 8; Higgins, "Imagining Christendom," 108n; Zacher, "Mandeville's Travels."

18. The three-thousand-line Metrical version of the *Travels* reduces and rearranges its Insular Latin source, while also adding a long section on Rome, and changes the narrative voice from first to third person (See *Metrical Version,* introduction and notes; Moseley, "Metamorphoses," 14–15; Higgins, *Writing East,* esp. 61–62, 127).

A stanzaic fragment (Bodleian Library, MS e Musaeo 160), prose epitome (British Library, MS Additional 37049), and extracts in Bodleian Library, MS Ashmole 751, and Bodleian Library, MS Digby 88, each in its own way emphasizes the theological and devotional elements in their Insular source (see Seymour, "English Epitome," "Marco Polo" [for e Musaeo 160], "Secundum" [for Ashmole 751]; and Horner, "Mandeville's Travels" [for Digby 88]; see also Moseley, "Metamorphoses," 10–13).

By contrast, the Bodley version (Bodleian Library, MS e Musaeo 116 and MS Rawlinson D.99), also from an Insular source, omits more serious episodes to concentrate on marvels and also changes the sequence of events (see *Bodley Version* and Seymour, "Medieval Redactor").

19. Cotton is divided into thirty-six chapters, but Egerton has none. Cotton contains passages not in Egerton, such as Lot sleeping with his daughters (74.20–33), just as Egerton has some not in Cotton, such as an interpolation about Thule and Saint Thomas of Canterbury (Egerton, 220, cf. note 3 at 149 [trans., 183]; see Letts, ed. 1:212–14). On Egerton, see Seymour, "Origin"; Higgins, *Writing East,* 24. The two texts

Variance is found within versions as well as between them. The most popular form of the *Travels* among Middle English readers was the so-called Defective version, which Hanna contended is the only one that "has any real claims to be the English *Mandeville*" ("Mandeville," 123), and yet Tamarah Kohanski has shown that the manuscripts of this version "are far too varied for a single exemplar to represent them usefully" (*Unchartered Territory*, 137ff., 147n).[20]

Iain Higgins has argued that "there is no necessarily 'authoritative' text" of the *Travels* (*Writing East*, 17). Instead, he refers to the work as the "mandevillian multi-text" and proposes it as a "model for reading medieval writing in its various forms of multiplicity" (viii, 65).[21] The *Travels* is a particularly useful model for *Piers*. Thinking of the two as "multitexts" is not anachronistically postmodern. Someone first wrote these distinct works, for they are not impersonal sites for competing discourses any more than they are the product of an infinite number of monkeys with an infinite number of quill pens.[22] Nevertheless, the original author, however important, is only one of the agents of a multitext. Just as the *Travels* and *Piers* are rewritings of existing material, so they in turn

---

have somewhat different textual traditions: see Seymour, *Sir John Mandeville*, 45; Hanna, "Mandeville," 124. Cotton is apparently closer to the French original, whereas Egerton's translation is generally considered more intelligent and skillful. For discussion of differences between the two texts, see Bennett, *Rediscovery*, 85–86; Higgins, *Writing East*, 24, 44, 57, 101–2.

20. Defective, which is so named because it lacks a long section about Egypt, is extant in about thirty-three manuscripts and several fragments, in contrast to the single manuscripts of Cotton and Egerton, and was the basis for all early printed editions. See Seymour, *Sir John Mandeville*, 43–44, and his EETS edition of the *Defective Version*, especially xi–xxvi, which, in addition to describing Defective in general, defines five sub-groups, and 186–215, which lists unique additions and lacunae in individual manuscripts.

Diversity within Defective includes presentation as well as content: British Library, MS Harley 3954, which also contains a *Piers* text, has a number of simple but lively illustrations that sensationalize the text by emphasizing incidents of nudity and violence, producing a sort of tabloid *Travels*. For other examples of variation within Defective, see Kohanski, "Two Manuscripts."

21. Kohanski also urges us to recognize the many shapes of the *Travels*: "[I]f we are going to call ourselves students of medieval books, we would be well advised to meet them on their own terms" (*Unchartered Territory*, 148).

22. Nor would I agree with one strain of the movement that calls itself (perhaps too optimistically) the New Philology, which sees *only* difference, as in the often-quoted dictum of Bernard Cerquiglini, "[M]edieval writing does not produce variants; it is variance." See the special issue of *Speculum* (65.1 [1990]), especially the introduction by Stephen Nichols from which the translated quotation by Cerquiglini comes (Nichols, "Introduction," 1). Even assuming that it is clear exactly what Cerquiglini means here, it is as misleading to celebrate random variance today as it was to celebrate organic unity yesterday. A multitext is neither one extreme nor the other.

were rewritten by others.[23] The *Travels* and *Piers*, to adapt Auden's phrase, became their readers, the former work appearing not only in many languages but also in a wide variety of individual shapes (long and short, prose and verse, pious and sensational) as it escaped from direct authorial control and became public writing.

Although the textual variations in *Piers* were not as extreme as those in the English *Travels*, they produced a similar multiplicity. All fifty surviving manuscripts of the poem have been modified, as individual cooks might modify a recipe for particular tastes or occasions, sometimes dramatically, as I have discussed in Chapter 2. For example, the A-version of *Piers* was supplemented in three manuscripts with forms of a passus 12 (the so-called John But ending), and in several others by the addition of a C-conclusion. Parts of C were skillfully rewritten in the Ilchester manuscript, and Huntington Library, MS HM 114, is a compendium of all three main versions. The readers of *Piers* not only rewrote the texts they received, sometimes so well that the authenticity of these variations is still in doubt, but they also created the individual programs of *ordinatio*, as previously discussed. Several *Piers* manuscripts have unique passus divisions and one C-text has a series of illustrations. Most have some form of annotation, with no program exactly like another even if produced in the same workshop: sometimes the annotation is heavy, sometimes light; it is regularly in the hand of the original scribe but often also in that of one or more later readers (see Benson and Blanchfield, *Manuscript*; Uhart, "Early Reception"). Even minor annotations can change the emphasis, if not the content, of a particular text, as an actor transforms a written part by intonation and gesture.

Recognizing *Piers* as a multitext means, first of all, not assuming that the poem has anything like the stability of a modern printed edition (or even of three or four printed editions). Like the *Travels*, *Piers* does not exist in a fixed form: it is one (a work) as well as many (individual texts), and also several (versions).[24] The original creation was remodeled by public reception and use. Most

---

23. Higgins demonstrates that the *Travels* is the result of "a considered, engaged, and sometimes inspired overwriting of its sources" (*Writing East*, 12). Compare Kohanski: "The author is not a single person but the combination of forces that produces a particular text: the original author, later authors (scribes, redactors), factors of earlier versions' reception, and more" (*Unchartered Territory*, 92–93). Earlier, Zacher had noted that Mandeville was a reader who wrote for other readers (*Curiosity*, 155).

24. I have adapted this terminology from Kohanski, who in discussing the *Travels* uses *work* to refer to all its forms, *version* to refer to a related group of manuscripts (such as Defective), and *text* to refer to a specific manuscript or printed edition (*Unchartered Territory*, 4n).

medieval readers of *Piers* would have known the poem in only a single copy, and yet each of these readers, however distinctive his or her text, would have believed that he or she had indeed read *Piers Plowman:* both Bodleian Library, MS Bodley 851 (the brief Z-text), and Bodleian Library, MS Douce 104 (a C-version with extensive notes and illustrations), are part of the same work.

The *Book of Margery Kempe* survives in a single manuscript, but it too demonstrates, in its own way, the difficulties within this period of establishing an authorial text.[25] If not really a multitext, Kempe's *Book* is certainly multilayered—or so we are told in its two opening prefaces (whose doubleness enacts multiplicity). The prefaces describe a tortured process of production: Kempe's dictation of her experiences was first taken down in a strange mixture of English and German—"neithyr good Englysch ne Dewch"—(4.15–16 [1.75])—by one who died soon after. A priest attempting to put this version into standard English found it incomprehensible (he was also intimidated by popular opposition to Kempe in Lynn). But after a third scribe, another priest, also failed to make a serviceable version, the first priest tried again and with Kempe's prayers and correction—"he red it ovyr beforn this creatur every word, sche sumtym helpyng where ony difficulte was" (5.10–12 [1.98–99])—established the first book of the *Book* as we know it, to which he added two prefaces and a second book about Kempe's later life.

Despite this detailed account, the actual responsibility for the composition of Kempe's *Book* is far from clear. We do not know the true identities of any of Kempe's scribes; it has been plausibly suggested that the first was her son (Hirsh, "Author and Scribe," 146) and the second her confessor and parish priest, Robert Spryngolde (Dillon, "Margery Kempe's Sharp Confessor/s"), but the evidence is not overwhelming in either case. Who then should be called the author of the *Book of Margery Kempe*?[26] Some argue that the priest who produced the first readable transcription is at least Kempe's collaborator (Hirsh, "Author

---

25. The printing history of the *Book* is brief but illustrates both the instability of medieval texts and their ability to inspire imaginary biographical speculation. Wynkyn de Worde's first edition (c. 1501) contains only Kempe's prayers and nothing about her life, as radical a reshaping as any of the versions of Mandeville, with the result that a later reprint by Henry Pepwell in 1521 can identify Kempe as an anchoress (see Meech in Kempe, *Book*, xlvi–xlviii). For the creation of this simpler, less troubled Margery Kempe in de Worde's translation, see the first chapter of Rebecca Schoff's forthcoming Harvard dissertation, "From Print to Manuscript."

26. Clarissa Atkinson if anything understated the case when she observed, "The relation of author and scribe in this work is complicated and uncertain" (*Mystic and Pilgrim*, 36).

and Scribe," 150, and Le Saux, "'Hir not lettyrd,'" 64–65). In addition to the prefaces that are presented as his, later chapters (such as 24 and 62) report incidents that clearly derive from his own knowledge (Goodman, "Piety," 347–48); other passages, especially Kempe's answers to accusations of heresy, also sometimes seem to be worded with a clerical knowingness (but see Goodman, ibid.). Feminist scholars, who have done so much to reawaken interest in Kempe, understandably claim her as the principal author, thus adding an important name to the small list of known medieval English woman writers.[27] Lynn Staley even argues that although Kempe may have adopted strategic tropes like a pretense of illiteracy and the need for male scribes, she is actually a highly sophisticated and literate writer worthy to be mentioned with Chaucer and Langland (*Dissenting Fictions*). This is an issue where the scattered and contradictory evidence resists any definitive judgment. However important the question of authorship of the *Book*, it can be (as it has been) decided only by critical fiat.[28] Julian Yates wonders if our desire to call Margery Kempe (or alternately the priest/scribe) an "author" is "not but one more attempt to inscribe her [and, I would add, her book] within a familiar set of categories" ("Mystic Self," 82n). Yates instead describes a process of composition and transmission involving "numerous layers of mediation" (84).

Like Kempe's *Book*, *Piers* is a multilayered, collaborative work in which authorship is diffused, even if the prevailing consensus is accepted that one person wrote the different versions of the poem in a particular order. If *Piers*, like the *Book*, is the work of a lifetime, each version must have been composed by a particular author (even if the same man) with unique experiences and in different historical situations. Moreover, as is also true for the *Travels*, others besides the author were responsible for individual shapes of the poem, either because a version was designed for and addressed to a specific audience or because it was a

27. See, for example, Sue Ellen Holbrook, who insisted that, whatever the contributions of others, "the text represents Margery Kempe as the chief maker of the book: she is its writer in the essential modern sense of the word" ("'About Her,'" 273).

28. Perhaps the authorship of the *Book of Margery Kempe* should be imagined as an extended movie credit: Colonel W. Butler-Bowden proudly presents a Mount Grace Production, *The Book of Margery Kempe*, based on the life and narration of Margery Kempe. Original story by a German-speaking Englishman; screenplay translated and amplified by scribe 2, with the assistance of scribe 3. Addition material supplied by Mrs. Kempe. Special effects provided by the Four Evangelists (as adapted by pseudo-Bonaventure). Cameo appearances by John Kempe, Archbishop Arundel, Julian of Norwich, the Virgin Mary, and a cast of hundreds of saints and sinners. The entire production supervised by God the Father and directed by Jesus Christ.

response to outside historical events such as the Rising of 1381. Even the Athlone editors, who make the strongest claims for three discrete authorial versions of *Piers*, concluded that in revising his work the poet incorporated many scribal readings from the manuscripts he had at hand and that the C-version was put in final form by someone other than the poet himself. As demonstrated in my second chapter, additional layers were incorporated into the text when scribes and annotators supplied new endings, conflated versions, rewrote passages, or reorganized and annotated their copies—when the work came into public use. The manuscript histories of *Mandeville's Travels* and the *Book of Margery Kempe* are contemporary analogues to the textual multiplicity of *Piers Plowman*. They demonstrate a dynamic, collaborative process of creation and adaptation in late medieval public writing not sufficiently recognized by modern readers.

Multiple Voices

In the previous chapter, I argued against autobiographical readings of the narrative "I" in *Piers Plowman*. The first person is only an intermittent voice in *Piers* and, even when present, is less a consistent character than a subjectivity that is both generic and fragmented. I cautioned against assuming that we can identify the accents of the author in the hubbub of voices he creates and argued that *Piers* is less directly didactic than it sometimes seems: instead, it contains debate, creating a forum in which no position is necessarily final. In their different kinds of public writing, *Mandeville's Travels* and the *Book of Margery Kempe* offer contemporary support for this understanding of *Piers*. They demonstrate that first-person narrative voices in late medieval England can be fictional, slippery, and unstable—used to organize miscellaneous material rather than to express clear authorial opinion.

As noted in my first chapter, R. W. Chambers defended autobiographical readings of *Piers* with an argument from literary history that has been accepted by many Langland scholars: he insisted that in medieval poetry such as *Piers* the first-person narrator is always to some degree an authorial self-portrait (often using his own name) and thus any idea that the dreamer Will does not represent the writer is "an anachronism" ("Robert," 442; cf. Preface, 17; "Three Texts," 131).[29] But if we move beyond visionary poetry to the more general category of

---

29. Kane strongly endorsed this position, although he also acknowledged that the exact degree of resemblance between literary narrator and historical poet may be difficult to determine (*Evidence*, 53ff., and "Autobiographical Fallacy"). See also Kerby-Fulton, "'Who Has Written This Book'" and "*Piers*."

late medieval public writing, *Mandeville's Travels* provides a striking example of a contemporary encyclopedic work whose prominent first-person narrator is entirely fictional.[30] As suspected by a few commentators as early as the seventeenth century and proved beyond question in the nineteenth, the figure of Sir John was woven out of borrowed and invented cloth. The *Travels* describes no actual human being. Some of Sir John's reported experiences are chronologically impossible, and many of his most "personal" moments, such as his intimate talk with the sultan or his terrifying journey through the Valley Perilous, are taken directly from other works.[31] Our best current information about the author of *Mandeville's Travels* is that he was not named Mandeville and did very little traveling. The *Travels* demonstrates that an invented narrator is not at all anachronistic in the discursive world that produced and received *Piers Plowman*.[32]

The narrating "I" of *Mandeville's Travels*, like that of *Piers*, is not only unreliable as an autobiographical source but unstable even as fiction, though this has not always been acknowledged. Just as Donaldson noted "the strong sense of personality" in *Piers*, Josephine Bennett claimed that "Sir John Mandeville is a personality who gives inner coherence and life to the book."[33] In fact, both figures

30. It is true that the *Travels* is different from *Piers* because it is prose rather than poetry and is not a dream vision; but the works of two other writers that Chambers compared with Langland differ from his in other ways ("Robert," 443; Preface, 19–20): Dante's *Commedia* is not in fact a dream, and Chaucer did not write alliterative verse. Langland's closest literary association is not with the likes of Chaucer and Dante but with those anonymous alliterative poets, such as the author of *Winner and Waster*, whose relationship to their narrators is almost wholly obscure.

31. For some of the anachronisms in the *Travels*, see Seymour, *Sir John Mandeville*, 16. For others and for borrowings in the *Travels*, see also the notes to the editions by Letts and by Warner (and the latter's introduction, xv–xxix).

32. As with the life of Langland, any life of Mandeville has had to be constructed almost entirely from information within the text itself. The lengthy biographical notice of Mandeville by the sixteenth-century antiquarian John Bale derives even more completely from the narrator's self-portrait than does the biography Bale created for "Robert" Langland discussed in my first chapter (see Haraszti, "Travels," 312).

The belief that Mandeville was indeed a genuine Englishman continues to be held, even by good scholars; see, for example, Bennett, *Rediscovery*, 176–204; [Moseley in translation of Egerton version of *Mandeville*, 10–11]. In a naive recent book, Giles Milton, a London journalist, insists that Sir John was exactly who he says he was and sets out to learn about him by retracing his journeys.

Some Continental candidates have been proposed as the true author of the *Travels*, especially two residents of Liège; a physician, Jean de Bourgogne, and a notary and notoriously unreliable chronicler, Jean d'Outremeuse. See Seymour, *Sir John Mandeville*, 2. See also Letts, *Sir John Mandeville*, 14–21; Hamelius, *Mandeville's Travels*, 2.1–13; Cameron, "Discovery"; Jackson, "Who Was Sir John Mandeville"; Phillips, "Quest." For Seymour's own candidate for the original Mandeville, Jean de Long, see Seymour, *Sir John Mandeville*, 23.

33. Donaldson, *C-Text and Its Poet*, 199; Bennett, *Rediscovery*, 5. Hanna also refers to Sir John's "definable personality" ("Mandeville," 121), and Moseley to his "attractive *persona*," claiming that its "stamp of a subjectivity" makes the material of the *Travels* memorable ("Metamorphoses," 5). See also Zacher, *Curiosity*, 131, 142; M. Campbell, *Witness*, 9; Westrem, "Two Routes," 72; Camargo, "Geography of Identity," 68.

are highly elusive. In contrast to the first-person tellers of the prologues to Chaucer's Wife of Bath's and Pardoner's Tales, those in *Piers* and the *Travels* often do little more than observe or listen to others, without taking much part in the action.[34] They are also inconsistent. Sir John is commonly described as cool and sophisticated by critics, but he is also capable of harsh, snap judgments, like that about the people of Tartary: "Thei beth right foule folk and of il kynde" (Defective, 55.3; Cotton, 94.8–9; Egerton, 64.27 [trans., 103]; not in Bodley; see Kohanski, *Unchartered Territory*, 187).[35] Moreover, his fabled tolerance toward Saracens and pagans coexists with a fierce bigotry toward Jews.[36] Sir John is an important analogue to the fragmented speaking subject of *Piers* defined by David Lawton, as discussed in the previous chapter, a subject whose multiple voices and views are revealed as early as the prologue. Nor does the "I" stabilize thereafter. The ignorant "doted daffe" scorned by Holy Church in passus 1 becomes an efficient, objective reporter of the action of Meed's proposed wedding in passus 2, and then a stern moralist on such topics as the decoration of churches and the responsibilities of mayors in passus 3.[37]

The plasticity of the narrative voice of the *Travels* became clear during the work's reception, even if we restrict our analysis to the English versions. The

---

34. Even though we learn more details about Sir John's personal life than about Will's, Kohanski notes that most of the personal information about him occurs in two short passages at the beginning and end of most versions of the *Travels* (Kohanski, *Unchartered Territory*, 56). About the Cotton version, Letts states, "I have counted only twenty-three specific personal statements" (*Sir John Mandeville*, 37). Howard comments that Sir John "gives no circumstantial details of his day-to-day activities in travel" ("World," 4; *Writers*, 63).

Our ignorance is even greater with Will, whose most intense interactions are with allegorical figures. In B and C we are told the names of his wife and daughter (which may be generic), but nothing about their life together. The one detailed account of Will in the nondream world comes from a single passage in one version (c 5.1–108), though the information there is often read into the other versions. Will, as Howard said about the "I" of the *Travels*, is often no more than "an impersonal Everyman" ("World," 2; *Writers*, 56).

35. Kohanski states that the narrator of the *Travels* "exists less as a character than a polyphony of voices" (*Unchartered Territory*, 156).

36. For the anti-Semitism of the *Travels*, see Higgins, *Writing East*, and Greenblatt, "Dome." This bigotry has sometimes been overlooked because of Sir John's tolerance for other religions: "The Sir John Mandeville who appears in the *Travels* is full of reverence for the God who made all things, secure in a firm faith, yet free from intolerance and narrow orthodoxy" (Bennett, *Rediscovery*, 5).

37. As Higgins puts it, the narrator of the *Travels* is a "textual fiction written into others' writings and sometimes depicted as doing their deeds," and thus the "author is not so much dead . . . as deeply and probably irretrievably encrypted" (*Writing East*, 8). Greenblatt associates whoever wrote the *Travels* not with "medieval masters of personae" like Chaucer and Dante, but with "post-modern artists bent on dismantling stable structures of literary identity and meaning" like Calvino or Barthes ("Dome," 160n). Greenblatt further argues that the *Travels* lacks both an authoritative text and person: "There is no original, no authorizing self, no authentic text; all texts are translations of fragments that are themselves translations. Still less is there an original experience, an extralinguistic meaning, a primal act of eyewitnessing that is subsequently copied, paraphrased, or imitated in Mandeville's collage of translations" (48–49).

"I" disappears entirely in the Metrical version, for instance, which is told in the third person. Other English scribes and adaptors, by contrast, give *more* emphasis to Sir John's voice by supplying original examples of it, adding such phrases as "I, John Mandeville, saw this" or "I, John Mandeville, say that this is true."[38] A revealing difference between the two English versions that are most commonly cited by modern critics occurs when the sultan promises Sir John a princess and great lordships if he will renounce his Christian faith and become a Muslim. Egerton has him reply simply, "bot I wald noght" (18.15 [trans., 59]).[39] An orthodox answer, but not so passionate as his words in Cotton: "but I thanke God I had no wille to don it for no thing that he behighte me" (24.22–23). The unsuspecting reader who knows only the Cotton version might take Sir John's emphatic rejection of apostasy (or is it self-defensive?) as an important insight into the psychology of the author. The real point, however, which is revealed only by careful comparison, is that the narrative voice in the *Travels* can be re-created by particular scribes and readers with the same flexibility we saw in the manuscripts of *Piers Plowman*.[40] In both works, the "I," far from being the private expression of the author, is a public instrument available to others.[41]

38. Thus the Bodley version generally abbreviates the text, but it repeatedly adds and expands first-person statements, such as this unique address to the reader just before the sultan's speech: "Trowith this wel, for this have I bothe herd and sen with mynne eyne and mynne eryn and myne felawys that were with me that weryn of dyvers regionys, for wete ye wel that al be it wondyr to youre heryng, I am not set to lye yow lesyngis. Trowith yif ye welyn" (75.28–32; the last sentence is not in the Rawlinson manuscript of Bodley).

39. Defective gives the sultan's offer without explicit mention of Sir John's rejection (21.30–22.1).

40. For other examples of difference in the representation of the narrative voice, see Kohanski, *Unchartered Territory*, 125ff.; Letts, *Sir John Mandeville*, 133. Egerton, but not Cotton (197.19; see Letts, ed., 1:190n), has the following sentence about fish in the Gravelley Sea: "I John Maundeuill ete of tham, and tharfore trowez it, for sikerly it es soth" (Egerton, 134.23–24 [trans., 169]). Bodley has a similar expression ("for I Jon Maundevile et of hem. It is soth. Trowe it if ye welyn" [101.13–14; the last two sentences are not in the Rawlinson manuscript of Bodley]), but not Defective (115.23). Earlier, Egerton (130.14–16 [trans., 165]) and Defective (111.4–7) both mention the marvel of a fruit that when ripe contains a small animal like a lamb, which is eaten by the residents of that land, but it is only Cotton that has the knight himself stop, taste, and comment: "Of that frute I have eten, alle though it were wondirfulle, but that I knowe wel that God is merveyllous in His wekes" (191.10–12). The original passages in both Egerton and Cotton turn Sir John from a reporter into a participant. They thus intensify each episode (a main purpose of all such "I" additions).

41. Although the main versions of *Piers* are presumably the work of the same author, first-person statements vary. These range from minor differences, such as the absence in C of A and B's defense of some minstrels ("synnelees, I leeve" [B pr.34, A pr.34]), to more significant changes, such as the absence in C of the B-narrator's justification for his poetic "makying" (B 12.20–28, though a different apology is offered in passus 5 of C).

The function of the first-person narrators in the *Travels* and *Piers* is less self-portrayal than organizational.[42] As mentioned earlier in this chapter, each lacks clear, logical structures and narrative coherence. There is no connection made between the Church of Saint Katherine on Mount Sinai and the court of the Great Khan, or between the pillar at which Jesus was scourged and the gold-digging ants of Ceylon, except that Sir John saw each. Likewise, the main link of the visions in *Piers* is that all are dreamed and reported by the narrator. Both *Piers* and the *Travels* contain a rich variety of lore and discourses, but because the form of each is so tenuous (neither has a plot as such), their only principle of unity is the claim that everything was experienced by a single individual.[43]

In contrast to *Mandeville's Travels*, the *Book of Margery Kempe* apparently presents the experiences of a real person, though the facts about Kempe's life found in her work are almost as meager as those about Langland's in *Piers*.[44] Nevertheless, her *Book* does provide convincing accounts of the city of Lynn and of historical figures, such as Julian of Norwich and Archbishop Arundel. Modern critics often call the work an autobiography (even the "first autobiography in English"), but that is a somewhat misleading designation.[45] Whatever genuine information about the actual Margery Kempe it may contain, the *Book* is anything but a full account of her life. It opens with Kempe's giving birth at twenty, and only in book 2 do we hear for the first (and last) time anything (and then not much) about the lives of even one of her fourteen children.[46] Kempe's individuality is further undercut because the *Book* generally refers to her in the third person as a "creature" of God and often emphasizes her resemblances to other holy women, including the Virgin Mary, Mary Magdalene, Bridget of Sweden, and Mary

---

42. Seymour briefly suggested this point in his edition of Cotton (*Mandeville's Travels*, xvi–xvii).

43. Similarly, the main purpose of the narrator in the *Canterbury Tales* (the pilgrim Chaucer) is not to supply autobiographical details about the poet (though many have looked to find them), but to provide a pretext for the variety of the tales.

44. The only extant contemporary historical record of Margery Kempe herself is as a member of the important Trinity Guild in Lynn in the late 1430s, which, assuming that this is indeed our Margery, suggests a social acceptance late in life one might not have predicted from her *Book*. Ample records do exist concerning her father, John Burnam (often spelled Brunham), who held the mayoralty and other responsible positions in Lynn, and her husband, John Kempe, a lesser presence in that city (Kempe, *Book*, 358–68).

45. Atkinson, *Mystic and Pilgrim*, 36; those who warn again treating the *Book* as simple autobiography include Sue Ellen Holbrook, in "'About Her,'" and Robert Ross, in "Oral Life."

46. Similarly, although her father's civic achievements are mentioned several times, we learn nothing about his personality or Kempe's relationship with him, in contrast to her relationships with various "ghostly" fathers.

d'Oignies. Gail Gibson has perceptively noted that at the moments when Kempe may seem to sound "most like her inimitable self," she is, in fact, closely imitating the popular *Meditations on the Life of Christ* by pseudo-Bonaventure ("St. Margaret," 146).[47]

Kempe, like the shadowy "I" of *Piers*, is more exemplary than individual. For all its local detail, her life follows a standard arc of sin and redemption, as outlined in the second preface: "A schort tretys of a creature sett in grett pompe and pride of the world, whech sythen was drawyn to ower Lord be gret poverte, sekenes, schamis, and gret reprevys" (5.33–6.1 [1.113–14]).[48] A similar pattern can be traced in *Piers*, though, significantly, without the redemption. The first inner dream (B 11.4ff.; C 11.166ff.), which is often taken to be one of the author's most personal statements, as we have seen, is less a portrait of an individual than the Christian understanding of the temptations experienced by all: lust of the flesh, lust of the eyes, and pride of life. This vision of how Fortune beguiles the narrator/dreamer until finally deserting him in old age is the general condition of human life rather than a specific authorial self-portrait.

In the previous chapter, I also argued that we can never be sure of the poet's own position in *Piers*, because the voices of the poem are so various and contradictory. *Mandeville's Travels* and *Kempe's Book* again provide contemporary analogues: they are public writing that is multivoiced as well as multitextual. As in *Piers*, the "I" of Sir John and the third-person of Kempe certainly can be didactic. Sir John often tells his audiences what he has learned on his travels, repeatedly using phrases such as "you must understand." Kempe lectures clerics and laity alike on their failings. Yet both works also contain a multitude of other voices, which express a range of opinions on diverse topics. Despite Kempe's prominence and tendency to hectoring, her *Book* allows others to speak as well (cf. Holbrook, "'About Her,'" 267); many of these individuals directly attack Kempe herself and her way of life, often quite persuasively. Few readers will not sympathize with the frustrations expressed by Kempe's traveling companions and her beleaguered husband or fail to understand why the friar at Saint Margaret's did not want her to disrupt his preaching with weeping and roaring.

47. Helen Taylor argues that because the *Book* is not purely autobiographical, it does not present a "coherent psyche which can be analyzed" ("*Mulier*," 365).

48. Greenspan claims that in the *Book*, as in other similar writing, "historial truth appears remade, as allegory" ("Autohagiography," 226). Harding similarly points to how the work "translates a medieval woman's experience into recognizable textual patterns": from sinner to saint, from Eve to Mary ("Medieval Women's Discourse," 204).

Most of the accusations against Kempe that are still made today (that she is hysterical, vain, hypocritical, sick, or simply tiresome) were first expressed, and expressed forcefully, by voices within the *Book* itself. The *Travels* is similarly dialogic. Sir John hears detailed and convincing criticism of the failures of Roman Catholicism from other Christians and non-Christians alike. There is no single source of authority in the *Travels*, but competing discourses have their say about the right way to live—from the opulent luxury of the khans to the asceticism of the Brahmins, as I shall show in more detail in the following section. No view is necessarily definitive, including the narrator's.[49]

Piers Plowman shares in this polyphony. Many voices speak in the poem, but their authority remains uncertain; none, not even Christ's, can be accepted as necessarily speaking for the author. In the B-version, for example, four separate speakers, not heard before or after, express various views about kingship (B pr.123–45; the passage is not in A and very different in C). A lunatic kneels and prays that Christ allow the king to rule in such a way that "leaute thee lovye"; an angel then descends to urge at length in Latin that the king temper justice with mercy. The following two speakers also speak in Latin: "a goliardeis, a gloton of wordes" says in answer to the angel that a ruler's proper function, as shown by etymology, is to rule and thus uphold the laws; and finally, and most briefly, "al the commune" declare that the king's will is their law. Critics have noted the differences between these positions, but their assessments of their validity also vary. Schmidt insists that the angel's words "sum up concisely L[angland's] view of proper social order," whereas the words of the "commune" are "ignorant" (*Vision*, 412–13). Yet the commune's speech not only concludes the passage but also is similar to what Donaldson took to be the authorial message about kingship in the fable of the rats that follows soon after (*C-Text and Its Poet*, 94). In a detailed analysis of the episode, Baldwin characterizes the views of both the angel and the lunatic as "a few platitudes," finds that the "commune" strikes a "discordant note," and values most the ideas of the goliard (*Theme of Government*, 12–13), though his words have been dismissed by other scholars as incomplete and amoral (Robertson and Huppé, *Piers Plowman*, 29–30; Wittig, *William Langland*, 44). As these varied judgments suggest, the debate over kingship

---

49. Higgins notes that Sir John often uses "they say" to support a statement of a particular people without having himself to vouch for its accuracy (*Writing East*, 75–76); Higgins also concludes that the *Travels* is "a textual space within which fundamentally distinct views of the world could be articulated" (264).

here is a genuine dialogue with no obvious resolution. In *Piers* a lunatic is not necessarily outranked by an angel. To claim one position as determinate in such an epistemological welter is reductive.

The Hunger episode during the plowing of the half acre suggests some of the difficulty of locating stable authorial meaning in *Piers*.[50] Although the figure Hunger is anything but consistent in words or deeds, readers have tried to make him so. Some, like Robert Frank ("'Hungry Gap'"), stress the physical reality of hunger in the Middle Ages, minimizing what the character says, whereas others such as Robert Kaske read him allegorically as the spiritual hunger for righteousness, ignoring his hoglike consumption ("Character"). David Aers claims that Langland's account abandons the "traditional" Christian view of poverty as a sanctified state for a "'new' ethos" that demands work from all ("Problems," 6–9). In a more recent piece, Aers perceptively notes argumentative inconsistencies in the episode, which he refers to as a "wobble," but still insists that the "*dominant* tendency" of the episode supports the newer ethos (*Community*, 45, 53, his emphasis).[51]

A detailed reading of what Hunger does and says, which I shall only outline here, suggests that "wobble" may be the key to the episode, as it is to much of the apparent exposition in *Piers*.[52] Hunger adopts too many contradictory roles for him to be reduced to any single authorial message. He enters the poem as a cruel avenger who wrings Waster "by the wombe" and savagely buffets the Bretoner (B 6.174–77; A 7.159–62; C 8.171–74), but when asked by Piers what to do with such beggars, he speaks like a social worker, advocating charity for those made destitute through misfortune: "Conforte hem with thi catel for Cristes love of hevene; / Love hem and lene hem—so lawe of kynde wolde" (B 6.220–21; A 7.206–7; C 8.230–31). Surprisingly caring words for such a brute. Even a distinction Hunger make between the deserving and nondeserving

---

50. My discussion here deals only with the B-version of the Hunger episode. For a longer treatment of these ideas, see my essay, with Elizabeth Passmore, "The Discourses of Hunger in *Piers Plowman*." For another view of the episode, see Hewett-Smith, "Allegory."

51. In a less directly political treatment, John Burrow also calls attention to a clash in the episode between strict and lenient views toward the poor. Piers feels both anger and pity toward beggars, whereas Hunger reassures him that "it is indeed right to discriminate between the truly disadvantaged and the frauds," which Burrow called a "somewhat unstable compromise" between justice and mercy (*Langland's Fictions*, 44). Like Aers, Burrow recognizes unresolved stresses in the text (his "unstable compromise" is reminiscent of Aers's "wobble"), but both insist on a generally coherent argument.

52. To choose another, minor example of such wobbles—is Study for or against Theology? She first says Theology has often annoyed her and is misty (B 10.182–85; A 11.137–40; C 11.128–31), but in A and B she then goes on to cite Theology to refute Cato and to urge us to love our enemies, a central Christian tenet (B.10.197ff.; A 11.149ff.; C, perhaps revealingly, eliminates this second passage).

poor is soon undermined in the B-version when he goes on to suggest unlimited and nonjudgmental charity ("Love hem and lakke hem noght") in which all are to be helped, even if "thei doon yvele" (B 6.224–25). A pitiless Simon Legree has become Saint Francis.

Nor is this the end of Hunger's roles. His talk with Piers ends almost bathetically with commonsensical dietary advice (don't drink on an empty stomach or overeat), before he again becomes a mute allegorical figure, who, ignoring his own recent advice, gorges himself into insensibility. The Hunger episode provides no clear lesson—or rather too many. No single voice or position dominates for long, as Hunger is explored from multiple perspectives. Here, as throughout *Piers Plowman*, the author's own views (even if they could be determined) are less important than the experience of readers as they navigate the exhilarating rapids of the text.

III. PUBLIC RELIGION

The Condition of Christianity

Voices in *Piers Plowman* condemn the condition of Christianity with a level of ferocity unmatched in other Ricardian poems. Even Julian of Norwich, for all her innovative theology, is respectful of the Church and generous toward her fellow Christians. In contrast, many passages in *Piers* suggest that all manner of things are far from well. The poem repeatedly shows us Christendom in disarray, fallen sharply away from its own past ideals and urgently needing reform. These complaints have led some to associate the poem with the most radical contemporary critics of the Church, such as Wyclif and the Lollards.[53] But there is no need to look for analogues in such heretical and persecuted quarters: *Mandeville's Travels* and the *Book of Margery Kempe* express similar laments about current Christian practices. They thus provide an important contemporary context for *Piers*, showing that its criticism is less extreme and idiosyncratic than often thought. Far from an aberrant voice crying in the wilderness of Malvern (or London), *Piers* shares with other late medieval English public writing the desire for a more authentic experience of God, participating in what Nicholas Watson has called "vernacular theology." The earnest *Book* and the entertaining *Travels*

53. The poem's first printer, Robert Crowley, believed Langland was indeed a follower of Wyclif and much recent scholarly work has dealt with his relationship to the Lollards: if most today agree that the author was essentially orthodox, he is nevertheless often taken to be something of a premature reformer. Rather than imagining Langland as some kind of Lollard, it is probably better to say, in David Lawton's phrase, that "Lollards had Langlandian sympathies" ("Lollardy," 793; cf. Hudson, *Premature Reformation*, 401).

ask many of the same questions about the state of Christendom as *Piers* and suggest some of the same remedies.

All three works were written by loyal Roman Catholics who nevertheless portray their secular and ecclesiastical leaders as wanting.[54] Margery is often dissatisfied with the clergy she meets: the inept confessor who bungles her confession at the beginning of the *Book*, the intolerant friar who bars her from attending his sermons, and the many high churchmen whose primary interest she believes to be worldly advancement.[55] Similar disappointment is expressed in the less devout *Travels*, whose preface attacks Christian lords for weakening the hold of the faith on the Holy Land because of their pride, covetousness, and envy (Defective, 4.20–23; Cotton, 2.34–3.1; Egerton, 2.13–14 [trans., 44]; not in Bodley). Later, the sultan of Jerusalem excoriates the Christian clergy: "youre prestis make no fors of Goddis service, for they schulde yeve good sample to men to do wel and thei yeveth yvel ensample" (Defective, 60.12–14; Cotton 100.22–24; Egerton, 69.7–9 [trans., 107]; Bodley, 77.9–12).[56] These sentiments are similar to criti-

---

54. The *Travels* compares exotic pagan practices with familiar Catholic ones that, it says, "we" use. For example, in an early account of Greek Orthodoxy, Sir John says, "And yf al it be so that men of the lond of Grece be cristene, yit hy varieth fro *oure* feith" (Defective, 12.18–19, my emphasis; Cotton, 13.6–7; Egerton, 9.19 [trans., 50]; Bodley, 13.8–10). Howard notes that there is "not a scrap of evidence" to suggest that Mandeville doubted that "the Church of Rome was the true church and its dogmas the true faith" (*Writers*, 69).

Margery Kempe, too, held orthodox beliefs, as she was eager to prove to anyone, secular or clerical, who dared to challenge them. When pressed on disputed issues of the day, such as the real presence and images, she shows herself to be anything but a Lollard.

55. Kempe, like Piers himself in the pardon scene, is often condescended to by the clergy, especially because she is a laywoman: "What kanst thow seyn of God?" sneers an old monk at Canterbury who wishes she were "closyd in an hows of ston" (27.28–33 [1.627–30]), and the vicar of Norwich (who later becomes a supporter), when first asked by Kempe for an hour or two after dinner to speak "in the lofe of God," replies with the superior tone of the Doctor of Divinity in *Piers* toward Patience: "What cowd a woman ocupyn an owyr or tweyn owyrs in the lofe of owyr Lord? I schal nevyr ete mete tyl I wete what ye can sey of owyr Lord God the tyme of on owyr" (38.21–28 [1.874–78]). But Kempe saves some of her sharpest criticism for high ecclesiastics. When the archbishop of York tells her that he has heard that she is a wicked woman, she stoutly replies, "Ser, so I her seyn that ye arn a wikkyd man. And yyf ye ben as wikkyd as men seyn, ye shal nevyr come in Hevyn les than ye amende yow whil ye ben her" (125.19–21 [1.2951–53]).

56. Unlike the other versions, Cotton uses the more general phrase "Cristene men" in this passage, but the context—"Yee scholde yeven ensample to the lewed peple"—makes clear that it is also referring to priests.

The sultan goes on to detail the disastrous effect of such clerical laxity on the laity, which is reminiscent of Gluttony's overindulgence instead of going to confession: "And therfore when the folk ["comownes" in Cotton] schulde gon on the holi day to chirche to serve God, thei goth to taverne to be in glotonye al day and alle night ete and drinke as bestis that witen not when thei have ynow" (Defective, 60.14–17; Cotton, 100.25–29; Egerton, 69.9–12 [trans., 107]; Bodley, 77.12–16). Anima in *Piers* makes a similar point when he says that although good clergy would make the Church a source of holiness, the result is only evil where "inparfit preesthode is, prechours and techeris" (B 15.92–95; C 16.241–45).

cisms of the learned and powerful, including bishops and rich lords, for which
Piers Plowman is so famous.[57]

More unsettling than anticlericism in all three works is the fear that
Christianity has lost its vitality. The Middle Ages has sometimes been called the
Age of Faith, but the public world of *Piers Plowman* is often only nominally
Christian, with few actually putting into practice their professed beliefs. On the
Field of Folk, some love God and their fellows, but most follow the world's
demands and their own self-interest. The sorry condition of contemporary
Christians is clear from the confession of the sins in the *visio;* even those who say
they want to do well hardly know how to begin. Gluttony's resolve to go to
church and confess his sins is easily undermined by the promise of hot spices,
and Covetise cannot be expected to make a good confession when he does not
even know what restitution means. Haukyn in the B-version may be the most
poignant example of how imperfectly ordinary laypeople live their faith. Called
the active man (and Activa Vita in C), Haukyn commits innumerable tawdry
sins that foul his baptismal coat. When Conscience and Patience offer to teach
him a more devout way (true confession and trust that the Lord will provide),
Haukyn finds it hard to take them seriously: "Thanne laughed Haukyn a litel,
and lightly gan swerye, / 'Whoso leveth you either, by Oure Lord, I leve noght
he be blessed'" (B 14.35–36). His condescending chuckle suggests how impractical and irrelevant he considers their spiritual advice: Haukyn knows some of the
vocabulary of Christianity, such as its oaths ("by Oure Lord") and the word
"blessed," but cannot follow its most central commands.

Despair over the public state of Christendom is not unique to *Piers;* it colors
both the *Travels* and the *Book.* Many go on pilgrimage with Kempe, but God is the
last thing they want to discuss at meals and they become outraged when she

57. The *Travels* also contains a letter from the Greeks who blame the Roman pope for his "grete
pruyde" and "grete covetise" (Defective, 12.32–33; Cotton, 13.22–23; Egerton, 10.2–3 [trans., 51]; Bodley,
13.23–24). Although the *Travels* is not as antipapal as the editor of the EETS edition of Cotton, Hamelius,
believed it to be, the narrator does comment that the priests at the Church of the Holy Sepulcher "knowe
not of addiciouns that many popes have maad" to the Mass (Defective, 31.26–27; Cotton, 58.30–31;
Egerton, 40.19–20 [trans., 79]); not in Bodley).

    Popes and cardinals are criticized in *Piers,* the latter being compared unfavorably to the virtues of the
same name (B pr.107; C pr.134; and B 19.414–22; C 21.413–21) and the former rarely seen as wholly positive, with the exception of Gregory. Although the narratorial "I" affirms its belief in the power of the
pope's pardon at the end of the *visio* ("Lordes forbode ellis"), good works are suggested as more reliable for
salvation (B 7.174ff.; A 8.158ff.; C 9.324ff.). Other characters in *Piers,* including the Doctor of Divinity (B
13.174–75; C 15.173–75), Haukyn (B 13.244–47), and especially the lewed vicory (B 19.432–33, C
21.431–32) make disparaging references to the papacy, though they themselves are hardly unspotted moral
exemplars.

insists on doing so.[58] Her flamboyant devotions are a frequent embarrassment to laypeople and clergy alike: they wish she were locked up or at least that she would stop going on so about spiritual matters. When Kempe tries to describe one of her revelations about the bliss of heaven, her friends (her friends!) reply, "'Why speke ye so of the myrth that is in Hevyn; ye know it not and ye have not be ther no mor than we,' and wer wroth wyth hir for sche wold not her no speke of wordly thyngys as thei dedyn and as sche dede beforntyme" (11.30–34 [1.253–55]).

Although the *Travels* is set largely in the non-Christian East, its accounts of those cultures reveal the tepid faith of the West. The sultan disputes Sir John's claim that Christians govern themselves well with a devastating account of their selfish and evil behavior. As already noted, he says that priests set bad examples and ordinary Christians act like beasts. The latter fight and deceive one another, acting contrary to Jesus' example of meekness, honesty, and charity: they prostitute "for a litel silver" their children, sisters, and wives, and "noon holdith his fey to other" (Defective, 60.17–27; Cotton, 100.30–101.7; Egerton, 69.6–19 [trans., 107–8]; Bodley, 77.19–28). The sultan insists that Christians have lost their lands to Islam because of "youre synnes"; and although acknowledging a prophecy that Christians will win the Holy Land again "when thei serve wel here God," he insists that as long as "thei lyve so foule as thei do, we have no drede of hem for here God wole not helpe hem" (Defective, 60.27–61.7; Cotton, 100.8–18; Egerton, 69.20–25 [trans., 108]; Bodley, 77.29–79.6). The promise of future Christian triumph seems very distant given this current infamy. Later, describing the suffering that Indians willingly endure for their pagan idols, Sir John notes that "a Cristene man, I trowe, durst not taken upon him the tenthe parte the peyne for love of oure lord Jhesu Crist" (Cotton, 129.23–26; Egerton, 87.21–23 [trans., 126]; Bodley, 95.16–20; Defective, 77.10–12, though vaguer).

Given such attenuated belief, does the faith have a future? Despite some hopeful prophecies of eventual success in the *Travels*, all three works give a powerful sense that Christianity's time, or at least its best time, has gone by. As befits its genre, the *Travels* expresses this decline, if not quite fall, in geographical terms.[59]

---

58. As Lynn Staley Johnson notes, late medieval English society is portrayed in the *Book* as "indifferent, if not hostile to spiritual development" ("Margery Kempe," 183).

59. The first image in the work, though not specifically religious, sets the tone. A gold apple once held in the hand of the statue of Justinian at Constantinople has fallen, symbolizing that the Eastern Emperor rules only a remnant of his former lands (Defective, 6.29–7.8; Cotton, 6.13–26; Egerton, 4.16–5.1 [trans., 46]; not in Bodley).

Christianity has literally lost ground, for Sir John is always visiting places formerly of the faith that are now pagan. It is not only Jerusalem that is lost: the Christian tide has also receded from other famous sites. Saint John's Patmos is held by the Turks (Defective, 14.26–28; Cotton, 16.5–6; Egerton, 12.56 [trans., 53]; not in Bodley); the Christian city of Tyre, where Jesus worked many miracles, has been destroyed (Defective, 18.12–15; Cotton, 20.27–30; Egerton, 15.10–12 [trans., 56]; Bodley, 23.33–25.1); and the Savior's own Nazareth is held by especially wicked and cruel Saracens (Cotton, 82.13–15; Egerton, 55.23–56.1 [trans., 94]; not in Defective or Bodley). The several lands conquered for Christianity by Constantine are noted, along with the pious hope, "when God wol," that they will be won again, but the present reality is defeat: a place where once there were "many goode holy men and holy heremytes" is now "in payems and Sarasyns hondis" (Defective, 30.28–31.4; Cotton, 57.35–58.5; Egerton, 40.3–6 [trans., 79]; Bodley, 55.24–26). Farther East, we hear in most versions that even the khans used to be Christians but have since renounced the faith (Cotton, 166.8–15; Egerton, 113.10–15 [trans., 149]; Bodley, 133.17–19; not in Defective, but see 98.9–11). The Holy Land, the center of the world according to the *Travels*, now retains only isolated physical traces of the great Christian drama of Incarnation: spots of Mary's nursing milk, for example (Defective, 24.27; Cotton, 51.35–52.2; Egerton, 36.14–15 [trans., 75]; Bodley, 51.4–8), or the left footprint made by Christ during his Ascension (Defective, 40.8–10; Cotton, 70.26–28; Egerton, 48.4–5 [trans., 87]; not in Bodley).

Holy sites or their images appear often in the *Book of Margery Kempe*, but only for Margery herself do they seem to come fully alive. Going into a church in Norwich, she sees an image of the Pietà and begins to weep and cry loudly at the thought of Christ's death on the cross and the compassion of his mother. A priest observing her remarks tartly, "Damsel, Jhesu is ded long sithyn." To which she replies, "Sir, hys deth is as fresch to me as he had deyd this same day, and so me thynkyth it awt to be to yow and to alle Cristen pepil. We awt evyr to han mende of hys kendnes and evyr thynkyn of the dolful deth that he deyd for us" (148.11–17 [1.3496–500]). For Kempe, Christ's Passion is not an ancient tale but a present reality. Yet her *Book* makes clear that the same is not true for her fellow Catholics. For many of them the faith is weak and distant, less immediate than worldly advancement or a good meal. Christianity is shown to have become routine in late medieval England. Her *Book* documents that many of her countrymen and -women, as the sultan says about Christians in general, "dispise and defoule the lawe, the which Jhesu yaf to ham for here salvacioun" (Defective, 60.26–27; Cotton, 100.6–7; Egerton, 69.19 [trans., 108]; Bodley, 77.26–28). But Kempe is a testimony that this need not be so: she speaks directly to God and enters into biblical history; the faith is alive and well to her in local churches and even on the public streets.

Kempe and Mandeville alert us to the strong sense of belatedness that also exists in *Piers Plowman*. Once, according to Anima in B, "Ellevene holy men al the world tornede / Into lele bileve"; now conversions should be easier because Christianity boasts "so manye maistres— / Preestes and prechours, and a pope above" (B 15.437–41). The sarcasm marks how far the faith has fallen. *Piers* honors Christian spiritual heroes—the apostles; the desert monks; Gregory; even the founders of two orders of friars, Francis and Dominic—but these exemplars are located in a remote past. No current champions appear, lay or clerical, except for Piers himself. Haukyn, who wishes he had died immediately after baptism because sin so constantly oppresses him, is the public face of contemporary Christendom. At least he bewails his condition, unlike the smug Doctor of Divinity at the dinner given by Conscience, who may have recently preached on temperance but now indulges in rich food and drink and scorns Patience's talk of loving one's enemies as impractical fantasy. At the end of the poem, the Barn of Unity (the Church in England) that had been built with such hope and effort is undermined from within and attacked from without.

The Worth of Other Religions

John Alford has remarked that the central question of *Piers Plowman* is one the dreamer asks Holy Church, "How may I save my soul?" ("Design," 35). Salvation is a public as well as a personal issue in the poem, involving not only the dreamer but also his fellow Catholics and others. The eternal fate of those who do not accept the faith is a persistent theme in the poem, which often discusses how non-Christians might be converted and even whether they are capable of earning divine favor on their own outside the Church. This last and most daring question, the possible salvation of righteous nonbelievers by their own efforts, has sparked some of the most interesting scholarship on *Piers*, which generally argues that the poet was influenced on this issue by elite scholastic thought. *Mandeville's Travels* and the *Book of Margery Kempe*, however, demonstrate that it is not necessary to adduce such erudite authorities, because the salvation of the heathen (and Jews and Muslims) was a familiar topic in public writing.

All three of our works take up the relatively uncontroversial matter of the conversion of those outside the Church. During Kempe's usual Good Friday devotions, she prayed not only for sinful Catholics and the souls in Purgatory, but also for "Jewys, Sarazinys, and alle fals heretikys that God for hys gret goodness schulde puttyn awey her blyndnes that thei myth thorw hys grace be turnyd to the feyth of Holy Chirche and ben children of salvacyon" (141.1–4 [1.3328–30]; see also 250.19–20 [2.717–18]). Conversions were assumed to be easier to bring about with fellow monotheists. Anima in *Piers* argues that because "Sarzens, scribes and Jewes" already have "a lippe of oure bileve," it ought to be "the lightloker" to teach them uniquely Christian doctrines such as the Trinity (B 15.500–502; C 17.252–54; cf. B 15.392).[60] The *Travels* is not quite so hopeful, because of "a hostility that borders on paranoia" toward the Jews (Higgins, *Writing East*, 81; cf. Greenblatt, "Dome," 50), but it does accept that Muslims have much in common with Christians and therefore sees the same opportunity expressed in *Piers*: "And for as myche as thei trowe nere oure fey, thei beth lightlich convertid to oure fey" (Defective, 58.24–25; Cotton, 98.30–32; Egerton, 67.25–68.2 [trans., 106]; Bodley, 73.13–15).

That believers in other traditions might be converted because they already share much with us does not, of course, deny the superiority of Christian doctrine (if not always its practice), but rather affirms it. Conscience makes this clear in the B-version when he says that if he were united with Clergy and Patience:

> "Ther nys wo in this world that we ne sholde amende,
> And conformen kynges to pees, and alle kynnes londes—
> Sarsens and Surre, and so forth alle the Jewes—
> Turne into the trewe feith and intil oon bileve."
>
> (B 13.208–11)

The true faith here, like the one belief, is, of course, Christianity and only Christianity. The dreamer/seeker had previously consoled himself by recalling that "Crist cleped us alle, come if we wolde— / Sarzens and scismatikes, and so he dide the Jewes" (B 11.119–20; C 11.55–56). Those addressed include a range of

---

60. But see Narin van Court, who argues that despite the sympathy toward Jews that scholars usually attribute to *Piers*, which is present in the B-version, the C-version was systematically revised to present them negatively.

non-Catholics, but the one who calls is Christ and his invitation is to the one, true, holy, and catholic Church.

In addition to imagining the conversion of Jews and Saracens to "our" faith, *Piers* contains a more daring conception: that non-Christians, pagans as well as monotheists, might win God's favor if they loyally followed their own particular beliefs. Thus they could achieve heaven not only by turning Christian but also by becoming their own best non-Christian selves. Answering the assertion of the narrative "I" that clerks have said that salvation is not possible "withouten Cristendom" (B 12.276), Imaginatif, after noting different kinds of baptism, ends his speech and the poem's third vision with a truly remarkable, if somewhat riddling, statement:

> "Ac truthe that trespased nevere ne traversed ayeins his lawe,
> But lyvede as his lawe taughte and leveth ther be no bettre,
> (And if ther were, he wolde amende) and in swich wille deieth—
> Ne wolde nevere trewe God but trewe truthe were allowed.
> And wher it worth or worth noght, the bileve is gret of truthe,
> And an hope hangynge therinne to have a mede for his truthe;
> For *Deus dicitur quasi dans eternam vitam suis, hoc est fidelibus.*
> *Et alibi, Si ambulauero in medio vmbre mortis . . .*
> The glose graunteth upon that vers a greet mede to truthe.
> And wit and wisdom," quod that wye, "was som tyme tresor
> To kepe with a commune—no catel was holde bettre—
> And muche murthe and manhod"—and right myd that he vanysshed.
>
> (B 12.284–95; C 14.209–14)

Scholars have often called attention to the extent to which Imaginatif here appears to be challenging conventional medieval thought that salvation is possible only within the Church.[61] Indeed, the C-version concludes the passage with a

---

61. Chambers argued that the poet's attempts to resolve his liberal views on the salvation of non-Christians with the harsher official position of the Church accounts for a fifteen-year gap between the A and B versions (see *Man's Unconquerable Mind*, 129–49). Frank called Imaginatif's position a "daring hope" (*Scheme*, 65) and noted, in contrast to such as Dunning ("Salvation"), that the passage is unusual in claiming that the righteous heathen are saved not by knowing the principles of Christian faith through divine inspiration but by adhering to the best faith they know (65n). In a careful analysis of the end of Imaginatif's speech in B, Whately argues that its ideas may derive from Thomas Aquinas and Nicholas of Lyra's concept that just pre-Christians could be saved by their "implicit" faith (minimal but sufficient) in redemption, but Whatley does admit that Imaginatif is unorthodox is applying the same dispensation to

different biblical quotation and an explicit acknowledgment that its argument may contradict clerical teaching:

> "*Quia super pauca fuisti fidelis* . . .
> And that is love and large huyre, yf the lord be trewe,
> And a cortesye more then covenant was, what so clerkes carpe!
> For al worth as God wol"—and therwith he vanschede.
>
> (c 14.214A–17)

But Imaginatif's own words go far beyond the usual medieval wish for conversion to suggest that God will reward nonbelievers for adhering to their own "truthe," as long as it is the best law available to them. The idea is presented in *Piers* only as the hope of a single (albeit important) character, but the insistent repetition of the key term *truth* implies, though it is not necessarily the poet's own position, that Imaginatif thinks that God would have to be false to himself not to reward such fidelity.

Scholars have sought to identify the sources of such a bold concept. Some have pointed to the extreme (and censured) argument of Uthred of Boldon that immediately before death all humans are given a moment of clear vision (*clara visio*) during which they may accept or reject God and thus determine their eternal fate (Frank, *Scheme*, 65n).[62] The most thorough treatment of the issue is by Janet Coleman (*Moderni*, 108–46). She cites advanced theologians such as Ockham and his followers, known as the *moderni*, who argued that grace might be offered by God to those who followed the best doctrine they knew (*facit quod in se est*), even if it was a non-Christian creed (119). Coleman asserts that this was a radical and rare concept, which she finds moderated in the C-version (142): "[T]he *modern* theologians were the only orthodox thinkers to postulate the *possibility* of salvation outside the Church" (186, her emphasis).

But the *Book* and especially the *Travels* contain ideas similar to those in *Piers*, demonstrating that these views were entertained by others besides elite academ-

---

post-Christian heathens ("*Piers Plowman* B 12.277–94," esp. 8–10; see also Whatley, "Uses of Hagiography," esp. 54–55). Much recent discussion had been on the opposition of faith to works; see Vitto, *Virtuous Pagan*, 62–63n. For the argument that Langland is less daring than I claim, see D. Baker, "Dialectic Form," esp. 272; and Minnis, "Looking." For a different discussion of the end, see Schmidt, "Covenant."

62. Russell also thought that Uthred was Langland's source, supporting his arguments with reference to revisions in the C-version ("Salvation").

ics. In this as elsewhere, the poem is more in accord with the general public culture than is often acknowledged. Nicholas Watson, in one of the few discussions
that includes all three of our works (along with others), has recently argued that
each presents what he calls a "vernacular theology" of universal salvation.
Watson's thesis is important but conflates two distinct ideas about salvation.
The first, an appeal to mercy, hopes that all humans will somehow be saved
regardless of their sins (as famously suggested by Julian of Norwich), whereas
the second, an appeal to justice, posits the possibility that non-Christians may
obtain salvation as a reward for faithful adherence to their own laws. Watson is
most interested in the first position and cites Christ's speech during the
Harrowing of Hell as the point at which "Langland can thus at last set out
explicitly his hope that all will finally be saved" ("Visions of Inclusion," 158). I
have already shown in the previous chapter the difficulty with accepting Christ's
words here as unproblematic, given their contrast with earlier demands in *Piers*
for some kind of human action to merit salvation and the pessimism of the
poem's final two passus. Universal salvation is a difficult concept for *Piers* to
accept or even to define (as it is difficult for Julian of Norwich); yet in both
works Christ hints at this possibility, though in neither it is made explicit how it
might be achieved. The most direct appeal for universal salvation is in Kempe's
Book, but, in contrast to *Piers* and Julian, Christ is firmly opposed. Kempe tells
her Savior that she cannot conceive of sinners "departyd fro thi gloryows face
wythowtyn ende" (141.25–26 [1.3343–44]), and therefore she prays that they
will receive the grace that she has been granted. But when Kempe refuses to
accept the reality of damnation, her stubbornness is punished with obscene
visions until she relents (chapter 59).

    If universal salvation was an open question in the public culture (what
Watson would call the vernacular culture) of late medieval England, that culture
may have been more willing to accept the equally radical idea of non-Christians
earning salvation. Not salvation for all, perhaps, but salvation for those who faith-
fully obey their own laws. Kempe rarely concerns herself with the spirituality of
non-Christians (though she has good things to say about the Muslims she meets
in the Holy Land), and thus for her any salvation outside the Church would presumably take the form of the public Christianity I shall discuss in the following
section of this chapter. The *Travels*, however, like *Piers*, has positive things to say
about those non-Christians who do their best (always excepting the Jews in the
Travels). Not only are the monotheist Saracens "trewe, for thei kepith wel the

comaundementis of here *Alkaron,* whiche God sente to hem by his messyngere Macomet" (Defective, 61.21–22; Cotton, 102.5–7; Egerton, 70.10–11 [trans., 108]; not in Bodley), but equally admirable are a variety of Eastern religions with no relationship whatsoever to the people of the Book.[63]

The most explicit argument that pagans may earn salvation by their own efforts is prompted by some followers of the Brahmins near the end of the *Travels*: "And yf al it be so that thei haveth not the artyclis of oure feith, nevertheles I trowe that God loves theyme well fore theire good entencioun and that he takes theire servyce to gree as he was of Job, whiche was a peynym whom he held for his trewe servaunt, and many other also" (Defective, 126.27–31; Cotton, 214.10–14; Egerton, 146.8–11 [trans., 180]; not in Bodley). This is followed by an assertion that closely echoes Imaginatif's hope: "I trowe that God loveth wel al these that loveth hym and serveth hym mekeliche and trewliche and that dispiseth veynglorye of the world as these men doth and as Job dide" (Defective, 126.31–33; Cotton, 214.14–18; Egerton, 146.11–13 [trans., 180]; not in Bodley).[64] Salvation is not necessarily universal or automatic; it must be earned by loving God and serving him "trewliche" or, as Cotton says, "in trouthe" (forms of the word—*truth*—repeatedly used by Imaginatif), but it appears to be achievable outside the Church: the *Travels* cites a vision of Saint Peter that is interpreted to mean that "that men schulde noght have many men in dispyt for their dyverse

63. The *Travels* contains long, detailed accounts of other religions that have no parallel in *Piers,* but its tolerance toward non-Christians is not automatic. Some pagan societies in the *Travels,* such as the Bedouin, are strongly censured as nasty and brutish (Defective, 23.1–2; Cotton, 47.7–8; Egerton, 33.8 [trans., 72]; Bodley, 45.11). Sir John is also less than reverent toward Muhammad, for he twice repeats the story that the prophet killed a holy hermit while drunk (Defective, 27.3–5, 62.21–63.9; Cotton, 52.12–14, 103.5–22; Egerton, 36.20–21, 70.28–71.11 [trans., 75, 109]; Bodley, 51.14–17, which omits the second version of the story), and he says that the prophet falsely attributed his fits of epilepsy to ecstasy while speaking with the angel Gabriel (Defective, 62.8–13; Cotton, 102.24–31; Egerton, 70.21–24 [trans., 109; not in Bodley). Of course, *Piers* accuses the prophet of even more spectacular fraud (B 15.398–410; C 17.165–82). Kohanski notes that "the voice of tolerance" in the *Travels* "does not completely eclipse the voice of the xenophobe" (*Unchartered Territory,* 197; see also Brandser, "*Mandeville's Travels*").

64. The boldness of Sir John's praise of pagan piety and his claim that it may win God's favor seems to have disconcerted some of the medieval redactors of the *Travels,* causing them to modify or eliminate its most generous passages (Higgins, *Writing East,* 234–38). Nevertheless, most of the English versions, including Cotton, Egerton, and the widely distributed Defective, follow the early French versions in presenting the case for the salvation of the heathen by their own merits (but note the omissions in Bodley just cited). Higgins asserts that belief in such salvation was not "an entirely unorthodox position" (*Writing East,* 232, see 224–34), and Thomas Hahn, who examined attitudes among theologians and in the Alexander romances toward the reputed good pagans of India, concludes that the "most striking and the most influential vision of the Indians as virtuous heathen in late medieval Europe occurs in *Mandeville's Travels*" ("Indians East and West, 80; cf. also Hahn, "Indian Tradition").

lawis, for we wote not whom God loveth ne whom he hatith" (Defective, 127.10–13; Cotton, 214.31–33; Egerton, 146.20–22 [trans., 180]; not in Bodley).

The significance of this for *Piers Plowman* is that it shows that the poet, and even more important, his readers, need not have been advanced theologians to be familiar with such nonstandard ideas, for they are also found in a widely known piece of vernacular writing, an entertaining travel book no less. One of the most audacious conceptions in *Piers* had permeated the general culture. Imaginatif's questioning of the Church's monopoly on salvation did not keep *Piers* from being widely read in England (by clerks and laypeople alike), just as the even more direct challenge in the *Travels* coexisted with an enormous readership throughout Europe. Daring ideas about alternatives to Christianity that were still worrying Continental inquisitors two centuries later are expressed in the public writing of late medieval England.[65]

A More Accessible Religion

Piers Plowman, Mandeville's Travels, and the *Book of Margery Kempe* are each pessimistic about the current state of Christianity and open to the possibility that salvation might be available outside the Church. In addition, the three make gestures toward a common religion for all that embodies the essence of Christianity without its institutional abuses or factional disputes. Each work in its own way attempts to imagine a faith that supplements but is not directly hostile (in contrast to Lollardy) to the established Church: a faith that brings the sacred into ordinary human activities, thus anticipating the later *devotio moderna.* The spirituality they imagine is inclusive and available to rich and poor, learned and uneducated, male and female, lay and cleric, Catholic and non-Catholic.

In the *Book of Margery Kempe* the search for an accessible religion expresses itself in a piety that finds the holy in the commonplace and everyday.[66] For despite its concern with religious issues and ecclesiastic practice, the *Book of Margery Kempe,* like *Piers Plowman,* never entirely leaves the concerns of the normal secular world. Margery repeatedly identifies herself as the wife of a respectable townsman of

65. For the trouble one man caused himself by following Sir John's views on this issue, see Carlo Ginsburg, "Cheese," 41ff. For an extreme argument that Mandeville is always very pro-Christian and shares the negative attitudes toward other peoples that later led to European colonization, see Brandser, "*Mandeville's Travels.*"

66. Beckwith refers to the "powerful and polemical claim for lay piety" made by Kempe ("Problems," 193).

Lynn, just as major figures in the poem such as Haukyn and Piers are married workingmen.

The importance in *Piers* of imagery that is associated with secular clothing and especially food and drink has often been discussed by critics.[67] Kempe's *Book* offers a later example of public writing in which these material necessities of daily life (see B 1.17–22; A 1.17–22; C 1.17–22) are used to approach the sacred in ways beyond the control of the institutional Church. Kempe scandalized many by wearing white clothes, as if she, a married mother of fourteen, were a virgin or a nun. As the archbishop of York says, "Why gost thu in white? Art thu a mayden?" (124.15 [1.2923]). In her younger days, Margery had worn showy, expensive clothes to attract attention (9.9–18 [1.190–96]), and now these white garments publicly proclaim to all her new religious vocation, which is not ordained by the Church (though she seeks episcopal endorsement for it), but at the explicit direction of Christ. *Piers,* unsurprisingly, often uses secular clothing to make a negative point: examples include Meed's extravagant dress (which the unreformed Margery might have envied) and the threadbare cloak of Covetise, which is scorned even by lice. But secular clothing can also have positive spiritual significance in the poem. For instance, Christ's decision, like that of many an Arthurian knight, to joust in another's armor (the body of Piers), not only points to the mystery of the Incarnation but also suggests that even an ordinary layperson may be of value to the divine and play a part in the Redemption.

In the Middle Ages, as now, food and drink, in the form of bread and wine, was transformed by priests (and only priests) into the body and blood of Christ. Margery Kempe was eager for this sanctioned sustenance (receiving the Eucharist more frequently than did most of her contemporaries), but she also often uses ordinary food and drink as if they were (or could be) part of a holy ritual. For her they become what might be called secular sacraments, not undertaken in opposition to the Church, but as supplementary devotions available in ordinary life. As others have noted, people often reveal themselves to be good by inviting Kempe to share a meal with them (see Siegmund-Schultze, "Some Remarks," 335). Her reconciliation with a former supporter, the Carmelite Friar Alayn of Lynn also occurs over dinner, one "of gret joy and gladnes, meche mor gostly than bodily, for it was sawcyd and sawryd wyth talys of Holy Scriptur"

---

67. See, for example, Kirk, *Dream Thought,* 197–98; Mann, "Eating and Drinking"; Schmidt, "Structural Imagery."

(170.21–23 [1.4039–40]). The famous scene during which Margery finally gets her husband, John, to agree to a chaste marriage opens with mention of a bottle of beer and cake they are carrying on their journey from York. These are more than merely particularizing details, for the episode ends with husband and wife consuming that food and drink at a roadside cross to celebrate their new status, as if the beer and cake had been transformed into their own particular communion meal: "knelyng undyr a cros, and sythen thei etyn and dronkyn togedyr in gret gladnes of spyryt" (25.17–18 [1.574–75]).

In *Piers Plowman*, food and drink are often misused, as by Gluttony in the tavern, or by those who amuse themselves at meals with ribald stories or vain theological speculation while ignoring the starving poor: those who drivel on with "hir guttes fullen," while outside stand the hungry (B 10.56–59; A 11.43–46; C 11.40–43). But food is also recognized in the poem as both necessary to life on earth and capable of taking on spiritual meaning. Bishops are told by Anima in the B-version to provide their flocks with "bodily foode" as well as "gostly foode" (B 15.575). Piers diverts his pilgrimage to try to provide the first kind by plowing the half acre, just as the Samaritan pays for the keep of the man he finds bleeding along the road. But ghostly food is also required, and the Samaritan observes that the wounded man will not be truly healed until he has been baptized in the blood of a "barn born of a mayde" and that he will only become strong after "he have eten al the barn and his blood ydronke" (B 17.94–98; C 19.86–90). The culmination of the food-and-drink imagery in *Piers*, which involves the laity more radically even than Kempe's sacramental secular meals, is the human Eucharist suggested during the Harrowing of Hell. Instead of mortals partaking of God's body and blood administered by the Church, human redemption is described as Christ's physical appetite *for us*. Declaring that love is his drink, he says that after his fight on the cross he still thirsts "for mannes soule sake," with a thirst that will not be slacked until the Day of Judgment (B 18.368–71; C 20.403–12). The C-text even more explicitly describes a communion that is not mediated by clerics but comes directly from a divine craving for common humanity: "Ac I wol drynke of no dische ne of deep clergyse, / Bote of comune coppes, alle Cristene soules" (C 20.405–6).[68]

Margery Kempe's most flamboyant religious devotion (and the source of much of the suspicion about her sincerity) is her weeping, sobbing, and even

---

68. A comparable image of Christ's physical hunger for humans is presented by Holy Church earlier in the poem during the sublime plant of peace passage (B 1.153–55; C 1.148–51).

roaring, especially when thinking of Christ's Passion. Such affective piety was encouraged by the late medieval Church, but Kempe takes it to melodramatic extremes and performs it in spaces that are public as well as private, secular as well as sacred: "so as God wolde visiten hir, sumtyme in the cherch, sumtyme in the strete, sumtym in the chawmbre, sumtyme in the felde" (69.14–16 [1.1594–95]). Although many individual clerics approve of her public weeping, the authority she claims for it is no church official but instead Christ himself, who tells her that tears of compunction, compassion, and devotion are his highest gifts on earth and most torment the Devil.

Weeping was commonly associated with female devotion, in part because it did not require official sanction, Latin education, or clerical status. It has rarely been discussed in relation to *Piers Plowman*, whose intellectual tone seems to have little in common with the tears so extravagantly shed by Kempe. Reading the *Book* with *Piers*, however, reveals that key moments in the poem are associated with this accessible devotion. Langland's account of the Crucifixion, for instance, emphasizes the blind knight Longinus, who pierced Christ's side on the cross. When Longinus realizes what he has done, we are told, he fell to his knees, begged for mercy, "and right with that he wepte" (B 18.91; C 20.94). Longinus's tears instantly bring him the salvation that is open to all who sincerely turn to God and repent, whether or not they are supported by the Christian clergy. Weeping is also the devotion that other important secular characters in the poem rely on when the Church fails them. After the pardon from Truth is challenged by a priest, Piers in the B-version announces a new spiritual life in which he will work less, pray more, and "wepen whan I sholde slepe" (B 7.121). Haukyn, the very model of the ordinary layman, is last seen weeping and wailing for his sins, as passionately as ever did Margery (B 14.332). Tears also mark significant moments for the narrative "I." He weeps in response to Repentance before the confession of sins (B 5.61; A 5.44; C 6.2), at the beginning of his first inner dream (B 11.4; C 11.166), and in response to sin's power to prevent God's mercy (B 16.272; C 18.289). The corruption of Holy Church at the end of the poem is clear when the evil friar causes Contrition to forget to cry and weep for his wicked works (B 20.370; C 22.370).[69] *Piers Plowman* is not as lachrymose as the *Book of Margery Kempe*, but it depicts tears as a devout and saving practice for the laity.

---

69. The Barn of Unity is protected by a moat full of repentant tears (B 19.381–82; C 21.380–81).

Whereas the *Book of Margery Kempe* describes the spiritualizing of secular life without ecclesiastic mediation, *Mandeville's Travels* suggests the value of a plain faith based on simple devotion and good deeds.[70] These attempts to imagine a more accessible religion suggest some of the ways in which belief and practice could be rethought in late medieval public writing and can help readers recognize and better understand similar ideas in *Piers Plowman*. One of the most admirable rulers in the *Travels* is the legendary Prester John, the priest-emperor of a sect of Christians who "haveth not alle the articlis of oure fey," but who nevertheless believe in the Trinity and are "right devoute and trewe everichon to other" (Defective, 115.10–13; Cotton, 197.1–5; Egerton, 134.14–16 [trans., 168]; Bodley, 99.25). What price orthodoxy, if, as we have seen the sultan charge, it fosters pride, covetousness, and envy, whereas those who lack it are devout to God and true to one another? The *Travels* reserves its greatest praise for the pagan Brahmins and some of their local followers, who exist in an almost Edenic state of grace: those on one island go naked and live, as the Egerton text puts it, "innocently in lewtee and in luffe and charitee" (Egerton, 145.21 [trans., 179]). Being "goode men and trewe and of good feye and lyf," they follow natural law: "And yf al thei be not cristen, yit by lawe of kynde thei beth ful of good vertues" (Defective, 125.2–3; Cotton, 211.2–5; Egerton, 144.1–3 [trans., 178]; Bodley, 111.28–113.1). The subsequent account of how the Brahmins keep the Ten Commandments and avoid deadly sin indicates that they have achieved Christ's two great commandments (to love God and to love one's neighbor) without the help of either the Church or Revelation. Although the followers of the Brahmins do not have "the artyclis of oure feith," Sir John insists that they are nevertheless loved by God for "theire good entencioun" (and for "hire gode feyth naturelle" according to Cotton) and God is pleased with their service as he was with that of "Job, whiche was a peynym" (Defective, 126.27–30; Cotton, 214.10–14; Egerton, 146.11–13 [trans., 180]; not in Bodley).

Piers Plowman is more pessimistic about the ability of any human group to be wholly acceptable to God. Set in a known (and known to be imperfect) England instead of in the distant (and idealizable) East, *Piers* portrays no actually existing ideal societies. Nevertheless, suggestions of a natural and simplified religion not unlike that of the Brahmins (the basic values of Christianity without its rigidity or clerical monopoly) are found throughout *Piers*, although these may be over-

70. In contrast, there are few works of corporeal mercy in the *Book of Margery Kempe*: Kempe's taking care of an old woman in Rome for six weeks and her husband in his dotage are the principal examples.

looked by readers because of the poem's intense engagement with questions of Christian doctrine. Holy Church herself suggests such a simple religion in her surprisingly open and nonsectarian definition of who is "a god by the Gospel" and "ylik to Oure Lord": it is "whoso is trewe of his tonge and telleth noon oother, / And dooth the werkes therwith and wilneth no man ille" (B 1.88–91; A 1.86–89; C 1.84–87; see Galloway, "Two Notes"). She declares that this is a standard available to all, "For Cristen and uncristen cleymeth it echone" (B 1.93; A 1.91; C 1.89). Such an unembellished religion resembles that practiced by Piers the plowman himself. Although a dutiful son of the Church, he announces himself a follower of Truth rather than a traveler to Christian shrines. His refusal to accede to clerical authority prompts the dispute with the priest at the end of the *visio* in A and B. This priest is scornful of Piers because he lacks Christian ordination and the ecclesiastical sanction to teach (B 7.135–36; A 8.122–23), but the pardon they argue over makes the simple (if demanding) claim that salvation depends on doing well, a promise apparently available to Christians of all ranks—and to non-Christians as well. As seen earlier during the formal confessions, the sins do not lack Christian teaching (often they know it perfectly well or are even clerics); rather they are without the natural piety toward God and decency toward fellow humans practiced by Mandeville's good pagans (and Piers). The poem expresses the same admiration found in the *Travels* for honest faith and good deeds, what the emperor Trajan calls "my lyvynge in truthe" (B 11.151).[71]

The virtues of the Brahmin followers that are listed in the Egerton text of the *Travels*—"lewtee," love, and charity (145.21 [trans., 179])—are precisely those central to *Piers*. The poem repeatedly associates holiness not with vain clerical figures like the Doctor of Divinity but with those like Patience who preach and then practice a simpler, nonsectarian way: "'*disce*,' quod he, '*doce*; *dilige inimicos* [*Deum* in C]'" (B 13.137; C 15.142). Throughout the poem we meet many who, like Mandeville's Brahmins, are naturally pleasing to God, including the poor, who are described as his minstrels (B 13.440; C 7.99). These stand in stark contrast to the friars, whose claims to Christian learning are not matched by their actions. The Samaritan, an image of Christ (though himself neither Christian

71. For a discussion of the "salvific power of ethical behavior" by non-Christians, with special reference to Trajan in *Piers*, see Grady, "Rule of Exceptional Salvation." See also Whatley: "Langland's conception of Christianity is at bottom ethical and social rather than sacramental or mystical" ("*Piers Plowman* B 12.277–94," 11).

nor Jew), demonstrates by his care for the man wounded by robbers that same natural righteousness Sir John finds in the best pagans. In *Piers* (as opposed to the *Travels*) no human society long sustains such values, as seen in the failures of the half acre and later of the Barn of Unity, but the poem nevertheless represents them as an ideal, as in the exemplary, if unreachable, social behavior imagined by Reason and Conscience (e.g., B 3.284–330; A 3.260–76; C 3.436–82; and B 4.113–33; A 4.100–116; C 4.108–30) or the long discussion of patient poverty in the *vita*.[72] If no paradise like the land of the Brahmins is discovered in *Piers*, the poem nevertheless ends with Conscience setting off once again in hopes someday to "have" Piers the plowman (B 20.386; C 22.386).

72. *Piers Plowman* is not finally as optimistic about the practical success of this natural religion as is the *Travels*, perhaps because it remains at home. Even Sir John cannot find an ideal community in Europe, only in remotest Asia.

5. Public Art

PARISH WALL PAINTINGS

I. MURALS IN THE PARISH
Parish Churches

In medieval Europe no space was more public than the parish church. Men, women, and children of all estates and levels of education came there for a range of common activities. First of all, they gathered for worship and prayer: as Margery Kempe's *Book* makes clear, the parish in the late Middle Ages was "the unrivalled centre of local religious life" (Kümin, "English Parish," 30), an institution that remained vigorous in England until (and indeed after) Henry VIII's secession from the Roman Church.[1] The parish was also the site of other public endeavors, especially in rural areas. In addition to housing Christ's body in the form of consecrated bread and wine, it might hold the village's fire-fighting equipment (Pounds, *History*, 466). Often "the only strongly built masonry structure in the parish," the church was where "parishioners were accustomed to store their few goods of value" and to which they "were likely to resort . . . in time of danger" (284). Medieval parish churches were "multi-purpose public buildings" that blurred modern distinctions between secular and ecclesiastical use (Kümin, "English Parish," 23).

Of course the effects of hierarchy and status were not left outside at the church porch. Social privilege shaped the parish as surely as it did all other areas of medieval life. Male clerics alone were allowed to celebrate Mass, rich laity erected private chantries and family chapels, and ordinary worshipers, like Chaucer's Wife of Bath, strove to take precedence in presenting their offerings.

---

1. See especially Duffy, *Stripping*; Pounds, *History*; and the individual essays in the collection edited by French, Gibbs, and Kümin, *The Parish in English Life, 1400–1600*. Duffy insists that, despite some privatizing trends, especially among the aristocracy and higher gentry, "the overwhelming impression left by the sources for late medieval religion in England is that of a Christianity resolutely and enthusiastically oriented towards the public and the corporate, and of a continuing sense of the value of cooperation and mutuality in seeking salvation" (*Stripping*, 131). Duffy sees the "Henrician religious revolution" (379) as a devastating attack on traditional religion, but others stress the continuity of parish life across this divide.

But if the parish did not erase traditional social divisions, it nevertheless permit-ted interaction and cooperation between different groups. The parish was the focus of such communal activity as the upkeep of roads and bridges, mainte-nance of law and order through the parish constable, and support for the infirm and indigent (Pounds, *History*, 4).[2]

In words that suggest Habermas's public sphere, French describes the local parish as "a meaningful forum for collective action" (French, "Fund-Raising," 115), and Kümin refers to the "self-governing parish community of the later Middle Ages," whose offices were held by peasants as well as by the gentry, thus offering even humble members an "unusual degree of responsibility and political power" ("English Parish," 24, 30). It was the laity, not the clergy, for instance, who were responsible for maintaining the church nave, as well as providing a "staggering list of objects" that were needed for the conduct of worship, from the missal itself to ropes for the tower bells (Duffy, *Stripping*, 133; cf. the decree in Shinners and Dohar, *Pastors*, 219–20). These obligations were met by the generos-ity of individual donors, but also by communal fund-raising, through such events as church ales and other moneymaking festivities (French, "Fund-Raising").

Parish Art

In addition to fostering cooperative social activities, the English parish church was a visual public space displaying the central images of Christianity. Today, surviving medieval church buildings are often quite plain: their clear windows and unplastered or whitewashed walls relieved only by needlepoint cushions on the pews or a few children's drawings in a corner. But colorful images of all kinds once filled medieval Catholic churches, as they still do in many parts of the world. Even a modest parish might have several wall paintings and statues (often clothed and even bejeweled), and perhaps some expensive stained glass. These images did more than merely decorate the church (although the word *image* in Middle English often refers specifically to carved figures, it could have the broader modern meaning that I shall use here). As Margaret Aston has shown, "The image was not peripheral to medieval Christianity. It was a central means for the individual to establish contact with God" (*England's Iconoclasts*,

---

2. In the introduction to *The Parish in English Life*, French, Gibbs, and Kümin note that the parish was the site of many common social efforts: "Poor relief, religious worship, neighbourhood and village celebra-tions, the collection of taxes, and a myriad of cultural interactions and negotiations were all organized and conducted within this fundamental unit" (3).

1:20). So intense was this relationship, that images became a special target of Lollards and then Protestants, and even orthodox writers were careful to distinguish their proper use (as educational and devotional signs) from their abuse (when worshipped for themselves).

Church art would have a special meaning for those unable to follow the Mass in Latin, and Pope Gregory I's claim that images are books for the illiterate was frequently cited in the Middle Ages.[3] But the visual was not used only by the uneducated. As Lawrence Duggan and others have shown, pictures cannot be "read" like books, because the two media do not communicate in the same way or with the same preci-sion (Duggan, "Art," esp. 242–44). Images can remind us of what we already know but, unlike writing, they are usually incomprehensible to those who have not previously been told their meaning, as the pilgrims in the *Tale of Beryn*, an anonymous continuation of Chaucer's *Canterbury Tales*, demonstrate while trying (and comically failing) to decode the stained-glass windows of Canterbury Cathedral. The Gregorian dichotomy between writing for the literate and images for the illiterate dissolves in medieval practice. Images were used at all levels of education and were as prevalent (if often more sophisticated) in cathedrals and monasteries as in parish churches.

Two other familiar medieval defenses for images are more relevant here: visual art was said both to aid the memory and to move the will. The Middle English *Dives and Pauper*, for instance, states that, in addition to being books for the lewed, images were ordained "to steryn manys mende to thynkyn of Cristys incarnacioun and of his passioun and of holye seyntys lyvys" as well as "to steryn mannys affeccioun and his herte to devocioun, for often man is more steryd be syghte than be heryng or redyngge" (1:82).[4] At the end of the Middle Ages, Bishop Reginald Pecock, in his *Repressor*, argues that humans need not only the "heereable rememoratiif signes" of Scripture and other devotional writing, but also visual "seable rememoratiif signes" (1:209), because sight "schewith and bringith into the ymaginacioun

---

3. "What writing (*scriptura*) does for the literate, a picture does for the illiterate looking at it, because the ignorant see in it what they ought to do; those who do not know letters read in it" (Gregory, as translated in L. Duggan, "Art," 227; cf. Camille, "Seeing and Reading," 26).

4. See Aston, "Lollards and Images." Saint Bonaventure also made similar arguments: images (*a*) are for the uneducated, but they also (*b*) arouse the emotions better than what is heard and (*c*) aid the memory (Binski, *Medieval Craftsmen* 35). Rosemary Woolf notes that Aquinas followed Aristotle in arguing for sight as the highest of the senses, asserting that what is seen by the eye excites more devotion than what is heard by the ear (*English Mystery Plays*, 88–89). For other contemporary defenses of images, see Owst, *Literature and Pulpit*, 137–48.

and into the mynde . . . of a man myche mater and long mater sooner, and with lasse labour and traveil and peine, than the heering of the eere doth" (1:212–13).

Wall Paintings

Among the many kinds of images that once adorned English parish churches, wall paintings tend to be neglected by cultural historians, though from the Norman Invasion to the Reformation they were the most popular form of ecclesiastical art.[5] Occasionally done in oil (as at South Newington, Oxfordshire), most English murals were executed in a limited number of earth tones derived from iron oxides, though clever mixing could produce a significant range of color.[6] If overlooked by modern scholars in favor of other parish media, wall paintings were the primary decoration of local churches—large and small, rural and urban. Wall paintings were cheaper than tapestry, colored window glass, or sculpture, and thus could be afforded even by poor parishes.[7] As one of the pioneers in this field declares: "It must be realized that all medieval churches in England were more or less completely painted. Not all had many figure subjects but most had some" (Rouse, *Wall Paintings*, 9). The current authority, David Park, echoes this judgment: "Mural painting was the most usual form of interior ornament, frequently covering every available surface" ("Wall Painting," 125). Hardham in Sussex is a rare surviving example of a fully painted church. Its twelfth-century murals, including narrative sequences of the Nativity, Saint George, and Adam and Eve, cover the entire nave and chancel.[8]

---

5. For instance, in a major article on parish piety in East Anglia, Duffy focuses almost exclusively on rood-screen painting, mentioning wall paintings only in passing ("Parish, Piety, and Patronage"). For evidence that wall paintings are beginning to attract more attention from medieval scholars, see the second chapter ("The Aesthetics of Suffering") in E. Ross, *Grief of God*, esp. 53–65.

The great period of English murals was between the twelfth and sixteenth centuries. There were Anglo-Saxon murals, but few survive. Perhaps the best extant example are the angels, once apparently part of a Christ in Majesty, at Nether Wallop, Hampshire (see Gem and Tudor-Craig, "'Winchester School'"). For this and other early paintings, see the introduction and essays in Cather, Park, and Williamson, *Medieval Wall Paintings*.

6. Lime white and charcoal black also made up the palette. Other colors, such as vermilion and blue, were expensive and rare. It used to be believed that twelfth-century England murals were genuine fresco (painting done on wet plaster to which the pigment bonded), but it now appears that this may not be so. Certainly almost all murals in the thirteenth through sixteenth centuries were done in the so-called *secco* technique, by which paint is applied onto plaster after it has dried. For the techniques of wall paintings, see Tristram, *Thirteenth*, 395–410; Caiger-Smith, *Mural Paintings*, 118–28; Rouse, *Wall Paintings*, 23–25; Babington, Manning, and Stewart, *Painted Past*, 15–20.

7. We know little about who created the murals in medieval parish churches, though it seems likely that most were painted by itinerant lay craftsmen (Park, "'Lewes Group,'" 233).

8. See Park, "'Lewis Group'"; Park has also produced a superb church guide for Hardham.

The ample wall surface available for painting, especially in older churches with few windows, meant that murals were not only more abundant than other kinds of parish art but also more diverse. The north and south walls and aisle pillars of the nave at Little Witchingham, Norfolk, for instance, have extensive remains of a Passion cycle as well as paintings of saints, foliage, and symbols of the Four Evangelists (Tudor-Craig, "Painting," 41, 43). Parish rood screens typically display a row of saintly portraits, but wall paintings also contained many other forms, including allegorical moralities, biblical stories, and abstract designs. The most ambitious schemes, including multilevel representations of the Last Judgment or the Seven Deadly Sins, have a monumentality rarely found in stained glass. And unlike statues, wall paintings are often strongly narrative, with multipaneled depictions of the life of Christ, the Virgin, and other holy men and women. Mural images proliferated in English parishes. New ones were added to those already there, and others were painted over old ones. The church at Willingham, Cambridgeshire, contains six layers of painting from the thirteenth to the seventeenth centuries (44).

The variety and ubiquity of English parish wall paintings make them especially valuable examples of public art. Their past neglect by many scholars, which this chapter is in part an attempt to remedy, is not surprising when we consider how few remain from a once vast inventory and in what poor shape most of those now are. Yet parish murals have survived better than the ambitious wall paintings that once decorated royal palaces, cathedrals, and monasteries in England. Those elite works for select audiences are now almost entirely gone except for a few tantalizing examples to suggest the masterpieces we have lost.[9] A beautiful twelfth-century Saint Paul can still be seen in Saint Anselm's Chapel at Canterbury Cathedral, for example, as can a striking thirteenth-century Wheel of Fortune in the choir of Rochester Cathedral.[10] None of the many wall paint-

9. Praising the thirteenth-century murals in the monastery at Horsham Saint Faith, Norfolk, in comparison to drawings by Matthew Paris, Park observes: "That relatively provincial wall paintings can surpass contemporary manuscripts produced at a leading English abbey with close Court connections, reminds us that the relative importance and innovation of wall paintings is consistently undervalued, particularly with respect to perfectly preserved manuscripts" ("Wall Painting," 127).

10. For the Paul image, see Rouse, *Wall Paintings*, illustration 19; for the Wheel of Fortune at Rochester, see Borenius and Tristram, *English Medieval Painting*, plate 38. For other mural remains in cathedrals, see especially the articles by Park ("Wall Paintings of Holy Sepulchre") and Park and Welford on Winchester ("Medieval Polychromy"), and by Park ("Simony and Sanctity") and Park and Howard ("Medieval Polychromy") on Norwich. Perhaps the most accessible monastic examples of wall painting, now under the care of English Heritage, are the powerful Italianate Last Judgment fragments and intricate Flemish Apocalypse sequence in the Chapter House of Westminster Abbey, both from the late fourteenth century. See Tristram, *Fourteenth*, 201–6; Turner, "Patronage"; and, most recently, Babington, Manning, and Stewart, *Painted Past*, 30–32, in which they call these paintings "equal to anything painted in Europe at the time" (10).

ings that Henry III commissioned are extant (Park, "Wall Painting," 127–28; Borenius, "Cycle"; Dixon-Smith, "Image and Reality"), and only scraps from the fourteenth-century royal work at Saint Stephen's Chapel in the Palace of Westminster, "the most ambitious decorative programme of the century" (Park, "Wall Painting," 129).[11] The murals that once decorated private residences in England have also largely disappeared. A remarkable exception is the series at Longthorpe Tower, a modest knight's home near Peterborough (Babington, Manning, and Stewart, *Painted Past*, 58–59; Rouse and Baker, "Wall Paintings").

Parish churches, especially those not extensively remolded, hold most of the surviving wall paintings of the English Middle Ages, but the loss of even these is so heavy that systematic study is difficult. After the Crown took control of the English Church, an order in Council in 1547 called for the "obliteration and destruction of popish and superstitious books and images, so that the memory of them shall not remain in their churches and houses" (cited in Rouse, *Wall Paintings*, 71). The reigns of Edward VI and Elizabeth I in particular saw the forcible removal of Catholic images from parishes, as iconoclasts were encouraged (and church wardens ordered) to destroy statues and whitewash walls, replacing mural images with the royal coat of arms as well as with writing such as the Ten Commandments and creed or biblical texts on the obligation to obey one's rulers.[12] In addition to deliberate destruction, a greater loss of murals may have been caused by well-meaning Victorians (Rouse, *Wall Paintings*, 9). In their desire to expose the beauty of interior stonework (which the Middle Ages almost always covered and decorated), these enthusiasts tore down tons of plaster, reducing to dust the forgotten paintings within.

11. For the paintings in Saint Stephen's Chapel, see Alexander and Binski, *Age of Chivalry*, catalogue no. 680 and no. 681; and Tristram, *Fourteenth*, 206–19, plates 1–6. A rare royal survivor is a fragmentary late fourteenth-century image of the archangel Michael and the Virgin with other saints from the Byward Tower in the Tower of London. See Tristram, *Fourteenth*, 193–94, plates 8b, 9a-b, 10; and Alexander and Binski, *Age of Chivalry*, catalogue no. 696.

12. See, for example, the Lord's Prayer, Ten Commandments, and creed at Chalfont Saint Giles, Buckinghamshire, and the Elizabethan royal arms at Saint Thomas, Salisbury, Wiltshire. In the age-old struggle between image and iconoclast, the latter appeared to triumph in sixteenth-century England, but the repressed has returned. The unintended result of Protestant whitewashing was that some murals were preserved for us from the ravages of time and changing taste. An especially poignant example of the inability of text to extinguish image can be seen at Binham Priory, Norfolk: the beautiful figures on a wooden screen overpainted with excepts from Tyndale's New Testament have become more visible in recent years as the superimposed words flake away (see Denton, "Image and History," 25).

In addition to the limited availability of English wall paintings, scholarship on parish murals has been fitful.[13] Nothing like a complete list of surviving works is available, though the Courtauld Institute under the direction of David Park is in the midst of a census. Even when an extant mural can be located, the result is often disappointing. Many churches contain only bits and pieces of the original work—frequently in bad shape. At Henham, Essex, a Romanesque head is found high up on the east wall of the chancel and a delicate but faint Gothic outline of the Virgin lower down on the north wall. Both may have once been part of major paintings—the Romanesque head has been compared to a surviving scheme in Canterbury Cathedral (Park, "Anglo-Saxon," 239)—but such fragments can tell us little now. Even extensive remains are often badly faded or have lost so much detail that they only hint at their original achievement, unlike the many fresco cycles still vivid in Italian churches. A twelfth-century Passion sequence with other subjects was accidentally discovered after a fire at Ickleton, Cambridgeshire, but the colors are so dim and the faces so lacking in feature that the paintings disappoint when first seen—time and imagination are required to appreciate their magnificence (see Park, "Romanesque Wall Paintings"). The nave of Croughton, Northhamptonshire, has an extraordinary early fourteenth-century life of the Virgin and Passion sequence that have been compared to the best contemporary drawing and to the Psalter of Robert of Isle (Tristram, *Fourteenth*, 73–75; cf. Tristram and James), but the undeniable expressiveness of the figures at Croughton is diminished by the survival of little more than silhouettes.[14]

13. The first attempt to list the murals of medieval England was by C. E. Keyser in the late nineteenth century: his work was published as a small pamphlet in 1871; a second edition appeared in 1872 and a third in 1883. In the 1940s and 1950s, E. W. Tristram produced three massive and indispensable studies of wall paintings, on the twelfth, thirteenth, and fourteenth centuries, respectively, illustrated with many of his own drawings. A. Caiger-Smith's 1963 book contains what is still one of the most practical lists of surviving murals, though his work (and even more that of Keyser and Tristram) is now dated and unreliable because important paintings continue to be discovered while others are newly restored or have faded with time (sometimes as the result of misguided attempts to preserve them). E. Clive Rouse, who did so much to record and conserve these works, reprinted more than a decade ago a fine short introduction to medieval English murals originally published in 1968 (*Wall Paintings*); and brief descriptions of many murals can be found in the individual county volumes of Nikolaus Pevsner's Penguin guides to the buildings of England, now being updated. The most thorough and reliable accounts of murals are often scholarly essays on individual churches.

14. Croughton is also unpleasantly fouled by excrement from the many bats that live in the church; the well-being of the bats, unlike that of the murals, is protected by English law.

II. PARISH MURALS AND *PIERS PLOWMAN*

Unlike other public cultural contexts, such as sermons and the drama, parish wall paintings have been rarely discussed in studies of *Piers Plowman*.[15] Yet no contemporary art was more accessible to the poet and his audience. In contrast to illuminations in expensive manuscripts (the images most frequently cited by scholars when discussing medieval literature), murals were not just for the privileged few, but would have been known from childhood to medieval people of every social and educational level.[16] Although the poet of *Piers Plowman* assumes literacy in his audiences, he must never have been confident about what any of them had actually read. But everyone had always seen wall paintings in local churches. They were one of the most widely shared cultural experiences of the time, providing a common artistic grammar, a familiar repertoire of images, and an aesthetic, which the poet draws on (whether consciously or not) for his own more challenging work.[17]

---

15. Only three articles known to me discuss *Piers Plowman* in relationship to English wall paintings. All are brief treatments that attempt to identify the source or influence of specific passages in the poem, with results that are either wrong or unconvincing.

Early in the past century Tristram claimed that the fairly common late medieval subject of Christ surrounded by tools and other daily objects, such as those as at Hessett, Suffolk, and Nether Wallop, was directly inspired by our poem and showed Piers the laborer as Christ ("Piers Plowman"; cf. Tristram, *Fourteenth*, 121–25). Charlotte D'Evelyn quickly disputed Tristram's argument and instead identified the tools as the instruments of the Passion. Subsequent research, however, has shown that the image is actually a warning to those who work or play on the Sabbath, like the merchants mentioned in Truth's pardon who "holde noght hir haliday as Holy Chirche techeth" (B 7.20; A 8.22; C 9.24). Rouse describes a similar image in San Miniato, Florence, with an accompanying inscription that identifies it as a warning against Sabbath breaking (*Wall Paintings*, 68; cf. Binski, *Medieval Craftsmen*, 15). A definitive study of the "Sunday Christ" has recently been published by Athene Reiss.

A section of a third article by Robert Kaske proposed that the mirror of Middle Earth in *Piers* (B 11.9; C 11.170) may have been suggested to Langland by wall paintings of the Wheel of Life near his Malvern home, such as the one still extant (but very obscure) at Kempley, Gloucestershire, though even Kaske admits that the evidence is not completely convincing ("Local Iconography," 162–67). The loss of so many medieval murals and our almost complete ignorance of the life of the poet of *Piers Plowman* make any attempt to identify the precise source of particular images in the work difficult if not impossible.

16. Literary scholars who use manuscript illuminations rarely establish (or even address) how accessible these images would have been to a poet such as Chaucer (even though his patrons owned such manuscripts), let alone to more humble writers and their readers. An example of the difference between elite and public art is dramatically shown at Thornham Parva in Suffolk. Today this little country church displays on its altar the Thornham Parva Retable, one of the great achievements of East Anglican medieval painting. In the Middle Ages, the retable was not in this or any other parish church, but probably on the high altar of the Dominican priory at Thetford. The noncloistered clergy and laypeople of Thornham instead had to make do with the wall paintings in the church (of the Nativity and the Life of Saint Edmund), whose vigorous, dramatic scenes are in many ways more like *Piers Plowman* than the courtly, iconic retable.

17. The degree to which the poet was or was not conscious of his use of parish wall paintings in specific passages of *Piers* is unknowable and probably not very significant, perhaps comparable to the influence on a modern writer of cinematic techniques or Freudian psychology.

In the rest of this chapter I largely ignore wall paintings in cathedrals, monasteries, and private buildings to concentrate on those in local churches. Parish murals were the public art most available to the author, and even more important, to the audience of *Piers Plowman*, regardless of status, learning, or sex. Pecock observes that, unlike books, parish images were on display to "men and wommen and children" at all times of day (*Repressor*, 1:214). During a famous passage in his *Festial*, John Mirk (or Mirc) declares in a homily for Corpus Christi that "ther ben mony thousaund of pepul that couth not ymagen in her hert how Crist was don on the rood, but as thai lerne hit be syght of ymages and payntours" (171). But then as now, the unlettered were not the only ones whose imagination needed the aid of visual stimulation, and the power of mural images would have affected even the educated clerics and literate laypeople whom John Burrow has identified as the primary audience of *Piers Plowman* ("Audience"; cf. Middleton, "Audience and Public").

I make four assumptions about English parish wall paintings for the purposes of this study. First, murals depended on the repetition of conventional themes to communicate with a general audience: although no two churches had identical mural schemes (and their quality varied greatly, sometimes within the same building), a relatively limited number of recognizable motifs were used.[18] Second, every extant image represents many that were once present. If several examples survive today, we can be reasonably confident that the image was common in the Middle Ages. Third, no great difference in the subjects of wall paintings occurs from one part of England to another (with the exception of regional saints and the occasional depiction of local crafts in images of the Sunday Christ and Saint Christopher), and therefore, murals now present largely in the east and south can represent the entire country. Fourth, discussion of murals and *Piers Plowman* need not be restricted to paintings that are precisely contemporary with the poem, because many earlier schemes survived unchanged into the fourteenth century and later works were often copies of earlier images.[19]

    18. See Camille: "The medieval artist's ability was measured not in terms of invention, as today, but in the capacity to combine traditional motifs in new and challenging ways" (*Image on the Edge*, 36).
    Parish murals can be roughly divided into five categories: (*a*) decorative schemes; (*b*) the Last Judgment or Doom; (*c*) narratives of the life of Christ, especially the Nativity and Passion; (*d*) lives or single figures of saints, apostles, and the Virgin, including the single most frequent image in parish churches, Saint Christopher carrying the Christ child; and (*e*) moralities, especially the Seven Deadly Sins and the Seven Works of Mercy. Rouse gives a slightly different list of categories (*Wall Paintings*, 35).

    19. Many twelfth-century mural schemes must have been visible in Langland's time, such as the Apocalypse scene in the chancel at Kempley near Malvern (the church mentioned by Kaske ["Local Iconography"] in connection with *Piers*, though he discussed a different and later image). I shall cite only those images that there is good reason to believe were painted before the third quarter of the fourteenth century, unless otherwise indicated.

My study may seem compromised from the start by the famous condemnation of stained glass and wall painting in *Piers Plowman* itself. Meed at
Westminster corruptly promises the friars that if they will go easy on lecher-
ous lords in confession, she will decorate their church: "Wowes do whiten and
wyndowes glazen, / Do peynten and portraye and paie for the makynge" (B
3.61–62; C 3.65–66).[20] Although the narrative "I" here goes on to condemn all
such prideful displays, the criticism of religious art may be less severe than it
first appears. Primarily concerned with the making of windows (though painting is mentioned), the lines are specifically aimed at those who use art to boast
about their good deeds, which should be known only to God: "To writen in
wyndowes of hir wel dedes" (B 3.65, cf. 69; C 3.69). Image making for the right
devotional reasons is not necessarily forbidden, any more than the biblical
citation that immediately follows in the B-version, which criticizes ostenta-
tious alms giving, is a prohibition against genuine charity (B 3.71–75). In representing Christian doctrine and stories, wall paintings are doing in images the
sort of thing *Piers Plowman* does in verse; not that the poem does not repeatedly question the propriety of its literary undertaking.

The connections I am suggesting between *Piers Plowman* and contemporary
paintings are rarely direct or explicit. More than fifty years ago, Morton
Bloomfield called for "a general study of the backgrounds" of *Piers* in such areas as
folklore, art, theology, and homilies: "The basic purpose is not to find sources,
necessarily, but to make possible a new understanding of the intellectual and social
atmosphere of fourteenth-century England" ("Present State," 25). As Bloomfield
urged, I am not here attempting to identify specific borrowings by the poet (nor
his direct influence on others), but I do aim to add to our knowledge "of the intellectual and social atmosphere" of the period.[21] English parish wall paintings can
contribute to both historicist and formalist studies of *Piers*. Murals bring us closer
to the culture of the poet and his original medieval audience, as they provide a per-

---

20. Caiger-Smith (*Mural Paintings*, 90) quotes the citation of Saint Bernard in *Jacob's Well* on the vanity of
painting walls while the poor are naked and needy.

21. Unlike Kaske in his article on local iconography cited previously, I do not speculate on the specific
paintings that might have been seen by the poet: see note 15 above. Nor, like V. A. Kolve, in *Chaucer and the
Imagery of Narrative*, do I discuss narrative images that readers might have formed in their minds as they experienced the poem. Indeed, I shall discuss only some aspects of the visual in *Piers*. Nevertheless, I am
encouraged by Kolve's call for new kinds of interdisciplinary scholarship: "We are only beginning to
understand the issues involved in using pictures as a means of recovering the meaning of literary texts, only
beginning the hard tasks of historical scholarship, methodological refinement, and sympathetic imagination necessary if we would restore what was once a vital and viable relation between the two" (3).

FIGURE I. *Tree of Seven Deadly Sins (detail of top). Hessett, Suffolk.*

spective from which to evaluate the poem and its literary differences from other contemporary writing.

Let me begin with an example that illustrates both kinds of analysis. By far the most stimulating discussion of *Piers Plowman* and the visual arts is that of Elizabeth Salter, though the only murals she mentions are Italian ("Visual Arts"). In one section of her essay, Salter argues that the exemplar for Langland's Tree of Charity at the beginning of B 16 (C 18) might have been illustrations of allegorical trees in religious treatises such as British Library, London, MS Additional 37049, though she also notes the difference between these simple drawings and the complexities that Langland creates (263–64). Indeed, the immediate inspiration of the poet might well have been some such manuscript, but allegorical trees would also have been widely known to him and to his audience from their frequent appearance on church walls. As Rouse notes, "The tree was a favourite motif" on walls as elsewhere (*Wall Paintings*, 61; cf. Caiger-Smith, "Mural Paintings," 50–53). Common mural examples from the second half of the fourteenth century are trees of the Seven Deadly Sins, like the one at Hessett, Suffolk (fig. 1), which has branches ending in dragon heads that support the individual sins, or the one at Hoxne, Suffolk; in addition to trees of sins there were also trees of the Seven Works of Mercy, such as the one at Barnby, Suffolk.[22] A different kind of tree on parish walls was the Tree of Jesse, tracing the genealogical ancestry of Jesus, as at Black Bourton, Oxfordshire, or Weston Longville, Norfolk.[23]

These murals provide a historical context for the Tree of Charity in *Piers Plowman* that has not previously been recognized. Analogues for the episode existed in the public space of parish art as well as in the narrower sphere of manuscript culture. More formally, the tree murals also remind us of how schematic *Piers* can be. For all its intellectual sophistication and daring, the poem keeps returning to diagrammatic allegories, such as Piers's account of the route to Truth (B 5.560–629; A 6.47–117; C 7.204–81) or the description of the castle made by Kind at the beginning of B 9 (A 10; C 11.128ff.). Nevertheless, as Salter reminds us, such visual images, whether from manuscripts or church walls, do not begin to equal the dynamism of Langland's poetry. Anima's initial description of the Tree of Charity in the B-version (16.4–9) associates each part with a virtue (e.g., the root is mercy and the leaves faithful words), similar to the simple didactic meanings that can be read out from the trees of sins or virtues (one branch holds an image of wrath, for example, and another lechery). When Piers the plowman is introduced in the poem, however, the dreamer/seeker falls into an inner dream, and the tree, which is now present, changes into what David Aers has called a disclosure rather than picture model (*Christian Allegory*, 79–107), a complex and shifting allegory: first the Trinity, then the three states of chastity, then those who lived before the birth of Christ. The genealogical and moral trees, which were separate images in contemporary wall paintings, are combined in the poem, so that a static diagram becomes something like a motion picture or the morphing of a computer image. Mural painting is the familiar, public base from which the poet creates his more complex art.

Parish wall paintings may also have helped the original readers of *Piers* to appreciate the irony of some of its "lessons." For example, early in the *vita*, the narrative "I" argues that works and learning are not necessary for salvation

22. The Hessett tree seems to be from c.1400 (Caiger-Smith, *Mural Paintings*, 173), though information in the church suggests a somewhat earlier date. Tristram notes that the Deadly Sins and Works of Mercy, along with the Doom, are the subjects "more often found after c.1350 than any others" (*Fourteenth*, 19–20) and discusses the frequency of trees of the Sins and of the Works in the fourteenth century (*Fourteenth*, 102).

23. For the thirteenth-century Jesse tree at Black Bourton, see Tristram, *Thirteenth*, plate 108b; for the later one at Weston Longville, see Tristram, *Fourteenth*, plates 22–24.

because those such as Mary Magdalene, King David, and the apostle Paul, who acted wickedly during their lives, are now in heaven (B 10.421–26; A 11.287–92; C 11.264–72). Alert readers, as discussed in my Chapter 2, might have recognized the fallacy of the reasoning here (bad actions, if sincerely repented, need not bring damnation) even before Imaginatif's correction in the next passus. But more ordinary medieval readers (unlike many modern critics) might have been guided by the murals. Parishioners who had seen the Magdalene and Paul portrayed so positively on their church walls would have been less likely to agree with the narrator's condemnation of them and thus to question his dismissal of the value of works and faith.

Yet if wall paintings can help define the historical horizon of expectation that an original medieval audience brought to *Piers* as well as aid modern critical analysis, they are not the key that will unlock all the poem's mysteries. Parish murals are simpler than *Piers Plowman,* and their interests often diverge. Saint Christopher carrying the Christ child is the most popular single subject in English churches, but Christopher is never mentioned in *Piers.* Also absent, but common on church walls, are icons and the lives of Saint Catherine and Saint Margaret: saints in general play only a limited role in the poem.[24] Conversely, the searching intellectualism and obsession with language of *Piers* is necessarily missing in wall paintings, as is its severe criticism of the state of contemporary society and the Church, especially the role of friars.

Despite such differences, *Piers Plowman* and medieval English wall paintings share much. Both are found on the margins between high and popular art and bridge the worlds of secular and religious experience. The poem and the paintings transmit aspects of elite culture to a broad, though not necessarily unsophisticated, public audience. Both use workaday media, alliterative verse or earth tones, to represent the most sacred truths of Catholic Europe.

III. THE THEOLOGY OF THE NAVE

Medieval parish churches of all sizes and importance made a distinction between the chancel, the domain of the clergy, and the nave, the place for the laity,

---

24. Although Paul as the porter of heaven's gate and Peter with his sword are mentioned at B 15.18 (c 16.167), exactly as they are portrayed in wall paintings. Peter welcomes the saved into the New Jerusalem in murals from the twelfth century (Clayton, Sussex) to the sixteenth (Wenhaston, Suffolk), and Paul is regularly identifiable by his holding a sword. Earlier in the poem the *Legenda Sanctorum* is cited in respect to the limitations of logic and law at B 11.218ff.; and, of course, other saints, from King Edmund to Francis, who were painted on parish walls, are mentioned in *Piers.*

frequently separating the two by a rood screen. In England, parishioners, as mentioned previously, were expected to maintain the public space of the nave: "At some date in the twelfth or thirteen century it became the practice to make the parishioners responsible for the building and upkeep of the nave, leaving to the rector the obligation to maintain the chancel. The parishioners thus came to take a proprietorial interest in the nave, which became their exclusive domain" (Pounds, *History*, 47–48; cf. Drew, *Organization*, 8; Kümin, "English Parish," 24; Binski, *Medieval Craftsmen*, 41).[25]

Often, though not always, there was a difference of mural subjects in the two spaces. As Tristram wrote about twelfth-century painting: "The nave, devoted to the laity, represented the world, and its walls were therefore reserved for the delineation of events more closely associated with ordinary human existence, including the earthly life of Christ, the Virgin, and the Saints. . . . The chancel was conceived as Heaven, as Heaven would be after the Last Day" (*Twelfth*, 9; cf. Caiger-Smith, *Mural Paintings*, 1–2). These different spheres are clearly seen at Kempley—only a few miles from the Malvern Hills—whose nave contains a variety of earthly subjects painted in the fourteenth century, whereas the chancel has a remarkably well-preserved twelfth-century vision of the New Jerusalem based on John's *Apocalypse*, with Christ in heavenly majesty adored by angels and apostles (Babington, Manning, and Stewart, *Painted Past*, 50–51; Caiger-Smith, *Mural Paintings*, plates 1 and 2).

Images that are even more of this world are the practical moralities found in many church naves. Some of these paintings are very pragmatic indeed, concerned with promoting good order in parish worship. For instance, a number of murals warn women (and apparently only women) against disputes and gossiping in church, including a lively fourteenth-century image at Melbourne, Derbyshire, which shows devils egging on two female parishioners.[26] An even commoner image seems directed primarily at men, warning them not to work or play on the

25. A decree of c. 1295–1313, which circulated widely and is "usually attributed" to Archbishop Robert Winchelsey, lays out the duties of parishioners and rectors. The former are "responsible for repairing the nave of the church: its length and breadth, its inside and outside, including its altars, images (especially the principal image in the chancel [this appears to mean the rood or crucifixion on the nave side of the chancel arch]), and windows"; whereas the latter are enjoined "by due law and custom" to maintain "the interior and exterior of the church's chancel" (translation in Shinners and Dohar, *Pastors*, 219–20). Duffy notes that west of the rood screen, including the screen itself, "was the responsibility—and the property—of the parish" ("Parish, Piety, and Patronage," 136).

26. On warnings against gossip, see Rouse, *Wall Painting*, 68 and illustration 78; Gill, "Female Piety," 108–10; Alexander and Binski, *Age of Chivalry*, catalogue no. 557 (the Melbourne image), who record nine examples of the subject in the thirteenth and fourteenth centuries (444).

Sabbath, because such blasphemy causes direct injury to the body of Christ. This so-called Sunday Christ, which Tristram wrongly associated directly with *Piers Plowman* (see note 15 above), survives in more than twenty parish examples, including a well-preserved fifteenth-century painting from Breage, Cornwall, showing a naked and bleeding Christ, whose wounds are inflicted by surrounding objects, from agricultural tools to a deck of playing cards, wrongly used on holy days.[27]

The traditional if not inevitable mural distinction between a Christianity of this world depicted in the nave and an otherworldly Christianity in the chancel reveals an important way in which *Piers Plowman* differs from other contemporary religious writing. Despite the intensity of its spirituality, *Piers* never abandons the earthly subjects and concerns of the public world. It has none of the mystical flights of works such as the *Cloud of Unknowing*, nor does it make any attempt to describe the divine realms, as is done with such ornamented virtuosity in *Pearl*. From the plowing of the half acre through the jousting of Christ at Jerusalem to the assault on the Barn of Unity (for all its apocalyptic coloring), *Piers Plowman* is concerned with the Christian life here on earth. Three of the most popular mural schemes of the nave are directly relevant to the public preoccupations of *Piers Plowman*: the first is a dramatic spectacle, the Doom or Last Judgment; the second is a narrative, the life of Christ; and the third is a moral scheme, the Seven Deadly Sins, which is often paired with the Seven Works of Mercy.

The Doom

The Doom or Day of Judgment, which depicts the Four Last Things that medieval Christians were always supposed to keep in mind (death, judgment, hell, and heaven), was the most prominent and dramatic scene in English parish wall painting.[28] A colorful fifteenth-century example is found at Saint Thomas, Salisbury, which because it was repainted in the modern era gives some sense of the impact of the Doom when new (fig. 2). As at Salisbury, the Last Judgment was normally placed over the chancel arch directly facing the congregation (Tristram, *Fourteenth*, 19). This liminal location suggests that the Doom was a

27. For the Breage painting, see Rouse, *Wall Paintings*, illustration 72; Caiger-Smith, *Mural Paintings*, plate 20.

28. At least seventy-eight English examples of the Doom are still extant (Caiger-Smith, *Mural Paintings*, 31). The elements of the Doom are based on Matthew 24:30–31; 25:31–34, 41, 46. See Caiger-Smith, *Mural Paintings*, 31–43. For a full discussion and catalogue of English Dooms, see the admirable study by Jane Ashby "Medieval Murals." For a general treatment of the topic in art and drama, which mentions wall paintings only in passing, see the collection of essays written by Bevington, Diehl, Emmerson, Herzman, and Sheingorn, especially Sheingorn's "For God Is Such a Doomsman."

FIGURE 2. *Doom or Last Judgment. Salisbury (Saint Thomas), Wiltshire.*

transitional subject between the chancel and the nave, portraying both the last day of humans on earth and their entrance into the eternity of heaven or hell. Many surviving Dooms are from the fifteenth century, but key elements of the scheme are found in murals at Clayton, Sussex that date from as early as the eleventh or twelfth century (Tristram, *Twelfth*, plates 36–43; A. M. Baker, "Wall Paintings"; Park, "'Lewes Group'"). Over the chancel arch is Christ in a mandorla displaying his wounds and flanked by the apostles (fig. 3). The painting at Clayton occupies three walls of the nave: on the north wall, the dead rise from their graves to be weighed for salvation or damnation by the archangel Michael, and Peter greets the saved, led by a bishop, as they enter the New Jerusalem; on the south wall the damned are driven into hell by a devil on a horse.

In a crude, fragmentary Doom from Ickleton, painted three centuries after the Clayton Doom, the Judgment is still recognizable (fig. 4): Christ, here sitting on a rainbow, remains at the center, but the apostles have been replaced by two beseeching figures, John the Baptist on his left (in other Dooms the figure is John the Apostle, as in Crucifixion scenes) and the Virgin on his right (in this case bar-

FIGURE 3. *Doom or Last Judgment (detail of Christ and Apostles). Clayton, Sussex.*

ing her breasts in supplication).[29] The more elaborate Salisbury Doom includes both the two beseechers and the apostles (see fig. 2). Another late Doom, from Wenhaston, Suffolk, painted on wood but also originally placed over the chancel arch, shows Christ with Mary and John (both unusually on the same side), and below, as on the walls of Clayton, the dead rising from their graves while Michael weighs souls to determine whether they will be ushered into heaven by Peter on Christ's right or herded into hell by devils on his left (fig. 5).

The Doom is a neglected contemporary cultural intertext for *Piers Plowman*. Critics have long recognized the dreamer's powerful desire to save his soul, but it has perhaps not been sufficiently appreciated that salvation and damnation were not just orthodox doctrine known intellectually by the poet and his audience, but the most vivid image in their local churches. The Day of Doom is repeatedly

29. Park, "Romanesque Wall Paintings," plate 14. By baring her breasts, Mary reminds her son that he once nursed like other men and thus appeals to him to have pity on his fellow humans. Other examples of Mary baring her breasts occur at North Cove, Suffolk (Rouse, *Wall Paintings*, illustration 69), and Chalgrove, Oxfordshire. On the motif, see Morgan, "Texts and Images," 95–97.

FIGURE 4. *Doom or Last Judgment (detail of Christ with Virgin and John the Baptist). Ickleton, Cambridgeshire.*

referred to in *Piers,* as at the anguished conclusion of Robert the Robber's plea: "Dampne me noght at Domesday for that I dide so ille!" (B 5.471; A 5.246; C 6.324). Truth's pardon, which is the focus of the end of the *visio,* is all about the Last Judgment: "*Et qui bona egerunt ibunt in vitam eternam; / Qui vero mala, in ignem eternum*" (B 7.110a–b; A 8.95–96; C 9.286–87). The same starkly opposed destinations the pardon offers are also portrayed in the Doom.[30] Near the end of poem in the long versions, during the important *redde quod debes* section of the penultimate passus, we hear of Christ's second coming, when he will judge humans "at domesday, bothe quyke and dede— / The goode to the Godhede and to greet joye, / And wikkede to wonye in wo withouten ende" (B 19.197–99; C 21.197–99).[31]

30. The repainted Doom at South Leigh, Oxfordshire, has banners above the angels who blow trumpets for the saved and for the damned respectively: the banner over the former reads, "venite benedicti patris mei"; over the latter, "discedite maledicti." Similar texts are found at Trotton, Great Bowden, and Stanningfield (see Ashby, "Medieval Murals").

31. Other references, direct or implicit, to the Day of Judgment include B 1.128–33 (A 1.117–22; C 1.129–33); B 5.20 (A 5.20; C 5.122); B 5.274 (C 6.297); B 5.293 (C 6.346); B 7.172 (A 8.156; C 9.321); B 7.188 (A 8.175; C 9.338); B 7.201 (A 8.185; C 9.351); B 10.358; B 11.134 (C 12.70); B 12.91; C 16.36; B 18.386 (C 20.427); B 20.294 (C 22.294).

Piers Plowman never describes the complete parish scheme of the Doom at any one place, but the poem often seems to depend on its audience's familiarity with specific elements. The opposing tower and dungeon at the very beginning of the poem may owe something to the staging of contemporary drama, as has been suggested (e.g., Carruthers, *Search*, 28), but readers might also have associated this awesome duality of good and evil places with the heaven and hell of the more frequently seen Doom. In many Last Judgments, as at Salisbury, the ramparts of heaven are near the top of the image, similar to Truth's "tour on a toft" (B pr.14; A pr.14; C pr.15); similarly, hell in the Doom is always at the bottom right, like Wrong's redoubt located in a "deep dale bynethe" (B pr.15; A pr.15; C pr.17).

The Doom also contains a rare mural-parallel to the criticism of social abuses in church and state so often found in *Piers Plowman*. Kings, queens, clergy, and bishops (whose otherwise naked figures reveal their offices by convenient if somewhat incongruous headgear) are welcomed into heaven in Last Judgments such as the one at Wenhaston (see fig. 5); but in other cases, such as the magnificent if restored Doom at South Leigh, those who hold these high ecclesiastical or royal positions are sent chained and protesting to hell, no doubt to the

FIGURE 5. *Doom or Last Judgment. Wenhaston, Suffolk.*

immense satisfaction of ordinary parishioners.[32] Avarice, which Yunck has identified as the "great, tawdry sin" of Langland's world ("Satire," 145) is explicitly
punished in many Dooms: an example is the bearded man with a money bag in one
hand and another hanging from his belt who is thrown headfirst into hell by a devil
in the fifteenth-century mural at Chesterton, Cambridgeshire. One of the most
dramatic examples of social criticism in parish wall paintings is an early thirteenth-
century Ladder of Salvation, a variation of the standard Doom, at Chaldon,
Surrey (fig. 6; see Caiger-Smith, *Mural Paintings*, plate 12), which shows the saved led to
heaven by angels, while devils torture a variety of tradesmen for their commercial sins.
A central victim (lower right) who receives special treatment is a man with money
bags around his waist who is holding a coin in one hand and from whose mouth other
coins fall. Such murals are as severe about social crimes as is *Piers Plowman.*

For all its potential terror (which is sometimes overemphasized by modern
commentators), the Doom tempers justice with mercy, most obviously by the

FIGURE 6. *Ladder of Salvation. Chaldon, Surrey.*

32. According to David Fowler, the "ominous conclusion" to the penultimate passus of the long versions of *Piers*, which suggests that the high and mighty are susceptible to damnation as well as salvation, is
parallel to "a feature from medieval drama" (*Bible*, 282). But the same warning also appears in parish murals.

addition of Mary and John as intercessors. Moreover, the Psychostasis, or weighing of souls by the archangel Michael, which is part of the early Doom at Clayton, tended to become an independent image in parish churches, often with the addition of the Virgin showing compassion for threatened sinners. Wenhaston has a late weighing that is still part of the Doom without the Virgin but with the Devil holding a scroll of indictment (see fig. 5), whereas Slapton, Northhamptonshire, has a separate weighing in which the Virgin intercedes by placing her prayer beads on the scale to weigh it down in favor of the soul being judged (fig. 7; see Breeze, "Virgin's Rosary"; Morgan, "Texts and Images," 48–51).[33]

The weighing of a soul at death by Saint Michael seems to be described near the end of the *visio* in *Piers Plowman*, when Truth promises merchants their own pardon if they use their profits for good causes:

FIGURE 7. *Saint Michael Weighing Soul with Virgin. Slapton, Northhamptonshire.*

33. That the weighing by Michael could be either part of the Doom or an independent image suggests that the medieval mind was able to hold simultaneously the idea that an individual soul was judged at the moment of its death and the idea that the final verdict was not rendered until the last day (see Gurevich, "Perceptions," 84–85).

"And I shal sende yow myselve Seint Michel myn angel,
That no devel shal yow dere ne drede in youre deying,
And witen yow fro wanhope, if ye wol thus werche,
And sende youre soules in saufte to my Seintes in joye."

(B 7.33–36; A 8.36–39; C 9.37–40)[34]

The familiar parish mural potentially evoked by these lines has not been noted by *Piers* scholars. Yet even if we grant the association, the relationship between painting and poetry is far from simple. Truth's Michael in *Piers* is as strict as Truth's pardon; he will only shield those merchants who work well. There is no leniency for those who fall short, perhaps because there is no Virgin to intercede for them. Or is she only deferred? In fact, Mary does appear at the end of the passus, offering a more merciful (though still demanding) hope for humans at the day of Doom:

Forthi I counseille alle Cristene to crie God mercy,
And Marie his moder be oure meene bitwene,
That God gyve us grace here, er we go hennes,
Swiche werkes to werche, the while we ben here,
That after oure deth day, Dowel reherce
At the day of dome, we dide as he highte.

(B 7.196–201; A 8.180–85; C 9.346–51).[35]

These lines are a powerful expression, repeated often in the poem, of the need for both works and mercy to achieve salvation: God's grace by way of Mary is shown to rescue humans not by the unmerited addition of her beads to

34. The weighing of souls is not explicitly mentioned in these lines, and the reference here might be to the traditional Christian belief that the saved were escorted to heaven by angels, especially archangels, as suggested to me by Kathleen Scott in a private letter; see Sheingorn, "And Flights of Angels." Given the popularity of the weighing in parish murals, the explicit naming of Saint Michael here would probably have suggested this image to a contemporary audience. For the weighing, see Caiger-Smith, *Mural Paintings*, 58–63. His plate 21 has a weighing with the Virgin from Swalcliffe, Oxfordshire.

35. Morgan argues that although Mary interceding with her beads at the weighing of souls occurs in the thirteenth-century *Legenda Aurea*, she does not appear in English visual art until the third quarter of the fourteenth century ("Texts and Images," 50–51). Even if this is correct (and others have dated some of these images earlier), Morgan himself notes that Mary as a general intercessor kneeling before the judging Christ is a prominent theme in thirteenth-century Dooms (95).

Michael's scale but by permitting us to act in such a way that Dowell can honestly testify on our behalf at Doomsday.

In accordance with the earthly theology of the nave, *Piers Plowman* does not describe either of the otherworldly destinations of the Doom. Perhaps more surprising than the absence of the New Jerusalem is the poet's failure to describe the terrors of hell, which are so prominent in parish Dooms and medieval art in general. The varied and dramatic punishments of the damned by devils, including the fiend riding over sinners in the early Clayton Doom and the energetic torture of commercial transgressors in the thirteenth-century Ladder of Salvation at Chaldon (see fig. 6), might seem to be exactly the kind of scene that would attract this poet, given his fierce indignation at social corruption and thirst for justice. But no such demonic retribution is shown in *Piers.*

Not that the lively devils of the Doom are wholly absent in *Piers Plowman,* but when they do appear, humans are not being damned by them but liberated from them. Fiends and fiendkins never triumphantly drag men and women to ruin in the poem; instead, they are themselves punished by Christ during the Harrowing of Hell. After the Crucifixion, the debate between the four daughters of God, and the speech of Book, the scene shifts to the entrance of hell where, as Truth reports, a "spirit" speaks "and bit unspere the yates" (B 18.261; C 20.270). The spirit, of course, is Christ, whose arrival at the entrance to hell immediately causes consternation among the devils: Satan correctly predicts that "care and combraunce is comen to us alle" (B 18.267; C 20.276). Although Lucifer maintains that he holds men and women in hell justly, Satan and Gobelyn acknowledge that humans were taken by guile and "thorugh treson were thei dampned" (B 18.293; C 20.324). Despite the tricks and schemes of the devils, they are soon mastered by Christ. He silences their objections, scatters them, and rescues their captives: "They dorste noght loke on Oure Lord, the leste of hem alle, / But leten hym lede forth what hym liked and lete what hym liste" (B 18.406–7; C 20.448–49). In *Piers,* the fiends of hell are not the oppressors of the Doom but are themselves oppressed.

The poem's optimism, which we saw in the previous chapter in respect to salvation, is further illustrated by comparing the work with the use of an identical visual image (the whalelike hell mouth) in two different parish mural schemes. The most frequent and dramatic appearance of the hell mouth in parish wall paintings is as the fearsome destination of sinners in the Doom, as at Wenhaston (fig. 8A). But the identical gaping mouth also appears in murals of the Harrowing of Hell, as in an early fourteenth-century painting at North Cove,

FIGURE 8A. *Hell Mouth (detail from Doom). Wenhaston, Suffolk.*

FIGURE 8B. *Harrowing of Hell. North Cove, Suffolk.*

Suffolk (fig. 8B).[36] Although both images would have been familiar to his audience, the poet significantly chooses to represent the scene of hope and exclude the
one of despair. *Piers* contains an extended account of the Harrowing in B 18
(C 20), but no other infernal scene. This emphasis has sometimes been queried by
critics: "Why did Langland concentrate on the Harrowing of Hell rather than,
say, the Incarnation or Passion in the culmination of the Do-bet section?"
(Bloomfield, *Apocalypse*, 123). But hell with its active devils is seen in *Piers* only in a
context of joy and compassion. We do not witness the harsh execution of justice
on the sinful, as in the Doom, but rather their salvation. In the Harrowing, Christ
not only frees Adam and the others imprisoned in hell, but also, as discussed in
the previous chapter, goes so far as to suggest the release of *"alle* mennes soules"
(B 18.373; C 20.414, my emphasis). Because of the moral intensity and social criticism of *Piers Plowman*, its stress on redemption and grace is often overlooked or
downplayed. Parish wall paintings can redress the balance and suggest how often
and how powerfully the poem portrays divine mercy and deliverance.

Christ and Longinus

The life of Christ was the most popular narrative sequence in parish wall paintings and, as in contemporary drama and Books of Hours, usually emphasized
the Nativity and Passion. In its several retellings of episodes from the story of
Christ, especially in B 16 (C 18), B 18 (C 20), and B 19 (C 21), *Piers Plowman* also
includes scenes from the ministry, which seem to have been rare on parish walls
(though a few occur in the thirteenth-century chancel murals at Brook, Kent),
but the primary emphasis in the poem, as in local churches, is on the birth and
death of Jesus.[37] For instance, the narrative in B 16 concludes with two of the

36. Other surviving examples of the Harrowing of Hell include a huge (though now very obscure)
thirteenth-century example at Brent Eleigh, Suffolk (which may not have had a hell mouth), and a fourteenth-century image at Chalgrove (see Tristram, *Fourteenth*, plate 32). A much later, though clearer (because
repainted) Harrowing is at Pickering, Yorkshire.

37. For the lack of ministry scenes in parish wall paintings, see Caiger-Smith, *Mural Paintings*, 65–66;
Rouse, *Wall Paintings*, 41, 44; E. Ross, *Grief of God*, 58.

For the Brook paintings of the life of Christ, see Tristram, *Thirteenth*, plates 127, 128, 130, 131, supplementary plates 39A, 39B. Other thirteenth-century mural lives of Christ include a Passion sequence at
Capel, Kent (Tristram, *Thirteenth*, plates 148, 149, supplementary plate 44), and Nativity and Passion
sequences at West Chiltington, Sussex (Tristram, *Thirteenth*, plates 155–57, supplementary plate 42C; Rouse,
Wall Paintings, illustration 45), and at Wiston, Suffolk (Tristram, *Thirteenth*, plates 188–89).

Two important fourteenth-century Nativity sequences are at Corby Glen, Lincolnshire (Rouse, *Wall Paintings*,
illustration 8), and Croughton, Northhamptonshire (Tristram, *Fourteenth*, plate 21). Important fourteenth-
century Passion sequences include those at Croughton and at Chalgrove (Tristram, *Fourteenth*, plates 30–33).

most common mural scenes from the Passion: the Last Supper and the Betrayal (B 16.139–59; cf. C 18.167–77, which has only the Betrayal).[38]

The longest Christological sequence in *Piers Plowman* occurs in B 18 (C 20), beginning at Palm Sunday and going through the Harrowing of Hell; it may be the most sustained narrative in the entire poem. The passus owes much to the liturgy of Holy Week, and its basic material would have been familiar to educated readers from the Bible and commentaries, but the striking visual moments created by the poet—such as "Thanne was Feith in a fenestre, and cryde '*A! Fili David!*'" (B 18.15; C 20.13) or "Thanne cam *Pilatus* with muche peple, *sedens pro tribunali*" (B 18.37; C 20.35)—resemble the images repeatedly found in local wall paintings, including Jesus' triumphant entrance into Jerusalem and his interrogation before Pilate.

Langland's account of the Crucifixion in this passus is certainly violent but relatively short and austere, without the cascading blood, lovingly described wounds, or heartbroken tears of the Virgin so frequent in contemporary spiritual writing by such as Richard Rolle, Margery Kempe, and Julian of Norwich:

> Nailed hym with thre nailes naked upon the roode,
> And poison on a poole thei putte up to hise lippes,
> And beden hym drynken his deeth-yvel—hise dayes were ydone.
>
> (B 18.51–53; C 20.51–53)

The Crucifixion is equally straightforward in many parish wall paintings, as in representative examples from the thirteenth, fourteenth, and fifteenth centuries from Great Tew, Oxfordshire, Croughton (Tristram and James, "Wall-Paintings," plate XLIV, n. 8), and Little Easton, Essex (fig. 9). Christ's execution is certainly harsh in these images, but his suffering is not especially emphasized because of the objective representation and because the Crucifixion is but one scene in a developing narrative. The climax of the sequence is not Christ's death, but rather, at Great Tew and Croughton, and perhaps once at Little Easton, his

---

38. The special attention given to Judas in B 16 (C 18) is thematically appropriate, for Judas represents the obdurate human sinfulness that makes Christ's Incarnation necessary. The poet could count on his audience's familiarity with such a meaning, whatever their other knowledge of the Bible, because it was so common on their church walls: sometimes dramatically, as in Judas's kiss of betrayal (a key image in English parish murals as elsewhere in Western art), sometimes comically, as in the mid-fourteenth-century paintings at Belchamp Walter, Essex, where Judas's character is revealed when he steals a fish for himself off the table during the Last Supper.

FIGURE 9. *Passion Sequence. Little Easton, Essex.*

Resurrection.[39] Even when the Crucifixion appears alone on church walls, as in an elegant early fourteenth-century reredos with the flanking figures of Mary and John painted above a monument at Turvey, Bedfordshire (fig. 10), there are few tears and little gore. The observer may identify affectively with the scene if desired, but this is not demanded or even overtly encouraged, as it is in contemporary lyrics and meditative images, especially in devotional texts, such as the emotional and bloody Crucifixion scene in the Holkham Bible Picture Book (British Library, London, MS Additional 47682, fol. 32v; reproduced in Salter, "Visual Arts," plate 3).[40] Parish murals suggest that the emotional constraint of *Piers,* which distinguishes it from the extreme affective piety of much late medieval spirituality, is not unique but shared with the public art of the local church nave.

39. The Crucifixion at Great Tew is one of fifteen scenes of the Passion; that at Croughton one of twelve (Tristram, *Fourteenth,* 163–65): both sequences begin with Christ's entrance into Jerusalem and end with his Resurrection. The sequence at Little Easton has six complete scenes extending from the Last Supper to the Deposition, fragments of two others are extant, and there seem to have been others now lost.

40. For an argument that wall paintings of the Crucifixion, including that at Turvey, were meant to evoke more empathy and sentiment than I claim here, see E. Ross, *Grief of God,* 54–55. David Aers, in *Powers,* chapter 2, has argued, in a different context and somewhat tendentiously, that the emphasis in *Piers* is not on the suffering body of Christ.

FIGURE 10. *Crucifixion. Turvey, Bedforshire.*

Although divine suffering is not wholly excluded from the Crucifixion scene in *Piers* (Christ is shown as swooning "pitousliche and pale" like a prisoner about to die [B 18.58; C 20.58]), the primary emphasis is rather on human benefit. This focus is created by the prominence in the passage of the blind knight Longinus, who, according to popular legend, developed from hints in the biblical narratives of the Crucifixion, was forced to spear Jesus' dead body on the cross. As Longinus does so, the blood from the Savior's body restores his sight, and he falls to his knees and begs for mercy:

> Ac ther cam forth a knyght with a kene spere ygrounde,
> Highte Longeus, as the lettre telleth, and longe hadde lore his sighte.
> Bifore Pilat and oother peple in the place he hoved.
> Maugree his manye teeth he was maad that tyme
> To justen with Jesus, this blynde Jew Longeus.
> For alle thei were unhardy, that hoved on horse or stode,
> To touchen hym or to tasten hym or taken hym doun of roode,
> But this blynde bacheler, that baar hym thorugh the herte.
> The blood sprong doun by the spere and unspered the knyghtes eighen.
> Thanne fil the knyght upon knees and cryde Jesu mercy.
>
> (B 18.78–87; C 20.80–89)

This powerful moment is frequently marked by the scribes and early readers of B-manuscripts of *Piers Plowman* (see Benson and Blanchfield, *Manuscripts*). The special attention to Longinus, which surprises some modern readers, would not have surprised the original audience of *Piers.* Although the poet may indeed be using a written source ("lettre") as he claims (B 18.79; C 20.81), even the unlearned among his readers would have known the story of Longinus from wall paintings, for it was one of the most common images in England parish churches, as it was in expensive manuscripts.[41]

Like the Harrowing of Hell, Longinus is an answer to the Doom. He is an example of God's mercy and redemption: Longinus's wicked (if unwilling) act brings salvation, a reversal best summed up in one single, punning line: "The blood sprong doun by the spere and unspered the knyghtes eighen" (B 18.86; C 20.88). The cruelty of the spearing is transformed into the mercy of the "unspearing" or unlocking of his blind eyes. This paradox of grace in *Piers* is also found in parish murals, which frequently show Longinus still with the spear in his hand as he points to his now opened eye. At Peakirk, Cambridgeshire, a wall painting from about 1360 is particularly complex and closely matches the passage in *Piers* (fig. 11). As Clive Rouse has demonstrated, four separate incidents (two bad and two good) are merged into a single image: Longinus is shown both attacking Jesus and kneeling in homage; he points to his healed left eye, while his right eye remains closed and blind ("St Pega"; see also *Wall Paintings*, 18 and illustration 5). The Peakirk image is crudely, if vigorously, painted, but it contains the fused layers of meaning, requiring unpacking by observers, as is so often found in the concentrated poetry of *Piers Plowman.* The Longinus scene is a triumph of Langland's literary skill, yet parish murals are an important contemporary public context from which his art developed.

The Deadly Sins and the Works of Mercy

One of the most common moral subjects among English wall paintings of the fourteenth and fifteenth centuries (as was common in other contemporary media) is perhaps the clearest expression of the worldly spirituality of the nave: the Seven Deadly Sins, a example of which from Hessett in the shape of a tree has already been cited (see fig. 1). The Seven Deadly Sins are often paired with

---

41. Longinus is pictured in surviving thirteenth- and fourteenth-century wall paintings at Croughton; Great Tew; Little Easton; North Cove; Duxford, Cambridgeshire; Gussage Saint Andrew, Dorset; Barnby (perhaps later) and Wissington, Suffolk; Wisborough Green, Sussex.

FIGURE 11. *Longinus and Crucifixion. Peakirk, Cambridgeshire.*

the Seven Works of Mercy, as in the monumental late fourteenth-century work from the time of *Piers Plowman* that covers the entire west wall at Trotton, Sussex (fig. 12).[42] Beneath a variant of the Doom, the sins (now rather faded) are, as at Hessett, personified as individual figures standing within dragon mouths, though at Trotton these issue not from a tree, but from the appropriate parts of a human body.[43] Balancing the man of sin on the left as we view the mural is the good man on the right, who is surrounded by medallions that depict scenes of the Seven Works of Mercy performed by women: clothing the naked, feeding the hungry, giving drink to the thirsty, welcoming strangers or housing the

42. Neither the Sins nor Works are recorded before the fourteenth century, but in his volume on wall paintings of that century Tristram lists more than a dozen of each (*Fourteenth*, 302–3). The extraordinary Trotton mural was dated about 1380 by Tristram (*Fourteenth*, 260; cf. Tudor-Craig, "Painting," 40–41), though Rouse, more vaguely, dated it to the "fourteenth or fifteenth century" (*Wall Paintings*, 65). For photographs and a watercolor of the Seven Deadly Sins at Arundel, West Sussex; Padbury, Buckinghamshire; and Ruislip, Middlesex, see Rouse, *Wall Paintings*, illustrations 73–75. Tristram noted that murals of the Works of Mercy are recorded at the Abbey of Bury St. Edmunds no later than about 1300 (*Fourteenth*, 97); for later examples of the Works of Mercy at Moulton and Potter Heigham, Norfolk, see Tristram, *Fourteenth*, plates 29B and 64A. For the prominence of women in this scheme, see Gill, "Female Piety and Impiety," esp. 102, 110–15.

43. The body at Trotton is male, but at Raunds, Northhamptonshire, the central figure from which the Sins issue is now certainly a woman, though this might have been altered during modern repainting.

FIGURE 12. *Seven Deadly Sins and Seven Works of Mercy. Trotton, Sussex.*

homeless, tending the sick, visiting prisoners, and burying the dead.[44] The list, widespread in medieval culture, was based on Matthew 25:35–46 (the same section that lies behind the Doom) and (for burying the dead) Tobit 1:17–18.

Like the Trotton mural, *Piers Plowman* is a sophisticated work of religious art whose morality is based on a stark duality of sin and good works: do well or do evil. For all its intellectual daring, the poem never forgets for long the basic system of the traditional sins: from the prologue, through Meed's marriage charter and Haukyn's confession, to the final apocalyptic passus, sin is shown as the fundamental obstacle that keeps human beings from following a truly Christian life. Moreover, the sins are repeatedly analyzed in *Piers Plowman* with a seriousness not found in other great Ricardian poems; they are more central than in Chaucer's *Canterbury Tales* (where a full treatment occurs only in the problematic Parson's Tale at the end) and are more directly presented as religious themes than in Gower's *Confessio Amantis.*

Unlike the Seven Deadly Sins, the Seven Works of Corporeal Mercy never appear as a formal list in *Piers Plowman*, but they lie behind the insistent calls in the

44. Caiger-Smith, in *Mural Paintings,* 54, notes that, strictly speaking, the Seven Deadly Sins are not polar opposite of the Works of Mercy, but of the Seven Virtues.

poem for love of one's neighbor to be expressed in practical deeds. Early examples
include Holy Church's statement that God commanded that food, drink, and clothing should be common to all (B 1.23ff.; A 1.23ff.; C 1.23ff.), and Sloth's admission
that he never visited the sick or those in prison (B 5.406; C 7.21). The repetition in
the Trotton mural of scrolls with the word *caritas* on either side of the central good
man and the depiction of various acts of charity suggests Langland's Samaritan in
B 17 (C 19) with his very material and merciful works on behalf of one in need.[45]

The Trotton mural, an elaborate representation of familiar images of sins and
good deeds, shows the visual conventions that lie behind *Piers* and suggests their popular reception. The personification of the sins as human figures, found at Trotton
and elsewhere, such as Hessett (wrath as a man with a switch, lust as a couple embrac-
ing), must have encouraged contemporary viewers to regard them not just as abstract
moral failings but also as living actors. It is as such that the sins appear in *Piers*, especially during their confessions in B 5 (A 5; C 6,7), which contain some of the most vivid
visual moments in the entire poem: Envy with his lean cheeks and body swollen with
rage (B 5.81–84; A 5.64–67) and Covetise wearing a threadbare coat deserted even by
lice (B 5.193–95; A 5.111–13; C 6.202–5). The sin in *Piers* most fully developed as a
rounded character is undoubtedly Gluttony (B 5.297–385; A 5.146–214;
C 6.349–440), who suffers what Derek Pearsall has called a "long and lost week-end"
of drunkenness (*Piers: C-Text*, 125n). Gluttony is given friends and family, not to mention a realistic body capable of appetites and afflictions, all of which seems a natural
development from the often dramatic portraits of the same sin in parish murals, as at
Trotton, where he is shown eagerly draining a large tankard (fig. 13)—a prelude to the
vomiting and unconsciousness he suffers in the poem.

The prominence given to the sins and acts of mercy in both the wall paintings and *Piers Plowman* reveals a public spirituality that expresses itself through
external acts toward others (cf. E. Ross, *Grief of God*, 65). The Works of Mercy
in particular represent that combination of the communal and the personal in
the poem noted by Robert Adams, in which social virtues are "the necessary
means by which individual pilgrims advance on their way to the Heavenly City"

45. The parallels between Trotton and *Piers Plowman* are sometimes striking, though there seems to have
been no direct relationship. In addition to the centrality of the Sins and Works in both, the painting also
emphasizes the three theological virtues, which are so prominent in B 16–17 (C 18–19). The mural not only
contains two scrolls labeled "caritas" next to the good man, but also one labeled "spes," reminiscent of the
appearance in the poem of Moses as Spes (B 17.1–15; C 19.1–18), and the top of the mural also contains a
rare image of Moses with his Ten Commandments. Finally, there was apparently once a third scroll visible
next to the good man, labeled "fides" (Tristram, *Fourteenth*, 260), and, of course, it is as Faith that Abraham
appears in passus B 16 (B 18).

FIGURE 13. *Gluttony (detail from Seven Deadly Sins). Trotton, Sussex.*

("Langland's Theology," 89). The theology of the nave addressed itself to individuals, but the behavior it advocates and condemns is largely concerned with public social conduct toward others (providing shelter and food to those in need or giving in to anger and covetousness).

IV. MURAL AESTHETICS

In addition to specific mural themes from the parish nave echoed in the poem, the general aesthetic of English wall paintings provides a significant stylistic analogue to *Piers Plowman. Piers* is a poem of visions, and Geoffrey Shepherd plausibly suggested that it may have been inspired by a series of actual showings, like those experienced by Julian of Norwich, whose meaning the poet had to try to work out (Shepherd, "Alliterative Poetry," esp. 73–74).[46] Although several critics have insisted that the poem has little or no sense of the visual (e.g., Woolf,

46. Kolve, who apparently did not know Shepherd's essay, made a similar point without mentioning Julian: "[Langland] seems characteristically to have begun by inventing a magisterial image—a Field of Folk spread out between a Tower of Truth and a Dungeon of Falsehood, the Wedding of Lady Mede, a vision of Middle Earth, the Barn of Unity—and then to have invented actions and dialogue that explore the complexity of the image's potential meaning" (*Chaucer,* 68).

"Non-Medieval Qualities," 115; J. M. Bowers, *Crisis*, 30–33; cf. Donaldson, "Apocalyptic Style," 74), many of the most important scenes in the poem are highly pictorial, designed to appeal to the eye. These include the opening juxtaposition of tower and dungeon with the Field of Folk between, Meed riding to London on the back of a sheriff, the angry tearing of the pardon, the vision of Middlearth, Haukyn's soiled coat, the patriarchs resting in Abraham's bosom, the light that Christ brings to hell, and the assaults on the Barn of Unity.

A particularly powerful image that occurs several times in *Piers Plowman* contrasts the rich eating in luxury to the miserable poor without: one example describes heedless clerks and laity feasting and driveling on about God, while "the carefulle may crie and carpen at the yate, / Bothe afyngred and afurst, and for chele quake" (B 10.58–59; C 11.42–43; cf. B 9.80–81). The same visual opposition of rich and poor (with a happier outcome) occurs as a prelude to the grand feast given by Conscience: whereas the Doctor of Divinity ("a maister" and said to resemble a friar in C) is quickly welcomed into Conscience's court, Patience in the guise of a pilgrim waits outside and "preyde mete *pur charite* for a povere heremyte" (B 13.25–30; C 15.30–36). These images of rich and poor derive ultimately from the biblical story of the different fates of the selfish Dives and the beggar Lazarus (Luke 16:19–31), which the poet refers to explicitly at B 14.122 (C 15.303), B 17.265–70 (expanded in C 19.231–52), and C 8.278–82. Dives and Lazarus was a common mural theme of Henry III's royal palaces and is still found in parish churches, such as a twelfth-century image at Hardham (now quite ruined) and a thirteenth-century one at Ulcombe, Kent, whose upper register (fig. 14) shows the rich man and his friends dining at an elaborate table, while to the right outside the house a servant with a snarling dog (at the lower right) drives away the poor man (now almost invisible).[47]

Character, Action, and Literariness

Piers Plowman has been considered nonvisual by some because it lacks the detailed settings of *Sir Gawain and the Green Knight* (such as Arthur's feasting hall and the lady's bedroom) or of Chaucer's works (such as Criseyde's palace and the house of John the carpenter in the *Miller's Tale*). It is true that events in *Piers* are rarely located in a particularized space and might be taking place almost anywhere. But

47. For a watercolor of the Ulcombe image, see Rouse, *Wall Paintings*, illustration 49. For Henry III's interest in the subject, see Caiger-Smith, *Mural Paintings*, 83; Park, "Wall Painting," 127; and especially Borenius, *Cycle*, 40–42, 48; Dixon-Smith, *Image and Reality*.

FIGURE 14. *Dives and Lazarus. Ulcombe, Kent.*

this does not mean that Langland lacks a visual sense, only that his may be different from that of other Ricardian poets. The absence of background detail in *Piers* was associated by Salter with manuscript drawings ("Visual Arts," 257–60), but the most common and accessible contemporary analogue is English parish murals, especially those of the thirteenth and fourteenth centuries, which, in contrast to the complex use of space in contemporary Italian *fresci*, either lack architecture entirely, as in the lives of the Virgin and Christ at Chalgrove (Tristram, *Fourteenth*, plates 30–40), or use a shallow and unrealistic frame, as in the Passion sequence from Little Easton whose arches are purely decorative (see fig. 9).[48]

The attention in both *Piers* and wall paintings is not on naturalistic setting but on characters, singly or in groups. The same emphasis is also found in the lively colored drawings that appear in the only fully illustrated manuscript of

48. The Chalgrove painter sometimes uses the architecture of the church rather than representing a genuine setting. For example, an executioner with a pail of tools preceding Christ carrying his cross is not climbing up Golgatha, but up a steep window arch on the north wall (Tristram, *Fourteenth*, plates 31). Similarly, at Croughton, Herod receiving the Wise Men sits on the left curve of a window arch, while one of the Wise Men's horses is led over the top and right side of the same arch (see Tristram and James, *Wall-Paintings*, plate 39, figure 1).

Piers: Bodleian Library, Oxford, MS Douce 104 (a C-text). The Douce draw-ings never portray background but instead show a series of expressive figures from the text, some of whom are relatively minor.[49] Characters in the written text of *Piers* also suggest those in wall paintings. Individuals in the poem are clearly defined even when allegorical (Meed, Gluttony, Study), though their full significance must always be explored and they may (as with Conscience and Piers the plowman) develop and change. Likewise, figures in parish murals are sometimes given written labels, or they are saints identified by their symbols (Margaret's dragon, Catherine's wheel), or they make emblem-atic gestures, as we saw with Gluttony's drinking in the Trotton scheme (see fig. 13). Like characters in the poem, those in wall paintings are strongly out-lined and often not modeled (a characteristic of English medieval art and also found in Douce 104), as in the magnificent early fourteenth-century image of Christ with the remains of a Doubting Thomas (only his hand being guided by Jesus to his own wound is extant) from a small, isolated church in Bradwell, Essex (fig. 15).[50]

The characters in parish murals and in *Piers* attract the eye through their phys-ical actions. With minimal background and setting, wall paintings instead accen-tuate human energy and movement. Two vivid examples are from the early four-teenth century. A powerful martyrdom of Thomas of Lancaster done in oil at South Newington, Oxfordshire, shows the executioner rising up on one leg with a sword above his head as he is about to bring down the fatal blow onto the head of his kneeling victim (Tristram, *Fourteenth*, plate 18). The second is the simpler but equally athletic image of Salome's dancing from Chalfont St. Giles, Buckinghamshire, in which she completely bends over backward like a gymnast

49. A replica of the manuscript has recently been published (*Piers Plowman: A Facsimile*) with an intro-duction by Derek Pearsall and a catalogue by Kathleen Scott. Elsewhere Scott notes that "the figures proj-ect liveliness of gesture and body movement" ("Illustrations," 12). See also Pearsall, "Manuscript Illustration."

50. Tristram noted that "line rather than form appears to have been a characteristic preoccupation of the English artist from pre-Conquest times to the middle of the fourteenth century" (*Twelfth*, 8). Rouse agreed that English wall painting, especially in the thirteenth and fourteenth centuries, was characterized by "sureness and purity of outline" (*Wall Paintings*, 21).

As with the delicate hand of Thomas in figure 15, the visual in *Piers*, as George Kane has argued (*Middle English*, 236), is often expressed by a focus on particular physical details, such as Piers the plowman's men-tion of "ye lovely ladies *with youre longe fyngres*" (B 6.10; C 8.9: the example and emphasis are Kane's). Mention is made of Thomas's hand probing Christ's side in *Piers* at B 19.170–71 (C 21.170–71). Hands are often highly expressive in both the poem and the murals.

FIGURE 15. *Christ with Hand of Doubting Thomas. Bradwell, Essex.*

(fig. 16).[51] The physicality of wall paintings is paralleled in *Piers Plowman*. The poem is famous for the vigor of its verbs of motion, as in the dreamer's assertion that lewed people "percen with a *Paternoster* the paleys of hevene" (B 10.462; A 11.312; C 11.299) or in Liar's pell-mell escape from the king's justice: "Lightliche Lyere leep awey thenne, / Lurkyng thorugh lanes, tolugged of manye" (B 2.216–17; A 2.177–78; C 225–26). The poem contains many abrupt, violent gestures at key moments, such as Piers's sudden first appearance to the folk, his tearing of the pardon, and Trajan's breaking out of hell. The illustrator of Douce 104 responded to the energy the poet often gives his characters, as seen in the portrait of a leaping Envy with his fist punching the air.[52]

51. Other examples of dramatic action by mural figure include Saint Dunstan's pinching the Devil's nose at Barton, Cambridgeshire (cf. Tudor-Craig, "Painting," 41), the stoning of Saint Stephen at Black Bourton, Oxford (Tristram, *Thirteenth*, plate 102), and the killing of Abel by Cain at Capel, Kent (Tristram, *Thirteenth*, plate 150). See also the more refined motions of two elegant censing angels from Brent Eleigh, which originally bracketed a statue of the Virgin and Child, and an especially violent image, which also emphasizes hands, in which Saint Catherine is flipped over the back of a torturer, one of the scenes in the saint's life at Castor, Cambridgeshire (Rouse, *Wall Paintings*, illustration 9).

52. Scott, figure 12, which she compares to scenes of the Flagellation of Christ ("Illustrations," 31), a violent image often depicted in wall paintings. See Lawlor on the importance of movement and gesture in the poem (*Piers Plowman*, 209ff.).

FIGURE 16. *Salome Dancing at Herod's Feast. Chalfont St. Giles, Buckinghamshire.*

Aesthetic difference may be as revealing as similarity. Thus parish murals also suggest the ways the poem transcends painting, for some of the most effective visual techniques in *Piers* are inescapably literary. For example, the second half of the first line of a description of hermits includes the kind of precise physical detail noted by those who praise this aspect of the poem: "Heremytes on an heep with hoked staves" (B pr.53; A pr.50; C pr.51); but the following line, which is equally visual, depends on being written for its effectiveness: "Wenten to Walsyngham—and hire wenches after" (B pr.54; A pr.51; C pr.52). In a painting, where everything is available to the eye at once, the delayed impact of the stinging insult in the second half-line would be lost.

Some of the most brilliant images in *Piers Plowman* are impossible to paint. An obvious example is Holy Church's sublime description of the Incarnation as the plant of peace:

> For hevene myghte nat holden it, so was it hevy of hymselve,
> Til it hadde of the erthe eten his fille.
> And whan it hadde of this fold flessh and blood taken,
> Was nevere leef upon lynde lighter therafter,

> And portatif and persaunt as the point of a nedle,
> That myghte noon armure it lette ne none heighe walles.
>
> (B 1.153–58; C 1.148–53)

The passage contains a number of precise images (from eating the earth to penetrating needles, from fragile leaves to high walls), but their cumulative and metaphysical power comes from our inability to make them form a single coherent picture (for a similar, if simpler, passage, cf. B 12.140–42; C 14.84–86).

The Trinity is an even more complex example of an unpaintable image in *Piers Plowman*. Representations of the triune God, especially in sculpture, were criticized by the Lollards, though a few murals of the subject survive today, such as those at Bradwell, Essex; Ducklington, Oxfordshire; and Wymington, Bedfordshire.[53] Each of these Trinity paintings portrays the Father and Son as humans and the Holy Spirit as a dove. Such relatively simple images of this central but difficult doctrine are far surpassed by the poet's metaphysical comparisons of the Trinity to a hand (B 17.137–203; C 19.112–68) and then to a torch (B 17.204ff.; C 19.169ff.). The long second passage, which continues to ring changes on the idea of fire until the very end of the passus (see the mention of the proverbial smoky house at B 17.343ff.; C 19.325ff.), contains a series of sharply visual moments, such as when the transformation of God's might into mercy is likened to the way that "Ysekeles in evesynges thorugh hete of the sonne / Melteth in a mynut while to myst and to watre" (B 17.228–29; C 19.194–95). The sheer variety of the poet's fire imagery in this passage (including a flaming torch, sparks from flint, and the evil burning of rich men) makes impossible any actual painting of what he has written—a way of suggesting the mystery of the Trinity itself.

Clashing Styles

If some of the sophisticated visual effects that could be achieved in writing are not possible in wall painting, others are closely parallel. The clash of different

53. For the Ducklington Trinity, see Tristram, *Fourteenth*, plate 58. The Wymington Trinity is probably from the fifteenth century and appears to have been repainted recently.

The most intriguing image of the Trinity I have seen in an English parish church is an early fourteenth-century mural from Little Kimble, Buckinghamshire, which shows a bearded man pointing to a triptych that contain miniatures of the Virgin and Child and, on the right, the Trinity (Caiger-Smith, *Mural Paintings*, 133; Tristram, *Fourteenth*, 188). Woolf noted that the Lollards considered representations of the Trinity to be a special abomination (*English Mystery Plays*, 99). Margaret Aston, in "Lollards and Images," supports this view (165ff.), but, while stressing that a wide variety of views were held by Lollards about images (137), she reminds us that the main burden of their criticism of image worship referred to sculpture (146).

literary registers is a notable feature of late medieval English poetry. The mystery plays repeatedly exploit contrasts between the mundane and the holy: in the *Second Shepherd's Play*, for example, the rustic slapstick of tossing Mak in a blanket gives way to the holy discourse between angel and Virgin. Chaucer's *Canterbury Tales* is built on similar oppositions: the noble and pageantlike *Knight's Tale* followed by the bawdy, idiomatic *Miller's Tale*; the restrained, spiritual *Second Nun's Tale* followed by the compulsive, materialist *Canon Yeoman's Tale*. *Piers Plowman* likewise repeatedly contrasts the coarse with the exalted, the pious with the wicked, Latin with the demotic. Holy Church is followed by Meed, and the hopeless sinners by the ideal Piers. These juxtapositions are in style as well as meaning. Holy Church's lines on the Incarnation just quoted above are among the most sublime in English poetry (B 1.153–58; C 1.148–53), but she also employs racy proverbs—"na moore merite in masse ne in houres / Than Malkyn of hire maydenhede" (B 1.183–84; A 1.157–58; C PR.178–79)—as well as personal insult: "Thow doted daffe!" (B 1.140; A 1.129; C 1.138).

The rapid changes of tone in *Piers Plowman* and other Ricardian writing may seem radical, even bewildering, to the modern reader, but a medieval audience would have been familiar with such stylistic variety and contrast from their local churches. The walls of a single parish often had murals from different periods executed with different degrees of skill, though it is now difficult to determine exactly which paintings would have been visible at any specific time. At Little Horwood, Buckinghamshire, a late Seven Deadly Sins mural is directly painted over earlier images of Saint Nicholas and what is apparently the death of Thomas Becket, whereas West Chiltington, Sussex, has paintings from the twelfth, thirteenth, and fourteenth centuries at different locations in the church, all or most of which might have been available to a late medieval parishioner. The north wall of the nave at Ickleton has a series of magnificent, if faded, early images of Christ's Passion with martyrdoms of the apostles beneath; in contrast, as previously mentioned, Ickleton's chancel arch has a relatively crude, if vigorous, fourteenth- or fifteenth-century Doom (see fig. 4). From an aesthetic point of view, the two schemes could hardly differ more, and yet they shared the same building and perhaps many of the same viewers.

The mixture of mural subjects and treatments so often found in medieval parish churches was rarely the result of a unified artistic conception, but rather of many individual decisions over a span of time, sometimes over centuries. The aesthetic difference is not an act of intention, but of reception. Yet there were other stylistic clashes in wall painting that, like those in *Piers Plowman*, are the product of a single act of creation. The church at Beckley, near Oxford, contains a variety of paintings. One complex image, all of it painted at the same time and perhaps by the same hand, creates meaning, as in contemporary writing, through discordant artistic registers: a contrast that is still observable, even though the work of the Beckley artist, as with other English murals, now more resembles a drawing than a painting. The middle of the composition is not remarkable in style or subject: it contains the remains of a conventional weighing of souls by the archangel Michael with Mary and a devil vying to influence the outcome.[54] The significant aesthetic opposition takes places above and below the weighing. At the top of the composition is a naked sinner being roasted on a spit (fig. 17); one faint animal-like devil stands over the victim's body, seasoning it as it turns, while below another devil (almost invisible) operates a bellows to keep up the fire. To the left another sinner (not shown) hangs upside down from a meat hook waiting his turn to be toasted. In contrast to this upper scene, the bottom of the composition, under a painted canopy and in front of an elaborate trefoil, shows a crowned Mary suckling a nimbed baby Jesus (fig. 18). The artistic effect of the Virgin and Child differs absolutely, except in skill, from the burning sinner above. Despite the loss of color and detail (no features on Mary's face remain and only a few on Jesus'), the elegant outline of the pair fully expresses their holy serenity. In contrast, the cruder (note the lack of proportion in the arms and legs), though lively, drawing of the roasting sinner communicates the grotesque, even comic, results of evil. Stylistic unity has been sacrificed in order to convey meaning: the ugliness and absurdity of sin as opposed to the pure hope of the Incarnation. The tonal shifts and discordances in the poetry of Chaucer or Langland are not foreign to parish wall paintings or other medieval art (see Heslop, "Romanesque Painting").

Complex Structures

Parish wall paintings are a contemporary context for the complexity of structure, as well as style, in *Piers Plowman*, suggesting the way the poem might have been approached by its original readers. Some of the best critics of the poem have pointed to its elusive form and genre: its puzzling mixture of allegory,

---

54. The remains at Beckley of a later, larger weighing to the left of the fourteenth-century weighing are further testimony to the redoing of images over time.

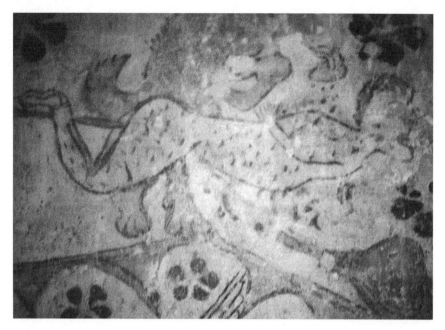

FIGURE 17. *Roasting of Sinner (detail). Beckley, Oxfordshire.*

description, and narrative, which often seems to lack any principle of organization. Thus C. S. Lewis asserts that Langland "hardly makes his poetry into a
poem" (*Allegory of Love*, 161), and Salter and Pearsall counsel us to accept that
"Langland is not committed to a narrative structure in any continuous way"
(edition of *Piers*, 32). Modern readers accustomed to Chaucer's skill at coherent
storytelling are often baffled by the narrative discontinuities of *Piers Plowman*
(see Benson, "Frustration"). But late medieval audiences familiar with the
cacophony of parish wall paintings might not have been so puzzled.

The programs of Romanesque murals were often highly unified (such as the
Last Judgment that fills three walls at Clayton), but such harmony was less
common in the following two centuries. David Park laments that by the thirteenth century the "coherence of organization and subject-matter of all but the
most major schemes begins to break down," resulting in an "odd diversity of
subjects" ("Wall Painting, 126; cf. 129). The church at Slapton,
Northhamptonshire, for example, is not large, but it contains a profusion of
different images. In addition to various decorative motifs and a Saint
Christopher mural (containing a coy mermaid looking at herself in a mirror),
the painting at Slapton includes the archangel Michael weighing a soul with the

FIGURE 18. *Virgin and Child (detail).*
Beckley, Oxfordshire.

Virgin intervening, as already mentioned (see fig. 7); Saint Francis receiving the stigmata; a Resurrection scene with donor; Saint Anne teaching the Virgin; the Devil urging on two gossiping women; the suicide of Judas from a tree; an Annunciation scene; an episode from the life of Saint Eligius; and the remains of a three-living-and-three-dead scene (in which three rich kings confront the three skeletons they shall become). There are fragments of other paintings and evidence that there were once many more.[55]

Additional parish churches that still preserve a wide variety of fourteenth-century imagery include Barton and Belchamp Walter. At Belchamp Walter, the east end of the north wall of the nave has a compressed Passion sequence (from the entrance into Jerusalem to Christ before Pilate) and below that a martyrdom of Saint Edmund, a pelican feeding her children with the blood from her own breast, and the three living and the three dead. Farther west on the north wall are

55. Tristram dated the paintings at Slapton "from c.1350 or just after the early part of the following century," without clearly explaining which paintings go with which dates (*Fourteenth*, 247). In a private communication, Miriam Gill judges the Saint Francis and some other images as fifteenth century, much of the rest of the painting as from the mid-fourteenth century (including Saint Eligius, Saint Anne, and the weighing), and the Annunciation and suicide of Judas as perhaps somewhat earlier. As always, it is difficult to know what images would have been visible at any one time.

a charming icon of the Virgin and Child and the rebirth of the phoenix. On the south wall are fragments of a Resurrection scene, and farther east the remains of a Seven Deadly Sins, with Pride in the center being attacked by Death with a lance.[56]

Whether or not one agrees with Park that such diversity of subjects is odd and a decline from twelfth-century coherence, it offers insight into the contemporary reception of *Piers Plowman*. Long experience with the public art of their local churches must have acclimated contemporaries to forms of organization that may seem peculiar to modern audiences. Parish wall paintings would have trained parishioners to make sense of stylistic and narrative variety within a single structure. The violent transitions and juxtapositions of disparate material in *Piers* might have been perfectly understandable to the first readers of the poem—as they may be to us when we are more familiar with the neglected cultural analogues painted on parish walls.[57]

Murals also reveal something about the way that *Piers Plowman* was experienced in its time. Unlike art in modern museums, wall paintings would not have been viewed by their original audience on only a few special occasions; instead, they were on permanent display in a public space and would have been seen again and again. It is equally unlikely that *Piers Plowman* was meant to be read straight through like a novel (which is why those who do so are so often disappointed, confused, or overwhelmed), but rather, like other religious treatises, it was intended to be consumed piecemeal, not necessarily always in the same order, and repeatedly. Elizabeth Kirk once remarked in my presence that Langland is one of those writers, like Proust, who should never be read for the first time. The wall paintings in local churches would never have been consciously seen for the first time, but, as with *Piers Plowman*, revealed their meanings gradually.

Indeed, a range of different meanings were available to the audiences of both the poem and the paintings. Although parish murals are orthodox in intent and may even have been used by preachers for instruction, their variety makes them susceptible to individual interpretation. Any observer could choose to look at

---

56. Belchamp Walter resembles *Piers Plowman* not only in its variety, but also in the centrality of Christ, whether represented directly (the Passion scenes), symbolically (the pelican), or by means of the human ills he came to remedy (the Deadly Sins).

57. Ellen Ross suggests that the murals at Chalgrove were designed to be read in a definite order (*Grief of God*, 56–57), though of course this may not have happened in practice. She does note that the arrangement of the murals at Great Tew, in contrast to Chalgrove, points to "the diversity of artistic structure" also found in Italian churches (59).

some rather than others and to understand them idiosyncratically. What lessons did women parishioners draw from images of the Virgin, for example, or from the frequent narratives of heroic female saints standing up to male authority? As modern criticism has shown us, *Piers Plowman*, despite its seeming didacticism, is also constantly open to multiple interpretations (why does Piers tear the pardon and what is doing well?), which is perhaps only truly possible in the comfort of a shared culture like that of late medieval Catholic England. English murals, whitewashed by the Tudors and often overlooked by modern scholars, are a major public context for *Piers Plowman*. To paraphrase Pecock, readers of the "heereable rememoratiif signes" of the poem can learn much from the "seable rememoratiif signes" of parish wall paintings.

6. Public Life

LONDON CIVIC PRACTICES

I. MALVERN AND CORNHILL

Malvern

Two hills mentioned in *Piers Plowman* have shaped the traditional biography of its author: the Malvern Hills, on the border of Worcestershire and Herefordshire, and Cornhill in the city of London. Most Langlandians from Skeat to the present have believed that the poet was brought up near the first and resided as an adult on the second. In truth, the two locales are more conspicuous in *Piers* scholarship than in the work itself. Malvern is mentioned a few times in the *visio*, though the speaker never says that that is where he lived, only that he had a vision there after much wandering (B pr.1–6; A pr.1–6; C pr.1–7). Cornhill is named but once—and only in the C-version. No special local knowledge about either Malvern or Cornhill is displayed in *Piers*, in contrast, for example, to the convincing detail about Oxford and Cambridge that Chaucer provides in his tales of the Miller and Reeve.

Yet little as these hills reveal about the private life of the author of *Piers*, both places (and especially the London site) clarify the poem's engagement with the public life of late medieval England. Malvern and Cornhill represent two striking geographical extremes in a work full of contrasts: Truth/Wrong, Holy Church/Meed, Christ/Satan. Rural Malvern is about as far west (the traditional locale of alliterative poetry) as one can go and still remain in England, whereas urban Cornhill is not only far to the east but also at the heart of the realm's capital city.

The Malvern Hills are never much more than a name in *Piers Plowman*. After being identified as the place of the initial dream (B pr.5; A pr.5; C. pr.6), they appear briefly and metaphorically later in the prologue in an insult to lawyers (B pr.215; A pr.88; C pr.163) and are then mentioned again in C only (5.110) and finally by all at the end of the *visio* (B 7.142; A 8.129; C 9.295). What we learn from these brief citations is the unsurprising information that the hills contain at least one brook and are often misty. Malvern is not named again in the poem, prompting Caroline Barron's observation that the references to it in *Piers* "barely justify the weight that has been placed upon them" by scholarship ("William Langland," 93).

In *Piers Plowman*, Malvern is primarily a sign of absence, pointing to two elite medieval institutions that go almost entirely unmentioned in the poem: knighthood and monasticism. Modern Malvern is a lovely Victorian resort town, associated with Edward Elgar, boarding schools, and bottled water, but in the Middle Ages it was "chiefly noteworthy for its great forest known as Malvern Chase, which pertained to the lordship of Hanley Castle, and for its Benedictine priory" (*Victoria History*, 4:124). Malvern Chase, occupying much of the eastern slope of the hills and the plain below, was originally a royal forest; later, when held by several important families, it continued to be used for knightly sport.[1] In addition to those who fought (or at least hunted) at Malvern, there were also those who prayed there—in particular, the monks at the priory of Great Malvern.[2]

Chase and cloister are both prominent in Florence Converse's novel *Long Will*, whose first scene has Prince Lionel pursuing game on the Malvern Hills and then describes the departure of Will from Great Malvern Priory. Converse seems to have added these episodes to her narrative because chivalry and monasticism, which are central to traditional conceptions of the Middle Ages (especially in fiction), are not very important in *Piers*. Although the poem's opening lines (with its May vision, "ferlies," tower, and dungeon) suggest romance, knights are rare in the rest of the poem and not especially efficacious when they are present. On the half acre, the knight volunteers to help Piers, but he proves incapable of controlling the wasters who ruin the communal effort, and Study

---

1. The designation Chase, as opposed to Forest, meant that Malvern was no longer owned by the king, though English royalty continued to hunt there. The lords of Malvern Chase and Hanley Castle included Clares, Despensers, and Mortimers. The most colorful was perhaps Gilbert de Clare, the famous Red Earl of Gloucester, who in the late thirteenth century ingeniously defended the rights of the Chase against the bishop of Hereford by digging a ditch angled so that escaping deer could not reenter the bishop's land. See Hurle, *Malvern Chase* and *Hanley Castle*; *Victoria History*, esp. 2:317–18, 4:93–96; Habington, *Survey*, 267–68; B. Smith, *History of Malvern*, 25–40.

2. The priory was extensively rebuilt in the fifteenth century and the truncated church today still contains some of its late medieval glories, including lively misericords and glass windows given by Richard III and Henry VII. See Nott, *Some of the Antiquities*, esp. 82–85; Pevsner, *Worcestershire*, 159–63; *Victoria History*, 2:136–43.

in the B-version blames lords and ladies for meanly eating in private so as not to
have to feed others (B 10.96–102). The only chivalric figure who succeeds in the
poem is Christ, the anti-knight, who, riding barefoot on an ass, conquers by
dying. That other Malvern institution, the monastery, is also missing in most of
the poem, which instead concentrates on clergy who are active in the world, such
as parish priests, bishops, and friars. An unusual reference to the cloister (and
school) as heaven on earth because "al is buxomnesse there and bokes" (B
10.299–302; C 5.152–55) is not as positive as sometimes assumed, for it prefaces
a strong attack on the present state of religion and the prediction that the abbot
of Abingdon will soon receive a knock. In sum, Malvern's elite worlds of
knights and monks are largely irrelevant to the more public, turbulent, and civic
life of *Piers Plowman.*

Because of its bucolic title, opening Malvern location, and other country settings such as the Field of Folk, half acre, and Barn of Unity, *Piers Plowman* is
often regarded as a celebration of rural life and virtues.[3] In a important essay,
Derek Pearsall has recently argued that Langland, "though he is conscious of
and minutely attentive to the economic and political life of the city, chooses
agrarian models for his allegorical ideals of community"; the reason being that
for all his "vivid and localized expression" of urban commerce, government, and
social relationships, the poet is not able to absorb them into his "traditional and
idealizing cast of mind" ("Langland's London," 185–86). Pearsall concludes
that London is "the problem of the poem, and one to which [Langland] found
no solution" (201). Without denying the force of this argument, I want to argue
instead that London practices are absolutely central to *Piers Plowman;* rather than
an merely an insoluble problem, urban life is used deliberately and eagerly by the
poet to express his greatest hopes as well as his deepest fears.

City and country are not necessarily antithetical in *Piers Plowman* or in
medieval culture. In the C-version the "I" declares that "I leve yn London and
opelond bothe" (C 5.44), and recent scholarship has stressed the continuity of
social and economic activities between rural and urban areas in the English
Middle Ages (see Rubin, "Religious Culture"; Patterson, *Subject of History,* chapter

---

3. Given Malvern's remote location, modern readers may assume that it is meant to stand for the
country in general as opposed to the city, though the poem offers a more extreme definition. Rather than
farmland, Malvern is presented in *Piers* as a wild, remote area, appropriate to a pseudohermit, and a place
of visions. Indeed, a wilderness is precisely how William of Malmesbury describes Malvern in his *De Gestis
Pontificum Anglorum* (285–86).

5). In *Piers,* it is often hard to tell whether a scene takes place in the city or in the country, and many occupy an allegorical nowhere space like the scenes in parish wall paintings. Even the Field of Folk contains London episodes, including parsons deserting their parishes for city silver (B pr.83–86; A pr.80–83; C pr.81–84), and the section ends with the cries of merchants in urban streets (B pr.226–30; A pr.104–8; C pr.227–31).

Nor is the poem's presentation of the country wholly positive. As many rogues and sharp practices are found on the farm as down city lanes. The agricultural world repeatedly produces sterile futility in *Piers:* the attempt to create a model community on the half-acre founders, and the poem concludes with the spiritual Barn of Unity under attack from Antichrist without and friars within. The steady, diligent work necessary for agricultural or monastic success is not the focus of *Piers Plowman.* Instead the narrative leaves the country, leaves Malvern, as it were, to search for another route to salvation. Like Lady Meed, it goes to London.[4]

Cornhill

Many readers of *Piers* have noted the importance of London in the poem. Skeat declared that "one great merit of the poem consists in its exhibition of *London* life and *London* opinions" and that "the *London* origin of, at any rate, the larger portion of the poem, is the true key to the right understanding of it" (*Three Parallel Texts,* 2:3, his emphasis). Barron has recently expressed a similar opinion: "Insofar as Langland's poem is rooted in time and place, it is rooted in the streets of London in the 1370s" ("William Langland," 93). Of course the city is never simple in *Piers* and always remains as dynamic and complex as the poem itself.[5] London both attracts and repels Langland, as he is attracted and repelled by minstrels, beggars, and those quintessentially urban figures, friars. The poet responds to the energy of the city (as in the lively street cries

---

4. Not that London, and specifically Cornhill, was unconnected to Malvern. The patrons of Saint Michael Cornhill, the only parish wholly within the ward of Cornhill, were the abbot and monks of Evesham, located only a few miles from the Malvern Hills, and Great Malvern itself was a dependency of Westminster Abbey.

5. There is medieval precedent for contradictory views of London. Two twelfth-century historians made very different judgments: William Fitzstephen had almost nothing but praise for the city, and Richard of Devizes nothing but criticism. See Scattergood, who notes that each follows a classical model ("Misrepresenting the City," 18–21). Translations of Fitzstephen's and Richard of Devizes's opposing positions are found at the beginning of Bailey's *Oxford Book of London,* 3–4.

at the end of the prologue), but he is also appalled by its vices, especially its commercial vices. If London is "the problem that the poem does not solve" (Pearsall, "Langland's London," 186), that is because the city is so embedded in the themes and concerns of *Piers* that any clear solution to the questions it raises is impossible.[6]

Attempting to achieve even a preliminary understanding of medieval London, either as an historical reality or as it seen in *Piers*, is no easy task. The approach I shall adopt here is to investigate one part of the city, Cornhill, using it as a cross-section for London as a whole. I initially chose Cornhill as a test site because it is mentioned in the poem in association with the narrative voice, and thus it seemed as good a place to start as any. As I have learned more about the area, I have come to believe that it offers more than just a convenient sample: in addition to being a manageable microcosm of late medieval London, Cornhill was the site of local public practices (religious, commercial, and judicial) that bring us to the heart of *Piers Plowman.*

As already noted, the name Cornhill appears only once in all the different versions of *Piers*, though at a significant point in the poem: between the trial of Meed and the confession of the sins. Here the C-version, and only the C-version, includes a scene in which the narratorial "I" enters into a long dialogue with Conscience and Reason about the way he is leading his life, prefaced by lines in which this figure locates himself in Cornhill:

6. The first extended urban scene in the poem, the trial of Meed, is something of a false step. It takes place not in the city of London itself but outside its walls and jurisdiction at Westminster, which, somewhat reminiscent of Malvern, was under the dual jurisdiction of those who pray, the abbey, and those who fight, the king and his court (see Rosser, "London and Westminster" and *Medieval Westminster*). But *Piers* does not reveal much detailed knowledge of either kingship or national government (Barron, "William Langland," 94–95).

Meed goes to Westminster to have her proposed marriage adjudicated because "there lawe is yshewed" (B 2.135; A 2.99; C 2.148), but in contrast to the practical law we shall see practiced on Cornhill, Westminster law in the poem is either hopelessly idealistic or utterly corrupt. The king's advisers are abstractions, Conscience and Reason, who advocate an unattainable justice. For example, when asked to be more merciful in the case Peace brings against Wrong, Reason says he will when lords love truth and hate harlotry and clerks covet to clothe and feed the poor (B 4.113–19; A 4.100ff., rewritten; C 4.108–14). In short—never. In direct opposition to such stern idealism, the court officials at Westminster are easily corrupted, willing to countenance any abuse for a little money. These extremes of good and evil at Westminster are in contrast to the more complex and believable legal and social behavior found on the streets of London itself and in *Piers Plowman*. Even Conscience admits that all the fine theories that he, Reason, and the king proclaim will not be realized "but the commune wole assente" (B 4.182; C 4.176). *Commune* has several overlapping meanings in *Piers*, but the public world of the commune of London is essential to the poem's most urgent social questions.

Thus I awaked, woet God, whan I wonede in Cornehull—
Kytte and I in a cote—yclothed as a lollare,
And lytel ylet by, leveth me for sothe,
Amonges lollares of Londone and lewede ermytes,
For I made of tho men as resoun me tauhte.

(c 5.1–5)

These lines and those that immediately follow have always provided the most fertile material for the Langland biographical myth.[7] Yet, despite the widespread modern assumption that the episode means that Langland actually lived in Cornhill, little attention has been paid to the area itself or to the associations it might have had for contemporary readers.[8]

Cornhill was located in the eastern part of the old city, and when the name appears in medieval London records (usually spelled "Cornhull" as in the C-text) it may refer to several related entities: the hill, the street, the ward, or several markets (Ekwall, *Street-Names*, 186–87). The summit of Cornhill is the highest point within the city, though it is admittedly not much of a rise. Cornhill Street ran east from the Poultry to the top of the hill and in the Middle Ages included the present Leadenhall Street as well (today this would be from the Bank Street tube stop to the Lloyd's building). Cornhill was one of the widest roads in medieval London, with two separate gutters running down it instead of the usual one. It was a continuation of Cheap Street (or West Cheap), and together

---

7. First used by Skeat, the passage was the foundation for Donaldson's influential life of the poet, and its importance is reaffirmed in the recent collection of essays edited by Justice and Kerby-Fulton (*Written Work*).

8. Whatever its personal relationship to the poet (and I do not assume anything), medieval Cornhill has much to say about the London context of the poem. To take a brief example, consider some of the names of those who crowd into Gluttony's tavern: "Cesse the Souteresse," "Tymme the Tynkere," "Hikke the Hakeneyman," "Clarice of Cokkeslane," "Rose the Dysshere," "Godefray of Garlekhithe," and "Griffyth the Walshe" (B 5.308–17; A 5.158–67; C 6.361–72). Modern readers are charmed by these striking names—the fourth and sixth of which specifically mention London sites, as do the variations "a rakiere of Chepe" (B 5.315; A 5.165) and "the hangeman of Tybourne" (c 6.367)—and so were the poem's early scribes and rubricators, who frequently called attention to them in medieval manuscripts of the poem. That the list is more than a poetical invention is shown by a similar one in the London city records that itemizes those accused of flouting city regulations on Cornhill in 1321–22. The names, with the same combination of a baptismal name and an occupation or place (though without the poem's use of nick-names and in Anglo-Norman French), include "Richard le Taillour," "William le Hosiere," "Roger Panyfader de Houndesdiche," "William de Abyndone," and "John de Suthwerk" (*Letter Book E*, fol. cxxx [*Calendar*, 156–57]). The customers of Gluttony's tavern have a historical authenticity that the allegorical Gluttony himself lacks.

they constituted the main east-west shopping thoroughfare of London; thus John Stow identified Cornhill as "part of the principall high streete" of London (*Survey*, 1:187). The ward of Cornhill, one of twenty-six divisions of the city that elected alderman and performed other municipal functions, was located on either side of the street on the western slope of the hill.

Because the speaker in c 5 refers to his living in Cornhill among lollars and lewed hermits (and because used-clothing markets were certainly located there), Cornhill is often assumed by modern scholars to be something of a downmarket slum, as in the note to Pearsall's edition that it "had something of a reputation as a resort of London vagabonds" (*Piers: C-Text*, 97n). This is misleading. Far from being seedy or marginal, Cornhill was part of the city's commercial center and always contained prosperous precincts. The magnificent Merchant Taylor's Hall was built in the late fourteenth century on the north side of the hill between Cornhill and Threadneedle Streets upon the site of a great mansion once owned by the powerful Crepin family; the Florentine House of Bardi had their headquarters in Lombard Street on the south side of the hill; and the imposing Leadenhall building (owned by the famous mercenary Sir John Hawkwood and then by Dick Whittington) sat on the top of the hill (Riley, *Memorials*, 183–85; Clode, 2:1; G. Williams, *Medieval London*, 98, 103–4, 247; Samuel and Milne, "'Ledene Hall,'" 39–42; Thomas, "Notes"). Gervase of Cornhill was among the wealthiest Londoners in the twelfth century, and in 1398 the executors of Walter Pynchon, a Cornhill merchant, listed jewels, silver, and gold belonging to him and his shop at the value of six hundred pounds (Riley, *Memorials*, 550; Britnell, *Commercialisation*, 34). A remarkably influential citizen of the late fourteenth century was Chaucer's friend John Philpot (or Philipot), who was an alderman from Cornhill in the 1370s and 1380s and mayor in 1378–79.[9] That the Royal Exchange was built in the middle of Cornhill in the sixteenth century and that the Bank of England now sits near one end of the street amidst some of the world's most powerful financial institutions is a natural development from the medieval district, however much this may seem to violate the values of *Piers Plowman*.

9. Ruth Bird noted that Philpot "was to achieve an influence and fame which in some ways exceeded those of his better known contemporary William Walworth" (*Turbulent London*, 3; cf. 47). Philpot lent money to the king and financed a private fleet to defeat pirates who were attacking English shipping. He was a London member of Parliament at least three times and was knighted for his part in resisting the Rising of 1381. See *Dictionary of National Biography*, s.v. "Philpot, Phelipot, or Pilpot, Sir John."

Public Cornhill

There were many uses of public space in medieval London, several of which I
shall be discussing, and among the most visible were ceremonial parades—by the
king, especially, but also by other municipal groups.[10] Cornhill was a major site
for such displays; the top of its hill has been identified by Glynne Wickham as
the crossing point for the "principal processional routes" that traversed the city
in the late Middle Ages (*Early English Stages*, 60 [fig. 9], see 53–54). One route, for
royal corteges and conveying important prisoners, ran from the Tower in the east
to Westminster in the west, going through Aldgate and then along Cornhill and
Cheap (see Kingsford, *Chronicles of London*, 221, 223, 258–59; Riley, *Memorials*, 640,
642). Royal entries into London usually followed a different route that also had
Cornhill as its hub; the king and his party approached the city across London
Bridge, then proceeded to the top of Cornhill along Gracechurch Street before
turning left down Cornhill Street into Cheap on the way to Saint Paul's or
Westminster.[11] As early as 1298, the fishmongers celebrated the military victory
of Falkirk by parading with carved and silver models of fish. Their route is not
certain, but according to Stow, it passed by the Leadenhall on Cornhill
(Withington, "'Royal-Entry,'" 621). Later processions over Cornhill include the
coronation of Richard II in 1377, which involved a staged pageant at Cheap with
the figure of an angel descending to the young sovereign, a scene possibly echoed
in *Piers Plowman* (B pr.128–31).[12] One of the most elaborate and best documented
of such spectacles was Henry VI's triumphal entry in 1432, for which Lydgate
wrote (or at least recorded) a series of allegorical pageants, including two performed on Cornhill.[13]

In addition to being the location of these royal entries, Cornhill was the site
of civic and religious public processions. For example, the medieval Midsummer

---

10. Hanawalt has commented on the prevalence of public display in medieval London: "We have
moved far from pageants and parades, away from rituals that all Londoners enjoyed. So much of London
life was lived in public that such ceremonies provide a good backdrop for outlining the history of London
society in the late Middle Ages" (*Growing Up*, 16).

11. Kipling argues that although such entries may have flattered the prince, their primary purpose "lay
in celebrating and renewing the communal political bond which united the sovereign and his people" (*Enter
the King*, 47). Wickham, anticipating Habermas's conception of medieval publicness, finds the purpose of
such street pageants to be "the physical manifestation of the ruler's person to the subjects assembled
within the capital city" (*Early English Stages*, 53).

12. For the 1377 coronation, see Wickham, *Early English Stages*, 54–55.

13. For this pageant, see Lydgate, "King Henry VI." See also Kingsford, *Chronicles*, 97–116, 302.

Watch included a unit that marched through the principal streets of London, traversing Cornhill both east and west (Stow, *Survey*, 1:101–3; cf. Lindenbaum, "Ceremony and Oligarchy"). The parish church of Saint Peter Cornhill was the point of origin for a major annual procession involving clergy and city officials that James Simpson has recently discussed in connection with *Piers Plowman.* To celebrate the supposed antiquity of this Cornhill church, the mayor, aldermen, and sheriffs of London gathered at Saint Peter's on the feast of Pentecost (Whitsun) and, along with the rectors of all other London churches, marched down Cornhill and Cheap to Saint Paul's. Simpson argues that this event has parallels with the Pentecostal scene in the penultimate passus of the long versions of *Piers* "in which liturgical and civic, or at least occupational, elements are inextricably interwoven" ("After Craftes Conseil," 109).[14]

In addition to encompassing such royal, municipal, and ecclesiastical processions, medieval London contained public spaces that allowed a variety of different social groups to meet and interact. This is not to say that the city was democratic in any way in which we would understand the term. All medieval Europe was a "deference society," and London was always strongly hierarchal, despite some challenges to its ruling oligarchy in the late fourteenth century. Only men (never women) were permitted to hold civic and guild offices, and only men who were prominent and prosperous (what the Anglo-Norman records call the great and the good). Yet, as some scholars have recently shown, the structure of power in London was not monolithic or absolutely closed: though kept from office, women belonged to and even helped to found guilds and achieved some measure of economic, if not political, power (Barron, "'Golden Age'"). The merchant elite that ran the city was not a static grouping but one constantly renewed by outsiders: few families were influential in the city for as long as three generations and many of the most successful citizens were immigrants from the provinces, such as the future mayor Dick Whittington.[15] Without disguising the rule of its merchant oligarchy, the London city records also repeatedly assert, at least rhetorically, the value of community and appeal to the common good and the

14. For the Saint Peter Cornhill procession, see *Letter Book H*, fol. cxlvi (*Calendar*, 188); *Liber Albus*, 29 (trans., 26); Riley, *Memorials*, 466, 651–53.

15. Barron, "Later Middle Ages," 56; see also Barron, "Richard Whittington," in which she argues that Whittington may not have been as destitute when he arrived in London as the legend has it. Whittington came from the West Country near Gloucester, the same general area where the Langland myth says that the poet was reared.

welfare of the people as a whole. For example, prices for a wide variety of goods and services (especially foodstuffs) were set by the city authorities to prevent price gouging (as well as to protect guild monopolies). Those who tried to charge more than these fixed prices or committed other commercial abuses were accused not only of offending the king and scandalizing the city but also of deceiving the people as a whole: *commune people* in the Anglo-Norman entries and *communis populi* in the Latin.[16]

Piers Plowman also recognizes both hierarchy and community. The hero of the poem is a plowman, but its speakers do not expect change from below. Calls for reform are usually addressed upward—especially to the rich and educated. At the same time, one of the poem's principal characters, Holy Church, goes beyond municipal attempts to ensure fair commercial prices by claiming that humans have a absolute right to food, drink, and clothing, just as the narratorial "I" and others frequently assert human responsibility for our neighbors. Of course, *Piers* is more than a simple reflection of contemporary social thought. It constantly complicates any endorsement of civic norms, as with its first-person narrator, who sometimes appears as a rebel to both hierarchy and community. Waking from the fourth vision of the B-version, for example, the speaker admits that others consider him a "lorel" (a wastrel), who has no respect for his social betters (B 15.1–10). In this he is rather like the "minstrels of hevene" of the C-version, who do not offer reverence even to the mayor.

The public life of late medieval London, which is both portrayed and challenged in *Piers Plowman*, is probably best approached through surviving city documents that record both civic ideals and actual municipal law cases and practices: these include the Plea and Memoranda Rolls, later collections of city customs such as the *Liber Albus*, and the so-called Letter Books. These working documents bring us closer to the daily life of the city than do monastic or aristocratic chronicles, though they have their own bias, being written by and for town officials. The special value of these records, especially the Plea and Memoranda Rolls and Letter Books, is that they describe a wide range of urban activities. In addition to accounts of major events, such as royal decrees and the Rising of 1381, there are more intimate and quirky notations. For example, one entry says that in 1364, Beatrice Langbourne was committed to the sheriffs

16. See, for example *Letter Book G*, fols. lxxviii, cxlib, ccxxxb (*Calendar*, 111, 178, 248; Riley, *Memorials*, 304, 318, 339); *Letter Book H*, fol. ccxxxviiib (*Calendar*, 174; Riley, *Memorials*, 456).

for calling an alderman, Simon de Worstede, "a false thief and a broken-down old yokel (*falsum latronem et rusticum veterem & defractum*) when he arrested her for throwing filth on the street" (Plea and Memoranda Roll A10, membr. 5 [*Calendar . . . 1364–1381,* 15]). Exactly seven years later, another record intriguingly reports that "John Stacy, servant of William Talbot, tailor, was committed to prison for going through Walbrook, contemptuously crying, 'Mew,' contrary to the ordinance" (Plea and Memoranda Roll A17, membr. 2 [*Calendar . . . 1364–1381,* 135]).

The London city documents indicate that the name Cornhill would have suggested three different kinds of public spaces to the original London audience of *Piers Plowman:* two important parish churches, major markets, and the principal city pillory. None of these sites has any necessary connection with the life of the author of *Piers,* but they are directly relevant to his poem and may explain why the speaker in c 5 locates himself on Cornhill. All three sites confirm Phythian-Adams's dictum that the "essence of culture in the late medieval city was that it was visual and public" (*Desolation,* 112).

II. PUBLIC INSTITUTIONS: CHURCHES, GUILDS, AND MARKETS

Saint Peter Cornhill and Saint Michael Cornhill

London is said to have contained as many separate parishes as any city in Christendom, and two of its oldest and richest churches were located in the ward of Cornhill: Saint Michael Cornhill and Saint Peter Cornhill.[17] The latter, as already noted, was the starting point for an annual civic and ecclesiastical procession on Pentecost. An entry for 1382 in a city Letter Book refers to the "ancient custom" (*l'annciene custume*) of this ceremony (*Letter Book H,* fol. cxlvi [*Calendar,* 188]; Riley, *Memorials,* 466), and a later record explains that Saint Peter had such pride of place because it was believed to be London's first church, founded in the second century as the archepiscopal seat of the kingdom (*Letter Book I,* fol. cciii [*Calendar,* 188]; Riley, *Memorials,* 651–53). In his *Survey of London,* a skeptical John Stow reproduced a tablet from Saint Peter's stating that "king *Lucius* founded the same church to be an Archbishops sea Metropolitane, & chief

17. Today Saint Michael and Saint Peter, Wren churches rebuilt after the London Fire, remain on their original sites. Because Cornhill can refer to the whole slope, other nearby churches, such as Saint Andrew Undershaft and Saint Christopher are often identified as being on Cornhill in city records. For accounts of Saint Michael's and Saint Peter's, see Stow, *Survey,* 1:194–98 (Stow's father and grandfather were buried in Saint Michael's); see also Hennessy, *Novum Repertorium,* 332–33, 374–75; Jenkinson, *London Churches.*

church of his kingdom, & that it so endured the space of 400 years, unto the coming of *Augustin* the Monk" (1:194).

The associations surrounding Saint Peter's might have been reason enough for the author of the C-version of *Piers Plowman* to locate its narrator in Cornhill. Piers, of course, is a form of the name of the apostle to whom the church was dedicated, and the name Saint Peter also suggests the plowman's roles as honest workman in the *visio* and pope in the *vita*. As the supposed metropolitan sea of England in Roman times, the parish is a metonymy for the Church itself (and the local equivalent of Saint Peter's in Rome). The state of the Church, of what is called "Seint Petres cherche" at the end of the *visio* in A and B (B 7.173; A 8.157), is a central concern of the poem from the early appearance of Holy Church to the assault on the Barn of Unity near the end. The supposed antiquity of Saint Peter Cornhill also suggests the heroic early days of Christianity, which are constantly contrasted in *Piers* to the corrupt present.

Parish Fraternities

In my previous chapter I discussed how parish churches, especially in rural areas, were significant public spaces for Christian imagery, as well as for the meeting and interaction of diverse social groups. London city church also undoubtedly had extensive murals, though almost no information about them has survived; evidence does exist, however, about other communal activities in the parish. Perhaps the public institution most relevant to *Piers Plowman* is the parish guild or fraternity. The general term *guild* when used about medieval London refers to three different if related organizations: merchant guilds that regulated large-scale, often foreign trade, craft guilds that oversaw manufacture and retail sales, and religious guilds that provided spiritual and social services—though in practice the boundaries between the three types were not always clear (McRee, "Civic Order," 70n).[18]

The golden age of London parish fraternities was exactly the time during which *Piers Plowman* was being written and most widely read. Barron notes that in the period 1350–1550 there are references to between 150 and 200 fraternities

18. Although London was not controlled by a single guild, as was the case in many other English towns, most of the city's aldermen (and thus its mayors) tended to come from a few important merchant guilds, whose leading members engaged in extensive foreign trading. The much more modest parish fraternities sometimes developed into craft guilds, but many remained primarily social, religious, and charitable societies (Barron, "Parish Fraternities," 14; cf. Barron and Wright, "Guild Certificates," 114; Rosser, "Workers' Associations").

within the parishes of London, Westminster, and Southwark; only five were def-
initely in existence before 1348 (the earliest being founded in 1339), whereas sev-
enty-four are mentioned for the first time between 1350 and 1400 ("Parish
Fraternities," 13, 23; cf. Rosser, "Communities," 33; Westlake, *Parish Gilds*, 28).
These figures support Sylvia Thrupp's contention that during the fourteenth
century the parishioners of most London's churches were able "to found and
keep alive at least one fraternity organization that had no direct connection with
a trade" (*Merchant Class*, 34).

Parish fraternities in late medieval London were not only numerous but also
inclusive in their membership. Fraternities consisted of women as well as men
and clerics as well as laypeople, though in both cases the latter were dominant
(Hanawalt, "Keepers of the Lights," 24–25; cf. Barron and Wright, "Guild
Certificates"). The very rich did not seem to need and the very poor could not
afford membership, but for a broad middle range of citizens "the parish fraternity was often the centre of their social and spiritual world" (Barron, "Parish
Fraternities," 30; cf. Holt and Rosser, "Introduction," 12; McRee, "Regulation,"
109–10; Thrupp, *Merchant Class*, 37). Fraternities offered a way for the late
medieval London laity to shape their local parishes: they "were essentially very
simple organisms, easily formed and readily adaptable to changing needs. This,
indeed, was one of their strengths" (Rosser, "Communities," 32). Fraternities
provided a collective version of the private chantries established by rich worshipers to say prayers for their souls after death. As "essentially communal
chantries," fraternities provided spiritual benefits (including memorial prayers)
to many in the parish (Barron, "Parish Fraternities," 23; cf. Unwin, *Gilds and
Companies*, 111; Westlake, *Parish Gilds*, 44).

Because they supplied a space for interaction between different occupations,
genders, and other social groupings, parish fraternities were public in one of the
principal senses in which I use the term in this book. Even Ben McRee, who has
challenged the argument that civic rituals, such as processions by fraternities, necessarily created social wholeness in their communities, notes the mixture of hori-
zontal and vertical forces at work in guilds: their initiation ceremonies insisted on
both equality (with other members) and subordination (to the authority of guild
officers).[19] Gervase Rosser convincingly argues that parish guilds were not just

19. "Unity or Division," esp. 190–94. Despite McRee's useful challenge to any easy nostalgia about the
past, his title suggests too rigid a dichotomy between unity and division.

mechanisms of social control from above but also institutions created and used by members for their own ends ("Crafts, Guilds," esp. 6–8; "Workers' Associations").[20] Rosser's description of the annual fraternity feast is reminiscent of Habermas's conception of the public sphere: because such feasts brought together a "diversity of members," they nurtured relationships between different groups and even created the possibility of a "forum for political discussion," especially among journeymen (Rosser, "Fraternity Feast," 440–43).[21]

Fraternities were an essential part of the public life of Cornhill. Barron notes that "in 1361 certain good men of the drapers of Cornhill, and other good men and women had founded a fraternity dedicated to the Blessed Virgin in the Hospital of St Mary of Bethlehem outside Bishopsgate" ("Parish Fraternities," 15n). Within the ward itself and in addition to private chantries, Saint Michael and Saint Peter Cornhill supported their own individual parish fraternities in the late fourteenth and fifteenth centuries.[22] Saint Michael's had a guild dedicated to Saint Anne by at least the 1380s and others, perhaps founded later, were dedicated to Saint Michael, to Saint Nicholas and Saint Katherine, and to the Name of Jesus.[23] My aim in what follows is not to claim any direct connection, autobiographical or otherwise, between Langland and the parish fraternities of Cornhill, only to show that the poem and the guilds share, in ideals and practices, the same public culture.

The Fraternity of Saint Peter

Much of our information about London parish fraternities comes from the self-description the government demanded from them in 1388–89: forty-five of

20. "Within a partially standardized constitution, the guilds exhibited enormous variety in the details of their collective religious rites, while at the same time they helped foster a richer internal spiritual life for the individual member. The satisfaction within a voluntary structure of this dual need, collective and individual, was the distinctive function of the pre-Reformation guild" (Rosser, "Communities," 45).

21. Rosser points to the "articulation of relations between artisan and gentry groups, and between town and countryside" ("Fraternity Feast," 442), though this may have been more true in provincial towns than in London. Rosser notes that four London guilds of journeymen met on the same day around 1400, which "suggests a degree of liaison with a view to facilitating the interchange of news at a time when large numbers of journeymen were gathering to drink together after their fraternity masses" (442–43). In "Workers' Associations," Rosser argues, in respect to journeymen, that the "practice of association in fraternities was clearly formative of habits of collective decision-making and action" (292).

22. For mention of a private chantry in Saint Michael's as early as 1291, see *Letter Book C*, fol. ii (*Calendar*, 3). A chantry was established in Saint Peter's in 1284 (Whittington, *Church of St. Peter*, 11).

23. Cf. Barron, "Parish Fraternities," 22n, 32, 32n. The 1388 will of John Cok, a chandler, includes a bequest to the fraternity of Saint Anne at Saint Michael's (*Calendar of Wills*, 2:266). The poll tax of 1379 lists ten chaplains at Saint Michael Cornhill: some probably served chantries, but others may have been fraternity chaplains (McHardy, *Church in London*, 9).

these documents are extant; ten of them are in English.²⁴ Few additional records
from late medieval London fraternities survive and these are generally scattered
and fragmentary (Barron, "Parish Fraternities," 18–19). A remarkable exception is
a complete fraternal rule from none other than Saint Peter Cornhill. A copy of
this document, which "in the incidental details it contains stands unrivalled"
(Westlake, *Parish Gilds*, 84), was included in a parish register of Saint Peter's compiled circa 1426 by John Sewarde, who will be discussed further in the following
section.²⁵ The rule itself is prefaced by a 1402 license from King Henry IV,
though there is some evidence that the guild was by then already in existence.²⁶
The Saint Peter rule does not directly imitate any other surviving guild record,
but it shares many of the general values and practices described in other London
certificates of 1388–89. I have already suggested that the mention of Cornhill
might have caused early readers of *Piers Plowman* to think of the parish of Saint
Peter because of the supposed antiquity of the church, its echo of Saint Peter's in
Rome, and its patron saint's resemblances to Piers the plowman. The fraternity of
Saint Peter Cornhill brings us even closer to the public themes in the poem.²⁷

24. Guilds throughout the country were required to respond, but my discussion concerns only those in
London. The best account of the London guild certificates, with complete texts of the ten English
returns, is in Barron and Wright, "Guild Certificates"; cf. also Westlake, *Parish Gilds*; Chambers and Daunt,
Book, 40–60. The authorities seem to have suspected fraternities of questionable political activity (perhaps
with some reason), which the returns are careful to minimize (Unwin, *Gilds and Companies*, 125).

The history of the guild certificates of 1388–89 reminds us that "power" is not always as dominant or
efficient as modern commentators sometime assume. Parliament petitioned in 1388 that guilds be abol-
ished because of fears that they were lawless confederacies, but the Crown did not agree to such annihila-
tion and many of the certificates it then demanded were either never sent it or subsequently lost (Barron
and Wright, "Guild Certificates," 108–9). Eventually the "anxieties about lawlessness, riots, and confed-
eracy which had inspired the original Commons' petition, seem to have abated" (118). Power sometimes
forgets or gets muddled.

25. Sewarde's register is now Guildhall Library, London, MS 4158A; extracts and summaries are in the
Sixth Report of the Royal Commission on Historical Manuscripts, 1: 407–18, which gives the complete rule in both
the original English and then an amplified Latin version made some months after, suggesting the maca-
ronic mixture of vernacular and learned languages in *Piers*. Quotations of the rule will be from the
Guildhall manuscript (cited by folio and slightly modernized) with additional citations to the report of
the Commission on Historical Manuscripts (by article, when applicable, and page number).

26. The rule says that the priest of the fraternity shall pray for its living and deceased members, "als he
hathe do to fore this tyme" (fol. 138a; article viii, 413).

27. James Simpson's important article, "After Craftes Conseil," calls attention, as previously noted, to
the annual Pentecost procession that originated at Saint Peter's. He argues that the parish fraternity was an
institution that, despite its limits (the ultimate craft in *Piers* is to love), provided a model for the just and
harmonious society that Langland imagines for London in the penultimate passus of the long versions of
his poem. I follow Simpson's general conclusions and try to extend them with specific reference to the rule
of the fraternity of Saint Peter, which he does not mention.

The rule of the fraternity of Saint Peter assumes a social inclusiveness (wide if not absolute) that is found in other parish fraternities and echoed in the attitudes and audience of *Piers*. Before the individual articles of the rule, the original founders of the guild are named several times (fols. 131a–135a; 411–12). They include one cleric, the parson of Saint Peter Cornhill (William Aghton); two high city officials (the aldermen William Brampton and William Askham); several other brethren; and most remarkable of all, three women: "Alianora Aghton, Alicia Gregory, & Alice atte Hale" (fol. 134a; 412). References to both the "brothers and sisters" and "bretherene and sisterne" of the fellowship and to "man or woman" and "he or she" appear frequently in the English rule (with equivalents in the Latin version), as they do in other certificates from 1388–89, for both sexes were members of most London fraternities; but the Saint Peter rule is unique as far as I know in listing women as founders.[28] In addition to differences in political rank, ecclesiastical status, and sex, the rule suggests inclusiveness in residence and craft. Of the two to four wardens to be elected every year, it is mandated that "half shall be chosen of the fysshemongers & half of the parisshe of Seint Petir" (fol 139b; article xi, 413). This indicates not only that the fraternity drew its membership from outside the parish itself, but also that, though the fishmongers were influential, other crafts were also represented.[29]

Parish fraternities, for all their social concerns, were, like *Piers Plowman*, religious at their core, intended to aid both individual and general salvation. The daily Masses and frequent prayers that the chaplain was required to say for the brothers and sisters of the Saint Peter fraternity, "quyke & deed," as well as "for all Christen" (fol. 135b; article i, 412), would have included the same devotional texts mentioned by the speaker of c 5 as part of his itinerant ministry: the *pater-*

28. On references in the certificates to both men and women, see Barron and Wright, "Guild Certificates," esp. 122, 123, 125, 129, 131, 132, 134, 136, 138, 139, and 144. On the surprise of finding women listed with men as founders here, see Barron, "Parish Fraternities," 31, in which she notes that the names of the women in the Saint Peter rule are different from those of the male founders "and so were not, we may presume, wives." Alianora Aghton has the same last name as the parson of Saint Peter's and was perhaps a sister in two senses. Inclusiveness goes only so far, however: there is no suggestion that wardens of the fraternity could be women nor, of course, could the fraternity chaplain. In the Latin version of the rule, sisters are mentioned with brothers as founders, but not named (fol. 147b; 414).

29. In a preface to the Latin version, some of the founders are more fully described, presumably by John Sewarde: for example, John Waleys, also called John Conyesburghe, is said to have been a poulterer, and Richard Stondone, also called Richard Manhale, a chandler (fol. 146a; 414). Later church records support this craft diversity: a 1547 inventory of ecclesiastical garb suggests that the drapers and grocers had a special connection with Saint Peter's, Cornhill, as their arms appeared on some of its copes (Walters, *London Churches*, 58, 575).

noster (said as part of the Mass), the primer (which includes the office of the dead and other prayers), *placebo, dirge,* and the seven penitential psalms (c 5.45–47).

The allegorical figure in *Piers* called Spes, who is also Moses, repeats Christ's claim that everything in both the law and the prophets is contained in two related commands: *Dilige Deum et proximum tuum* (love God and your neighbor, from Matthew 22:37–40). All who act this way, says Spes, will escape harm from the Devil: "I have saved with this charme / Of men and of wommen many score thousandes" (B 17.10–19; C 19.12–22).[30] These two great commandments likewise summarize the guild practices described in the rule of Saint Peter Cornhill and other fraternities. The first, the love and worship of God, was expressed through the many Masses, prayers, and other rituals performed by the guild priest: a Latin preface to the English rule of the Saint Peter fraternity declares that the guild was dedicated to the honor of God as well as to the apostle Peter (fol. 133a; 412).[31] The London guild return from Saint James Garlickhithe also begins "in the worship of god almighti" and then continues on to suggest the second command by noting that the fraternity had been founded "for amendement of her lyves and of her soules & to noriche more love bytwene the bretheren & sustren" (Barron and Wright, "Guild Certificates," 134).

The love of God at the center of parish fraternities was expected to be demonstrated by public behavior in the world. The "amendement" of lives and souls sought by the guilds is precisely the kind of Christian reform often called for in *Piers Plowman*, and, as in the poem, manifests itself by doing well. The Saint Peter fraternity priest was required to "be able of cunnyng, that is to say, of redyng & syngyng," as well as being "of covenable undirstondyng & honest of conversacioun" (fol. 135b; article i, 412), and he could be removed if found to be a "notorie lechour or an nyght wandrer" or a "taverne or alehous haunter or otherwyse criminous or mysproude or debate maker" (fol. 136b; article iv, 412). Similarly, any member of the fraternity who proved to be a "comune contectour, hasardour, lechour, chider, fals usurour, or useth ony othir shrewed tacches" was to be expelled (fol. 144a; article xx, 414). These requirements of minimal good conduct are reminiscent of the virtuous pagans in *Mandeville's Travels* and parallel Thought's first definition of Do-well in *Piers Plowman:*

30. Note the mention of women as well as men, so characteristic of fraternal documents.

31. The preface to the Latin version of the rule likewise states that the fraternal chantry with its chaplains was created, "in honorem dei et ipsius beati Petri" (fol. 147a; 414).

Whoso is trewe of his tunge and of his two handes,
And thorugh his labour or thorugh his land his liflode wynneth,
And is trusty of his tailende, taketh but his owene,
And is noght dronkelewe ne deynous, Dowel hym folweth.

(B 8.80–83; C 10.78–81)

The poem and the rule agree on some of the basic public acts that will find favor with God (and one's fellow Christians): using language honestly; doing your job well (the second line of the quotation in C speaks of those who "thorw lele labour lyveth"); and avoiding vices such as theft, drunkenness, prideful quarreling with others, and lechery (B's possible pun on *tail* in "tailende" is made explicit in C: "trewe of his tayl").

The second of the two great commandments (to love one's neighbor) was equally advocated by the London parish guilds, which urged members to live at peace with one another (Barron, "Parish Fraternities," 25). The Saint Peter rule requires that any debate between members be mediated by the wardens and others in order to produce "unite & accorde bytwene the parties" (fols. 144b–145a; article xxii, 414), just as the Garlickhithe fraternity's ambition, as we have seen, was "to noriche more love bytwene the bretheren & sustren."[32] Fraternal love in the Saint Peter rule (as in other rules) was imagined to extend beyond the calming of internal disputes to active charity. If any member of the fraternity should "yfalle in myschief & poverete by godys sonde and noght thurgh his owen evell governaunce" and was not able to support himself, he was to be entitled to eight pence a week from the fraternity's common "box" (fols. 142b–143a; article xviii, 413).[33]

A similar practical love of one's fellows is repeatedly advocated in *Piers Plowman*: examples include Hunger's counsel that Piers support those whom "Fortune hath apeired / Other any manere false men" (B 6.218–19; A 7.204–5; C 8.229–30); the assertion that Truth's pardon applies fully to men and women who cannot work because of old age or children, if they "taken this myschief mekeliche" (B 7.98–102;

---

32. For other examples in the London returns that urge such fraternal amity, see Barron and Wright, "Guild Certificates," 125, 130, 135. Simpson finds an echo in *Piers* B 19.251–52 (C 21.251–52): "And alle he lered to be lele, and ech a craft love oother, / And forbad hem alle debat—that noon be among hem" ("After Craftes Conseil," 119).

33. Barron notes that a common characteristic of guild ordinances of the period was "the declared intention to assist financially the sick and needy members of the fraternity" ("Parish Fraternities," 26). Apparently only a small percentage of fraternal funds was actually used for such charity, however, perhaps because the generous intent of the rules turned out to be too expensive (27).

A 8.82–86; C 9.175–86, which expands the different kinds of "meschief"); Wit's criticism of Christians in the B-version who do not, like the Jews, "eyther helpeth oother of hem of that that hym nedeth" (B 9.86); and the Samaritan's rescue and care for the man he finds grievously wounded by the roadside (B 17.64ff.; C 19.65ff.). The charity promised by the Saint Peter fraternity is by no means unconditional, however: the recipient had to have been a guild member for at least seven years (fol. 143a; article xviii, 413), and the legitimacy of any request was to be investigated by the wardens (fol. 143b; article xix, 414). Both requirements are reminiscent of the mixture of strictness and generosity in *Piers*, as it explores what is to done about beggars and others who claim to be in need (see, for example, Aers, "Problems").

A love of neighbor that crosses traditional social boundaries is an ideal shared by London fraternities such as Saint Peter's and *Piers Plowman*, though powerfully expanded in the latter. The Saint Peter rule mentions, as we have seen, praying "for all Christen," but most of its attention is on the welfare of its own members. *Piers* builds on the real, if limited, fellowship of the guild to imagine one great public fraternity open to all, with Christ as its warden. Trajan first announces this new community in declaring that "alle are we Cristes creatures, and of his cofres riche, / And bretheren as of oo blood, as wel beggeres as erles" (B 11.198–99; cf. C 12.110–11), but it is given most authoritative expression by Christ himself, who in the climactic Harrowing of Hell scene tells the devils that he shares a profound brotherhood of blood with his fellow humans: "Ac alle that beth myne hole bretheren, in blood and in baptisme, / Shul noght be dampned to the deeth that is withouten ende" (B 18.378–79; C 20.419–20).[34]

---

34. Although food and clothing have long been recognized as important thematic symbols in *Piers Plowman*, as noted in relation to the *Book of Margery Kempe* in Chapter 4, guild practices are a neglected public context for this theme. Food and clothing were two major ways that a fraternity asserted its identity and unity (see McRee, "Unity or Division"). At Saint Peter's, as at other London guilds, the annual feast followed church services at which all members were required to wear the fraternity's special livery (fols. 138b-39b; articles x and xi, 413).

Piers can be read as critical of such fraternal consumption of food and clothing. The showy livery of the guilds, though ostensibly a symbol of community, might have reminded the poem's readers of Meed's ravishing clothing and other prideful attire in the poem (e.g., B 4.116; A 4.102; C 4.111; and B 11.240), as opposed to the simple dress of Lady Holy Church. Similarly, the lavish fraternity feast perhaps resembles the Doctor of Divinity's enthusiastic gluttony at the dinner held by Conscience rather than Patience's satisfaction with the nourishment of biblical verses (though apparently the poor were often invited to fraternal feasts as *Piers* more than once recommends [Rosser, "Fraternal Feast," 436]).

In addition to criticizing inappropriate feasting and livery, *Piers Plowman* transforms both. Christ shows his unity with other humans by coming to the crucial joust at Jerusalem dressed not in knightly finery but humbly in "Piers armes" or *humana natura* (B 18.22–23; C 20.21–22) and, after his fight against death, proclaims that his drink is "love" and that he will not slake his thirst until "I drynke right ripe must, *resureccio mortuorum*" (B 18.366–71; C 20.403–12), the ultimate communal feast of human salvation (see the reference at C 20.406 to "comune coppes, alle Christen soules").

In addition to enlarging the concept of guild brotherhood, *Piers Plowman* echoes other elements of the London fraternities, once again making clear that whether or not its author ever dwelled on Cornhill, he shares elements of its public culture. For example, both the Saint Peter rule and the poem describe lay superiority over ecclesiastics. *Piers* contains many warnings about the dangers of bad clergy (e.g., B 15.94–95; C 16.244–45), and Clergy forsees a king who will come to correct monks and canons (B 10.316–19; cf. C 5.168–71). No contemporary churchman in the poem has the authority of the plowman Piers, whose greater spirituality is made clear during his debate with the priest over the meaning of Truth's pardon and whose importance continues to grow: he is later equated with Christ in the B-version (B 15.212), and Conscience's final, mysterious vow is not to rest "til I have Piers the Plowman" (B 20.386; C 22.386).

Of course there were no ideal figure like Piers in the London parish fraternities, but they, in their own way, also propose a measure of lay authority.[35] The first article of the Saint Peter rule, as already noted, asserts that the priest hired for the fraternity should be honest, well educated, and of good habits (fols. 135b–136a; article i, 412), and this article and the following two explain in great detail the many services the priest is to perform for the members of the guild.[36] In short, the laity instruct their clergyman in his duties and terms of employment (Barron, "Parish Fraternities," 33). If the priest becomes old or incapacitated, the guild promises to support him, but should he fall into vice and not reform, he will be removed "in presence of these wardeyns & parisshens of Seint Petres chirche" (fol. 136b; article iv, 412). The parson, a member of the fraternity and who would have to work closely with its priest, is certainly involved in this hiring and disciplining, but so are the wardens on behalf of the general membership (Barron, "Parish Fraternities," 33). In both *Piers Plowman* and the London fraternities, religious power is not exclusively in clerical hands but shared with the laity.

Saint Peter's School and Library

Two other institutions at the church of Saint Peter's further define the public world that Cornhill shares with *Piers Plowman*: a famous grammar school and a

---

35. The Saint Peter rule is the most explicit account we have about the terms by which fraternities employed their own priests (Barron, "Parish Fraternities," 34).

36. Rosser argues that the priest of Saint Peter's guild had no easy sinecure but was "kept busy almost hourly" by the Masses and prayers he was required to offer for the living and the dead ("Communities," 42).

library. Although both probably belong to a later period when *Piers* was being read rather than written, there are hints, as with the parish guild, that both might have existed earlier in some form. For example, A. G. Little mentioned in a review, without citing his evidence, that there was a grammar school at Saint Peter Cornhill "about 1225, when a Franciscan friar 'taught letters' in the church" (529).[37] This suggests that learning in late medieval London might have been more widely and publicly available than is generally believed and may help to explain both the composition and reception of a work like *Piers Plowman*. Stow reported a library "of olde time builded of stone" attached to Saint Peter's (*Survey*, 1:194), though it may not have been formally established until the mid-fifteenth century.[38] According to Stow, the books of the library were no longer at the church in his time, but two volumes associated with Saint Peter Cornhill are accessible today. The first (Guildhall Library, London, MS 4158A) is a late thirteenth-century illuminated Latin Bible with corrections in a fourteenth-century hand that contains a fifteenth-century rubrication stating that the book belongs to the chantry of the Holy Trinity "in ecclesia sancti Petri super Cornhull in London" (Ker, *Medieval Manuscripts*, 1:262). The other extant manuscript (British Library, London, MS Royal 13.D.1), formerly bound with a mid-fourteenth century psalter, is a miscellany of historical, geographical, and religious works in Latin and in English with two early inscriptions that both declare, "Liber ecclecsie sancti Peter super Cornehill" (fols. 1b, 2b).[39] Whether or not there was an organized library at Saint Peter's that Langland could have known, the contents of the two remaining books from the church suggest the kinds of texts that would have been known and used by the creator and early readers of *Piers Plowman*.

37. Sylvia Thrupp suggested that although three approved schools existed in London from the twelfth century (at Saint Paul's, Saint Mary Arches, and Saint Martin le Grand), there many have been others (*Merchant Class*, 156). Barron notes the "remarkable range of educational opportunities open to children of both sexes in London" ("Expansion of Education," 220) and concludes that "by the later fourteenth century, it is clear that this monopoly of grammar school teaching in London was being challenged" (226). Barron lists several schoolmasters working in Cornhill in the early fifteenth century (227).

38. John Coote, the rector of Saint Peter Cornhill and a supporter of grammar schools, was succeeded in 1448 by Hugh Damlett, a learned Cambridge man with a large library: "It may have been Damlett who was responsible for the creation, at St. Peter's, of the parish library later repaired by the executors of Sir John Crosby, who died in 1476" (Barron, "Expansion of Education," 231).

39. The Royal manuscript closely resembles, in format and contents, University Library, Cambridge, MS Dd.1.17 (Crick, 180–81). The Cambridge manuscript also contains *Mandeville's Travels* and an early copy of the B-version of *Piers Plowman*.

The other institute at Saint Peter Cornhill was a grammar school. Whatever the date of the original founding of the school, it was under the direction of John Sewarde (who, we will recall, compiled the register that contains the rule of the fraternity of Saint Peter) by at least 1404, and we know that he remained there until 1435. A recent study by Caroline Barron describes Sewarde in terms that make his erudition and interests sound like those that would have been shared by the author and audience of *Piers* ("Expansion of Education"; see also Galbraith, "John Sewarde"). According to Barron, Sewarde "challenged the clerical hold on Latin learning: here was a layman reading and composing in Latin, writing letters and verses to a group of learned scholars both lay and clerical" ("Expansion of Education," 228). The guild and school of Saint Peter Cornhill suggest that *Piers Plowman* is less eccentric and marginal than sometimes assumed but instead participates in, or at least anticipates, specific elements of the public culture of late medieval London and of Cornhill in particular.

The Markets of Cornhill

The most ubiquitous, and in many ways the most important, public spaces in medieval London were its numerous markets and shops. From Roman times, the city had always been famous as a great commercial center.[40] Then, as now, traders and their guilds controlled the square mile, whereas universities, important monasteries, and the court were located outside the walls. The most profitable London business was the large-scale importing and exporting of commodities (including wool, wine, and spices) by rich capitalists (merchants in the proper sense), such as the late fourteenth-century Cornhill alderman and mayor John Philpot. On a more modest level, London also contained England's most extensive and varied retail markets. These supplied the country with a range of luxury goods, in addition to providing the metropolis with its daily needs, especially food. Retail activity took place in or right off the street (whether from small individual shops, collective markets, or even wandering vendors), resulting in the interaction of many levels of society.[41] All this buying and selling was

40. The Roman historian Tacitus described London as full of merchants and famous for its commerce (Merrifield, *London*, 42), and Bede wrote of the city as an emporium for many nations (*Corporation of London*, 1–2). According to Derek Keene, the primary role of medieval London was "as a centre of commerce, a role which the city had fulfilled since the Roman period" ("Medieval London," 100).

41. Keene has noted that much trading took place in the public space of the street and that London shops were small in size and great in number ("Shops," esp. 32–34). Retail sales in the streets were often undertaken by women, who were known as hucksters (Barron, "Golden Age," 47).

under the close supervision and detailed regulations of craft guilds and city officials: "The unique feature of medieval urban administration lay in the jurisdiction that city authorities claimed over trade and industry" (Thrupp, *Merchant
Class*, 92).

The major markets and shopping areas of London were well established by
the beginning of the fourteenth century (Alley, *Caveat*, 1; Keene, "Shops," 29).
Cheap, more properly Westcheap, near the Guildhall and at the very center of
the city, was the single most important commercial street in London, and
Cornhill, immediately to the east, was its continuation for shopping, as it was for
ceremonial processions. The two areas are often linked in London documents.
Between Cheap and Cornhill, the city established in the late thirteenth century
the covered Stockes Market (Alley, *Caveat*, 4–5), and, in the reign of Edward I,
country bakers were allowed to sell their wares only on Cornhill or at the market
cross at Cheap (*Liber Albus*, lxvii–lxviii). Cheap and Cornhill contained the only
two officially permitted "common markets" of London, at which a variety of
victuals were sold between the two gutters in these unusually wide roads.[42]

Cornhill also had its own special markets. The large mansion known as
Leadenhall, at the top of the hill, was not yet owned by the city government in
the fourteenth century, though it was already being used for public functions,
including legal proceedings in a law court.[43] The Leadenhall was also an officially designated place of trade. All poulterers from outside London, for
instance, were confined to it, whereas city poulterers were required to sell from
their own houses, at the Poultry, or along the west wall of Saint Michael
Cornhill.[44] Cornhill was also the principal market for bows, and carts that sold
firewood, timber, and charcoal had to locate themselves there.[45] Blacksmiths who
did not sell their work from their shops were confined to a spot halfway up the
hill, and Thames fish taken east of London Bridge had to be sold on Cornhill.[46]

42. See *Letter Book D*, fol. cv (*Calendar*, 229; Riley, *Memorials*, 75); *Letter Book F*, fol. clib (*Calendar*, 179); *Liber
Albus*, xliv–xlv, 260–61. Cf. Alley, 4, 8, 9.

43. *Calendar of Early Mayor's Court Rolls*, 145n; *Letter Book E*, fol. ci (*Calendar*, 119); cf. Thomas, "Notes."

44. For out-of-town poulterers assigned to sell at the Leadenhall in Cornhill, see *Letter Book F*, fol. ciib
(*Calendar*, 123; Riley, *Memorials*, 220–21). Cf. also Alley, *Caveat*, 4, 10; *Corporation of London*, 147.

45. For the regulations that bows, firewood, and charcoal were to be sold at Cornhill, see *Liber Albus*,
xliv, lxxxv–lxxxvi, 272–73, 732.

46. For blacksmiths' work sold at Cornhill, see *Letter Book G*, fol. cclxxxv (*Calendar*, 291; Riley, *Memorials*,
361); and for fish, see *Letter Book H*, fol. ccxxxvii (*Calendar*, 338–39; Riley, *Memorials*, 508); *Calendar of Select Pleas
. . . 1381–1412*, 75.

Despite the many respectable markets that existed on Cornhill, there is some justification for the belief held by most Langland scholars that the district was one of vagrants and dishonest trading. The fifteenth-century poem "London Lyckpeny," much influenced by *Piers Plowman*, tells of a country visitor whose hood is snatched at Westminster only to be offered back to him for sale later the same day among "mutch stolen gere" on Cornhill (line 86). The city records contain many references to a market for secondhand clothes and furniture on Cornhill (e.g., *Liber Custumarum*, xcviii, 426–27), which Rechlesseness in the C-version mentions in unique lines on the transitoriness of material wealth: "Upholderes on the Hulle [Cornhill] shal have hit to sulle" (c 12.220). The city authorities tried several times, apparently without much success, to ban the holding of this traditional market after dark (as well as a similar one at Cheap), from fear that such evening markets, called "evynchepynges," allowed the selling of old and stolen clothes by candlelight as if new.[47]

"London Lyckpeny" reminds us that even if markets are public, they are not necessarily democratic or just. The country visitor finds that both the shops in London and the courts of Westminster are closed to him because he is poor— as stated in the poem's refrain, which is some version of "for lack of money I might not speed." The Meed episode in *Piers Plowman* reveals a similar corruption of Westminster law, and commercial fraud is denounced throughout the poem. In *Piers*, London is often seen as a wicked place, ruled only by personal gain: for instance, the sweetness of its silver lures priests to leave their parishes (b pr.86; a pr.83; c pr.84). The poem repeatedly shows getting and spending as nothing more than selfishness at the expense of public good and the poor. Truth's pardon to Piers includes merchants only grudgingly in the margins and only if they use their winnings for the common welfare (b 7.18–32; a 8.20–35; c 9.22–36). In the confession of the sins, Envy says he was a trader in London, where he slandered the goods of others (b 5.128–29; c 6.95–96). Covetise describes a variety of fraudulent schemes practiced by himself and his wife; not all take place in London, but there are many parallels in the city records to such activities as his wife's adulteration of ale (b 5.215–21; a 5.133–39; c 6.225–31).[48]

---

47. See *Letter Book E*, fols. cxxx, cxxxiib (*Calendar*, 156–57, 161–62); *Letter Book G*, fol. ccxxxb (*Calendar*, 248; Riley, *Memorials*, 339); *Letter Book H*, fol. cclxxviii (*Calendar*, 391; Riley, *Memorials*, 532–33); Plea and Memoranda Roll A1a, membr. 1 (*Calendar . . . 1323–1364*, 1–2).

48. See also the brewer in the penultimate passus of the long versions of *Piers*, who declares that he will not be ruled by justice as long as he can sell adulterated ale (b 19.400–405; c 21.399–404).

Covetise also describes a clever trick he was taught by drapers whereby cloth is pinned to make ten or twelve yards measure as thirteen (B 5.205–10; A 5.123–28; C 6.215–20), echoing an accusation by the London drapers in 1394 against one of their number, John Derlyng of Cornhill, that he had a false yard measure for cloth, "in deceit of the people and to the scandal of the whole mistery" (Plea and Memoranda Roll A36, membr. 6 [*Calendar of Select Pleas . . . 1381–1412*, 220]).⁴⁹

Yet, despite its exposures of market frauds, *Piers* finds little that is simple or unredeemable in such public commerce. James Simpson ("Spirituality") and Linda Georgianna ("Love So Dearly") have shown that economic language can be used by both Langland and Chaucer to convey profound spiritual meaning, and, of course, mercantile as well as agricultural imagery is found in the New Testament. It is the usurer not the prudent saver, after all, who wins salvation in the parable of the talents. When Covetise in A and B swears to Repentance that he will give up his fraudulent business practices, including false weighing and "wikked chaffare," he does not forswear the idiom of the marketplace, but says that he and his wife will go to Walsingham and ask the "Roode of Bromholm" there to "brynge me out of dette" (B 5.224–27; A 5.142–45).

In the unique passage from the C-version in which the poetic "I"-speaker claims to live on Cornhill, the mercantile world and not the agricultural world offers the speaker his only chance of salvation. When accused of loafing by Conscience and Reason, the narrator/dreamer declares that he is unsuited to work in the fields. Agricultural success depends on long, steady application, and clearly this figure has no chance of achieving that. He is more like the wasters on Piers's half acre; or, more precisely, he is an urban layabout, accused by Conscience of begging in cities (C 5.90). But all is not lost. The speaker, like a Cornhill merchant rather than a plowman, still imagines succeeding in business. He tells Conscience and Reason that he knows he has wasted and misspent his time. But, like one who has often traded ("ychaffared") and lost until finally

---

49. A particularly ingenious fraud occurred in 1327 when a group of bakers were accused of committing falsehood, malice, and deception ("falsitate, malicia & deceptione") at the expense of the common people because when dough was brought to be baked in their ovens, they shaped the loaves on "molding-boards" that had secret holes through which servants hidden below were able to steal some of the dough. Although indignant over this fraud, the writer of the account cannot help but marvel at its ingenuity: the hole is said to have been made "shrewdly and skillfully" ("prudenter artificioseque"). The story was recorded in Latin in both a Plea and Memoranda Roll, A1b membr. (16) (*Calendar . . . 1323–64*, 44) and the *Assize of Bread*, fols. 79b-80a (*Munimenta Guildhall* 3: 416–20; Riley, *Memorials*, 162–65).

pulling off a spectacular trade ("bouhte suche a bargayn") that will make up for all his past failures, the speaker hopes to win a "gobet of his [i.e., God's] grace" and "bigynne a tyme / That alle tymes of my tyme to profit shal turne" (c 5.92–101). Amid the markets of Cornhill, the dreamer does not lose a hood like the traveler in "London Lyckpeny," but imagines the ultimate deal that he has long sought: saving his soul.

III. THE PILLORY AND THE CROSS
The Cornhill Pillory and Piers Plowman

In addition to possessing its important churches and markets, medieval Cornhill was a principal London site for the public punishment of the pillory. Although today the pillory is little more than a quaint metaphor for abuse, it was once a fearsome and common judicial instrument. Those pilloried were made to stand on a raised platform and exposed to pelting from spectators even as their head and hands were confined in a wooden frame.[50] So harrowing was this punishment that the condemned were rarely subjected to it for more than a single hour at a time.[51]

According to John Stow, a pillory was placed on top of the Tun, a stone building located in the middle of the street and ward of Cornhill, when this structure, formerly a municipal lockup, was made into a water conduit in 1401 (Survey, 1:188–91). It has not always been recognized that the 1401 pillory was not something new, for a pillory on or near the Tun had existed throughout the fourteenth century.[52] Cornhill may not have been the only place for such pun-

---

50. For a general account of the pillory in England, see Beattie, Crime, 464–68. The pillory is a somewhat different instrument from the stocks, which confined the feet of a sitting offender and seem to have been most commonly used to restrain rather than dramatically to display victims, often as a temporary prison (as with Kent in King Lear). There was clearly some overlap between the two punishments (Andrews, Bygone Punishments, 173–79), and the instruments are sometimes mentioned together. In Piers Plowman, the king's reference to punishing Wrong—"he shal reste in my stokkes / As long as I lyve" ("he lyve" in all B mss; B 4.108–9; A 4.95–96; C 4.103–4)—suggests imprisonment rather than the limited public display of the pillory.

51. I know of no medieval account that records in detail the actual experience of the pillory, but a proclamation in 1456 by the mayor of London on behalf of the king commands spectators not to throw "any maner thyng," such as "eggis, stonys, bones," at those being pilloried but to let them stand there "in peas," suggesting how dangerous the practice could be (Journals of the Court of Common Council, 6, fol. 104, in the Corporation of London Records Office; I owe this reference to the index at the Corporation compiled by Caroline Barron; cf. the citation in Thrupp, Merchant Class, 25). In his short poem "Against Millers and Bakers," John Lydgate describes a baker exhibited on the pillory and pelted by eggs (3–4).

52. The recent London atlas edited by Mary Lobel appears to suggest that the Cornhill pillory dates only from 1401 (City of London, 83).

ishment in medieval London, but the surviving evidence suggests that it was the most prominent. The relevant Letter Books, Plea and Memoranda Rolls, and London Chronicles for the fourteenth and fifteenth centuries contain dozens of references to the pillory. In most cases an actual location is not specified (probably because everyone knew it), but when a place is mentioned it is almost invariably Cornhill.[53] Located on the main east-west thoroughfare of the city and amid many busy markets, Cornhill was an appropriate place for this public humiliation.

The medieval pillory was the penalty for a variety of municipal offenses, including prostitution, pimping, vagrancy, and minor theft, but London records make clear that its primary purpose was relatively narrow: to expose and punish crimes against truth. Those sentenced to the pillory were often directly accused of falsehood and deceit ("falsitate & deceptione").[54] John Carpenter's *Liber Albus*, a 1419 collection of medieval London civic precedents, prefaces a list of actual judicial cases with a heading that makes clear that the pillory was a response to social untruth: "Judicia pillorii pro mendaciis, scandalis, falsitatibus & deceptionibus" ("Judgments of the pillory for lies, slanders, falsehoods, and deceits").[55]

53. An early reference to the pillory on Cornhill (1318) is found in *Letter Book E*, fol. lxxxii (*Calendar*, 96; Riley, *Memorials*, 129); see also *Letter Book F*, fol. lvb (*Calendar*, 67–68; Riley, *Memorials*, 212); *Letter Book H*, fols. cxliii, cxcivb (*Calendar*, 181, 272; Riley, *Memorials*, 459–60, 486). See also Kingsford, *Chronicles* (Vitellius A xvi), 187, 198. For mention of the stocks on Cornhill, see Plea and Memoranda Roll A21, membr. 10b (*Calendar . . . 1364–1381*, 222).

A rare reference to a London location for the pillory other than Cornhill occurs in *De Antiquis Legibus Liber* (*Chronicles of the Mayors and Sheriffs of London*): the entry for 1269 notes that the "pillory that stood in Chepe (*in foro*)" was broken (121, trans., 127); the entry for the next year reports that a new pillory had been erected there (125; trans., 131). Certainly London pillories were located elsewhere in the seventeenth and eighteenth centuries, such as at Charing Cross (Beattie, *Crime*, 465; Andrews, *Punishments*, 56–58).

54. For examples of this formula, see *Letter Book G*, fols. cxxxiib, cxxxviib (*Calendar*, 171, 175; Riley, *Memorials*, 318, 319); *Letter Book H*, fol. cxxxviiib (*Calendar*, 174; Riley, *Memorials*, 456); and Plea and Memoranda Roll A21, membr. 10b (*Calendar . . . 1364–81*, 221–22), which refers to punishment on the stocks at Cornhill.

55. *Liber Albus*, fol. 288b (599; trans., 517), quoted in the form of the original Latin heading, which is written in red. For the *Liber Albus*, see Kellaway, "John Carpenter's Liber Albus." The second part of the heading associates the sentence of the pillory with other punishments, showing that the distinction between them was not always clear-cut and that the actual sentence for a specific criminal act was often *ad hoc*: "et alia judicia, imprisonamenta, forisfacture, fines & combustiones diversarum rerum" ("as also, other judgments, imprisonments, forfeitures, fines, and burnings of divers things"). A crime that elsewhere had merited the pillory was sometimes satisfied, as the list that follows in the *Liber Albus* demonstrates, by imprisonment, a fine, forfeiting or burning the false item, or even the promise not to commit the crime again.

Commercial fraud was the crime most frequently punished by the pillory in medieval London. Tradesmen were exhibited on it for swindles such as selling short-weighted bags of coal or charcoal, defective bowstrings, and counterfeit metal ornaments made to appear more precious than they were.[56] The pillory was the penalty for deceptions involving the basic necessities of food and drink, with bakers a particular target.[57] Those convicted of selling meat, fowl, and fish unfit for human consumption were sent to the pillory, often with their rotten goods ordered to be burned at their feet.[58]

The pillory was also the penalty for more general infractions against truth, such as cheating at checkers or dice and practicing sorcery, soothsaying, or other magic arts.[59] Those who used false language were also so exposed. Various forgers (of letters, pardons, deeds, bonds, even papal bulls) were sentenced to the pillory, as were those whose speech slandered others or whose deception could cause political unrest.[60] Also subject to the punishment were those guilty of imposture. The London records document the display on the pillory of those convicted of pretending to be royal, civic, and ecclesiastical officials, as well as

56. See, for example, *Letter Book H*, fols. cxxvib, cxcivb (*Calendar*, 156, 272; Riley, *Memorials*, 446, 486); *Letter Book G* fol. cclxxxviii (*Calendar*, 293; Riley, *Memorials*, 363). Sometimes the trickery could be quite elaborate. In 1414, a soldier offered a Southwark pelterer a box containing sixteen gold nobles and a necklace as a pledge for furs worth a hundred shillings. At the exchange, however, the soldier substituted a box full of sand and stones. After confessing that he had acted with deception, the soldier was sentenced to stand in the pillory for one hour on each of three market days (*Letter Book I*, fol. cxxxvb [*Calendar*, 128–29; Riley, *Memorials*, 599–600]).

57. The collection of London documents regulating the making and selling of bread known as the *Liber Assisa de Panis* (*Assize of Bread*), now in the London Records Office at the Guildhall, includes a long list of those sentenced to the pillory as well as a rare drawing of the instrument (fol. 126b). Extracts from the *Assisa*, including references to the punishment of the pillory, are printed as Appendix I to volume 3 of the *Munimenta Gildhallae Londoniensis*, 411–29.

58. For examples of those sent to the pillory for selling putrid meat, see *Letter Book F*, fol. cliiib (*Calendar*, 181; Riley, *Memorials*, 240–41) and *Letter Book G*, fol. vib (*Calendar*, 8; Riley, *Memorials*, 270–71); for selling putrid fowl, see *Letter Book F*, fol. cxciv (*Calendar*, 226–27; Riley, *Memorials*, 266–67) and *Letter Book G*, fol. cxxxviii (*Calendar*, 176; Riley, *Memorials*, 328); for selling putrid fish, see *Letter Book H*, fol. cxlv (*Calendar*, 185; Riley, *Memorials*, 464).

59. For examples of the penalty of the pillory for cheating with a false checkerboard and with false dice, see *Letter Book H*, fol. cxxxviiib (*Calendar*, 174; Riley, *Memorials*, 455–57). For the pillory for sorcery and soothsaying, see *Letter Book H*, fols. cxliii, ccxlviii (*Calendar*, 181, 351; Riley, *Memorials*, 462–63, 518–19).

60. For various examples of forgeries punished by the pillory, see *Letter Book H*, fols. livb, cxxv, cclixb (*Calendar*, 54, 152, 365; Riley, *Memorials*, 404–5, 442–43, 527–29). For the forgery of papal bulls in 1412, see *Letter Book I*, fol. cxv (*Calendar*, 105; Riley, *Memorials*, 587–89). For the sentencing to the pillory of John de Hakford, who falsely claimed in 1364 that there was a widespread conspiracy to slay the important men and officials of London, see *Letter Book G*, fols. cxxxviiib–cxxxix (*Calendar*, 176–77; Riley, *Memorials*, 315–16).

others who fraudulently claimed to be what they were not, such as a hermit, a physician, or the son of an earl.[61]

Piers Plowman twice explicitly mentions the penalty of the pillory, both times during the important Meed episode. The first example occurs after the king orders that Meed's corrupt companions—False and Favel and their fellows, such as Gyle—be caught and severely punished (B 2.193–203; A 2.154–64; C 2.204–14). The king then instructs the constable about the treatment of one last villain:

> "And if ye lacche Lyere, lat hym noght ascapen
> Er he be put on the pillory, for any preyere, I hote."
>
>   (B 2.204–5; A 2.167–68; C 2.215–16).

Threatened only with the pillory, Liar may seem to be getting off easier than the other related forms of fraud (False and Favel are ordered to be hanged and Gyle to be beheaded), but the form of his sentence is appropriate. As the king's conditional phrasing suggests (*"if* ye lacche Lyere," my emphasis), Liar is portrayed as being as elusive as he is protean: he is everywhere and nowhere, successively taken in by pardoners, doctors, spicers, minstrels, and friars. The king does not imagine that Liar, as opposed to his companions, can be destroyed, but only flushed out of his hiding places and publicly exposed on the pillory so that all may see and beware of him.

The second explicit mention of the punishment of the pillory in *Piers Plowman* concerns civic rather than royal government. After an account of Meed's corrupt dealing with friars, a speaking voice, which may or may not be identified with the author, abruptly and with no clear transition addresses mayors, who are described as those "That menes ben bitwene / The kyng and the comune to kepe the lawes" (B 3.76–77; A 3.65–66; the lines at C 3.77–78 differ). As the term "menes" makes clear, mayors occupied a crucial position in medieval society, a point at which ideas of hierarchy and fraternity intersected. The office was the primary link between the sovereign and the urban

---

61. For examples of those who pretended to be ecclesiastical, civic, or royal officials, see *Letter Book G*, fol. cxlviiib (*Calendar*, 183; Riley, *Memorials*, 320–21), *Letter Book H*, fols. xxvib, ccix (*Calendar*, 18–19, 295; Riley, *Memorials*, 390–91, 489–90). For impostors pretending to be a hermit, physician, and the son of the earl of Ormound, see, respectively, *Letter Book I*, fol. cxiiib (*Calendar*, 104; Riley, *Memorials*, 584); *Letter Book H*, fols. cxlv, ccxixb (*Calendar*, 184, 312; Riley, *Memorials*, 464–66, 496–98).

community.[62] The speaker in *Piers* urges mayors to employ the pillory for those who cheat the poor, especially in regard to the most basic necessities of life—food and drink:

> To punysshe on pillories and on pynynge stooles
> Brewesters and baksters, bochiers and cokes—
> For thise are men on this molde that moost harm wercheth
> To the povere peple that parcelmele buggen.
> For thei poisone the peple pryveliche and ofte,
> Thei richen thorugh regratrie and rentes hem biggen
> With that the povere peple sholde putte in hire wombe.
>
> (B 3.78–84; A 3.67–73; C 3.79–83)

The offenses mentioned here were commonly punished in medieval London by the pillory or, for women, the "pynyng stoole."[63] The description of food sellers as those who "poisone the peple pryveliche and ofte" would fit the malefactors sent to the pillory for marketing spoiled food. The passage also echoes city ordinances against forestalling (buying up victuals before the general public had an opportunity to purchase them) and against certain kinds of retail reselling of food "parcelmele," also known as "regratrie."[64] The poor are the chief concern of these lines in *Piers*; likewise, in the *Statute of Bakers* forestallers are

62. *Piers Plowman* states this most powerfully in Holy Church's simile in B and C in which mayors are compared to nothing less than God's love: "Forthi is love ledere of the Lordes folk of hevene, / And a meene, as the mair is, inmiddes the kyng and the commune" (B 1.159–60; C 1.154–55).
When the office of mayor is mentioned in *Piers* the primary reference is probably to London, though what is said is general enough to apply to other English towns. Caroline Barron has noted that in contrast to his "simplistic" ideas about kingship, "Langland does have some quite specific and well-understood things to say about the local government he had experienced at first hand, namely the government of the City of London." She adds that about "the duties of the mayor of London Langland is often quite specific" ("William Langland," 95).

63. See Pearsall, *Piers: C-Text*, p. 69, note to C 3.79. The "pynyng stoole" was also called the "cucking stool" and was perhaps related to the *thewe*, which is what the London city records call the pillory for women. For mention of the *thewe* on Cornhill, see *Letter Book H*, fol. cxcivb (*Calendar*, 271–72; Riley, *Memorials*, 484–86). Both the *thewe* for women and the pillory for men are glossed in the margins of city records by the same Latin word: *collistrigium*.

64. For "forestalling" and "regrating," see Alley, *Caveat*, 5–6. A fourteenth-century book of London civic practices, the *Liber Custumarum*, insists that regrators not be allowed to buy basic foodstuffs from wholesalers before they have been offered to the city's great lords and good citizens: "les graunz seignours de la terre, e les bones genz de la ville" (193). For poulterers given various sentences, including the pillory, for forestalling, see Plea and Memoranda Roll A6, membr. 4 (*Calendar . . . 1323–1364*, 232).

blamed because in addition to deceiving the rich, they oppress the poor for private gain: the pillory is the punishment for a second offense (203–4).

The scene I have been discussing concludes with Meed trying to persuade the mayor to take silver and other presents "regratiers to mayntene," urging him to "love hem echone, / And suffre hem to selle somdel ayeins reson" (B 3.87–92; A 3.76–81; C 3.115–20), which is then followed by a biblical quotation from Job 15:34: *"Ignis devorabit tabernacula eorum qui libenter accipiunt munera"* (B 3.96; A 3.85; C 3.124).[65] Before this final warning, C inserts a stronger passage on the vengeance from on high that awaits the mercantile deceit and official negligence that causes "many sondry sorwes in citees" (C 3.86–114). Yet despite these invocations of divine wrath, the primary concern here, as always in *Piers Plowman*, is on human actions in the world. Following the Meed episode, *Piers* moves on to the confession of the sins, during which Covetise reveals that he and his wife are guilty, as noted in the previous section, of the kinds of commercial frauds that were punished by the pillory and the *thewe*. Indeed, Covetise's wife is known as "Rose the Regrater" (B 5.222; A 5.140; C 6.232).

The Public Spectacle of the Pillory

The London pillory was civic theater, a drama of justice performed before the citizens of the city.[66] The pillory brought untruth into the light and exposed it. Justice had to be seen to be done, both to reassure the town that offenders would not escape and to deter others from similar offenses.[67] At the center of this spectacle was the mute body of the prisoner himself. When brought to trial, defen-

65. As we might expect, *Piers* is franker about municipal corruption than are the London records, which were under the control of those in power. These dignitaries seem to have been more concerned with punishing slanders against themselves than in exposing official wrongdoing. A rare notation of the punishment of a London officer (a beadle) for corruption is found in Plea and Memoranda Roll A5, membr. 24 (*Calendar . . . 1323–1364*, 212).

66. The title of this section obviously refers to the second chapter of Michel Foucault's important *Discipline and Punish*. I cannot claim to deal with all the implications of Foucault's challenging study of public executions, but I have profited from his emphasis on the search for truth in such spectacles, on the importance of the body, and on the use of theater to manifest power and make spectators complicit. Some of my conclusions differ from Foucault's, in part because my subject is pillorying rather than execution and also because the official records available to me, unlike Foucault's, describe little of what actually happened at these spectacles but only what London courts ordered to happen.

67. In a mid-fourteenth-century Plea and Memoranda Roll, it is recorded that John Godard, who pretended to be a purveyor for the Prince of Wales, was sentenced to the pillory for three hours (an unusually harsh penalty) as an example to others: "exemplum aliorum" (Roll A7, membr. 5; *Calendar . . . 1323–1364*, 251). In 1382, Robert Berewold was put on the pillory for soothsaying and defamation to warn others not to do the like (*Letter Book H*, fol. clv [*Calendar*, 198; Riley, *Memorials*, 472–73]).

dants could admit their guilt, proclaim their innocence, or offer mitigating evidence, but once sentenced to the pillory, they fell silent and were not heard from again. No longer permitted their own words or gestures, they were displayed and defined by others and subject to the gaze and ridicule of spectators.[68]

In 1376, John Outlawe (possessing as allegorical a name as any character in *Piers*) was accused by two brothers of luring them into playing a board game called "quek" at the home of Nicholas Prestone, a tailor. After losing steadily, the brothers discovered that the board and its dice were rigged. Brought into court before the mayor and alderman, Prestone denied ownership of the board or knowledge that it was crooked. He was not believed. Both he and Outlawe were committed to prison and the jury determined they should repay the brothers what had been stolen from them. A second jury later found the pair guilty of fraud: "Therefore it was awarded that Nicholas Prestone and John Outlawe should have the punishment of the pillory, to stand thereon for one hour in the day; and that the said false chequer-board should be burnt beneath them, the Sheriff causing the reason for their punishment to be proclaimed. And after that, Prestone and Outlawe were to be taken back to the Prison of Newgate, there to remain until the Mayor and Aldermen should give orders for their release."[69]

This example is representative of many London pillory cases from the period when *Piers* was being written and first read. The humiliation of being displayed was often only part of the total punishment, its public aspect: Prestone and Outlawe were also fined and imprisoned. On the pillory itself even these clever tricksters became inert: their crime was proclaimed by the sheriff, and, in a further piece of stagecraft, a token of their crime was displayed and burned.[70] An even more elabo-

---

68. The primary object of the pillory was not to effect inner change in the criminal, as would be true with the later penal disciplines explored by Foucault, nor to produce admission of guilt (that had already happened or was made unnecessarily by a jury), as in sacramental confessional. Although Beattie refers to the experience of the pillory as a "form of public penance" (*Crime*, 464), the condemned apparently said nothing; the punishment was instead directed against him, aiming to bring about, as Beattie himself notes, "the participation of the community in the denunciation of the offender and his deed" (614).

69. *Letter Book H*, fols. xxxiib–xxxiii (*Calendar*, 25; Riley, *Memorials*, 395–96). I have added proper names to Riley's somewhat abbreviated translation.

70. As noted above, those who sold defective goods in London often had them burned at their feet as they stood on the pillory, as the checkerboard is here. Lies of speech or writing were also represented semiotically on the pillory. Those guilty of forgery had the counterfeit documents burned or tied to their bodies. A special sign was used to indicate false speech: a whetstone hung around the prisoner's neck, apparently in reference to proverbs about liars filing their tongues or lies having a sharp edge. In 1383 William Berham was sentenced to the pillory with two whetstones: a large one for slandering the mayor and a smaller one for lying about an ordinary citizen (*Letter Book H*, fol. clxii [*Calendar*, 212; Riley, *Memorials*, 476–77]).

rate public spectacle associated with the medieval London pillory was the noisy and ceremonial parading of prisoners from Newgate, the main municipal prison on the west edge of the city, through Cheap to Cornhill in the east. In 1382 John Stratton was convicted of forgery and other deceits and sent to "the prison of Newgate, and from thence on the same day should be led through Chepe with trumpets and pipes to the pillory on Cornhill, and be put upon the same for one hour of the day; after which, he was to be taken back to the prison aforesaid, there to remain until the morrow, when he was again to be taken to the pillory, with trumpets and pipes, and be put upon the same for one hour of the day."[71]

The pillory was a secular punishment, not a religious one. The criminal's body, not his mind or heart, was its object. The pillory was not concerned with inner reformation (though that might happen) but with controlling external behavior. In a challenging article on London and Chaucer's *Cook Tale*, David Wallace compares the reuniting of the criminal with a symbol of his crime on the pillory, what he calls the "imaging of justice," to Dante's use of *contrapasso* in the *Inferno*. Wallace finds the procedure an anticipation of divine justice: "an hour in the pillory warns of, prefigures, an eternity of punishment" ("Chaucer," 64). Instead of the pillory as a mirror of divine justice, however, I want to stress it as an expression of public earthly justice.

The medieval pillory punished social crimes, lies and commercial fraud against others, and was meant to have a practical, social result. The state of the offender's soul or his eternal destination were matters for other jurisdictions. Rather than a final judgment, the pillory was part of a graded scale of sanction designed to keep civic order in London. It was an intermediate penalty, more serious than some others, such as fines, but not as drastic as actual expulsion from the community (itself a social, rather than a spiritual sanction). Thus a London proclamation concerning victualers in 1363 asserts that none should conceal the products he had to sell: "on pain of paying, the first time, half a mark to the Chamber; and of being put on the pillory the second time."[72] The

71. *Letter Book H*, fol. cxliii (*Calendar*, 181; Riley, *Memorials*, 459). This is the kind of procession referred to by Chaucer, though without specific mention of the pillory, when he describes Perkyn in the *Cook's Tale* as "somtyme lad with revel to Newegate" (1 4402). The Letter Books and Plea and Memoranda Rolls contain references to several such processions from Newgate to the pillory, though other accounts of the punishment of the pillory do not mention them.

72. *Letter Book G*, fol. cviii (*Calendar*, 151; Riley, *Memorials*, 312). Fraudulent bakers were also subject to increasingly severe punishments: drawn on a hurdle for a first offense, put on the pillory for a second, and banished from their trade for a third (*Liber Albus*, 265 [fol. 199]; trans., 232).

bakers with their false molding boards noted previously were to forswear their profession only if they repeated their crime (see note 49 above).

Descriptions of pillory cases in the London records emphasize its punishments as a communal sanction; it was a response to fraud that deceived and damaged "all the City" or "all the people" or "the common people" (which I take to mean the people in general), though other formulas note more specific insults to officials such as the mayor or the sovereign.[73] The first mention of the pillory in *Piers,* when the king orders that Liar be put on it, reminds us that the crown was the ultimate guarantee of the law in England (cf. Foucault, *Discipline and Punish,* 47ff.). Indeed, the privileges of hierarchy could influence this punishment, as they did every other aspect of medieval life. Sylvia Thrupp has argued that the humiliation of the pillory was primarily suffered by the poor and powerless, whereas for those better off, "money and position could nearly always protect an offender's personal dignity" (*Merchant Class,* 24).[74] Yet Thrupp also noted some exceptions to the deference to status, especially under the mayoralty of John of Northampton in the 1380s, as in cases of forgery, which "was considered so heinous that it brought several people to the pillory who were well above the rank of those ordinarily convicted" (25). Although appeals in the London records to the welfare of the whole community and to the common people should probably be treated with some skepticism, they nevertheless suggest the importance given, at least rhetorically, to the public welfare.

Piers as Poetic Pillory

Piers Plowman has often been read as if it were a kind of poetic pillory: that is, a poem demanding strict social justice. And, indeed, much in *Piers* is intended, like the pillory, to expose, denounce, and reform frauds against the community, such as Meed's corruption of civil and religious law. Whatever its other interests, *Piers* is a significant political poem, though there has been much disagreement about

---

73. For examples of the phrases cited, see "all the city" ("tocius civitatis"), *Assize of Bread* (fol. 79b; *Munimenta Guildhall* 3:417); "to the prejudice of all the people" ("tocius populi"), *Letter Book G,* fol. cxiii (*Calendar,* 156; Riley, *Memorials,* 314); and "deceit of the common people" ("communis populi"), *Letter Book G,* fols. cxxxiib, ccxcii (*Calendar,* 171, 297; Riley, *Memorials,* 317, 367).

74. Those sentenced to the pillory (and worse) were sometimes excused from the penalty because they were servants of the king; see, for example, *Letter Book H,* fol. clivb (*Calendar,* 197; Riley, *Memorials,* 471–72). Thrupp adds: "Commercial fraud among merchants rarely came before the city courts because their own companies were supposed to deal with the problem, and cases that received public notice were not severely punished" (*Merchant Class,* 24).

its precise ideology.[75] If John Ball's letter is to be credited, *Piers* was used by the rebels during the Rising of 1381 to support their demands for social reform, though some recent scholars have emphasized the poem's essentially conservative views. What is not in question is that *Piers* frequently condemns deceit and dishonesty and demands their punishment and correction.

Justice is a common theme in the poem. Meed is put on trial, and Piers calls on Hunger to deal harshly with slackers during the plowing of the half acre, though he later relents. The *visio* concludes with the stark verdict of Truth's pardon: only those who do well will be saved; those who do evil will be damned eternally. The *vita* is less legalistic and more psychological than the *visio*, but here also *Piers* can be seen as a poetic pillory in its desire to expose fraud and assess blame. The specific crimes liable to the pillory are rarely mentioned in this part of the poem, but it does denounce and urge the correction of misdeeds by rich lords and clergy, who would not normally be at risk of punishment from the instrument because of their status.[76]

Piers and the pillory threaten a stern justice to wrongdoers, but both also practice a scrupulous justice. That special element of English law, the jury, provided a check against official pressure for convictions, and jurors apparently took pains to discover the facts of a case and to make the punishment fit the crime. Some accused were found innocent, and the responsibility of the guilty was often measured with a nice precision. When several poulterers were indicted in 1350 for forestalling, one was found not guilty, most were sent to prison, but another, who had been previously convicted of a similar crime, was made to suffer the additional penalty of the pillory (Plea and Memoranda Roll A6, membr. 4a [*Calendar . . . 1323–1364*, 232]). In a 1382 case, a man who falsely accused a woman of theft is made to confess his libel, but the greater punishment of the

---

75. Early readers of *Piers Plowman* often regarded it as a "satire" against current conditions and the Church, as in Puttenham's comments in 1589 (DiMarco, *Reference Guide*, 11). Middleton traced the critical heritage of treating the poet as a reformer ("Introduction," 4–12). Critics who have dealt with the political elements of the poem, especially its interest in secular law and social justice in various forms, include Aers, "Problems"; Alford, "Literature and Law"; Baldwin, *Theme of Government*; Chadwick, *Social Life*; Kean, "Justice" and "Love"; and Stokes, *Justice*.

76. The character in the *vita* who comes from the stratum of society most commonly pilloried in medieval London is undoubtedly the B-version's Haukyn, who is a baker among other things and thus practiced one of the crafts frequently so punished. Haukyn's confession is essentially religious and not judicial (about sin rather than crime), but, like others put on the pillory, he admits to commercial fraud (B 13.357ff.), says he wanted men to believe him to be what he was not (B 13.280), and stands exposed to Will with stains on his coat that are reminiscent of the tokens of crime regularly displayed on the pillory.

pillory is given to a second man, who had first implicated the woman by means of sorcery (*Letter Book H*, fol. clv [*Calendar*, 198; Riley, *Memorials*, 472–73]).

Piers contains the same kind of nuanced judgment. The frequent call in the penultimate passus for *Redde quod debes* suggests that each debt is unique—pay what *you* owe. Sometimes *ac* (or "but") seems to be the most important word in the poet's vocabulary as he explores the intricacies of a particular question. Because of their faults, merchants are not granted a full pardon from Truth, though that is not the poem's final statement about them: "Ac under his secret seel Truthe sente hem a lettre" (B 7.23; A 8.25; C 9.27), detailing precisely how they also might gain salvation. Another passage about the rich contains a series of *ac*s that reveal a lawyerly attempt to define exactly the different possibilities of guilt or innocence for individual members of this class (B 14.145, 155, 170).

Piers is most like a pillory in its fundamental concern with truth. Offenses against this quality (fraud in act or word), as I have shown, link most of the crimes of the pillory in medieval London. *Piers Plowman*, of course, is all about truth, though because it is a poetic and not a judicial pillory, it has a much broader view of the concept than can be found in the civic courts. Truth is the theme of Holy Church's teaching at the beginning of the poem, and the value she identifies with both God and love: "Whan alle tresors arn tried . . . treuthe is the beste" (B 1.85; A 1.83; C 1.81). Truth is a key concept in late medieval culture and carries a complex series of personal, chivalric, and religious meanings (see Green, *Crisis*). Whereas *Piers* exploits all these aspects (especially the religious), its view can be as pragmatic and communal as those behind the pillory. In contrast to more idealistic treatments by other Ricardian poets such as Chaucer or the *Gawain*-poet, truth in *Piers Plowman* never abandons the everyday social world. In the *visio*, Holy Church's initial abstractions give way to Reason's call for the folk to go on a pilgrimage to Truth, which takes the material form of the communal plowing of the half acre. In response to Truth's pardon, the rest of the poem is occupied with the practical question of what it is to do well, better, and best in this world. One of the heroes of this later part of the poem is Trajan, the Roman emperor, who asserts that he was saved not by clerical prayers but by his active good deeds, his "lyvynge in truthe" (B 11.151; cf. B 11.158 and C 12.92).

The Pillory and the Cross

Although *Piers Plowman* can be read as a political poem that pillories crimes of untruth against society and especially the poor, it is much more. Despite its thirst for justice, *Piers* nevertheless extends its sympathy to those who are guilty under the law: those who cannot always manage to live up to the truth and find themselves subject to punishment. The example of Trajan is not enough. Although an exemplar of just behavior, the emperor is detached from the effects of sin and the need for redemption so central to the poem: he is too perfect. Trajan certainly has no reason to fear the pillory. With his indomitable right-eousness, he is on the other side: a judge like the king or mayor, as suggested by his reference to the "leautee of my laweful domes" (B 11.145; C 12.81, with "lawes demynge" instead of "laweful domes"). But *Piers Plowman* is about the guilty as well as the innocent, Haukyn as well as Trajan, and it contains another instru-ment of public punishment with a very different message from that of the pil-lory: the cross.

Whereas the pillory is explicitly mentioned only twice at the beginning of the poem (and perhaps also suggested by the reference to Cornhill in the C-version), the cross or "rood" is constantly mentioned, culminating in the Crucifixion scene in passus B 18 (C 20), which many regard as the most important passus of the poem.[77] Indeed, after going on to describe the Harrowing of Hell and the four daughters of God, the passus ends by again returning to the cross, which it presents as a sovereign protector, as the narratorial "I" (in one of his most per-sonal moments) describes waking on Easter morning:

> And callede Kytte my wif and Calote my doghter:
> "Ariseth and go reuerenceth Goddes resurexion,
> And crepeth to the cros on knees, and kisseth it for a juwel.
> For Goddes blissede body it bar for oure boote,
> And it afereth the fend—for swich is the myghte,
> May no grisly goost glide there it shadweth."
>
> (B.18.428–33; C 20.472–78)

Obviously crucifixion differs from pillorying because its ultimate purpose is death, but the two penalties do share a number of general similarities. Both instruments display the victim in roughly the same position, standing erect with

---

77. Examples of references to Christ's "cros" in the B-version alone include 5.240, 5.465, 8.59, 10.415, 12.192, 15.446, 15.531, 15.540, 15.578, 16.164, 17.6, 19.63, 19.142, 19.200, and 19.324. Examples of refer-ences to the cross as "rood" in the B-version include 4.185, 5.103, 5.227, 5.455, 11.73, 15.536, 15.543, 17.39, 19.326, and 20.43.

arms spread to the side (more widely with the cross). Both are public punishments enacted on the body of the criminal. In the first stanza of an alliterative poem from the Vernon manuscript (which also includes an A-version of *Piers*), the Virgin Mary's address to the cross show that the similarity was well recognized in Langland's time: "Cros, thou dost no trouthe, / On a pillori my fruit to pinne" ("Disputation," lines 5–6).

The description of Christ's Crucifixion in *Piers*, which is based on the Gospels, contains significant parallels to accounts of the judgment of the pillory in the London records. In contrast to late medieval meditative accounts of the Passion that focus almost entirely on Christ's unmerited suffering, *Piers* clearly describes the event as a judicial proceeding. Pilate presides as judge, like a London mayor, "*sedens pro tribunali*" in order to "deme hir botheres righte" (B 18.37–38; C 20.35–36).[78] Christ in the poem is then accused of one of the crimes against truth frequently punished by the London pillory—using the magic arts: "'*Crucifige*,' quod a cachepol, 'I warante hym a wicche'" (B 18.46; C 20.46; Christ is accused of sorcery earlier at B 16.120; C.18.150; and later of being a witch at B 18.69 and of practicing sorcery at C 20.71). The crown of thorns (here called a "garland"), which is next described (B 18.47–50; C 20.47–50), also suggests the pillory: it resembles those physical symbols of the crime that were frequently displayed with the guilty party on the pillory. Specifically, this token refers to Jesus' claim to be "Crist and kynges sone" (B 18.55; "Godes sone" in C 20.55), an extreme example of pretending to be someone you are not, one of the offenses against truth subject to punishment by the pillory.[79]

As was true for those on the medieval London pillory, Christ is virtually silent on the cross, except for his last words, "*Consummatum est*" (B 18.57; C 20.57), and his body is acted upon by others: "Nailed hym with thre nailes naked upon the roode" (B 18.51; C 20.51). In accordance with Gospel accounts, most of the mocking of Jesus in the poem occurs before the Crucifixion and not (as seems to have been true with the pillory) during the punishment itself.

78. The trial is more biased and raucous in *Piers* than in a typical pillory case. Instead of officials and a jury in search of a careful verdict, "al the court," which seems to include spectators as well as "the justice," cry for the punishment of crucifixion before they have heard the evidence (B 18.38–39; C 20.37–38).

79. The specific accusation against Christ (that he had claimed he would destroy the temple and then rebuild it [B 18.40–45; C 20.39–45]) can be seen as an accusation of witchcraft, as already noted, or of fraudulent lying that might result in political unrest, both of which crimes merited the pillory in medieval London.

Nevertheless, *Piers* emphasizes an act of disrespect to Christ's body at least as bad as the taunting or egg and stone throwing on the pillory: the piercing of his side by Longinus (B 18.78ff.; C 20.80ff.). Like Mary in the Vernon poem, the poet of *Piers*, whether consciously or not, seems to have associated the ancient punishment of crucifixion with the more familiar experience of the pillory.

The Pillory Transformed

If the shadow of the cross lies behind the pillory in *Piers*, its account of Christ's Passion finally suggests a profound difference between the instruments. Discourses, images, and practices associated with the pillory become richer and more positive in the poem. Criminal is transformed into supernatural ruler, punishment into mercy, jeering spectators into redeemed brothers, and hierarchal social control into a profound sense of community. The threat of the pillory is replaced by the hope of the cross. The transformation is most evident with the blind knight Longinus. Longinus's assault may resemble that of a spectator attacking a constrained body on the pillory, but the result of his act is not pain for the other but, as seen in the previous chapter, his own physical (and spiritual) healing. Instead of humiliating the condemned man, Longinus himself is humbled as blood opens his eyes, causing him to kneel and beg for mercy from one he now recognizes to be not a malefactor but "rightful Jesu" (B 18.86–91; C 20.88–94). A secular act of punishment becomes a divine act of salvation.

Although the Crucifixion in *Piers* is presented as a judicial event like pillorying, the author also associates it with other discourses. The most persistent is that of chivalry, for the poem repeatedly refers to Christ's time on the cross as a joust.[80] At the beginning of the Crucifixion passage, Christ is said to look like "the kynde of a knyght that cometh to be dubbed" (B 18.13; C 20.11). Instead of a felon, he is a warrior (and soon a king), who before his Ascension from the earthly Jerusalem throws open the doors of the New Jerusalem to all. Christ's joust is a very different public spectacle from that of the pillory, full of joy instead of suffering, success rather than shame: "Thanne was Feith in a fenestre, and cryde "*A, Fili David,* / As dooth an heraud of armes whan aventrous cometh

---

80. This trope begins as early as the account of the Incarnation two passus before the Crucifixion itself (B 16.95; C 18.129), and it continues in the next passus, which describes Abraham, Moses, the Samaritan, and the narrative "I" as all hurrying to "a justes in Jerusalem" (B 17.52; C 19.52). Foucault also notes an element of the joust in the interrogation and execution of the prisoners he discusses (*Discipline and Punish,* 40–41, 51–52).

to justes" (B 18.15–16; C 20.13–14). A scene of punishment is described as a glo-
rious chivalric adventure. Moreover, Christ is a unique knight, lacking the arro-
gance of the class as he rides "barefoot on an asse" without "spores other spere"
(B 18.11–12; C 20.9–10).[81] And, for all his modesty, he deals with issues that go
far beyond civic law and order: the opponent he seeks to defeat is no less than
"the fend and fals doom to deye" (B 18.28; C 20.27).

In this spectacle of redemption, elements associated with the London pillory
are radically redefined. The derisive revelry that often accompanied the procession of the prisoner to and from Newgate, for instance, appears in the poem
only as its opposite (there is no mention of Christ carrying his cross): the hymns
of praise sung to Jesus as he first enters the city on Palm Sunday: "Olde Jewes of
Jerusalem for joye thei songen, / *Benedictus qui venit in nomine Domini*" (B 18.17–18;
C 20.15–16). The shame and social degradation stressed in late medieval meditative accounts of the Passion (as they are in London records of the pillory) are in
Piers not finally suffered by Jesus but by his Jewish judges and spectators, who, we
are told by not less than Abraham, will lose their freedom because of their
"foule vileynye." The Jews are doomed to become landless thralls, like those
repeat offenders banished from London after their criminal behavior was not
corrected by the pillory (B 18.92–109; C 20.95–112).

The helplessness of the contemporary pilloried one is transformed by *Piers*
into Christ's power and mercy. If the crown put on Jesus' head suggests the
tokens of crime often displayed on the pillory, such intended mockery makes
fools of its perpetrators, for it is a true sign of divine majesty. Instead of being
returned to Newgate prison, as frequently happened after the public spectacle in
London, Christ goes to the prison of hell and liberates its prisoners from their
eternal sentence and establishes instead a new, temporary lockup, "my prisone
Purgatorie," which is not a place of punishment, like Newgate or the Tun on
Cornhill, but of genuine reformation: "Thei shul be clensed clerliche and clene
wasshen of hir synnes" (B 18.392–93; not in C).

Fraud was the principal target of the London pillory: the sort of "falsnesse,"
"gile," and deceit ("men to deceyve") of which Christ had earlier accused Judas
during his betrayal in the garden (B 16.154–56; c.18.172–74, without "gile"). A
specific class of offenses often mentioned in the London records, as noted previously, was pretending to be someone you were not: an official of the king, for

---

81. For the tradition of the Christ-knight in *Piers*, see St.-Jacques, "Christ-Knight"; Waldron, "Langland's
Originality."

example, or a earl's son. In the Crucifixion scene in *Piers*, such deception by Jesus is not only insisted upon but even highly praised. Both a knight and a lord's son, Jesus fights not in his own colors but "in Piers armes" in order that he "be noght biknowe here for *consummatus Deus*" (B 18.22–24; C 20.21–23). In contrast to the fraud punished on the pillory, which the London records denounce because of its cheating of the city and its residents, Christ's fraud is of the people (he fights in the human form of a plowman), but, most important, for the people—to save them from eternal death and damnation. And whereas the London pretenders claimed to be someone more important, Christ pretends to be someone less important: an ordinary human plowman.

Although the pillory punished crimes against truth, the Crucifixion scene in *Piers* goes so far as to raise questions about even that high virtue. Truth, one of the four daughters of God who appear between the Crucifixion and Harrowing, advocates a strict justice that is as wrongheaded as that insisted upon by her equally severe sister Righteousness:

> At the bigynnyng God gaf the doom hymselve—
> That Adam and Eve and alle that hem suwede
> Sholden deye downrighte, and dwelle in peyne after.
> (B 18.190–92; C 20.195–97).

But the law of the cross is very different from that of the pillory. Mercy and Peace, not Truth and Righteousness, understand how it works, which is very different from London civic justice. Instead the cross is more like the ways of poetry (B 18.142; C 20.144), intoxication (B 18.187; C 20.192), or the even liturgy, the last of which teaches that Adam's fall was happy because its final result was not punishment but the redemption of the cross (B 18.217–28; C 20.226–37).

The language of medieval justice spoken during the Passion scene in *Piers* appears primarily in the mouths of various devils. When Christ demands the souls of Adam and his descendants, Lucifer insists that they are his "by right and by reson" (B 18.277; C 20.300) and appeals to the "lawe" made by God forbidding the eating of the apple (B 18.284; C 20.306, which also contains an additional reference to "treuthe" at 20.311). The other devils acknowledge, however, that their claim over humans is shaky because it is based on "treson": "It is noght graithly geten, ther gile is the roote" (B 18.289–91; rewritten at C 20.319–22).

That fiends should practice the kind of fraud punished by the pillory is unre-markable, but it is a shock that Christ is so accused. The Devil complains that when alive, Jesus pretended, like many condemned to the pillory, to be someone he was not (a human being): "and som tyme I asked / Wher he were God or Goddes sone—he gaf me short answere" (B 18.296–97; C 20.330–31). The C-version is even more explicit about this deceit when the Devil equates the trick-ing of Adam and Eve by Satan (a separate fiend) with Christ's disguise as a man: "And as thowe [Satan] bigyledest Godes ymages in goynge of an addre, / So hath God bigiled us alle in goynge of a weye" (C 20.326–27). When Christ finally speaks, he quickly transcends such narrow legalistic categories. He does begin by insisting that the "Olde Lawe" that "gilours be bigiled" is a good one (B 18.339–40; C 20.381–82), and in the B-version asserts that his death allows him to "by right and by reson raunsone here my liges" (B 18.350), but he then goes far beyond the strict justice of such equal requiting. Instead of guile for guile, Christ asserts a reward for humans completely out of proportion to the devils' crime: grace for guile. This is a mercy that does more than merely temper justice, it overwhelms it in imagery of burgeoning generosity: "Now bigynneth thi gile ageyn thee to turne / And my grace to growe ay gretter and widder" (B 18.362–63; C 20.399–400). Later, Christ makes clear that whereas he has no intention of abolishing justice, he will restrict it to a single locale: "Ac my rightwisnesse and right shal rulen al helle, / And mercy al mankynde bifore me in hevene" (B 18.397–98; C 20.439–40). In the eternal realms, the law and jus-tice associated with the pillory are literally hellish.

Commercial fraud was a major concern of the London pillory, but despite the genuine indignation in *Piers* at the abuses of retail trade, especially against the poor, the poem also, as we have seen before, presents these same urban practices posi-tively. Although mercantile imagery is not explicitly used in the Crucifixion scene in *Piers*, Christ is a kind of urban trader who buys humans from the wily devils of hell at the price of his death. Moreover, in contrast to the food and drink that were sold spoiled or piecemeal in London as expensive "regratrie," making its sellers liable to the pillory, the nourishment offered by Christ is available to all humans and wholly healthy. Lucifer, as "doctour of deeth," must consume his own bitter brew ("drynk that thow madest"), suggesting the brewers and other victualers deserving of the pillory because "thei poisone the peple pryveliche and ofte" (B 3.82); but the refreshment associated with Christ is vivifying: identifying himself as "lord of lif," he declares that "love is my drynke, / And for that drynke today, I deide upon erthe" (B 18.364–67; C 20.401–4). The imagery here is dazzling, Christ is both *corpus christi*, the food of eternal life eaten by the faithful at the Eucharist, and one who himself hungers and thirsts for human beings. The strict control of food that was such a feature of medieval London life and was enforced by the pillory, is utterly transgressed by Christ's unregulated appetite and free offer of his own body: this is indeed love and not law.

By his actions, Christ shows himself far more magnanimous than the well-meaning monarch we saw attempting to deal with Meed at Westminster, who concentrates on having his laws obeyed and wrongdoers condemned, or than the sovereign whose terrible revenge Foucault sees behind the scaffold (*Discipline and Punish*, 47–49). Rather than simply a king, Christ is "kyng of kynges" (B 18.385; C 20.426), one who uses his overwhelming power to pardon rather than to pun-ish. He cites justice only to supersede it, noting the custom that if a king is pres-ent when a felon is about to suffer death or other punishment, "Lawe wolde he yeve hym lif, and he loked on hym" (B 18.382–84; C 20.423–25). But it is not just to demonstrate his royal prerogative that Christ pardons evildoers in *Piers* (cf. Foucault, *Discipline and Punish*, 53); instead, it is primarily because of the deep kinship he feels with fellow humans: "For we beth bretheren of blood" (B 18.377; C 20.419). This king's subjects become his brothers. The fundamental tension in medieval society between ideals of hierarchy and community, which the London records continually note and act out in crude and cruel legalistic prac-tices like the pillory, here meet and are reconciled (like the disputatious four daughters of God during their final carol) in a moment of visionary redemption. The public becomes the personal and also the universal and the divine.

Bibliography

ABBREVIATIONS

EETS   *Early English Text Society*
JEGP   *Journal of English and Germanic Philology*
MLR   *Modern Language Review*
MP   *Modern Philology*
NQ   *Notes and Queries*
PMLA   *Publications of the Modern Language Association*
TLS   *Times Literary Supplement*
YES   *Yearbook of English Studies*
YLS   *Yearbook of Langland Studies*

Editions of Piers Plowman are listed under the names of their editors.

Adams, Robert. "Editing and the Limitations of the *Durior Lectio.*" *YLS* 5 (1991): 7–15.
———. "Editing *Piers Plowman B*: The Imperative of an Intermittently Critical Edition." *Studies in Bibliography* 45 (1992): 31–68.
———. "Langland's *Ordinatio*: The *Visio* and the *Vita* Once More." *YLS* 8 (1994): 51–84.
———. "Langland's Theology." In *A Companion to Piers Plowman*, ed. John Alford, 87–114. Berkeley and Los Angeles: University of California Press, 1988.
———. "The Reliability of the Rubrics in the B-Text of *Piers Plowman.*" *Medium Aevum* 54 (1985): 208–31.
Aers, David. *Chaucer, Langland, and the Creative Imagination*. London: Routledge, 1980.
———. "Christ's Humanity and *Piers Plowman*: Contexts and Political Implications." *YLS* 8 (1994): 107–25.
———. *Community, Gender, and Individual Identity: English Writing, 1360–1430*. London: Routledge, 1988.
———. *Piers Plowman and Christian Allegory*. London: Arnold, 1975.
———. "*Piers Plowman* and Problems in the Perception of Poverty: A Culture in Transition." *Leeds Studies in English*, n.s., 14 (1983): 5–25.
———. "Reflections on the 'Allegory of the Theologians,' Ideology, and *Piers Plowman.*" In *Medieval Literature: Criticism, Ideology, and History*, ed. David Aers, 58–73. New York: St. Martin's, 1986.
———. "A Whisper in the Ear of Early Modernists; or, Reflections on Literary Critics Writing the 'History of the Subject.'" In *Culture and History, 1350–1600*, ed. David Aers, 177–202. Detroit: Wayne State University Press, 1992.

Aers, David, and Lynn Staley. *The Powers of the Holy: Religion, Politics, and Gender in Late Medieval English Culture.* University Park: Pennsylvania State University Press, 1996.

Alexander, Jonathan, and Paul Binski, eds. *The Age of Chivalry: Art in Plantagenet England, 1200–1400.* London: Weidenfeld and Nicolson, 1987.

Alford, John A. "The Design of the Poem." In *A Companion to Piers Plowman,* ed. John Alford, 29–65. Berkeley and Los Angeles: University of California Press, 1988.

———. "Literature and Law in Medieval England." *PMLA* 92 (1977): 941–51.

———. "Improving the Text." In *English Romanticism: Preludes and Postludes,* ed. Donald Schoonmaker and John A. Alford, 1–19. East Lansing, Mich.: Colleagues Press, 1993.

———. Review of *Piers Plowman: The B Version,* ed. George Kane and E. Talbot Donaldson. *Speculum* 52 (1977): 1002–5.

———. "The Role of the Quotations in *Piers Plowman.*" *Speculum* 52 (1977): 80–99.

Alley, Hugh. *Hugh Alley's Caveat: The Markets of London in 1598.* Ed. Ian Archer, Caroline Barron, and Vanessa Harding. London: London Topographical Society, 1988.

Andrews, William. *Bygone Punishments.* London, 1899.

———. *Punishments in the Olden Time.* London: W. Stewart, n.d. [1881].

De Antiquis Legibus Liber: Cronica Maiorum et Vicecomitum Londoniarum. Ed. Thomas Stapleton. London: Camden Society, 1846. Translated as *Chronicles of the Mayors and Sheriffs of London.* Trans. Henry T. Riley. London: Trübner, 1863.

Arn, Mary-Jo. "Langland's Characterization of Will in the B-Text." *Dutch Quarterly Review* 11 (1981): 287–301.

Ashby, Jane E. "English Medieval Murals of the Doom: A Descriptive Catalogue and Introduction." Master's thesis, York University, Medieval Studies, 1980.

Astell, Ann W. "'Full of Enigmas': John Ball's Letters and *Piers Plowman.*" In *Political Allegory in Late Medieval England,* 44–72. Ithaca: Cornell University Press, 1999.

Aston, Margaret. *England's Iconoclasts.* 2 vols. Oxford: Clarendon Press, 1988.

———. "Lollards and Images." In *Lollards and Reformers: Images and Literacy in Late Medieval Religion,* 135–92. London: Hambledon, 1984.

Atkinson, Clarissa W. *Mystic and Pilgrim: The Book and the World of Margery Kempe.* Ithaca: Cornell University Press, 1983.

Babington, Caroline, Tracy Manning, and Sophie Stewart. *Our Painted Past: Wall Paintings of English Heritage.* London: English Heritage, 1999.

Bailey, Paul, ed. *The Oxford Book of London.* Oxford: Oxford University Press, 1995.

Baker, A. M. "The Wall Paintings in the Church of St. John the Baptist, Clayton." *Sussex Archaeological Collections* 108 (1970): 58–81.

Baker, Denise N. "Dialectic Form in *Pearl* and *Piers Plowman.*" *Viator* 15 (1984): 263–73.

Baldwin, Anna P. *The Theme of Government in Piers Plowman.* Cambridge, England: Brewer, 1981.

Bale, John. *Index Britanniae Scriptorum . . . John Bale's Index of British and Other Writers.* Ed. R. L. Poole. Oxford, 1902.

Balibar, Etienne. "Subjection and Subjectivation." In *Supposing the Subject,* ed. Joan Copjec, 1–15. London: Verso, 1994.

Bannister, Arthur T. "William Langland's Birthplace." *TLS,* 7 September 1922, 569.

Barr, Helen. *Signes and Sothe: Language in the Piers Plowman Tradition.* Cambridge, England: Brewer, 1994.

Barron, Caroline M. "The Expansion of Education in Fifteenth-Century London." In *The Cloister and the World: Essays in Medieval History in Honour of Barbara Harvey*, ed. John Blair and Brian Golding, 219–45. Oxford: Clarendon Press, 1996.

———. "The 'Golden Age' of Women in Medieval London." *Reading Medieval Studies* 15 (1989): 35–58.

———. "The Later Middle Ages: 1270–1520." In *The City of London from Prehistoric Times to c. 1520*, ed. Mary D. Lobel, 42–56. The British Atlas of Historical Towns 3. Rev. ed. Oxford: Oxford University Press, 1991.

———. "The Parish Fraternities of Medieval London." In *The Church in Pre-Reformation Society: Essays in Honour of F. R. H. Du Boulay*, ed. Caroline Barron and Christopher Harper-Bill, 13–37. Dover, N.H.: Boydell Press, 1985.

———. "Richard Whittington: The Man Behind the Myth." In *Studies in London History Presented to Philip Edmund Jones*, ed. A. E. J. Hollaender and William Kellaway, 197–248. London: Hodder and Stoughton, 1969.

———. "William Langland: A London Poet." In *Chaucer's London*, ed. Barbara A. Hanawalt, 91–109. Minneapolis: University of Minnesota Press, 1992.

Barron, Caroline M., and Laura Wright. "The London Middle English Guild Certificates of 1388–9." *Nottingham Medieval Studies* 39 (1995): 108–45.

Barthes, Roland. *Mythologies*. Trans. Annette Lavers. New York: Hill and Wang, 1972.

Beattie, J. M. *Crime and the Courts in England, 1660–1800*. Oxford: Clarendon Press, 1986.

Beckwith, Sarah. "A Very Material Mysticism: The Medieval Mysticism of Margery Kempe." In *Medieval Literature: Criticism, Ideology, and History*, ed. David Aers, 34–57. New York: St. Martin's, 1986.

———. "Problems of Authority in Late Medieval English Mysticism: Language, Agency, and Authority in the Book of Margery Kempe." *Exemplaria* 4 (1992): 171–99.

Belsey, Catherine. *The Subject of Tragedy: Identity and Difference in Renaissance Drama*. London: Routledge, 1985.

Bennett, Josephine Waters. *The Rediscovery of Sir John Mandeville*. New York: MLA, 1954.

Benson, C. David. "An Augustinian Irony in 'Piers Plowman.'" *NQ*, n.s., 23 (1976): 51–54.

———. "The Frustration of Narrative and the Reader in *Piers Plowman*." In *Art and Context in Late Medieval English Narrative*, ed. Robert Edwards, 1–15. Cambridge, England: Brewer, 1994.

Benson, C. David, and Lynne Blanchfield. *The Manuscripts of Piers Plowman: The B-Version*. Cambridge, England: Brewer, 1997.

Benson, C. David, and Elizabeth Passmore. "The Discourses of Hunger in *Piers Plowman*." In *Satura: Studies in Medieval Literature in Honour of Robert R. Raymo*, ed. Nancy M. Reale and Ruth E. Sternglantz, 150–52. Donnington, Linc., England: Saun Tyas, 2001.

Bevington, David, Huston Diehl, Richard Kenneth Emmerson, Ronald Herzman, and Pamela Sheingorn. *Homo, Memento Finis: The Iconography of Just Judgment in Medieval Art and Drama*. Kalamazoo, Mich.: Medieval Institute Publications, 1985.

Binski, Paul. *Medieval Craftsmen: Painters*. University of Toronto Press, 1991.

Bird, Ruth. *The Turbulent London of Richard II*. London: Longmans, 1949.

Blackman, Elsie. "Notes on the B-Text MSS. of *Piers Plowman*." *JEGP* 17 (1918): 489–545.

Bloomfield, Morton. *Piers Plowman as a Fourteenth-Century Apocalypse*. New Brunswick: Rutgers University Press, n.d. [1961].

———. "Present State of *Piers Plowman* Studies." *Speculum* 14 (1939): 215–32. Reprinted with corrections in *Style and Symbolism in Piers Plowman: A Modern Critical Anthology*, ed. Robert J. Blanch, 3–25. Knoxville: University of Tennessee Press, 1969.

———. "Was William Langland a Benedictine Monk?" *Modern Language Quarterly* 4 (1943): 57–61.

Blythe, Joan. "*Transitio* and Psychoallegoresis in *Piers Plowman*." In *Allegoresis*, ed. J. Stephen Russell, 133–55. New York: Garland, 1988.

Bodley Version of Mandeville's Travels. Ed. M. C. Seymour. EETS, o.s., 253. London: Oxford, 1963.

Borenius, Tancred. "The Cycle of Images in the Palaces and Castles of Henry III." *Journal of the Warburg and Courtauld Institutes* 6 (1943): 40–50.

Borenius, Tancred, and E. W. Tristram. *English Medieval Painting*. 1927. Reprint, New York: Hacker Art Books, 1976.

Bowers, John M. *The Crisis of Will in Piers Plowman*. Washington, D.C.: Catholic University of American Press, 1986.

———. "*Piers Plowman* and the Police: Notes Toward a History of the Wycliffite Langland." *YLS* 6 (1992): 1–50.

———. "*Piers Plowman*'s William Langland: Editing the Text, Writing the Author's Life." *YLS* 9 (1995): 65–90.

Bowers, Terence N. "Margery Kempe as Traveler." *Studies in Philology* 97 (2000): 1–28.

Brandser, Kristin. "*Mandeville's Travels*: A Medieval Stockpile of Representations." In *Proceedings of the Third Dakotas Conference on Earlier British Literature*, ed. Bruce E. Brandt, 25–34. Brookings: South Dakota State University, 1995.

Breeze, Andrew. "The Virgin's Rosary and St Michael's Scales." *Studia Celtica* 24/25 (1989/90): 91–98.

Brewer, Charlotte. "Authorial vs. Scribal Writing in *Piers Plowman*." In *Medieval Literature: Texts and Interpretation*, ed. Tim William Machan, 59–89. Binghamton, N.Y.: Medieval and Renaissance Texts and Studies, 1991.

———. *Editing Piers Plowman: The Evolution of the Text*. Cambridge: Cambridge University Press, 1996.

———. "Editing *Piers Plowman*." *Medium Aevum* 65 (1996): 286–93.

———. "George Kane's Processes of Revision." In *Crux and Controversy in Middle English Textual Criticism*, ed. A. J. Minnis and Charlotte Brewer, 71–96. Cambridge, England: Brewer, 1992.

———. "Response [to John Bowers, "Editing the Text"]." *YLS* 9 (1995): 91–94.

———. "The Textual Principles of Kane's A Text." *YLS* 3 (1989): 67–90.

———. "Walter William Skeat (1835–1912)." In *Medieval Scholarship: Biographical Studies on the Formation of a Discipline*, ed. Helen Damico with Donald Fennema and Karmen Lenz. Vol. 2, 139–49. New York: Garland, 1998.

Bright, Allan H. *New Light on "Piers Plowman."* With a preface by R. W. Chambers. London: Oxford University Press, 1928.

———. "William Langland's Birthplace." *TLS*, 12 March 1925, 172.

———. "William Langland's Early Life." *TLS*, 5 November 1925, 739.

———. "William Langland's Early Life." *TLS*, 9 September 1926, 596.

Britnell, Richard H. *The Commercialisation of English Society, 1000–1500*. 2d ed. Manchester: Manchester University Press, 1996.

Brogan, T. V. F., ed. *The New Princeton Handbook of Poetic Terms*. Princeton: Princeton University Press, 1994.

Brooke-Rose, Christine. "Ezra Pound: Piers Plowman in the Modern Waste Land." *Review of English Literature* 2 (1961): 74–88.

Burrow, John A. "The Action of Langland's Second Vision." *Essays in Criticism* 15 (1965): 247–68. Reprinted in *Style and Symbolism in Piers Plowman: A Modern Critical Anthology*, ed. Robert J. Blanch, 209–27. Knoxville: University of Tennessee Press, 1969.

———. "The Audience of *Piers Plowman.*" *Anglia* 75 (1957): 373–84.

———. "Autobiographical Poetry in the Middle Ages: The Case of Thomas Hoccleve." (Gollancz Lecture.) *Proceedings of the British Academy* 67 (1982): 389–412.

———. *Langland's Fictions.* Oxford: Clarendon Press, 1993.

———. "Langland *Nel Mezzo Del Cammin.*" In *Medieval Studies for J. A. W. Bennett*, ed. P. L. Heyworth, 21–41. Oxford: Clarendon Press, 1981.

———. Review of *Piers Plowman: The B Version*, ed. George Kane and E. Talbot Donaldson. *TLS*, 21 November 1975, 1380–81.

Butturff, Douglas. "Satire in Mandeville's Travels." *Annuale Medievale* 13 (1972): 155–64.

Caiger-Smith, A. *English Medieval Mural Paintings.* Oxford: Clarendon Press, 1963.

Calendar of Coroners Rolls of the City of London, A.D. 1300–1378. Ed. Reginald R. Sharpe. London: Richard Clay, 1913.

Calendar of Early Mayor's Court Rolls . . . of the City of London (1298–1307). Ed. A. H. Thomas. Cambridge: Cambridge University Press, 1924.

Calendar of Letter-Books . . . of the City of London: Letter-Book C [1291–1309]. Ed. Reginald R. Sharpe. London: John Edward Francis, 1901.

Calendar of Letter-Books . . . of the City of London: Letter-Book D [1309–14]. Ed. Reginald R. Sharpe. London: John Edward Francis, 1902.

Calendar of Letter-Books . . . of the City of London: Letter-Book E [1314–37]. Ed. Reginald R. Sharpe. London: John Edward Francis, 1903.

Calendar of Letter-Books . . . of the City of London: Letter-Book F [1337–52]. Ed. Reginald R. Sharpe. London: John Edward Francis, 1904.

Calendar of Letter-Books . . . of the City of London: Letter-Book G [1352–74]. Ed. Reginald R. Sharpe. London: John Edward Francis, 1905.

Calendar of Letter-Books . . . of the City of London: Letter-Book H [1375–99]. Ed. Reginald R. Sharpe. London: John Edward Francis, 1907.

Calendar of Letter-Books . . . of the City of London: Letter-Book I [1400–1422]. Ed. Reginald R. Sharpe. London: John Edward Francis, 1909.

Calendar of Plea and Memoranda Rolls . . . 1323–1364. Ed. A. H. Thomas. Cambridge: Cambridge University Press, 1926.

Calendar of Plea and Memoranda Rolls . . . 1364–1381. Ed. A. H. Thomas. Cambridge: Cambridge University Press, 1929.

Calendar of Select Pleas and Memoranda . . . 1381–1412. Ed. A. H. Thomas. Cambridge: Cambridge University Press, 1932.

Calendar of Wills Proved and Enrolled in the Court of Hustings, London, A.D. 1258–A.D. 1688. Ed. Reginald R. Sharpe. 2 vols. London: John C. Francis, 1889–90.

Calhoun, Graig. *Habermas and the Public Sphere.* Cambridge: MIT Press, 1992.

Camargo, Martin. "*The Book of John Mandeville* and the Geography of Identity." In *Marvels, Monsters, and Miracles*, ed. Timothy S. Jones and David A. Sprunger, 67–84. Kalamazoo, Mich.: Medieval Institute Publications, 2002.

Cameron, Kenneth W. "A Discovery in *John de Mandevilles.*" *Speculum* 2 (1936): 351–59.

Camille, Michael. *Image on the Edge: The Margins of Medieval Art.* Cambridge: Harvard University Press, 1992.

———. "Seeing and Reading: Some Visual Implications of Medieval Literary and Illiteracy." *Art History* 8 (1985): 26–49.

Campbell, Mary B. *The Witness and the Other World.* Ithaca: Cornell University Press, 1988.

Campbell, Thomas. *Specimens of the British Poets.* Vol. 1. London: John Murray, 1819.

Cargill, Oscar. "The Langland Myth." *PMLA* 50 (1935): 36–56.

Carruthers, Mary. *The Search for St. Truth: A Study of Meaning in Piers Plowman.* Evanston: Northwestern University Press, 1973. See also Schroeder, Mary C.

Cather, Sharon, David Park, and Paul Williamson, eds. *Early Medieval Wall Paintings and Painted Sculpture in England.* British Series 216. Oxford: BAR, 1990.

Chadwick, D[orothy]. *Social Life in the Days of Piers Plowman.* 1922. New York: Russell and Russell, 1969.

Chambers, R. W. "The Authorship of 'Piers Plowman.'" *MLR* 5 (1910): 1–32.

———. "Incoherencies in the A- and B-texts of *Piers Plowman* and Their Bearing on the Authorship." *London Mediaeval Studies* 1 (1937): 27–39.

———. "Long Will, Dante, and the Righteous Heathen." *Essays and Studies* 9 (1924): 50–69.

———. *Man's Unconquerable Mind.* London: Cape, 1939.

———. Preface to *New Light on 'Piers Plowman,'* by Allan H. Bright, 9–31. London: Oxford University Press, 1928.

———. "Robert or William Longland?" *London Mediaeval Studies* 1 (1939): 430–62.

———. "The Original Form of the A-Text of 'Piers Plowman.'" *MLR* 6 (1911): 302–23.

———. "The Three Texts of 'Piers Plowman,' and Their Grammatical Forms." *MLR* 14 (1919): 129–51.

Chambers, R. W., and Marjorie Daunt, eds. *A Book of London English, 1384–1425.* 1931. Reprint, Oxford: Clarendon Press, 1967.

Chambers, R. W., and J. H. G. Grattan. "The Text of 'Piers Plowman.'" *MLR* 4 (1909): 357–89.

———. "The Text of 'Piers Plowman.'" *MLR* 26 (1931): 1–51.

———. "The Text of 'Piers Plowman': Critical Methods." *MLR* 11 (1916): 257–75.

Chessell, Del. "The Word Made Flesh: The Poetry of William Langland." *Critical Review* 14 (1971): 109–24.

Chronicles of the Mayors and Sheriffs of London. See *De Antiquis Legibus Liber.*

Clode, Charles M. *The Early History of the Guild of Merchant Taylors.* 2 vols. London: Harrison, 1888.

Clopper, Lawrence M. "The Contemplative Matrix of *Piers Plowman* B." *Modern Language Quarterly* 46 (1985): 3–28.

———. "Langland's Markings for the Structure of *Piers Plowman.*" *MP* 85 (1988): 245–55.

———. "The Life of the Dreamer, the Dreams of the Wanderer in *Piers Plowman.*" *Studies in Philology* 86 (1989): 261–85.

———. "Need Men and Women Labor? Langland's Wanderer and the Labor Ordinances." In *Chaucer's England,* ed. Barbara A. Hanawalt, 110–29. Minneapolis: University of Minnesota Press, 1992.

———. "A Response to Robert Adams, 'Langland's *Ordinatio.*'" *YLS* 9 (1995): 141–46.

Coleman, Janet. *Piers Plowman and the Moderni.* Rome: Edizioni di Storia e Letteratura, 1981.

Converse, Florence. *Long Will.* 1908. Reprint, London: Dent, 1948.

The Corporation of London: Its Origin, Constitution Powers, and Duties. London: Oxford University Press, 1950.

[Cotton version of Mandeville]. See *Mandeville's Travels.*

Coulton, G. G. *Medieval Panorama.* Cambridge: Cambridge University Press, 1938.

Crick, Julia C., ed. *The Historia Regum Britannie of Geoffrey of Monmouth.* Vol. 3, *A Summary Catalogue of the Manuscripts.* Cambridge, England: Brewer, 1989.

Crowley, Robert, ed. *The Vision of Pierce Plowman, now fyrste imprynted.* 1505 [1550]. London: David Paradine, 1976.

Dahl, Eric. *"Diuerse Copies Haue it Diuerselye:* An Unorthodox Survey of *Piers Plowman* Textual Scholarship from Crowley to Skeat." In *Suche Werkis to Werche: Essays on Piers Plowman,* ed. Míceál F. Vaughan, 53–80. East Lansing, Mich.: Colleagues Press, 1993.

Dawson, Christopher. "The Vision of Piers Plowman." In *Medieval Essays,* 212–40. 1934 (as *Medieval Religion*). Reprint, Garden City, N.Y.: Image, 1959.

The Defective Version of "Mandeville's Travels." Ed. M. C. Seymour. EETS, o.s., 319. Oxford: Oxford University Press, 2002.

De Looze, Laurence. *Pseudo-Autobiography in the Fourteenth Century.* Gainesville: University Press of Florida, 1997.

Denton, Jeffrey. "Image and History." In *Age of Chivalry: Art in Plantagenet England, 1200–1400,* ed. Jonathan Alexander and Paul Binski, 20–25. London: Weidenfeld and Nicolson, 1987.

D'Evelyn, Charlotte. *"Piers Plowman in Art." Modern Language Notes* 34 (1919): 247–49.

Dickman, Susan. "Margery Kempe and the Continental Tradition of the Pious Woman." In *Medieval Mystical Tradition in England . . . 1984,* ed. Marion Glasscoe, 150–68. Cambridge, England: Brewer, 1984.

Dillon, Janette, "Margery Kempe's Sharp Confessor/s." *Leeds Studies in English,* n.s., 27 (1996): 131–37.

———. *"Piers Plowman:* A Particular Example of Wordplay and its Structural Significance." *Medium Aevum* 50 (1981): 40–48.

DiMarco, Vincent. "Godwin on Langland." *YLS* 6 (1992): 123–35.

———. "Eighteenth-Century Suspicions Regarding the Authorship of *Piers Plowman." Anglia* 100 (1982): 124–29.

———. *Piers Plowman: A Reference Guide.* Boston: G. K. Hall, 1982.

"Disputation Between Mary and the Cross." In *The Minor Poems of the Vernon MS,* ed. F. J. Furnivall. Vol. 2, 612–26. EETS, o.s., 117. London: Kegan Paul, 1901.

Dives and Pauper. Ed. Priscilla Heath Barnum. Vol. 1, pt. 1. EETS, o.s., 275. London: Oxford University Press, 1976.

Dixon-Smith, Sally. "The Image and Reality of Alms-Giving in the Great Halls of Henry III." *Journal of the British Archaeological Association* 152 (1999): 79–96.

Donaldson, E. Talbot. "Apocalyptic Style in *Piers Plowman* B XIX–XX." *Leeds Studies in English,* n.s., 14 (1983): 74–81.

———. "Chaucer the Pilgrim." (1954). In *Speaking of Chaucer,* 1–12. London: Athlone Press, 1970.

———. "MSS R and F in the B-Tradition of *Piers Plowman." Transactions of Connecticut Academy of Arts and Sciences* 39 (1955): 179–212.

———. "'Piers Plowman': Textual Comparison and the Question of Authorship." In *Chaucer und Seine Zeit,* ed. Arno Esch, 241–47. Tübingen: Niemeyer, 1968.

———. *Piers Plowman: The C-Text and Its Poet.* 1949. Reprint, London: Frank Cass, 1966.

———. "The Texts of *Piers Plowman:* Scribes and Poets." *MP* 50 (1953): 269–73.

Dove, Mary. *The Perfect Age of Man's Life.* Cambridge: Cambridge University Press, 1986.

Doyle, A. I. "Remarks on Surviving Manuscripts of *Piers Plowman*." In *Medieval English Religious and Ethical Literature: Essays in Honour of G. H. Russell*, ed. Gregory Kratzmann and James Simpson, 35–48. Cambridge, England: Brewer, 1986.

Drew Charles. *Early Parochial Organisation in England: The Origins of the Office of Churchwarden*. St. Antony's Hall Publications, no. 7. York: Berthwick Institute of Historical Research, 1954.

Duffy, Eamon. "The Parish, Piety, and Patronage in Late Medieval East Anglia: The Evidence of Rood Screens." In *The Parish in English Life, 1400–1600*, ed. Katherine L. French, Gary G. Gibbs, and Beat A. Kümin, 133–62. Manchester: Manchester University Press, 1997.

———. *The Stripping of the Altars: Traditional Religion in England c.1400–c.1580*. New Haven: Yale University Press, 1992.

Duggan, Hoyt N. "The Authenticity of the Z-Text of *Piers Plowman*: Further Notes on Metrical Evidence." *Medium Aevum* 56 (1987): 25–45.

Duggan, Lawrence. "Was Art Really the 'Book of the Illiterate'?" *Word and Image* 5 (1989): 227–51.

Dunning, T. P. "Langland and the Salvation of the Heathen." *Medium Aevum* 12 (1943): 45–54.

———. *Piers Plowman: An Interpretation of the A-Text*. 1937. Reprint, Westport, Conn.: Greenwood, 1971. 2d ed., rev. and ed. by T. P. Dolan. Oxford: Clarendon Press, 1980.

Dutschke, C. W., et al. *Guide to Medieval and Renaissance Manuscripts in the Huntington Library*. Vol. 1. San Marino, Ca.: Huntington Library, 1989.

Edgar, Andrew, and Peter Sedgwick, eds. *Key Concepts in Cultural Theory*. London: Routledge, 1999.

Edwards, A. S. G. "Observations on the History of Middle English Editing." In *Manuscripts and Texts*, ed. Derek Pearsall, 34–48. Cambridge, England: Brewer, 1987.

———. "*Piers Plowman* in the Seventeenth-Century: Gerard Langbaine's Notes." *YLS* 6 (1992): 141–44.

[Egerton version of *Mandeville*]. *The Buke of John Maundeuill*. Ed. George F. Warner. Westminster: Roxburghe Club, 1889.

[Egerton version of *Mandeville*, translation]. *The Travels of Sir John Mandeville's Travels*. Trans. C. W. R. D. Moseley. London: Penguin, 1983.

Ekwall, Eilert. *Street-Names of the City of London*. Oxford: Clarendon Press, 1954.

Elliott, R. W. V. "The Langland Country." In *Piers Plowman: Critical Approaches*, ed. S. S. Hussey, 226–44, 345–48. London: Methuen, 1969.

Embree, Dan, and Elizabeth Urquhart. "*The Simonie*: The Case for a Parallel-Text Edition." In *Manuscripts and Texts*, ed. Derek Pearsall, 49–59. Cambridge, England: Brewer, 1987.

Foucault, Michel. *Discipline and Punish: The Birth of the Prison*. Trans. Alan Sheridan. 2d ed. New York: Vintage, 1995.

———. "What Is an Author?" In *Aesthetics, Method, and Epistemology*, ed. James D. Faubion, 205–22. Essential Works of Foucault, vol. 2. New York: New Press, 1998.

Fowler, David C. *The Bible in Middle English Literature*. Seattle: University of Washington Press, 1984.

———. "A New Edition of the B text of *Piers Plowman*." *YES* 7 (1977): 23–42.

Fowler, Elizabeth. "Civil Death and the Maiden: Agency and the Conditions of Contract in *Piers Plowman*." *Speculum* 70 (1995): 760–92.

Frank, Robert Worth, Jr. "The 'Hungry Gap,' Crop Failure, and Famine: The Fourteenth-Century Agricultural Crisis and *Piers Plowman*." *YLS* 4 (1990): 87–104.

———. *Piers Plowman and the Scheme of Salvation: An Interpretation of Dowel, Dobet, and Dobest*. 1957. Reprint, Hamden, Conn.: Archon, 1969.

Fredell, Joel. "Margery Kempe: Spectacle and Spiritual Governance." *Philological Quarterly* 75 (1996): 137–66.

French, Katherine L. "Parochial Fund-Raising in Late Medieval Somerset." In *The Parish in English Life, 1400–1600*, ed. Katherine L. French, Gary G. Gibbs, and Beat A. Kümin, 115–32. Manchester: Manchester University Press, 1997.

French, Katherine L., Gary G. Gibbs, and Beat A. Kümin, eds. *The Parish in English Life, 1400–1600.* Manchester: Manchester University Press, 1997.

Galbraith, V. H. "John Sewarde and His Circle: Some London Scholars of the Early Fifteenth Century." *Medieval and Renaissance Studies* 1 (1941–43): 85–104.

Galloway, Andrew. "*Piers Plowman* and the Schools." *YLS* 6 (1992): 89–107.

———. "Two Notes on Langland's Cato: *Piers Plowman* B 1.88–91; 4.20–23." *English Language Notes* 25 (1987): 9–12.

———. "Uncharacterizable Entities: The Poetics of Middle English Scribal Culture and the Definitive *Piers Plowman*." *Studies in Bibliography* 52 (1999): 59–84.

Geertz, Clifford. *The Interpretation of Cultures.* New York: Basic Books, 1973.

Gem, Richard, and Pamela Tudor-Craig, "A 'Winchester School' Wall-Painting at Nether Wallop, Hampshire." *Anglo-Saxon England* 9 (1981): 115–36.

Georgianna, Linda. "Love So Dearly Bought: The Terms of Redemption in *The Canterbury Tales*." *Studies in the Age of Chaucer* 12 (1990): 85–116.

Gibson, Gail M. "St. Margaret: *The Book of Margery Kempe*." In *Equally in God's Image: Women in the Middle Ages*, ed. Julia B. Holloway and Constance S. Wright, 144–63. New York: Peter Lang, 1996.

Gill, Miriam. "Female Piety and Impiety: Selected Images of Women in Wall Paintings in England After 1300." In *Gender and Holiness*, ed. Samantha J. E. Riches and Sarah Salih, 101–20. London: Routledge, 2001.

Ginsburg, Carlo. *The Cheese and the Worms: The Cosmos of a Sixteenth-Century Miller.* Trans. John Tedeschi and Anne Tedeschi. New York: Penguin, 1982.

Godden, Malcolm. *The Making of Piers Plowman.* London: Longman, 1990.

Godwin, William. *The Life of Geoffrey Chaucer, the Early English Poet.* 2 vols. London: Phillips, 1803.

Goodman, Anthony. "The Piety of John Brunham's Daughter, of Lynn." In *Medieval Women*, ed. Derek Brewer, 347–58. Oxford: Blackwell, 1978.

Grady, Frank. "*Piers Plowman, St. Erkenwald*, and the Rule of Exceptional Salvation." *YLS* 6 (1992): 61–86.

Gray, Douglas. "Popular Religion and Late Medieval English Literature." In *Religion in the Poetry and Drama of the Late Middle Ages in England*, ed. Piero Boitani and Anna Torti, 1–28. Cambridge, England: Brewer, 1990.

Green, Richard Firth. *A Crisis of Truth: Literature and Law in Ricardian England.* Philadelphia: University of Pennsylvania Press, 1999.

———. "The Lost Exemplar of the Z-Text of *Piers Plowman* and Its 20-Line Pages." *Medium Aevum* 56 (1987): 307–9.

Greenblatt, Stephen. "From the Dome of the Rock to the Rim of the World." *Marvellous Possessions: The Wonder of the New World*, 26–51, 156–65. Chicago: University of Chicago Press, 1991.

Greenspan, Kate. "Autohagiography and Medieval Women's Spiritual Autobiography." In *Gender and Text in the Later Middle Ages*, ed. Jane Chance, 217–36. Gainesville: University Press of Florida, 1996.

Greetham, D. C. "Reading in and Around *Piers Plowman*." In *Texts and Textuality*, ed. Philip Cohen, 25–57. New York: Garland, 1997.

Grindley, Carl James. "Reading *Piers Plowman* C-Text Annotations: Notes Toward the Classification of Printed and Written Marginalia in Texts from the British Isles 1300–1641." In *The Medieval Professional Reader at Work: Evidence from Manuscripts of Chaucer, Langland, Kempe, and Gower*, ed. Kathryn Kerby-Fulton and Maidie Hilmo, 73–141. Victoria: University of Victoria, 2001.

Gurevich, Aaron. "Perceptions of the Individual and the Hereafter in the Middle Ages." In *Historical Anthropology of the Middle Ages*, ed. Jana Howlett, 65–89. Cambridge: Polity Press, 1992.

Habermas, Jürgen. *The Structural Transformation of the Public Sphere: An Inquiry into a Category of Bourgeois Society*. Trans. Thomas Burger and Frederick Lawrence. Cambridge: MIT Press, 1989.

Habington, Thomas. *A Survey of Worcestershire*. Ed. John Amphlett. Oxford: Worcester Historical Society, 1895.

Hahn, Thomas. "The Indian Tradition in Western Medieval Intellectual History." *Viator* 9 (1978): 213–34.

———. "Indians East and West: Primitivism and Savagery in English Discovery Narratives of the Sixteenth Century." *Journal of Medieval and Renaissance Studies* 8 (1978): 77–114.

Hales, John W. "Langland, William." In *Dictionary of National Biography*. Vol. 11, 545–49. 1892. London: Oxford University Press, 1921–22.

Hamelius, Paul, ed. *Mandeville's Travels*. See *Mandeville's Travels*.

Hanawalt, Barbara A. *Growing Up in Medieval London*. New York: Oxford University Press, 1993.

———. "Keepers of the Lights: Late Medieval English Parish Gilds." *Journal of Medieval and Renaissance Studies* 14 (1984): 21–37.

Hanna, Ralph, III. "Annotating *Piers Plowman*." *Text* 6 (1994): 153–63.

———. "Emendations to a 1993 'Vita de Ne'erdowel.'" *YLS* 14 (2000): 185–98.

———. "Mandeville." In *Middle English Prose*, ed. A. S. G. Edwards, 121–32. New Brunswick: Rutgers University Press, 1984.

———. "'Meddling with Makings' and Will's Work." In *Late-Medieval Religious Texts and Their Transmission: Essays in Honour of A. I. Doyle*, ed. A. J. Minnis, 85–94. Cambridge, England: Brewer, 1994.

———. "MS. Bodley 851 and the Dissemination of *Piers Plowman*." In *Pursuing History: Middle English Manuscripts and Their Texts*, 195–202, 312–14. Stanford: Stanford University Press, 1996.

———. "On the Versions of *Piers Plowman*." In *Pursuing History: Middle English Manuscripts and Their Texts*, 203–43, 314–19. Stanford: Stanford University Press, 1996.

———. "Producing Manuscripts and Editions." In *Crux and Controversy in Middle English Textual Criticism*, ed. A. J. Minnis and Charlotte Brewer, 109–30. Cambridge, England: Brewer, 1992.

———. "The Scribe of Huntington HM 114." *Studies in Bibliography* 42 (1989): 120–33.

———. "Studies in the Manuscripts of *Piers Plowman*." *YLS* 7 (1993): 1–25.

———. *William Langland*. Authors of the Middle Ages 3. Aldershot: Variorum, 1993.

———. "Will's Work." In *Written Work: Langland, Labor, and Authorship*, ed. Steven Justice and Kathryn Kerby-Fulton, 23–66. Philadelphia: University of Pennsylvania Press, 1997.

Haraszti, Zoltan. "The Travels of Sir John Mandeville." *Boston Public Library Quarterly* 2 (1950): 306–16.

Harding, Wendy. "Medieval Women's Unwritten Discourse on Motherhood: A Reading of Two Fifteenth-Century Texts." *Women's Studies* 21 (1992): 197–209.

Hennessy, George. *Novum Repertorium Ecclesiasticum Parochiale Londinense, or London Diocesan Clergy Succession.* London: Sonnenschein, 1898.

Heslop, T. A. "Romanesque Painting and Social Distinction: The Magi and the Shepherds." In *England in the Twelfth Century,* ed. David Williams. Woodbridge, Suffolk: Boydell, 1990. 137–52.

Hewett-Smith, Kathleen. "Allegory on the Half Acre: The Demands of History." *YLS* 10 (1996): 1–22.

Heyck, T. W. *The Transformation of Intellectual Life in Victorian England.* London: Croom Helm, 1982.

Higgins, Iain. "Imagining Christendom from Jerusalem to Paradise: Asia in *Mandeville's Travels.*" In *Discovering New Worlds,* ed. Scott D. Westrem, 91–114. New York: Garland, 1991.

———. *Writing East: The "Travels" of Sir John Mandeville.* Philadelphia: University of Pennsylvania Press, 1997.

Higonnet, Patrice. *Paris: Capital of the World.* Trans. Arthur Goldhammer. Cambridge: Harvard University Press, 2002.

Hill, Thomas D. "Universal Salvation and Its Literary Context in *Piers Plowman* B 18." *YLS* 5 (1991): 65–76.

Hirsh, John. "Author and Scribe in *The Book of Margery Kempe.*" *Medium Aevum* 44 (1975): 145–50.

Hobsbaum, Philip. "Piers Plowman Through Modern Eyes." *Poetry Review* 61 (1971): 335–62.

Holbrook, Sue Ellen. "'About Her': Margery Kempe's Book of Feeling and Working." In *The Idea of Medieval Literature,* ed. James Dean and Christian Zacher, 265–84. Newark: University of Delaware Press, 1992.

Holt, Richard, and Gervase Rosser. "Introduction: The English Town in the Middle Ages." In *The English Medieval Town: A Reader in English Urban History, 1200–1540,* ed. Richard Holt and Gervase Rosser, 1–28. London: Longman, 1990.

Home, Gordon. *Mediaeval London.* 1927. Reprint, London: Bracken Books, 1994.

Hopkins, Edwin M. "The Character and Opinions of William Langland as Shown in 'The Vision of William Concerning Piers the Plowman.'" *Kansas University Quarterly* 2 (1894): 233–88.

———. "Notes on Piers Plowman." *Kansas University Quarterly* 7 (1898): 1–26.

Horner, Patrick J. "*Mandeville's Travels:* A New Manuscript Extract." *Manuscripta* 24 (1980): 171–75.

Howard, Donald. "The World of Mandeville's Travels." *YES* 1 (1971): 1–17.

———. *Writers and Pilgrims: Medieval Pilgrimage Narratives and Their Posterity.* Berkeley and Los Angeles: University of California Press, 1980.

Hudson, Anne. "The Legacy of *Piers Plowman.*" In *A Companion to Piers Plowman,* ed. John A. Alford, 251–66. Berkeley and Los Angeles: University of California Press, 1988.

———. "Middle English." In *Editing Medieval Texts: English, French, and Latin Written in England,* ed. A. G. Rigg, 34–57. New York: Garland, 1977.

———. *The Premature Reformation: Wycliffite Texts and Lollard History.* Oxford: Clarendon Press, 1988.

———. "The Variable Text." In *Crux and Controversy in Middle English Textual Criticism,* ed. A. J. Minnis and Charlotte Brewer, 49–60. Cambridge, England: Brewer, 1992.

Huot, Sylvia. *The "Romance of the Rose" and Its Medieval Readers.* Cambridge: Cambridge University Press, 1993.

Hurle, Pamela. *Hanley Castle: Heart of Malvern Chase.* London: Phillimore, 1978.

———. *Malvern Chase: Its Origins, Law and Legacy.* 3d ed. Malvern: Malvern Museum, 1993.

Hussey, S. S. Introduction to *Piers Plowman: Critical Approaches,* ed. S. S. Hussey, 1–26. London: Methuen, 1969.

Jack, A. S. "The Autobiographical Elements in *Piers the Plowman.*" *JEGP* 3 (1901): 393–414.

Jackson, Isaac. "Who Was Sir John Mandeville?" *Modern Language Review* 23 (1928): 466–68.

James, Stanley. *Back to Langland.* London: Sands, 1935.

Jenkinson, Wilberforce. *London Churches before the Great Fire.* London: SPCK, 1917.

Jewitt, Llewellynn. "The Pillory, and Who They Put in It." *Reliquary* 1 (1861): 209–24.

Johnson, Lynn Staley. "Margery Kempe: Social Critic." *Journal of Medieval and Renaissance Studies* 22 (1992): 159–84. [See also Staley, Lynn.]

Journals of the Court of Common Council. Corporation of London Records Office. Guildhall, London.

Jusserand, J. J. *Piers Plowman: A Contribution to the History of English Mysticism.* Trans. M. E. R. Rev. ed. London: Unwin, 1894.

———. "*Piers Plowman:* The Work of One or of Five." *MP* 6 (1909): 271–329.

———. "*Piers Plowman,* The Work of One or of Five: A Reply." *MP* 7 (1910): 289–326.

Justice, Steven. "The Genres of *Piers Plowman.*" *Viator* 19 (1988): 291–306.

———. *Writing and Rebellion: England in 1381.* Berkeley and Los Angeles: University of California Press, 1994.

———. "Introduction: Authorial Work and Literary Ideology." In *Written Work: Langland, Labor, and Authorship,* ed. Steven Justice and Kathryn Kerby-Fulton, 1–12. Philadelphia: University of Pennsylvania Press, 1997.

Justice, Steven, and Kathryn Kerby-Fulton, eds. *Written Work: Langland, Labor, and Authorship.* Philadelphia: University of Pennsylvania Press, 1997.

Kane, George. "The Autobiographical Fallacy in Chaucer and Langland Studies." Chambers Memorial Lecture. London: H. K. Lewis, 1965. Reprinted in Kane, *Chaucer and Langland.* Berkeley and Los Angeles: University of California Press, 1989. 1–14, 242–45.

———. "'Good' and 'Bad' Manuscripts: Texts and Critics." *Studies in the Age of Chaucer, Proceedings* 2 (1986): 137–45.

———. *Middle English Literature: A Critical Study of the Romances, the Religious Lyrics, Piers Plowman.* London: Methuen, 1951.

———, ed. *Piers Plowman: The A Version.* London: Athlone Press, 1960. Rev. ed., 1988.

———. *Piers Plowman: The Evidence for Authorship.* London: Athlone Press, 1965.

———. "'Piers Plowman': Problems and Methods of Editing the B-Text." *MLR* 43 (1948): 1–25.

———. "The Text." In *A Companion to Piers Plowman,* ed. John A. Alford, 175–200. Berkeley and Los Angeles: University of California Press, 1988.

———. "The 'Z Version' of *Piers Plowman.*" *Speculum* 60 (1985): 910–30.

Kane, George, and E. Talbot Donaldson, eds. *Piers Plowman: The B Version.* London: Athlone Press, 1975. Rev. ed., 1988.

Kaske, R. E. "The Character Hunger in *Piers Plowman.*" In *Medieval English Studies Presented to George Kane,* ed. Edward Donald Kennedy, Ronald Waldron, and Joseph S. Wittig, 187–97. Cambridge, England: Brewer, 1988.

———. "Langland and the *Paradisus Claustralis.*" *Modern Language Notes* 72 (1957): 481–83.

———. "*Piers Plowman* and Local Iconography." *Journal of the Warburg and Courtauld Institutes* 31 (1968): 159–69.

Kean, P. M. "Justice, Kingship and the Good Life in the Second Part of *Piers Plowman.*" In *Piers Plowman: Critical Approaches,* ed. S. S. Hussey, 76–110. London: Methuen, 1969.

———. "Love, Law, and *Lewte* in *Piers Plowman.*" *Review of English Studies,* n.s., 15 (1964): 241–61.

Keene, Derek. "Medieval London and Its Region." *London Journal* 14, no. 2 (1989): 99–111.

———. "Shops and Shopping in Medieval London." In *Medieval Art, Architecture, and Archaeology in London*, ed. Lindy Grant, 29–46. British Archaeological Association Conference Transaction for 1984. Leeds: British Archaeological Association, 1990.

Kellaway, William. "John Carpenter's Liber Albus." *Guildhall Studies in London History* 3 (1978): 67–84.

Kempe, Margery. *The Book of Margery Kempe.* Ed. Sanford B. Meech and Hope Emily Allen. EETS, o.s., 212. London: Oxford University Press, 1940.

Kempshall, M. S. *The Common Good in Late Medieval Political Thought.* Oxford: Clarendon, 1999.

Ker, N. R. *Medieval Manuscripts in British Libraries:* London. Vol. 1. Oxford: Clarendon Press, 1969.

Kerby-Fulton, Kathryn. "Langland and the Bibliographic Ego." In *Written Work: Langland, Labor, and Authorship*, ed. Steven Justice and Kathryn Kerby-Fulton, 67–143. Philadelphia: University of Pennsylvania Press, 1997.

———. "Piers Plowman." In *The Cambridge History of Medieval English Literature*, ed. David Wallace, 513–38. Cambridge: Cambridge University Press, 1999.

———. "Professional Readers of Langland at Home and Abroad: New Directions in the Political and Bureaucratic Codicology of *Piers Plowman*." In *New Directions in Later Medieval Manuscript Studies*, ed. Derek Pearsall, 103–29. York: York Medieval Press, 2000.

———. *Reformist Apocalypticism and Piers Plowman.* Cambridge: Cambridge University Press, 1990.

———. "'Who Has Written This Book?': Visionary Autobiography in Langland's C-Text." In *Medieval Mystical Tradition in England: Exeter Symposium V,* ed. Marion Glasscoe, 101–16. Cambridge, England: Brewer, 1992.

Kerby-Fulton, Kathryn, and Denise L. Despres. *Iconography and the Professional Reader: The Politics of Book Production in the Douce Piers Plowman.* Minneapolis: University of Minnesota Press, 1999.

Kerby-Fulton, Kathryn, and Steven Justice. "Langlandian Reading Circles and the Civil Service in London and Dublin, 1380–1427." *New Medieval Literatures* 1 (1997): 59–83.

Keyser, Charles E. *A List of Buildings in Great Britain and Ireland Having Mural and Other Painted Decorations.* 3d ed. London: HMSO, 1883.

Kingsford, Charles L., ed. *Chronicles of London.* 1905. Reprint, Dursley, England: Alan Sutton, 1977.

Kipling, Gordon. *Enter the King: Theatre, Liturgy, and Ritual in the Medieval Civic Triumph.* Oxford: Clarendon Press, 1998.

Kirk, Elizabeth D. *The Dream Thought of Piers Plowman.* New Haven: Yale University Press, 1972.

Kohanski, Tamarah. *The Book of John Mandeville: An Edition of the Pynson Text with Commentary on the Defective Versions.* Medieval and Renaissance Texts and Studies 231. Tempe: Arizona Center for Medieval and Renaissance Studies, 2002.

———. "Two Manuscripts of *Mandeville's Travels.*" *NQ*, n.s., 42 (1995): 269–70.

———. *Unchartered Territory: New Perspectives on "Mandeville's Travels."* Ph.D. diss., University of Connecticut, 1993.

———. "'What Is a "Travel Book," Anyway?': Generic Criticism and *Mandeville's Travels.*" *LIT* 7 (1996): 117–30.

Kolve, V. A. *Chaucer and the Imagery of Narrative.* Stanford: Stanford University Press, 1984.

Knott, Thomas A. "An Essay Toward the Critical Text of the A-Version of 'Piers the Plowman.'" *MP* 12 (1915): 389–421.

Kruger, Steven F. "Mirrors and the Trajectory of Vision in *Piers Plowman.*" *Speculum* 66 (1991): 74–95.

Kümin, Beat. "The English Parish in a European Perspective." In *The Parish in English Life, 1400–1600*, ed. Katherine L. French, Gary G. Gibbs, and Beat A. Kümin, 15–32. Manchester: Manchester University Press, 1997.

Latini, Brunetto. *The Book of the Treasure (Li livres dou tresor)*. Trans. Paul Barrette and Spurgeon Baldwin. New York: Garland, 1993.

Lawler, Traugott. "The Pardon Formula in *Piers Plowman:* Its Ubiquity, Its Binary Shape, Its Silent Middle Term." *YLS* 14 (2000): 117–52.

———. "A Reply to Jill Mann, Reaffirming the Traditional Relation Between the A and B Versions of *Piers Plowman*." *YLS* 10 (1996): 145–80.

Lawlor, John. *Piers Plowman: An Essay in Criticism*. London: Arnold, 1962.

Lawton, David A. "Lollardy and the 'Piers Plowman' Tradition." *MLR* 76 (1981): 780–93.

———. "The Subject of *Piers Plowman*." *YLS* 1 (1987): 1–30.

Leicester, H. Marshall. *The Disenchanted Self: Representing the Subject in the Canterbury Tales*. Berkeley and Los Angeles: University of California Press, 1990.

Le Saux, Françoise. "'Hir not lettyrd': Margery Kempe and Writing." In *Writing and Culture*, ed. Balz Engler, 53–68. Tübingen: Narr, 1992.

Letts, Malcolm. "A German Manuscript of Mandeville's 'Travels' Dated 1433." *MLR* 50 (1955): 57–60.

———, ed. *Mandeville's Travels: Texts and Translations*. See *Mandeville's Travels*.

———. *Sir John Mandeville: The Man and His Book*. London: Batchworth Press, 1949.

Lewis, C. S. *The Allegory of Love: A Study in Medieval Tradition*. 1936. Reprint, London: Oxford University Press, 1948.

Liber Albus. Vol. 1 of *Munimenta Gildhallae Londoniensis*. Ed. Henry T. Riley. Rolls Series. London, 1859.

Liber Albus: The White Book of the City of London. Trans. Henry Thomas Riley. London: Richard Griffin, 1861.

Liber Custumarum. Vol. 2 of *Munimenta Gildhallae Londoniensis*. Ed. Henry T. Riley. Rolls Series. London, 1860.

Lindenbaum, Shelia. "Ceremony and Oligarchy: The London Midsummer Watch." In *City and Spectacle in Medieval Europe*, ed. Barbara A. Hanawalt and Kathryn L. Reyerson, 171–88. Minneapolis: University of Minneapolis Press, 1994.

Little, A. G. Review of *Schools of Medieval England*, by A. F. Leach. *English Historical Review* 30 (1915): 525–29.

Lobel, Mary D., ed. *The City of London from Prehistoric Times to c. 1520*. The British Atlas of Historic Towns 3. Rev. ed. Oxford: Oxford University Press, 1991.

"London Lyckpeny." *The Oxford Book of Late Medieval Verse and Prose*. Ed. Douglas Gray, 16–19, 419–20. Oxford: Clarendon Press, 1985.

Longo, Joseph A. "*Piers Plowman* and the Tropological Matrix: Passus XI and XII." *Anglia* 82 (1964): 291–308.

Lydgate, John. "Against Millers and Bakers." In *The Minor Poems of John Lydgate: Part II*, ed. Henry N. MacCracken, 448–49. EETS, o.s., 192. 1934. Reprint, London: Oxford University Press, 1961.

———. "King Henry VI's Triumphal Entry into London." In *The Minor Poems of John Lydgate: Part II*, ed. Henry N. MacCracken, 630–48. EETS, o.s., 192. 1934. Reprint, London: Oxford University Press, 1961.

McGann, Jerome J. *A Critique of Modern Textual Criticism.* Chicago: University of Chicago Press, 1983.

Machan, Tim William. "Editing, Orality, and Late Middle English Texts." In *Vox Intexta: Orality and Textuality in the Middle Ages,* ed. A. N. Doane and C. B. Pasternack, 229–45. Madison: University of Wisconsin Press, 1991.

———. "Middle English Text Production and Modern Textual Criticism." In *Crux and Controversy in Middle English Textual Criticism,* ed. A. J. Minnis and Charlotte Brewer, 1–18. Cambridge, England: Brewer, 1992.

McHardy, A. K. *The Church in London 1375–1392.* London: London Record Society, 1977.

McRee, Ben R. "Religious Gilds and Civic Order: The Case of Norwich in the Late Middle Ages." *Speculum* 67 (1992): 69–97.

———. "Religious Gilds and Regulation of Behavior in Late Medieval Towns." In *People, Politics, and Community in the Later Middle Ages,* ed. Joel Rosenthal and Colin Richmond, 108–22. New York: St Martin's Press, 1987.

———. "Unity or Division? The Social Meaning of Guild Ceremoney in Urban Communities." In *City and Spectacle in Medieval Europe,* ed. Barbara A. Hanawalt and Kathryn L. Reyerson, 189–207. Minneapolis: University of Minneapolis Press, 1994.

Mandeville's Travels. See also *Bodley Version; Defective Version;* Egerton version of *Mandeville;* Egerton version, translation; and *Metrical Version.*

Mandeville's Travels. Ed. Paul Hamelius. 2 vols. EETS, o.s., 153, 154. London: Oxford University Press, 1919, 1923. [Cotton version].

Mandeville's Travels: Texts and Translations. Ed. Malcolm Lett. 2 vols. 2d series, 101–2. London: Hakluyt Society, 1953. [modernized Egerton and other versions].

Mandeville's Travels. Ed. M. C. Seymour. Oxford: Clarendon Press, 1967. [Cotton version].

Manly, John M. "The Authorship of *Piers Plowman.*" *MP* 7 (1909): 83–144.

———. "The Authorship of *Piers The Plowman.*" *MP* 14 (1916): 315–16.

———. "The Lost Leaf of 'Piers the Plowman.'" *MP* 3 (1906): 359–66.

———. "*Piers the Plowman* and Its Sequence." In *Cambridge History of English Literature,* ed. A. W. Ward and A. R. Waller. Vol. 2, 1–42. 1908. Reprint, Cambridge: Cambridge University Press, 1912.

———. *Some New Light on Chaucer.* London: Bell, 1926.

Mann, Jill. *Chaucer and Estates Satire.* Cambridge: Cambridge University Press, 1973.

———. "Eating and Drinking in 'Piers Plowman.'" *Essays and Studies,* n.s., 32 (1979): 26–43.

———. "The Power of the Alphabet: A Reassessment of the Relation Between the A and B Versions of *Piers Plowman.*" *YLS* 8 (1994): 21–49.

Matheson, Lister. Review of *William Langland,* by Ralph Hanna III. *YLS* 8 (1994): 192–94.

Mauss, Marcel. "The Subject: The Person." *Sociology and Psychology: Essays.* Trans. Ben Brewster, 59–94. London: Routledge, 1979.

Meech, Sanford. See Kempe, Margery.

Meroney, Howard. "The Life and Death of Longe Wille." *ELH* 17 (1950): 1–35.

Merrifield, Ralph. *London: City of the Romans.* Berkeley and Los Angeles: University of California Press, 1983.

The Metrical Version of Mandeville's Travels. Ed. M. C. Seymour. EETS, o.s., 269. London: Oxford University Press, 1973.

Middle English Dictionary. Ann Arbor: University of Michigan Press, 1956–99.

Middleton, Anne. "The Audience and Public of 'Piers Plowman.'" In *Middle English Alliterative Poetry and Its Literary Background: Seven Essays.* ed. David Lawton, 101–23, 147–54. Cambridge, England: Brewer, 1982.

———. "The Idea of Public Poetry in the Reign of Richard II." *Speculum* 53 (1978): 94–114.

———. "Introduction: The Critical Heritage." In *A Companion to Piers Plowman,* ed. John A. Alford, 1–25. Berkeley and Los Angeles: University of California Press, 1988.

———. "Narration and the Invention of Experience: Episodic Form in *Piers Plowman.*" In *The Wisdom of Poetry: Essays in Early English Literature in Honor of Morton W. Bloomfield,* ed. Larry D. Benson and Siegfried Wenzel, 91–122, 280–83. Kalamazoo, Mich.: Medieval Institute Publications, 1982.

———. *"Piers Plowman." A Manual of the Writings in Middle English, 1050–1500.* Ed. Albert E. Hartung. Vol. 7, 2211–34. New Haven, Conn.: Connecticut Academy of Arts and Sciences, 1986.

———. "William Langland's 'Kynde Name': Authorial Signature and Social Identity in Late Fourteenth-Century England." In *Literary Practice and Social Change in Britain, 1380–1530,* ed. Lee Patterson, 15–82. Berkeley and Los Angeles: University of California Press, 1990.

Minnis, A. J. "Looking for a Sign: The Quest for Nominalism in Chaucer and Langland." In *Essays on Ricardian Literature in Honour of J. A. Burrow,* ed. A. J. Minnis, Charlotte C. Morse, and Thorlac Turville-Petre, 142–78. Oxford: Clarendon Press, 1997.

———. *Medieval Theory of Authorship.* 2d ed. Philadelphia: University of Pennsylvania Press, 1988.

Mirk, John. *Mirk's Festial: A Collection of Homilies.* Ed. Theodor Erbe. *EETS* e.s. 96. London: Kegan Paul, 1905.

Moore, Samuel. "Studies in *Piers the Plowman.*" *MP* 11 (1913): 177–93; 12 (1914): 19–50.

Morgan, Nigel. "Texts and Images of Marian Devotion in Fourteenth-Century England." In *England in the Fourteenth Century: Proceedings of the 1991 Harlaxton Symposium,* ed. Nicholas Watson, 34–57. Harlaxton Medieval Studies 3. Stamford: Paul Watkins, 1993.

———. "Texts and Images of Marian Devotion in Thirteenth-Century England." In *England in the Thirteenth Century: Proceedings of the 1989 Harlaxton Symposium,* ed. W. M. Ormrod, 69–103. Harlaxton Medieval Studies 1. Stamford: Paul Watkins, 1991.

Morrall, E. J. "Michel Vesler and His German Translation of Mandeville's 'Travels.'" *Durham University Journal* 24 (1963): 16–22.

Moseley, C. W. R. D. "The Metamorphoses of Sir John Mandeville." *YES* 4 (1974): 5–25.

———, ed. *The Travels of Sir John Mandeville.* See Egerton version.

Munimenta Gildhallae Londoniensis. Ed. Henry T. Riley. Rolls Series. 3 vols. London, 1859–62.

Muscatine, Charles. *Poetry and Crisis in the Age of Chaucer.* Notre Dame: University of Notre Dame Press, 1972.

Narin van Court, Elisa. "The Hermeneutics of Supersession: The Revision of the Jews from B to the C Text of *Piers Plowman.*" *YLS* 10 (1996): 43–87.

Nichols, Stephen G. "Introduction: Philology in a Manuscript Culture." *Speculum* 65 (1990): 1–10.

Nitecki, Alicia K. "Figures of Old Age in Fourteenth-Century English Literature." In *Aging and the Aged in Medieval Europe,* ed. Michael Sheehan, 107–16. Toronto: Pontifical Institute of Mediaeval Studies, 1990.

Nolan, Barbara. *The Gothic Visionary Perspective.* Princeton: Princeton University Press, 1977.

Nott, James. *Some of the Antiquities of "Moche Malverne."* Malvern: John Thompson, 1885.

The Orcherd of Syon. Ed. Phyllis Hodgson and Gabriel M. Liegely. Vol. 1. *EETS*, o.s., 258. London: Oxford University Press, 1966.

Orme, Nicholas. "Langland and Education." *History of Education* 11 (1982): 251–66.

Orsten, Elisabeth M. "The Ambiguities in Langland's Rat Parliament." *Mediaeval Studies* 23 (1961): 216–39.

Owst, G. R. *Literature and Pulpit in Medieval England.* 2d ed. 1961. Oxford: Blackwell, 1966.

Park, David. "Anglo-Saxon or Anglo-Norman? Wall Paintings at Wareham and Other Sites in Southern England." In *Early Medieval Wall Paintings and Painted Sculpture in England*, ed. Sharon Cather et al., 225–47. Oxford: BAR, 1990.

———. "The 'Lewes Group' of Wall Paintings in Sussex." *Anglo-Norman Studies* 6 (1983): 201–37.

———. "Romanesque Wall Paintings at Ickleton." In *Romanesque and Gothic: Essays for George Zarzecki.* Vol. 1, 159–69. Bury St Edmunds, England: Boydell, 1987.

———. "Simony and Sanctity: Herbert Losinga, St Wulfstan of Worcester, and Wall-Paintings in Norwich Cathedral." In *Studies in Medieval Art and Architecture Presented to Peter Lasko*, ed. D. Buckton and T. A. Heslop, 157–70. London: Stroud and London, 1994.

———. "Wall Painting." In *Age of Chivalry: Art in Plantagenet England, 1200–1400*, ed. Jonathan Alexander and Paul Binski, 125–30. London: Weidenfeld and Nicolson, 1987.

———. "The Wall Paintings of the Holy Sepulchre Chapel." *British Archaeological Association Conference Transactions* 6 (1983): 38–62.

Park, David, and Helen Howard. "The Medieval Polychromy." In *Norwich Cathedral: Church, City, and Diocese, 1096–1996*, ed. Ian Atherton et al., 379–409. London: Hambledon Press, 1996.

Park, David, and Peter Welford. "The Medieval Polychromy of Winchester Cathedral." In *Winchester Cathedral: Nine Hundred Years, 1093–1993*, ed. John Clark, 123–38. Chichester: Phillimore, 1993.

Parkes, M. B. "The Influence of the Concepts of *Ordinatio* and *Compilatio* on the Development of the Book." In *Medieval Learning and Literature: Essays Presented to Richard William Hunt*, ed. J. J. G. Alexander and M. T. Gibson, 115–41. Oxford: Clarendon Press, 1976.

Patterson, Lee. *Chaucer and the Subject of History.* Madison: University of Wisconsin Press, 1991.

———. "The Logic of Textual Criticism and the Way of Genius: The Kane-Donaldson *Piers Plowman* in Historical Perspective." In *Textual Criticism and Literary Interpretation*, rd. Jerome J. McGann, 55–91, 212–19. Chicago: University of Chicago Press, 1985.

Pearsall, Derek. *An Annotated Critical Bibliography of Langland.* Ann Arbor: University of Michigan Press, 1990.

———. "Authorial Revision in Some Late-Medieval English Texts." In *Crux and Controversy in Middle English Textual Criticism*, ed. A. J. Minnis and Charlotte Brewer, 39–48. Cambridge, England: Brewer, 1992.

———. "Editing Medieval Texts: Some Developments and Some Problems." In *Textual Criticism and Literary Innterpretation*, ed. Jerome J. McGann, 92–106. Chicago: University of Chicago Press, 1985.

———. "The 'Ilchester' Manuscript of *Piers Plowman.*" *Neuphilologische Mitteilungen* 82 (1981): 181–93.

———. "Langland's London." In *Written Work: Langland, Labor, and Authorship*, ed. Steven Justice and Kathryn Kerby-Fulton, 185–207. Philadelphia: University of Pennsylvania Press, 1997.

———. "Manuscript Illustration of Late Middle English Literary Texts, with Special Reference to the Illustration of *Piers Plowman* in Bodleian Library MS Douce 104." In *Suche Werkis to*

Werche: Essays on Piers Plowman, ed. Míceál F. Vaughan, 191–210. East Lansing: Colleagues
   Press, 1993.

———, ed. *Piers Plowman by William Langland: An Edition of the C-Text.* York Medieval Texts, 2d series.
   Berkeley and Los Angeles: University of California Press, 1978.

———. "*Piers Plowman* Forty Years On." In *Langland, the Mystics, and the Medieval English Religious Tradition,*
   ed. Helen Phillips, 1–9. Cambridge, England: Brewer, 1990.

———. "Texts, Textual Criticism, and Fifteenth Century Manuscript Production." In *Fifteenth-
   Century Studies,* ed. R. F. Yeager, 121–36. Hamden, Conn.: Archon, 1984.

———. "Theory and Practice in Middle English Editing." *Text* 7 (1994): 107–26.

Pecock, Reginald. *The Repressor of Over Much Blaming of the Clergy.* Ed. Churchill Babington. 2 vols. Rolls
   Series. London: Longman, 1860.

Pevsner, Nikolaus. *Worcestershire.* The Buildings of England. 1968. Reprint, London: Penguin, 1992.

Phillips, J. R. S. "The Quest for Sir John Mandeville." In *The Culture of Christendom,* ed. Marc
   Anthony Meyer, 243–55. London: Hambeldon Press, 1993.

Phythian-Adams, Charles. *Desolation of a City: Coventry and the Urban Crisis of the Late Middle Ages.*
   Cambridge: Cambridge University Press, 1979.

Piers Plowman: A Facsimile of Bodlein Library, Oxford, MS Douce 104. Introduction by Derek Pearsall, catalogue by Kathleen Scott. Cambridge, England: Brewer, 1992.

Pile, Steve, and Nigel Thrift, eds. *Mapping the Subject.* London: Routledge, 1995.

Porter, Roy. Introduction to *Rewriting the Self,* ed. Roy Porter, 1–14. London: Routledge, 1997.

Pounds, N. J. G. *A History of the English Parish: The Culture of Religion from Augustine to Victoria.* Cambridge:
   Cambridge University Press, 2000.

Raabe, Pamela. *Imitating God: The Allegory of Faith in Piers Plowman B.* Athens: University of Georgia
   Press, 1990.

Raw, Barbara. "Piers and the Image of God in Man." In *Piers Plowman: Critical Approaches,* ed. S. S.
   Hussey, 143–79. London: Methuen, 1969.

Reiss, Athene. *The Sunday Christ: Sabbatarianism in English Medieval Wall Painting.* British Series 292.
   Oxford: BAR, 2000.

Rigg, A. G., and Charlotte Brewer, eds. *Piers Plowman: The Z Version.* Toronto: Pontifical Institute of
   Medieval Studies, 1983.

Riley, Henry Thomas, ed. *Memorials of London and London Life, in the XIIIth, XIVth, and XVth Centuries.*
   London: Longmans, 1868.

Robertson, D. W., Jr. *Preface to Chaucer.* Princeton: Princeton University Press, 1962.

Robertson, D. W., Jr., and Bernard F. Huppé. *Piers Plowman and Scriptural Tradition.* Princeton:
   Princeton University Press, 1951.

Robinson, Peter M. W. "Redefining Critical Editions." In *The Digital Word,* ed. George Landow and
   Paul Delany, 271–91. Cambridge: MIT Press, 1993.

Ross, Ellen M. *The Grief of God: Images of the Suffering Jesus in Late Medieval England.* New York: Oxford
   University Press, 1997.

Ross, Robert C. "Oral Life, Written Text: The Genesis of The Bookof Margery Kempe." *YES* 22
   (1992): 226–37.

Rosser, Gervase. "Communities of Parish and Guild in the Late Middle Ages." In *Parish, Church, and
   People: Local Studies in Lay Religion 1350–1750,* ed. S. J. Wright, 29–55. London: Hutchinson,
   1988.

———. "Crafts, Guilds, and the Negotiaton of Work in the Medieval Town." *Past and Present* 154 (1997): 3–31.

———. "Going to the Fraternity Feast: Commensality and Social Relations in Late Medieval England." *Journal of British Studies* 33 (1994): 430–46.

———. "London and Westminster: The Suburb in the Urban Economy in the Later Middle Ages." In *Towns and Townspeople in the Fifteenth Century*, ed. John A. F. Thomson, 45–61. Gloucester: Sutton, 1988.

———. *Medieval Westminster: 1200–1540.* Oxford: Clarendon Press, 1989.

———. "Workers' Associations in English Medieval Towns." In *Les métiers au Moyen Âge: Aspects économiques et sociaux*, ed. Pascale Lambrechts and Jean-Pierre Sosson, 283–305. Louvain, 1994.

Rouse, E. Clive. *Medieval Wall Paintings.* 4th ed. Princes Risborough, Bucks., England: Shire Publications, 1991.

———. "Wall Paintings in the Church of St Pega, Peakirk, Northamptonshire." *Archaeological Journal* 110 (1954): 135–49.

Rouse, E. Clive, and Audrey Baker. "The Wall Paintings at Longthorpe Tower." *Archaeologia* 96 (1955): 1–57.

Rouse, E. Clive, and Audrey Baker. "The Wall Paintings at Longthorpe Tower." *Archaeologia* 96 (1955): 1–57.

Rubin, Miri. "Religious Culture in Town and Country: Reflections on a Great Divide." In *Church and City, 1000–1500*, ed. David Abulafia, Michael Franklin, and Miri Rubin, 3–22. Cambridge: Cambridge University Press, 1992.

Russell, George H. "'As They Read It': Some Notes on Early Responses to the C-Version of *Piers Plowman*." *Leeds Studies in English*, n.s., 20 (1989): 173–89.

———. "The Evolution of a Poem: Some Reflections on the Textual Tradition of *Piers Plowman*." *Arts* (Sydney) 2 (1962: 33–46.

———. "The Imperative of Revision in the C Version of *Piers Plowman*." In *Medieval English Studies Presented to George Kane*, ed. Edward Donald Kennedy, Ronald Waldron, and Joseph S. Wittig, 233–42. Cambridge, England: Brewer, 1988.

———. "The Salvation of the Heathen: The Exploration of a Theme in *Piers Plowman*." *Journal of the Warburg and Courtauld Institutes* 29 (1966): 101–16.

———. "Some Aspects of the Process of Revision in *Piers Plowman*." In *Piers Plowman: Critical Approaches*, ed. S. S. Hussey, 27–49, 326–28. London: Methuen, 1969.

———. "Some Early Responses to the C-Version of *Piers Plowman*." *Viator* 15 (1984): 275–300.

Russell, George, and George Kane, eds. *Piers Plowman: The C Version.* London: Athlone Press, 1997.

Russell, George H., and Venetia Nathan. "A *Piers Plowman* Manuscript in the Huntington Library." *Huntington Library Quarterly* 26 (1963): 119–30.

St.-Jacques, Raymond. "Langland's Christ-Knight and the Liturgy." *Révue de l'Université d'Ottawa* 37 (1967): 146–58.

———. "Langland's *Christus Medicus* Image and the Structure of *Piers Plowman*." *YLS* 5 (1991): 111–27.

Saintsbury, George. "Langland and Gower." In *A Short History of English Literature.* London: Macmillan, 1898. 131–38.

Salter, Elizabeth. "Alliterative Verse and *Piers Plowman*." In *Fourteenth-Century English Poetry: Contexts and Readings*, 86–116. Oxford: Clarendon Press, 1983.

———. "Langland and the Contexts of 'Piers Plowman.'" *Essays and Studies*, n.s., 32 (1979): 19–25, 199–202.

———. "*Piers Plowman* and the Visual Arts." In *Encounters: Essays on Literature and the Visual Arts*, ed. John Dixon Hunt, 11–27. London: Studio Vista, 1971. Reprinted in Salter, *English and International: Studies in the Literature, Art, and Patronage of Medieval England*. Ed. Derek Pearsall and Nicolette Zeeman. Cambridge: Cambridge University Press, 1988. 256–66.

Salter, Elizabeth, and Derek Pearsall, eds. *Piers Plowman*. York Medieval Texts. Evanston: Northwestern University Press, 1969.

Samuel, Mark, and Gustav Milne. "The 'Ledene Hall' and Medieval Market." In *From Roman Basilica to Medieval Market*, ed. Gustav Milne, 39–50. London, HMSO, 1992.

Samuels, M. L. "Dialect and Grammar." In *A Companion to Piers Plowman*, ed. John A. Alford, 201–21. Berkeley and Los Angeles: University of California Press, 1988.

———. "Langland's Dialect." *Medium Aevum* 54 (1985): 232–47.

Sawday, Jonathan. "Self and Selfhood in the Seventeenth Century." In *Rewriting the Self*, ed. Roy Porter, 29–48. London: Routledge, 1997.

Scase, Wendy. *Piers Plowman and the New Anticlericalism*. Cambridge: Cambridge University Press, 1989.

———. "Two *Piers Plowman* C-Text Interpolations: Evidence for a Second Textual Tradition." *NQ*, n.s., 34 (1987): 456–63.

———. "Writing and the Plowman: Langland and Literacy." *YLS* 9 (1995): 121–31.

Scattergood, John. "Misrepresenting the City: Genre, Intertextuality and Fitzstephen's *Description of London* (c. 1173)." In *Reading the Past: Essays on Medieval and Renaissance Literature*, 15–36. Dublin: Four Courts Press, 1996.

Schmidt, A. V. C. *The Clerkly Maker: Langland's Poetic Art*. Piers Plowman Studies 4. Cambridge, England: Brewer, 1987.

———. "'A Covenant More Than Courtesy': A Langlandian Phrase in Its Context." *NQ*, n.s., 31 (1984): 153–56.

———. "Langland's Structural Imagery." *Essays in Criticism* 30 (1980): 311–25.

———, ed. *Piers Plowman: A Parallel-Text Edition of the A, B, C and Z Versions*. Vol. 1. London: Longman, 1995.

———, ed. *The Vision of Piers Plowman*. 1978. 2d ed. Everyman. London: Dent, 1995.

Schroeder, Mary C. "The Character of Conscience in *Piers Plowman*." *Studies in Philology* 67 (1970): 13–30. [See also Carruthers, Mary.]

Scott, Kathleen. "The Illustrations of *Piers Plowman* in Bodleian Library MS. Douce 104." *YLS* 4 (1990): 1–86.

Sewell, William H., Jr. "The Concept(s) of Culture." In *Beyond the Cultural Turn*, ed. Victoria E. Bonnell and Lynn Hunt, 35–61. Berkeley and Los Angeles: University of California Press, 1999.

Seymour, M. C. "The Early English Editions of *Mandeville's Travels*." *Library*, n.s., 19 (1964): 202–7.

———. "The English Epitome of *Mandeville's Travels*." *Anglia* 84 (1966): 27–58.

———. "English Manuscripts of *Mandeville's Travels*." *Edinburgh Bibliographical Society Transactions* 4 (1966): 169–98.

———. "Mandeville and Marco Polo: A Stanzaic Fragment." *Journal of the Australasian Universities Language and Literature Association* 21 (1964): 39–52.

———. "A Medieval Redactor at Work." *NQ* 206 (1961): 169–71.

———. "The Origin of the Egerton Version of *Mandeville's Travels*." *Medium Aevum* 30 (1961): 159–69.

———. "The Scribal Tradition of Mandeville's Travels: The Insular Version." *Scriptorium* 18 (1964): 34–48.

———. "Secundum Iohannem Maundvyle." *English Studies in Africa* 4 (1961): 148–58.

———. *Sir John Mandeville*. Authors of the Middle Ages 1. Aldershot: Variorum, 1993.

Sheingorn, Pamela. "'And Flights of Angels Sing Thee to Thy Rest': The Soul's Conveyance to the Afterlife in the Middle Ages." In *Art into Life*, ed. Kathleen L. Scott and Carol G. Fisher, 155–82. East Lansing: Michigan State University Press, 1995.

———. "'For God Is Such a Doomsman': Origins and Development of the Theme of Last Judgment." *Homo, Memento Finis: The Iconography of Just Judgment in Medieval Art and Drama*, 15–58. Kalamazoo, Mich.: Medieval Institute Publications, 1985.

Shepherd, Geoffrey. "The Nature of Alliterative Poetry in Late Medieval England." Gollancz Memorial Lecture. *Proceedings of the British Academy* 56 (1970): 57–76.

Sherbo, Arthur. "Walter William Skeat (1835–1912) in the *Cambridge Review*." *YLS* 3 (1989): 109–30.

Shinners, John, and William J. Dohar, eds. *Pastors and the Care of Souls in Medieval England*. Notre Dame: University of Notre Dame Press, 1998.

Shuger, Debora. "The 'I' of the Beholder: Renaissance Mirrors and the Reflexive Mind." In *Renaissance Culture and the Everyday*, ed. Patricia Fumerton and Simon Hunt, 21–41. Philadelphia: University of Pennsylvania Press, 1999.

Siegmund-Schultze, Dorothea. "Some Remarks on the Book of Margery Kempe." *Fifteenth-Century Studies* 7 (1983): 329–44.

Simpson, James. "'After Craftes Conseil Clotheth Yow and Fede': Langland and London City Politics." In *England in the Fourteenth Century: Proceedings of the 1991 Harlaxton Symposium*, ed. Nicholas Rogers, 109–27. Harlaxton Medieval Studies 3. Stamford, Lincs., England: P. Watkins, 1993.

———. *Piers Plowman: An Introduction to the B-Text*. London: Longman, 1990.

———. "The Power of Impropriety: Authorial Naming in *Piers Plowman*." In *William Langland's "Piers Plowman": A Book of Essays*, ed. Kathleen M. Hewett-Smith, 145–65. New York: Routledge, 2001.

———. "Spirituality and Economics in Passus 1–7 of the B-Text." *YLS* 1 (1987): 83–103.

Sixth Report of the Royal Commission on Historical Manuscripts. Part 1. London: Eyre and Spottiswoode, 1877.

Skeat, Walter W. "Langland." *Encyclopaedia Britannica*. 9th ed. Vol. 14, 285–86. New York: Scribners, 1882.

———, ed. *Parallel Extracts from Forty-Five Manuscripts of Piers Plowman*. EETS, o.s., 17. London: Trübner, 1866.

———. "Section VIII." In *History of English Poetry*, by Thomas Warton. Rev. ed. Ed. W. Carew Hazlitt. Vol. 2, 244–63. London: Reeves and Turner, 1871.

———, ed. *The Vision of William Concerning Piers the Plowman in Three Parallel Texts*. 2 vols. Oxford: Oxford University Press, 1886.

———, ed. *The Vision of William concerning Piers Plowman . . . Text A*. EETS, o.s., 28. London: Trübner, 1867.

———, ed. *The Vision of William concerning Piers the Plowman . . . Text B*. EETS, o.s., 38. London: Trübner, 1869.

————, ed. *The Vision of William concerning Piers the Plowman . . . Text C. EETS*, o.s., 54. London: Trübner, 1873.

————, ed. *The Vision of William concerning Piers the Plowman . . . Notes, etc.* Part IV. *EETS*, o.s., 67, 81. London: Trübner, 1877, 1884.

————, ed. *The Vision of William concerning Piers the Plowman.* 1869. 10th ed., 1923. Oxford: Clarendon Press, 1968. [Student edition].

————, trans. *The Vision of Piers the Plowman.* 1905. Reprint, London: Chatto and Windus, 1992.

Smith, Brian S. *A History of Malvern.* 1964. Reprint, Malvern: Alan Sutton, 1978.

Smith, Paul. *Discerning the Subject.* Theory and History of Literature 55. Minneapolis: University of Minnesota Press, 1988.

Somerset, Fiona. *Clerical Discourse and Lay Audience in Late Medieval England.* Cambridge: Cambridge University Press, 1998.

Spearing, A. C. *Medieval to Renaissance in English Poetry.* Cambridge: Cambridge University Press, 1985.

————. "Poetic Identity." In *A Companion to the Gawain-Poet*, ed. Derek Brewer and Jonathan Gibson, 35–51. Cambridge, England: Brewer, 1997.

————. "The Poetic Subject from Chaucer to Spenser." In *Subjects on the World's Stage*, ed. David G. Allen and Robert A. White, 13–37. Newark: University of Delaware Press, 1995.

————. "A Ricardian 'I': The Narrator of 'Troilus and Criseyde.'" In *Essays on Ricardian Literature: In Honour of J. A. Burrow*, ed. A. J. Minnis, Charlotte C. Morse, Thorlac Turville-Petre, 1–22. Oxford: Clarendon Press, 1997.

Spitzer, Leo. "Note on the Poetic and the Empirical 'I' in Medieval Authors." *Traditio* 4 (1946): 414–22.

Staley, Lynn. *Margery Kempe's Dissenting Fictions.* University Park: Pennsylvania State University Press, 1994. *See also* Johnson, Lynn Staley.

Stanley, E. G. "The B Version of 'Piers Plowman': A New Edition." *NQ*, n.s., 23 (1976): 435–47.

Statute concerning Bakers (Statutum de Pistoribus). In *The Statutes of the Realm.* Vol. 1, 202–4. London: Dawsons, 1810.

Sternberg, Meir. *The Poetics of Biblical Narrative.* 1985. Reprint, Bloomington: Indiana University Press, 1987.

Stokes, Myra. *Justice and Mercy in Piers Plowman: A Reading of the B Text Visio.* London: Croom Helm, 1984.

Stow, John. *A Survey of London.* Ed. Charles L. Kingsford. 2 vols. Oxford: Clarendon Press, 1908.

Strohm, Paul. *Social Chaucer.* Cambridge: Harvard University Press, 1989.

Stroud, Theodore A. "Manly's Marginal Notes on the 'Piers Plowman' Controversy." *Modern Language Notes* 64 (1949): 9–12.

Sturges, Robert S. "Textual Scholarship: Ideologies of Literary Production." *Exemplaria* 3 (1991): 109–31.

Tavormina, M. Teresa. *Kindly Similitude: Marriage and Family in Piers Plowman.* Cambridge, England: Brewer, 1995.

Taylor, Charles. *Sources of the Self.* Cambridge: Harvard University Press, 1989.

Taylor, Helen Clare. "'Mulier, Quid Ploras?' Holy Tears in *The Book of Margery Kempe*." *Mediaevalia* 19 (1996): 363–84.

Taylor, Sean. "The F Scribe and the R Manuscript of *Piers Plowman* B." *English Studies* 77 (1996): 530–48.

Thomas, A. H. "Notes on the History of the Leadenhall, A.D. 1195–1488." *London Topographical Society* 13 (1923): 1–22.

Thorne, J. R. "Piers or Will: Confusion of Identity in the Early Reception of *Piers Plowman.*" *Medium Aevum* 60 (1991): 273–84.

Thrupp, Sylvia L. *The Merchant Class of Medieval London.* 1948. Reprint, Ann Arbor: University of Michigan Press, 1962.

Tristram, E. W. *English Medieval Wall Painting: The Thirteenth Century.* 2 vols. Oxford: Oxford University Press, 1950.

———. *English Medieval Wall Painting: The Twelfth Century.* Oxford: Oxford University Press, 1944.

———. *English Wall Painting of the Fourteenth Century.* London: Routledge, 1955.

———. "Piers Plowman in English Wall-Painting." *Burlington Magazine* 31 (October 1917): 135–40.

Tristram, E. W., and M. R. James. "Wall-Paintings in Croughton Church, Norhamptonshire." *Archaeologia* 76 (1927): 179–204.

Tudor-Craig, Pamela. "Painting in Medieval England: The Wall-to-Wall Message." *History Today* 37 (November 1987): 39–45. Reprinted in *Age of Chivalry,* ed. Nigel Saul, 106–19. New York: St. Martin's, 1992.

Turner, Brian. "The Patronage of John of Northhampton: Further Studies of the Wall-Paintings in Westminster Chapter House." *Journal of the British Archaeological Association* 138 (1985): 89–100.

Turville-Petre, Thorlac. Review of *Piers Plowman: The B Version,* ed. George Kane and E. Talbot Donaldson. *Studia Neophilologica* 49 (1977): 153–55.

———. "Sir Adrian Fortescue and His Copy of *Piers Plowman.*" *YLS* 14 (2000): 29–48.

Uhart, Marie-Claire. "The Early Reception of *Piers Plowman.*" Ph.D. diss., University of Leicester, 1986.

Unwin, George. *The Gilds and Companies of London.* 4th ed. London: Frank Cass, 1963.

Usk, Adam. *The Chronicle of Adam Usk: 1377–1421.* Ed. C. Given-Wilson. Oxford: Clarendon Press, 1997.

Vance, Eugene. "Augustine's *Confessions* and the Grammar of Selfhood." *Genre* 6 (1973): 1–28.

Vaughan, Míceál F. "The Ending(s) of *Piers Plowman* A." In *Suche Werkis to Werche: Essays on Piers Plowman: In Honor of David C. Fowler,* ed. Míceál F. Vaughan, 211–41. East Lansing, Mich.: Colleagues Press, 1993.

Victoria History of the County of Worcestershire. Ed. J. W. Willis-Bund and William Page. Vols. 2 and 4. London, 1906, 1924.

Vitto, Cindy L. *The Virtuous Pagan in Middle English Literature.* Transactions of the American Philosophical Society 79, part 5. Philadelphia, 1989.

Waldron, R. A. "Langland's Originality: The Christ-Knight and the Harrowing of Hell." *Medieval English Religious and Ethical Literature.* Ed. Gregory Kratzmann and James Simpson, 66–81. Cambridge, England: Brewer, 1986.

Wallace, David. "Chaucer and the Absent City." In *Chaucer's London,* ed. Barbara A. Hanawalt, 59–90. Minneapolis: University of Minnesota Press, 1992.

Walters, H. B. *London Churches at the Reformation: With an Account of their Contents.* London: SPCK, 1939.

Warner, George, ed. *The Buke of John Maundeuill.* [See Egerton version of *Mandeville*].

Watson, Nicholas. "Visions of Inclusion: Universal Salvation and Vernacular Theology in Pre-Reformation England." *Journal of Medieval and Early Modern Studies* 27 (1997): 145–87.

Weldon, James. "*Ordinatio* and Genre in MS CCC 201: A Mediaeval Reading of the B-Text of *Piers Plowman.*" *Florilegium* 12 (1993): 159–75.

Westlake, H. F. *The Parish Gilds of Mediaeval England.* London: SPCK, 1919.

Westrem, Scott. "Two Routes to Pleasant Instruction in Late-Fourteenth-Century Literature." In *The Work of Dissimiltude: Essays from the Sixth Citadel Conference on Medieval and Renaissance Literature,* ed. David G. Allen and Robert A. White, 67–80. Newark: University of Delaware Press, 1992.

Whatley, Gordon. "*Piers Plowman* B 12.277–94: Notes on Language, Text, and Theology." *MP* 82 (1984): 1–12.

———. "The Uses of Hagiography: The Legend of Pope Gregory and the Emperor Trajan in the Middle Ages." *Viator* 15 (1984) 25–63.

Whitaker, Thomas Dunham, ed. *Visio Willí de Petro Ploughman . . . , or The Vision of William concerning Piers Plouhman, and the Visions of the Same concerning the Origin, Progress, and Perfection of the Christian life.* London: John Murray, 1813.

Wickham, Glynne. *Early English Stages: 1300 to 1660.* Vol. 1. London: Routledge, 1959.

William of Malmesbury. *De Gestis Pontificum Anglorum.* Ed. N. E. S. A. Hamilton. Rolls Series. 1870. Reprint, N.p.: Kraus, 1964.

Williams, Gwyn A. *Medieval London: From Commune to Capital.* London: Athlone Press, 1963.

Williams, Raymond. *Keywords: A Vocabulary of Culture and Society.* Rev. ed. New York: Oxford University Press, 1985.

Windeatt, B. A. "The Scribes as Chaucer's Early Critics." *Studies in the Age of Chaucer* 1 (1979): 119–41.

Withington, Robert. "The Early 'Royal-Entry.'" *PMLA* 32 (1917): 616–23.

Wittig, Joseph S. "'Piers Plowman' B, Passus IX–XII: Elements in the Design of the Inward Journey." *Traditio* 28 (1972): 211–80.

———. *William Langland Revisited.* New York: Twayne, 1997.

Wogan-Brown, Nicholas Watson, Andrew Taylor, and Ruth Evans, eds. *The Idea of the Vernacular: An Anthology of Middle English Literary Theory, 1280–1520.* University Park: Pennsylvania State University Press, 1999.

Wood, Robert A. "A Fourteenth-Century London Owner of *Piers Plowman.*" *Medium Aevum* 53 (1984): 83–90.

Woolf, Rosemary. *The English Mystery Plays.* London: Routledge, 1972.

———. "Some Non-Medieval Qualities of *Piers Plowman.*" *Essays in Criticism* 12 (1962): 111–25.

Wright, Thomas, ed. *The Vision and Creed of Piers Ploughman.* 2 vols. London: Pickering, 1842.

Yates, Julian. "Mystic Self: Margery Kempe and the Mirror of Narrative." *Comitatus* 26 (1995): 75–93.

Yunck, John A. "Satire." In *A Companion to Piers Plowman,* ed. John A. Alford, 135–54. Berkeley and Los Angeles: University of California Press, 1988.

Zacher, Christian. *Curiosity and Pilgrimage: The Literature of Discovery in Fourteenth-Century England.* Baltimore: Johns Hopkins University Press, 1976.

———. "Mandeville's Travels." In *A Manual of the Writings in Middle English,* ed. Albert E. Hartung. Vol. 7, sec. 9: Travel and Geographical Writing. New Haven: Conn. Academy of Arts and Sciences, 1986. 2239–41, 2452–57.

Zink, Michel. *The Invention of Literary Subjectivity.* Trans. David Sices. Baltimore: Johns Hopkins University Press, 1999.

Zumthor, Paul. "Autobiography in the Middle Ages?" *Genre* 6 (1973): 29–48.

Index